Constitutional Law

Second Edition

2008 Supplement

ASPEN PUBLISHERS

2008 Supplement

Constitutional Law

Second Edition

Erwin Chemerinsky
Dean and Distinguished Professor of Law
University of California, Irvine, School of Law

Law & Business

AUSTIN   BOSTON   CHICAGO   NEW YORK   THE NETHERLANDS

Aspen Publishers
Attn: Permissions Department
76 Ninth Avenue, 7th Floor
New York, NY 10011-5201

To contact Customer Care, e-mail customer.care@aspenpublishers.com, call 1-800-234-1660, fax 1-800-901-9075, or mail correspondence to:

Aspen Publishers
Attn: Order Department
PO Box 990
Frederick, MD 21705

Printed in the United States of America.

1 2 3 4 5 6 7 8 9 0

ISBN 978-0-7355-7204-1

Library of Congress Cataloging-in-Publication Data

Chemerinsky, Erwin.
  Constitutional law/Erwin Chemerinsky.—2nd ed.
    p. cm.
  Includes index.
  ISBN 0-7355-4946-X (casebook)
  ISBN 978-0-7355-7204-1 (supplement)
  1. Constitutional law—United States—Cases. I. Title.

  KF4549.C44 2005
  342.73—dc22

                                                                2005007712

About Wolters Kluwer Law & Business

Wolters Kluwer Law & Business is a leading provider of research information and workflow solutions in key specialty areas. The strengths of the individual brands of Aspen Publishers, CCH, Kluwer Law International and Loislaw are aligned within Wolters Kluwer Law & Business to provide comprehensive, in-depth solutions and expert-authored content for the legal, professional and education markets.

CCH was founded in 1913 and has served more than four generations of business professionals and their clients. The CCH products in the Wolters Kluwer Law & Business group are highly regarded electronic and print resources for legal, securities, antitrust and trade regulation, government contracting, banking, pension, payroll, employment and labor, and healthcare reimbursement and compliance professionals.

Aspen Publishers is a leading information provider for attorneys, business professionals and law students. Written by preeminent authorities, Aspen products offer analytical and practical information in a range of specialty practice areas from securities law and intellectual property to mergers and acquisitions and pension/benefits. Aspen's trusted legal education resources provide professors and students with high-quality, up-to-date and effective resources for successful instruction and study in all areas of the law.

Kluwer Law International supplies the global business community with comprehensive English-language international legal information. Legal practitioners, corporate counsel and business executives around the world rely on the Kluwer Law International journals, loose-leafs, books and electronic products for authoritative information in many areas of international legal practice.

Loislaw is a premier provider of digitized legal content to small law firm practitioners of various specializations. Loislaw provides attorneys with the ability to quickly and efficiently find the necessary legal information they need, when and where they need it, by facilitating access to primary law as well as state-specific law, records, forms and treatises.

Wolters Kluwer Law & Business, a unit of Wolters Kluwer, is headquartered in New York and Riverwoods, Illinois. Wolters Kluwer is a leading multinational publisher and information services company.

Contents

Preface

The second edition of the casebook was published in May 2005 and covers cases through the end of October Term 2003, which concluded in June 2004. Thus, this supplement covers the last four years of the Supreme Court, October Terms 2004, 2005, 2006, and 2007. It is the last supplement to this edition, as a new edition is planned for the spring of 2009.

This has been a time of momentous developments on the Supreme Court, occasioned by the death of Chief Justice William Rehnquist and the retirement of Justice Sandra Day O'Connor. There are two new members of the Court, Chief Justice John Roberts and Justice Samuel Alito.

The three years also have seen many major developments, which are reflected in the cases included in this supplement. Some of the most important include the following:

- *Heller v. District of Columbia*, concerning the meaning of the second Amendment (Chapter 1)
- *Hein v. Freedom from Religion*, concerning taxpayer standing to challenge government expenditures. (Chapter 1)
- *Gonzales v. Raich*, on the scope of Congress's commerce power and whether Congress may prohibit the cultivation and possession of small amounts of marijuana for medicinal purposes. (Chapter 2)
- *Hamdan v. Rumsfeld*, on the legality of the military tribunals created to try those held as enemy combatants in Guantanamo Bay, Cuba. (Chapter 3)
- *Boumediene v. Bush*, on whether non-citizens detained as enemy combatants can be denied access to federal habeas corpus relief (Chapter 3)
- *Philip Morris USA v. Williams*, on when punitive damage awards violate due process. (Chapter 6)
- *Kelo v. City of New London*, on what constitutes a taking for "public use" and whether a taking for economic development purposes is "public use." (Chapter 6)
- *Parents Involved in Community Schools v. Seattle School Dist. No. 1*, on the ability of schools to use race as a factor in assigning students to achieve desegregation. (Chapter 7)
- *Gonzales v. Carhart*, on the constitutionality of the Federal Partial Birth Abortion Ban Act. (Chapter 8)
- *Crawford v. Marion County Election Board*, on whether a requirement for photo identification for voting is constitutional
- *Randall v. Sorrell*, on the constitutionality of a state law restricting campaign contributions and expenditures, and *Federal Election Commission v. Wisconsin Right to Life, Inc.*, on whether a key provision of the Bipartisan Campaign Finance Reform Act of 2002 is constitutional. (Chapter 9)

- *Morse v. Frederick*, concerning the constitutionality of punishing student speech. (Chapter 9)
- *McCreary County v. ACLU of Kentucky* and *Van Orden v. Perry*, on whether Ten Commandment displays violate the Establishment Clause. (Chapter 10)

In addition to being important clarifications of the doctrines in these areas, these cases raise important underlying questions about how these constitutional provisions—and all of the Constitution—should be interpreted.

With two new Justices, there is the prospect of the Court reconsidering many areas of constitutional law in the years ahead. It is an exciting time to be studying constitutional law. I look forward to continuing to do annual supplements and a new edition every several years. I welcome comments and suggestions from those using this book.

Erwin Chemerinsky

July 2008

Chapter 1

The Federal Judicial Power

B. Limits on the Federal Judicial Power

1. Interpretive Limits (casebook p. 14)

The casebook uses the Second Amendment as a way to examine the debate over constitutional interpretation. In considering the meaning of the Second Amendment, there can be arguments over the text, over the original meaning, over precedent, and over social policy. Each of these is very much disputed in interpreting the Second Amendment and there is an ongoing debate, for this provision and all of constitutional law, as to which sources are relevant in constitutional interpretation.

The casebook used two recent federal court of appeals cases to illustrate this. But in June 2008, the Supreme Court handed down its most important Second Amendment decision. In reading the case, it is important to compare the majority and the dissents as to their underlying views concerning constitutional interpretation.

DISTRICT OF COLUMBIA v. HELLER
128 S.Ct. 2783 (2008)

Justice SCALIA delivered the opinion of the Court.

We consider whether a District of Columbia prohibition on the possession of usable handguns in the home violates the Second Amendment to the Constitution.

I

The District of Columbia generally prohibits the possession of handguns. It is a crime to carry an unregistered firearm, and the registration of handguns is prohibited. See D.C.Code §§ 7-2501.01(12), 7-2502.01(a), 7-2502.02(a)(4) (2001). Wholly apart from that prohibition, no person may carry a handgun without a license, but the chief of police may issue licenses for 1-year periods. See §§ 22-4504(a), 22-4506. District of Columbia law also requires residents to keep their lawfully owned firearms, such as registered long guns, "unloaded and dissembled or bound by a trigger lock or similar device" unless they are located in a place of business or are being used for lawful recreational activities. See § 7-2507.02.[1]

Respondent Dick Heller is a D.C. special police officer authorized to carry a handgun while on duty at the Federal Judicial Center. He applied for a registration certificate for a handgun that he wished to keep at home, but the District refused. He thereafter filed a lawsuit in the Federal District Court for the District of Columbia seeking, on Second Amendment grounds, to enjoin the city from enforcing the bar on the registration of handguns, the licensing requirement insofar as it prohibits the carrying of a firearm in the home without a license, and the trigger-lock requirement insofar as it prohibits the use of "functional firearms within the home."

II

We turn first to the meaning of the Second Amendment.

A

The Second Amendment provides: "A well regulated Militia, being necessary to the security of a free State, the right of the people to keep and bear Arms, shall not be infringed." In interpreting this text, we are guided by the principle that "[t]he Constitution was written to be understood by the voters; its words and phrases were used in their normal and ordinary as distinguished from technical meaning."

The two sides in this case have set out very different interpretations of the Amendment. Petitioners and today's dissenting Justices believe that it protects only the right to possess and carry a firearm in connection with militia service. Respondent argues that it protects an individual right to possess a firearm unconnected with service in a militia, and to use that arm for traditionally lawful purposes, such as self-defense within the home.

The Second Amendment is naturally divided into two parts: its prefatory clause and its operative clause. The former does not limit the latter grammatically, but rather announces a purpose. The Amendment could be rephrased, "Because a well regulated Militia is necessary to the security of a free State, the right of the people to keep and bear Arms shall not be infringed." Although this structure of the Second Amendment is unique in our Constitution, other legal documents of the founding era, particularly individual-rights provisions of state constitutions, commonly included a prefatory statement of purpose.

---

1. There are minor exceptions to all of these prohibitions, none of which is relevant here. [Footnote by the Court]

Logic demands that there be a link between the stated purpose and the command. The Second Amendment would be nonsensical if it read, "A well regulated Militia, being necessary to the security of a free State, the right of the people to petition for redress of grievances shall not be infringed." But apart from that clarifying function, a prefatory clause does not limit or expand the scope of the operative clause.

1. Operative Clause.

a. "Right of the People." The first salient feature of the operative clause is that it codifies a "right of the people." The unamended Constitution and the Bill of Rights use the phrase "right of the people" two other times, in the First Amendment's Assembly-and-Petition Clause and in the Fourth Amendment's Search-and-Seizure Clause. The Ninth Amendment uses very similar terminology. All three of these instances unambiguously refer to individual rights, not "collective" rights, or rights that may be exercised only through participation in some corporate body.

What is more, in all six other provisions of the Constitution that mention "the people," the term unambiguously refers to all members of the political community, not an unspecified subset. This contrasts markedly with the phrase "the militia" in the prefatory clause. As we will describe below, the "militia" in colonial America consisted of a subset of "the people"—those who were male, able bodied, and within a certain age range. Reading the Second Amendment as protecting only the right to "keep and bear Arms" in an organized militia therefore fits poorly with the operative clause's description of the holder of that right as "the people."

We start therefore with a strong presumption that the Second Amendment right is exercised individually and belongs to all Americans.

b. "Keep and bear Arms." We move now from the holder of the right—"the people"—to the substance of the right: "to keep and bear Arms."

Before addressing the verbs "keep" and "bear," we interpret their object: "Arms." The 18th-century meaning is no different from the meaning today. The 1773 edition of Samuel Johnson's dictionary defined "arms" as "weapons of offence, or armour of defence." 1 Dictionary of the English Language 107 (4th ed.) (hereinafter Johnson). Timothy Cunningham's important 1771 legal dictionary defined "arms" as "any thing that a man wears for his defence, or takes into his hands, or useth in wrath to cast at or strike another." 1 A New and Complete Law Dictionary (1771). The term was applied, then as now, to weapons that were not specifically designed for military use and were not employed in a military capacity.

Some have made the argument, bordering on the frivolous, that only those arms in existence in the 18th century are protected by the Second Amendment. We do not interpret constitutional rights that way. Just as the First Amendment protects modern forms of communications, and the Fourth Amendment applies to modern forms of search, the Second Amendment extends, prima facie, to all instruments that constitute bearable arms, even those that were not in existence at the time of the founding.

We turn to the phrases "keep arms" and "bear arms." Johnson defined "keep" as, most relevantly, "[t]o retain; not to lose," and "[t]o have in custody." Webster defined it as "[t]o hold; to retain in one's power or possession." No party has apprised us of an idiomatic meaning of "keep Arms." Thus, the most natural reading of "keep Arms" in the Second Amendment is to "have weapons."

The phrase "keep arms" was not prevalent in the written documents of the founding period that we have found, but there are a few examples, all of which favor viewing the right to "keep Arms" as an individual right unconnected with militia service.

From our review of founding-era sources, we conclude that this natural meaning was also the meaning that "bear arms" had in the 18th century. In numerous instances, "bear arms" was unambiguously used to refer to the carrying of weapons outside of an organized militia. The most prominent examples are those most relevant to the Second Amendment: Nine state constitutional provisions written in the 18th century or the first two decades of the 19th, which enshrined a right of citizens to "bear arms in defense of themselves and the state" or "bear arms in defense of himself and the state." It is clear from those formulations that "bear arms" did not refer only to carrying a weapon in an organized military unit.

Justice Stevens places great weight on James Madison's inclusion of a conscientious-objector clause in his original draft of the Second Amendment: "but no person religiously scrupulous of bearing arms, shall be compelled to render military service in person." He argues that this clause establishes that the drafters of the Second Amendment intended "bear Arms" to refer only to military service. It is always perilous to derive the meaning of an adopted provision from another provision deleted in the drafting process. In any case, what Justice Stevens would conclude from the deleted provision does not follow. It was not meant to exempt from military service those who objected to going to war but had no scruples about personal gunfights. Quakers opposed the use of arms not just for militia service, but for any violent purpose whatsoever—so much so that Quaker frontiersmen were forbidden to use arms to defend their families, even though "[i]n such circumstances the temptation to seize a hunting rifle or knife in self-defense ... must sometimes have been almost overwhelming." Thus, the most natural interpretation of Madison's deleted text is that those opposed to carrying weapons for potential violent confrontation would not be "compelled to render military service," in which such carrying would be required.

Finally, Justice Stevens suggests that "keep and bear Arms" was some sort of term of art, presumably akin to "hue and cry" or "cease and desist." This suggestion usefully evades the problem that there is no evidence whatsoever to support a military reading of "keep arms." And even if "keep and bear Arms" were a unitary phrase, we find no evidence that it bore a military meaning. Although the phrase was not at all common (which would be unusual for a term of art), we have found instances of its use with a clearly nonmilitary connotation.

c. Meaning of the Operative Clause. Putting all of these textual elements together, we find that they guarantee the individual right to possess and carry weapons in case of confrontation. This meaning is strongly confirmed by the historical background of the Second Amendment. We look to this because it has always been widely understood that the Second Amendment, like the First and Fourth Amendments, codified a pre-existing right. The very text of the Second Amendment implicitly recognizes the pre-existence of the right and declares only that it "shall not be infringed."

There seems to us no doubt, on the basis of both text and history, that the Second Amendment conferred an individual right to keep and bear arms. Of course the right was not unlimited, just as the First Amendment's right of free speech was no. Thus, we do not read the Second Amendment to protect the right of citizens to carry arms for any sort of confrontation, just as we do not read the First Amendment to protect the right of citizens to speak for any purpose. Before turning to limitations upon the individual right, however, we must determine whether the prefatory clause of the Second Amendment comports with our interpretation of the operative clause.

2. Prefatory Clause.

The prefatory clause reads: "A well regulated Militia, being necessary to the security of a free State. . . . "

a. "Well-Regulated Militia." In United States v. Miller (1939), we explained that "the Militia comprised all males physically capable of acting in concert for the common defense." That definition comports with founding-era sources.

Petitioners take a seemingly narrower view of the militia, stating that "[m]ilitias are the state- and congressionally-regulated military forces described in the Militia Clauses (art. I, § 8, cls. 15-16)." Although we agree with petitioners' interpretive assumption that "militia" means the same thing in Article I and the Second Amendment, we believe that petitioners identify the wrong thing, namely, the organized militia. Unlike armies and navies, which Congress is given the power to create ("to raise . . . Armies"; "to provide . . . a Navy," Art. I, § 8, cls. 12-13), the militia is assumed by Article I already to be in existence. Congress is given the power to "provide for calling forth the militia," § 8, cl. 15; and the power not to create, but to "organiz[e]" it-and not to organize "a" militia, which is what one would expect if the militia were to be a federal creation, but to organize "the" militia, connoting a body already in existence, ibid., cl. 16. This is fully consistent with the ordinary definition of the militia as all able-bodied men.

Finally, the adjective "well-regulated" implies nothing more than the imposition of proper discipline and training.

b. "Security of a Free State." The phrase "security of a free state" meant "security of a free polity," not security of each of the several States as the dissent below argued. There are many reasons why the militia was thought to be "necessary to the security of a free state." First, of course, it is useful in repelling invasions and suppressing insurrections. Second, it renders large standing armies unnecessary-an argument that Alexander Hamilton made in favor of federal control over the militia. Third, when the able-bodied men of a nation are trained in arms and organized, they are better able to resist tyranny.

3. Relationship between Prefatory Clause and Operative Clause

We reach the question, then: Does the preface fit with an operative clause that creates an individual right to keep and bear arms? It fits perfectly, once one knows the history that the founding generation knew and that we have described above. That history showed that the way tyrants had eliminated a militia consisting of all the able-bodied men was not by banning the militia but simply by taking away the people's arms, enabling a select militia or standing army to suppress political opponents. This is what had occurred in England that prompted codification of the right to have arms in the English Bill of Rights.

It is therefore entirely sensible that the Second Amendment's prefatory clause announces the purpose for which the right was codified: to prevent elimination of the militia. The prefatory clause does not suggest that preserving the militia was the only reason Americans valued the ancient right; most undoubtedly thought it even more important for self-defense and hunting. But the threat that the new Federal Government would destroy the citizens' militia by taking away their arms was the reason that right—unlike some other English rights—was codified in a written Constitution. Justice Breyer's assertion that individual self-defense is merely a "subsidiary interest" of the right to keep and bear arms is profoundly mistaken. He bases that assertion solely upon the prologue-but that can only show that self-defense had little to do with the right's codification; it was the central component of the right itself.

B

Our interpretation is confirmed by analogous arms-bearing rights in state constitutions that preceded and immediately followed adoption of the Second Amendment. Four States adopted analogues to the Federal Second Amendment in the period between independence and the ratification of the Bill of Rights. Two of them—Pennsylvania and Vermont—clearly adopted individual rights unconnected to militia service.

North Carolina also codified a right to bear arms in 1776. Many colonial statutes required individual arms-bearing for public-safety reasons—such as the 1770 Georgia law that "for the security and defence of this province from internal dangers and insurrections" required those men who qualified for militia duty individually "to carry fire arms" "to places of public worship."

The 1780 Massachusetts Constitution presented another variation on the theme: "The people have a right to keep and to bear arms for the common defence. . . . " Once again, if one gives narrow meaning to the phrase "common defence" this can be thought to limit the right to the bearing of arms in a state-organized military force. But once again the State's highest court thought otherwise. Writing for the court in an 1825 libel case, Chief Justice Parker wrote: "The liberty of the press was to be unrestrained, but he who used it was to be responsible in cases of its abuse; like the right to keep fire arms, which does not protect him who uses them for annoyance or destruction."

We therefore believe that the most likely reading of all four of these pre-Second Amendment state constitutional provisions is that they secured an individual right to bear arms for defensive purposes.

Between 1789 and 1820, nine States adopted Second Amendment analogues.

The historical narrative that petitioners must endorse would thus treat the Federal Second Amendment as an odd outlier, protecting a right unknown in state constitutions or at English common law, based on little more than an overreading of the prefatory clause.

C

Justice Stevens relies on the drafting history of the Second Amendment—the various proposals in the state conventions and the debates in Congress. It is dubious to rely on such history to interpret a text that was widely understood to codify a pre-existing right, rather than to fashion a new one. But even assuming that this legislative history is relevant, Justice Stevens flatly misreads the historical record.

It is true, as Justice Stevens says, that there was concern that the Federal Government would abolish the institution of the state militia. That concern found expression, however, not in the various Second Amendment precursors proposed in the State conventions, but in separate structural provisions that would have given the States concurrent and seemingly nonpre-emptible authority to organize, discipline, and arm the militia when the Federal Government failed to do so.

D

We now address how the Second Amendment was interpreted from immediately after its ratification through the end of the 19th century. Three important founding-era legal scholars interpreted the Second Amendment in published writings. All three understood it to protect an individual right unconnected with militia service. We have found only one early 19th-century commentator who clearly conditioned the right to keep and bear arms upon service in the militia-and he recognized that the prevailing view was to the contrary.

The 19th-century cases that interpreted the Second Amendment universally support an individual right unconnected to militia service. Many early 19th-century state cases indicated that the Second Amendment right to bear arms was an individual right unconnected to militia service, though subject to certain restrictions.

In the aftermath of the Civil War, there was an outpouring of discussion of the Second Amendment in Congress and in public discourse, as people debated whether and how to secure constitutional rights for newly free slaves. Since those discussions took place 75 years after the ratification of the Second Amendment, they do not provide as much insight into its original meaning as earlier sources. Yet those born and educated in the early 19th century faced a widespread effort to limit arms ownership by a large number of citizens; their understanding of the origins and continuing significance of the Amendment is instructive.

Blacks were routinely disarmed by Southern States after the Civil War. Those who opposed these injustices frequently stated that they infringed blacks' constitutional right to keep and bear arms. Needless to say, the claim was not that blacks were being prohibited from carrying arms in an organized state militia. It was plainly the understanding in the post-Civil War Congress that the Second Amendment protected an individual right to use arms for self-defense. Every late-19th-century legal scholar that we have read interpreted the Second Amendment to secure an individual right unconnected with militia service.

E

We now ask whether any of our precedents forecloses the conclusions we have reached about the meaning of the Second Amendment. Justice Stevens places overwhelming reliance upon this Court's decision in United States v. Miller (1939). Miller did not hold that and cannot possibly be read to have held that. The judgment in the case upheld against a Second Amendment challenge two men's federal convictions for transporting an unregistered short-barreled shotgun in interstate commerce, in violation of the National Firearms Act. It is entirely clear that the Court's basis for saying that the Second Amendment did not apply was not that the defendants were "bear[ing] arms" not "for . . . military purposes" but for "nonmilitary use." Rather, it was that the type of weapon at issue was not eligible for Second Amendment protection. Beyond that, the opinion provided no explanation of the content of the right.

This holding is not only consistent with, but positively suggests, that the Second Amendment confers an individual right to keep and bear arms (though only arms that "have some reasonable relationship to the preservation or efficiency of a well regulated militia"). Had the Court believed that the Second Amendment protects only those serving in the militia, it would have been odd to examine the character of the weapon rather than simply note that the two crooks were not militiamen. Miller stands only for the proposition that the Second Amendment right, whatever its nature, extends only to certain types of weapons.

It is particularly wrongheaded to read Miller for more than what it said, because the case did not even purport to be a thorough examination of the Second Amendment. The respondent made no appearance in the case, neither filing a brief nor appearing at oral argument; the Court heard from no one but the Government.

We conclude that nothing in our precedents forecloses our adoption of the original understanding of the Second Amendment.

III

Like most rights, the right secured by the Second Amendment is not unlimited. From Blackstone through the 19th-century cases, commentators and courts routinely explained that the right was not a right to keep and carry any weapon whatsoever in any manner whatsoever and for whatever purpose. For example, the majority of the 19th-century courts to consider the question held that prohibitions on carrying concealed weapons were lawful under the Second Amendment or state analogues. Although we do not undertake an exhaustive historical analysis today of the full scope of the Second Amendment, nothing in our opinion should be taken to cast doubt on longstanding prohibitions on the possession of firearms by felons and the mentally ill, or laws forbidding the carrying of firearms in sensitive places such as schools and government buildings, or laws imposing conditions and qualifications on the commercial sale of arms.

We also recognize another important limitation on the right to keep and carry arms. Miller said, as we have explained, that the sorts of weapons protected were those "in common use at the time." We think that limitation is fairly supported by the historical tradition of prohibiting the carrying of "dangerous and unusual weapons."

It may be objected that if weapons that are most useful in military service— M-16 rifles and the like—may be banned, then the Second Amendment right is completely detached from the prefatory clause. But as we have said, the conception of the militia at the time of the Second Amendment's ratification was the body of all citizens capable of military service, who would bring the sorts of lawful weapons that they possessed at home to militia duty. It may well be true today that a militia, to be as effective as militias in the 18th century, would require sophisticated arms that are highly unusual in society at large. Indeed, it may be true that no amount of small arms could be useful against modern-day bombers and tanks. But the fact that modern developments have limited the degree of fit between the prefatory clause and the protected right cannot change our interpretation of the right.

IV

We turn finally to the law at issue here. As we have said, the law totally bans handgun possession in the home. It also requires that any lawful firearm in the home be disassembled or bound by a trigger lock at all times, rendering it inoperable.

As the quotations earlier in this opinion demonstrate, the inherent right of self-defense has been central to the Second Amendment right. The handgun ban amounts to a prohibition of an entire class of "arms" that is overwhelmingly chosen by American society for that lawful purpose. The prohibition extends, moreover, to the home, where the need for defense of self, family, and property is most acute. Under any of the standards of scrutiny that we have applied to enumerated constitutional rights, banning from the home "the most preferred firearm in the nation to 'keep' and use for protection of one's home and family," would fail constitutional muster.

We must also address the District's requirement (as applied to respondent's handgun) that firearms in the home be rendered and kept inoperable at all times. This makes it impossible for citizens to use them for the core lawful purpose of self-defense and is hence unconstitutional. The District argues that we should interpret this element of the statute to contain an exception for self-defense. But we think that is precluded by the unequivocal text, and by the presence of certain other enumerated exceptions: "Except for law enforcement personnel . . . , each registrant shall keep any firearm in his possession unloaded and disassembled or bound by a trigger lock or similar device unless such firearm is kept at his place of business, or while being used for lawful recreational purposes within the District of Columbia." D.C.Code § 7-2507.02. The non-existence of a self-defense exception is also suggested by the D.C. Court of Appeals' statement that the statute forbids residents to use firearms to stop intruders.

Justice Breyer moves on to make a broad jurisprudential point: He criticizes us for declining to establish a level of scrutiny for evaluating Second Amendment restrictions. He proposes, explicitly at least, none of the traditionally expressed levels (strict scrutiny, intermediate scrutiny, rational basis), but rather a judge-empowering "interest-balancing inquiry" that "asks whether the statute burdens a protected interest in a way or to an extent that is out of proportion to the statute's salutary effects upon other important governmental interests."

We know of no other enumerated constitutional right whose core protection has been subjected to a freestanding "interest-balancing" approach. The very enumeration of the right takes out of the hands of government—even the Third Branch of Government—the power to decide on a case-by-case basis whether the right is really worth insisting upon. A constitutional guarantee subject to future judges' assessments of its usefulness is no constitutional guarantee at all. Constitutional rights are enshrined with the scope they were understood to have when the people adopted them, whether or not future legislatures or (yes) even future judges think that scope too broad. We would not apply an "interest-balancing" approach to the prohibition of a peaceful neo-Nazi march through Skokie. The First Amendment contains the freedom-of-speech guarantee that the people ratified, which included exceptions for obscenity, libel, and disclosure of state secrets, but not for the expression of extremely unpopular and wrong-headed views. The Second Amendment is no different. Like the First, it is the very product of an interest-balancing by the people—which Justice Breyer would now conduct for them anew. And whatever else it leaves to future evaluation, it surely elevates above all other interests the right of law-abiding, responsible citizens to use arms in defense of hearth and home.

Justice Breyer chides us for leaving so many applications of the right to keep and bear arms in doubt, and for not providing extensive historical justification for those regulations of the right that we describe as permissible. But since this case represents this Court's first in-depth examination of the Second Amendment, one should not expect it to clarify the entire field. And there will be time enough to expound upon the historical justifications for the exceptions we have mentioned if and when those exceptions come before us.

In sum, we hold that the District's ban on handgun possession in the home violates the Second Amendment, as does its prohibition against rendering any lawful firearm in the home operable for the purpose of immediate self-defense. Assuming that Heller is not disqualified from the exercise of Second Amendment rights, the District must permit him to register his handgun and must issue him a license to carry it in the home.

* * *

We are aware of the problem of handgun violence in this country, and we take seriously the concerns raised by the many amici who believe that prohibition of handgun ownership is a solution. The Constitution leaves the District of Columbia a variety of tools for combating that problem, including some measures regulating handguns. But the enshrinement of constitutional rights necessarily takes certain policy choices off the table. These include the absolute prohibition of handguns held and used for self-defense in the home. Undoubtedly some think that the Second Amendment is outmoded in a society where our standing army is the pride of our Nation, where well-trained police forces provide personal security, and where gun violence is a serious problem. That is perhaps debatable, but what is not debatable is that it is not the role of this Court to pronounce the Second Amendment extinct.

Justice STEVENS, with whom Justice SOUTER, Justice GINSBURG, and Justice Breyer join, dissenting.

The question presented by this case is not whether the Second Amendment protects a "collective right" or an "individual right." Surely it protects a right that can be enforced by individuals. But a conclusion that the Second Amendment protects an individual right does not tell us anything about the scope of that right.

Guns are used to hunt, for self-defense, to commit crimes, for sporting activities, and to perform military duties. The Second Amendment plainly does not protect the right to use a gun to rob a bank; it is equally clear that it does encompass the right to use weapons for certain military purposes. Whether it also protects the right to possess and use guns for nonmilitary purposes like hunting and personal self-defense is the question presented by this case. The text of the Amendment, its history, and our decision in United States v. Miller (1939), provide a clear answer to that question.

The Second Amendment was adopted to protect the right of the people of each of the several States to maintain a well-regulated militia. It was a response to concerns raised during the ratification of the Constitution that the power of Congress to disarm the state militias and create a national standing army posed an intolerable threat to the sovereignty of the several States. Neither the text of the Amendment nor the arguments advanced by its proponents evidenced the slightest interest in limiting any legislature's authority to regulate private civilian uses of firearms. Specifically, there is no indication that the Framers of the Amendment intended to enshrine the common-law right of self-defense in the Constitution.

In 1934, Congress enacted the National Firearms Act, the first major federal firearms law. Upholding a conviction under that Act, this Court held that, "[i]n the absence of any evidence tending to show that possession or use of a 'shotgun having a barrel of less than eighteen inches in length' at this time has some reasonable relationship to the preservation or efficiency of a well regulated militia, we cannot say that the Second Amendment guarantees the right to keep and bear such an instrument." United States v. Miller. The view of the Amendment we took in Miller—that it protects the right to keep and bear arms for certain military purposes, but that it does not curtail the Legislature's power to regulate the nonmilitary use and ownership of weapons—is both the most natural reading of the Amendment's text and the interpretation most faithful to the history of its adoption.

Since our decision in Miller, hundreds of judges have relied on the view of the Amendment we endorsed there; we ourselves affirmed it in 1980. See Lewis v. United States (1980). No new evidence has surfaced since 1980 supporting the view that the Amendment was intended to curtail the power of Congress to regulate civilian use or misuse of weapons. Indeed, a review of the drafting history of the Amendment demonstrates that its Framers rejected proposals that would have broadened its coverage to include such uses.

The opinion the Court announces today fails to identify any new evidence supporting the view that the Amendment was intended to limit the power of Congress to regulate civilian uses of weapons. Unable to point to any such evidence, the Court stakes its holding on a strained and unpersuasive reading of the Amendment's text; significantly different provisions in the 1689 English Bill of Rights, and in various 19th-century State Constitutions; postenactment commentary that was available to the Court when it decided Miller; and, ultimately, a feeble attempt to distinguish Miller that places more emphasis on the Court's decisional process than on the reasoning in the opinion itself.

Even if the textual and historical arguments on both sides of the issue were evenly balanced, respect for the well-settled views of all of our predecessors on this Court, and for the rule of law itself, would prevent most jurists from endorsing such a dramatic upheaval in the law.

In this dissent I shall first explain why our decision in Miller was faithful to the text of the Second Amendment and the purposes revealed in its drafting history. I shall then comment on the postratification history of the Amendment, which makes abundantly clear that the Amendment should not be interpreted as limiting the authority of Congress to regulate the use or possession of firearms for purely civilian purposes.

I

The text of the Second Amendment is brief. It provides: "A well regulated Militia, being necessary to the security of a free State, the right of the people to keep and bear Arms, shall not be infringed."

Three portions of that text merit special focus: the introductory language defining the Amendment's purpose, the class of persons encompassed within its reach, and the unitary nature of the right that it protects.

"A well regulated Militia, being necessary to the security of a free State"

The preamble to the Second Amendment makes three important points. It identifies the preservation of the militia as the Amendment's purpose; it explains that the militia is necessary to the security of a free State; and it recognizes that the militia must be "well regulated." In all three respects it is comparable to provisions in several State Declarations of Rights that were adopted roughly contemporaneously with the Declaration of Independence. Those state provisions highlight the importance members of the founding generation attached to the maintenance of state militias; they also underscore the profound fear shared by many in that era of the dangers posed by standing armies.

The preamble thus both sets forth the object of the Amendment and informs the meaning of the remainder of its text. Such text should not be treated as mere surplusage, for "[i]t cannot be presumed that any clause in the constitution is intended to be without effect." Marbury v. Madison (1803).

The Court today tries to denigrate the importance of this clause of the Amendment by beginning its analysis with the Amendment's operative provision and returning to the preamble merely "to ensure that our reading of the operative clause is consistent with the announced purpose." That is not how this Court ordinarily reads such texts, and it is not how the preamble would have been viewed at the time the Amendment was adopted.

"The right of the people"

The centerpiece of the Court's textual argument is its insistence that the words "the people" as used in the Second Amendment must have the same meaning, and protect the same class of individuals, as when they are used in the First and Fourth Amendments. According to the Court, in all three provisions— as well as the Constitution's preamble, "the term unambiguously refers to all members of the political community, not an unspecified subset." But the Court itself reads the Second Amendment to protect a "subset" significantly narrower than the class of persons protected by the First and Fourth Amendments; when it finally drills down on the substantive meaning of the Second Amendment, the Court limits the protected class to "law-abiding, responsible citizens." But the class of persons protected by the First and Fourth Amendments is not so limited; for even felons (and presumably irresponsible citizens as well) may invoke the protections of those constitutional provisions. The Court offers no way to harmonize its conflicting pronouncements.

"To keep and bear Arms"

Although the Court's discussion of these words treats them as two "phrases"—as if they read "to keep" and "to bear"—they describe a unitary right: to possess arms if needed for military purposes and to use them in conjunction with military activities.

As a threshold matter, it is worth pausing to note an oddity in the Court's interpretation of "to keep and bear arms." Unlike the Court of Appeals, the Court does not read that phrase to create a right to possess arms for "lawful, private purposes." Instead, the Court limits the Amendment's protection to the right "to possess and carry weapons in case of confrontation." No party or amicus urged this interpretation; the Court appears to have fashioned it out of whole cloth. But although this novel limitation lacks support in the text of the Amendment, the Amendment's text does justify a different limitation: the "right to keep and bear arms" protects only a right to possess and use firearms in connection with service in a state-organized militia.

The term "bear arms" is a familiar idiom; when used unadorned by any additional words, its meaning is "to serve as a soldier, do military service, fight." 1 Oxford English Dictionary 634 (2d ed.1989). It is derived from the Latin arma ferre, which, translated literally, means "to bear [ferre] war equipment [arma]."

The Amendment's use of the term "keep" in no way contradicts the military meaning conveyed by the phrase "bear arms" and the Amendment's preamble. To the contrary, a number of state militia laws in effect at the time of the Second Amendment's drafting used the term "keep" to describe the requirement that militia members store their arms at their homes, ready to be used for service when necessary. The Virginia military law, for example, ordered that "every one of the said officers, non-commissioned officers, and privates, shall constantly keep the aforesaid arms, accoutrements, and ammunition, ready to be produced whenever called for by his commanding officer." "[K]eep and bear arms" thus perfectly describes the responsibilities of a framing-era militia member.

* * *

When each word in the text is given full effect, the Amendment is most naturally read to secure to the people a right to use and possess arms in conjunction with service in a well-regulated militia. So far as appears, no more than that was contemplated by its drafters or is encompassed within its terms. Even if the meaning of the text were genuinely susceptible to more than one interpretation, the burden would remain on those advocating a departure from the purpose identified in the preamble and from settled law to come forward with persuasive new arguments or evidence. The textual analysis offered by respondent and embraced by the Court falls far short of sustaining that heavy burden.

Indeed, not a word in the constitutional text even arguably supports the Court's overwrought and novel description of the Second Amendment as "elevat [ing] above all other interests" "the right of law-abiding, responsible citizens to use arms in defense of hearth and home."

II

The proper allocation of military power in the new Nation was an issue of central concern for the Framers. The compromises they ultimately reached, reflected in Article I's Militia Clauses and the Second Amendment, represent quintessential examples of the Framers' "splitting the atom of sovereignty."

It is strikingly significant that Madison's first draft omitted any mention of nonmilitary use or possession of weapons. Rather, his original draft repeated the essence of the two proposed amendments sent by Virginia, combining the substance of the two provisions succinctly into one, which read: "The right of the people to keep and bear arms shall not be infringed; a well armed, and well regulated militia being the best security of a free country; but no person religiously scrupulous of bearing arms, shall be compelled to render military service in person."

Madison's decision to model the Second Amendment on the distinctly military Virginia proposal is therefore revealing, since it is clear that he considered and rejected formulations that would have unambiguously protected civilian uses of firearms. When Madison prepared his first draft, and when that draft was debated and modified, it is reasonable to assume that all participants in the drafting process were fully aware of the other formulations that would have protected civilian use and possession of weapons and that their choice to craft the Amendment as they did represented a rejection of those alternative formulations.

Madison's initial inclusion of an exemption for conscientious objectors sheds revelatory light on the purpose of the Amendment. It confirms an intent to describe a duty as well as a right, and it unequivocally identifies the military character of both. The objections voiced to the conscientious-objector clause only confirm the central meaning of the text.

The history of the adoption of the Amendment thus describes an overriding concern about the potential threat to state sovereignty that a federal standing army would pose, and a desire to protect the States' militias as the means by which to guard against that danger. But state militias could not effectively check the prospect of a federal standing army so long as Congress retained the power to disarm them, and so a guarantee against such disarmament was needed. As we explained in Miller: "With obvious purpose to assure the continuation and render possible the effectiveness of such forces the declaration and guarantee of the Second Amendment were made. It must be interpreted and applied with that end in view." The evidence plainly refutes the claim that the Amendment was motivated by the Framers' fears that Congress might act to regulate any civilian uses of weapons. And even if the historical record were genuinely ambiguous, the burden would remain on the parties advocating a change in the law to introduce facts or arguments "'newly ascertained,'" the Court is unable to identify any such facts or arguments.

[IV]

The Court concludes its opinion by declaring that it is not the proper role of this Court to change the meaning of rights "enshrine[d]" in the Constitution. But the right the Court announces was not "enshrined" in the Second Amendment by the Framers; it is the product of today's law-changing decision. The majority's exegesis has utterly failed to establish that as a matter of text or history, "the right of law-abiding, responsible citizens to use arms in defense of hearth and home" is "elevate[d] above all other interests" by the Second Amendment.

Until today, it has been understood that legislatures may regulate the civilian use and misuse of firearms so long as they do not interfere with the preservation of a well-regulated militia. The Court's announcement of a new constitutional right to own and use firearms for private purposes upsets that settled understanding, but leaves for future cases the formidable task of defining the scope of permissible regulations. Today judicial craftsmen have confidently asserted that a policy choice that denies a "law-abiding, responsible citize[n]" the right to keep and use weapons in the home for self-defense is "off the table." Given the presumption that most citizens are law abiding, and the reality that the need to defend oneself may suddenly arise in a host of locations outside the home, I fear that the District's policy choice may well be just the first of an unknown number of dominoes to be knocked off the table.

I do not know whether today's decision will increase the labor of federal judges to the "breaking point" envisioned by Justice Cardozo, but it will surely give rise to a far more active judicial role in making vitally important national policy decisions than was envisioned at any time in the 18th, 19th, or 20th centuries.

The Court properly disclaims any interest in evaluating the wisdom of the specific policy choice challenged in this case, but it fails to pay heed to a far more important policy choice-the choice made by the Framers themselves. The Court would have us believe that over 200 years ago, the Framers made a choice to limit the tools available to elected officials wishing to regulate civilian uses of weapons, and to authorize this Court to use the common-law process of case-by-case judicial lawmaking to define the contours of acceptable gun control policy. Absent compelling evidence that is nowhere to be found in the Court's opinion, I could not possibly conclude that the Framers made such a choice.

Justice Breyer, with whom Justice Stevens, Justice Souter, and Justice Ginsburg join, dissenting.

We must decide whether a District of Columbia law that prohibits the possession of handguns in the home violates the Second Amendment. The majority, relying upon its view that the Second Amendment seeks to protect a right of personal self-defense, holds that this law violates that Amendment. In my view, it does not.

I

The majority's conclusion is wrong for two independent reasons. The first reason is that set forth by Justice Stevens-namely, that the Second Amendment protects militia-related, not self-defense-related, interests. These two interests are sometimes intertwined. To assure 18th-century citizens that they could keep arms for militia purposes would necessarily have allowed them to keep arms that they could have used for self-defense as well. But self-defense alone, detached from any militia-related objective, is not the Amendment's concern.

The second independent reason is that the protection the Amendment provides is not absolute. The Amendment permits government to regulate the interests that it serves. Thus, irrespective of what those interests are—whether they do or do not include an independent interest in self-defense—the majority's view cannot be correct unless it can show that the District's regulation is unreasonable or inappropriate in Second Amendment terms. This the majority cannot do.

In respect to the first independent reason, I agree with Justice Stevens, and I join his opinion. In this opinion I shall focus upon the second reason. I shall show that the District's law is consistent with the Second Amendment even if that Amendment is interpreted as protecting a wholly separate interest in individual self-defense. That is so because the District's regulation, which focuses upon the presence of handguns in high-crime urban areas, represents a permissible legislative response to a serious, indeed life-threatening, problem.

Thus I here assume that one objective (but, as the majority concedes, not the primary objective) of those who wrote the Second Amendment was to help assure citizens that they would have arms available for purposes of self-defense. Even so, a legislature could reasonably conclude that the law will advance goals of great public importance, namely, saving lives, preventing injury, and reducing crime. The law is tailored to the urban crime problem in that it is local in scope and thus affects only a geographic area both limited in size and entirely urban; the law concerns handguns, which are specially linked to urban gun deaths and injuries, and which are the overwhelmingly favorite weapon of armed criminals; and at the same time, the law imposes a burden upon gun owners that seems proportionately no greater than restrictions in existence at the time the Second Amendment was adopted. In these circumstances, the District's law falls within the zone that the Second Amendment leaves open to regulation by legislatures.

[II]

I therefore begin by asking a process-based question: How is a court to determine whether a particular firearm regulation (here, the District's restriction on handguns) is consistent with the Second Amendment? What kind of constitutional standard should the court use? How high a protective hurdle does the Amendment erect?

The question matters. The majority is wrong when it says that the District's law is unconstitutional "[u]nder any of the standards of scrutiny that we have applied to enumerated constitutional rights." How could that be? It certainly would not be unconstitutional under, for example, a "rational basis" standard, which requires a court to uphold regulation so long as it bears a "rational relationship" to a "legitimate governmental purpose." The law at issue here, which in part seeks to prevent gun-related accidents, at least bears a "rational relationship" to that "legitimate" life-saving objective.

Respondent proposes that the Court adopt a "strict scrutiny" test, which would require reviewing with care each gun law to determine whether it is "narrowly tailored to achieve a compelling governmental interest." But the majority implicitly, and appropriately, rejects that suggestion by broadly approving a set of laws-prohibitions on concealed weapons, forfeiture by criminals of the Second Amendment right, prohibitions on firearms in certain locales, and governmental regulation of commercial firearm sales—whose constitutionality under a strict scrutiny standard would be far from clear.

Indeed, adoption of a true strict-scrutiny standard for evaluating gun regulations would be impossible. That is because almost every gun-control regulation will seek to advance (as the one here does) a "primary concern of every government-a concern for the safety and indeed the lives of its citizens." The Court has deemed that interest, as well as "the Government's general interest in preventing crime," to be "compelling," see and the Court has in a wide variety of constitutional contexts found such public-safety concerns sufficiently forceful to justify restrictions on individual liberties. Thus, any attempt in theory to apply strict scrutiny to gun regulations will in practice turn into an interest-balancing inquiry, with the interests protected by the Second Amendment on one side and the governmental public-safety concerns on the other, the only question being whether the regulation at issue impermissibly burdens the former in the course of advancing the latter.

I would simply adopt such an interest-balancing inquiry explicitly. The fact that important interests lie on both sides of the constitutional equation suggests that review of gun-control regulation is not a context in which a court should effectively presume either constitutionality (as in rational-basis review) or unconstitutionality (as in strict scrutiny). Rather, "where a law significantly implicates competing constitutionally protected interests in complex ways," the Court generally asks whether the statute burdens a protected interest in a way or to an extent that is out of proportion to the statute's salutary effects upon other important governmental interests. Any answer would take account both of the statute's effects upon the competing interests and the existence of any clearly superior less restrictive alternative. Contrary to the majority's unsupported suggestion that this sort of "proportionality" approach is unprecedented, the Court has applied it in various constitutional contexts, including election-law cases, speech cases, and due process cases.

In applying this kind of standard the Court normally defers to a legislature's empirical judgment in matters where a legislature is likely to have greater expertise and greater institutional factfinding capacity. Nonetheless, a court, not a legislature, must make the ultimate constitutional conclusion, exercising its "independent judicial judgment" in light of the whole record to determine whether a law exceeds constitutional boundaries.

[III]

A

No one doubts the constitutional importance of the statute's basic objective, saving lives. But there is considerable debate about whether the District's statute helps to achieve that objective.

First, consider the facts as the legislature saw them when it adopted the District statute. As stated by the local council committee that recommended its adoption, the major substantive goal of the District's handgun restriction is "to reduce the potentiality for gun-related crimes and gun-related deaths from occurring within the District of Columbia." The committee concluded, on the basis of "extensive public hearings" and "lengthy research," that "[t]he easy availability of firearms in the United States has been a major factor contributing to the drastic increase in gun-related violence and crime over the past 40 years." It reported to the Council "startling statistics," regarding gun-related crime, accidents, and deaths, focusing particularly on the relation between handguns and crime and the proliferation of handguns within the District.

The committee informed the Council that guns were "responsible for 69 deaths in this country each day," for a total of "[a]pproximately 25,000 gun-deaths . . . each year," along with an additional 200,000 gun-related injuries. Three thousand of these deaths, the report stated, were accidental. A quarter of the victims in those accidental deaths were children under the age of 14. And according to the committee, "[f]or every intruder stopped by a homeowner with a firearm, there are 4 gun-related accidents within the home."

In respect to local crime, the committee observed that there were 285 murders in the District during 1974—a record number. The committee report furthermore presented statistics strongly correlating handguns with crime. Of the 285 murders in the District in 1974, 155 were committed with handguns. Ibid. This did not appear to be an aberration, as the report revealed that "handguns [had been] used in roughly 54% of all murders" (and 87% of murders of law enforcement officers) nationwide over the preceding several years. Ibid. Nor were handguns only linked to murders, as statistics showed that they were used in roughly 60% of robberies and 26% of assaults. "A crime committed with a pistol," the committee reported, "is 7 times more likely to be lethal than a crime committed with any other weapon." The committee furthermore presented statistics regarding the availability of handguns in the United States, and noted that they had "become easy for juveniles to obtain," even despite then-current District laws prohibiting juveniles from possessing them.

Next, consider the facts as a court must consider them looking at the matter as of today. Petitioners, and their amici, have presented us with more recent statistics that tell much the same story that the committee report told 30 years ago. At the least, they present nothing that would permit us to second-guess the Council in respect to the numbers of gun crimes, injuries, and deaths, or the role of handguns.

From 1993 to 1997, there were 180,533 firearm-related deaths in the United States, an average of over 36,000 per year. Over that same period there were an additional 411,800 nonfatal firearm-related injuries treated in U.S. hospitals, an average of over 82,000 per year. Of these, 62% resulted from assaults, 17% were unintentional, 6% were suicide attempts, 1% were legal interventions, and 13% were of unknown causes.

The statistics are particularly striking in respect to children and adolescents. In over one in every eight firearm-related deaths in 1997, the victim was someone under the age of 20. Firearm-related deaths account for 22.5% of all injury deaths between the ages of 1 and 19. More male teenagers die from firearms than from all natural causes combined. Persons under 25 accounted for 47% of hospital-treated firearm injuries between June 1, 1992 and May 31, 1993.

Handguns are involved in a majority of firearm deaths and injuries in the United States. From 1993 to 1997, 81% of firearm-homicide victims were killed by handgun. In the same period, for the 41% of firearm injuries for which the weapon type is known, 82% of them were from handguns. Firearm Injury and Death From Crime 4. And among children under the age of 20, handguns account for approximately 70% of all unintentional firearm-related injuries and deaths. In particular, 70% of all firearm-related teenage suicides in 1996 involved a handgun.

Handguns also appear to be a very popular weapon among criminals. In a 1997 survey of inmates who were armed during the crime for which they were incarcerated, 83.2% of state inmates and 86.7% of federal inmates said that they were armed with a handgun. Statistics further suggest that urban areas, such as the District, have different experiences with gun-related death, injury, and crime, than do less densely populated rural areas. A disproportionate amount of violent and property crimes occur in urban areas, and urban criminals are more likely than other offenders to use a firearm during the commission of a violent crime.

Finally, the linkage of handguns to firearms deaths and injuries appears to be much stronger in urban than in rural areas. "[S]tudies to date generally support the hypothesis that the greater number of rural gun deaths are from rifles or shotguns, whereas the greater number of urban gun deaths are from handguns."

Finally, consider the claim of respondent's amici that handgun bans cannot work; there are simply too many illegal guns already in existence for a ban on legal guns to make a difference. In a word, they claim that, given the urban sea of pre-existing legal guns, criminals can readily find arms regardless. Nonetheless, a legislature might respond, we want to make an effort to try to dry up that urban sea, drop by drop. And none of the studies can show that effort is not worthwhile.

In a word, the studies to which respondent's amici point raise policy-related questions. They succeed in proving that the District's predictive judgments are controversial. But they do not by themselves show that those judgments are incorrect; nor do they demonstrate a consensus, academic or otherwise, supporting that conclusion.

Thus, it is not surprising that the District and its amici support the District's handgun restriction with studies of their own. One in particular suggests that, statistically speaking, the District's law has indeed had positive life-saving effects. See Loftin, McDowall, Weirsema, & Cottey, Effects of Restrictive Licensing of Handguns on Homicide and Suicide in the District of Columbia, 325 New England J. Med. 1615 (1991). Others suggest that firearm restrictions as a general matter reduce homicides, suicides, and accidents in the home. Still others suggest that the defensive uses of handguns are not as great in number as respondent's amici claim.

Respondent and his amici reply to these responses; and in doing so, they seek to discredit as methodologically flawed the studies and evidence relied upon by the District. The upshot is a set of studies and counterstudies that, at most, could leave a judge uncertain about the proper policy conclusion. But from respondent's perspective any such uncertainty is not good enough. That is because legislators, not judges, have primary responsibility for drawing policy conclusions from empirical fact. And, given that constitutional allocation of decisionmaking responsibility, the empirical evidence presented here is sufficient to allow a judge to reach a firm legal conclusion.

In particular this Court, in First Amendment cases applying intermediate scrutiny, has said that our "sole obligation" in reviewing a legislature's "predictive judgments" is "to assure that, in formulating its judgments," the legislature "has drawn reasonable inferences based on substantial evidence." And judges, looking at the evidence before us, should agree that the District legislature's predictive judgments satisfy that legal standard. That is to say, the District's judgment, while open to question, is nevertheless supported by "substantial evidence."

There is no cause here to depart from [that] standard for the District's decision represents the kind of empirically based judgment that legislatures, not courts, are best suited to make. In fact, deference to legislative judgment seems particularly appropriate here, where the judgment has been made by a local legislature, with particular knowledge of local problems and insight into appropriate local solutions.

For these reasons, I conclude that the District's statute properly seeks to further the sort of life-preserving and public-safety interests that the Court has called "compelling."

B

I next assess the extent to which the District's law burdens the interests that the Second Amendment seeks to protect. Respondent and his amici, as well as the majority, suggest that those interests include: (1) the preservation of a "well regulated Militia"; (2) safeguarding the use of firearms for sporting purposes, e. g., hunting and marksmanship; and (3) assuring the use of firearms for self-defense. For argument's sake, I shall consider all three of those interests here.

1

The District's statute burdens the Amendment's first and primary objective hardly at all. As previously noted, there is general agreement among the Members of the Court that the principal (if not the only) purpose of the Second Amendment is found in the Amendment's text: the preservation of a "well regulated Militia." What scant Court precedent there is on the Second Amendment teaches that the Amendment was adopted "[w]ith obvious purpose to assure the continuation and render possible the effectiveness of [militia] forces" and "must be interpreted and applied with that end in view."

2

The majority briefly suggests that the "right to keep and bear Arms" might encompass an interest in hunting. But in enacting the present provisions, the District sought "to take nothing away from sportsmen." And any inability of District residents to hunt near where they live has much to do with the jurisdiction's exclusively urban character and little to do with the District's firearm laws. For reasons similar to those I discussed in the preceding subsection—that the District's law does not prohibit possession of rifles or shotguns, and the presence of opportunities for sporting activities in nearby States—I reach a similar conclusion, namely, that the District's law burdens any sports-related or hunting-related objectives that the Amendment may protect little, or not at all.

3

The District's law does prevent a resident from keeping a loaded handgun in his home. And it consequently makes it more difficult for the householder to use the handgun for self-defense in the home against intruders, such as burglars. As the Court of Appeals noted, statistics suggest that handguns are the most popular weapon for self defense. To that extent the law burdens to some degree an interest in self-defense that for present purposes I have assumed the Amendment seeks to further.

C

In weighing needs and burdens, we must take account of the possibility that there are reasonable, but less restrictive alternatives. Are there other potential measures that might similarly promote the same goals while imposing lesser restrictions? Here I see none.

The reason there is no clearly superior, less restrictive alternative to the District's handgun ban is that the ban's very objective is to reduce significantly the number of handguns in the District, say, for example, by allowing a law enforcement officer immediately to assume that any handgun he sees is an illegal handgun. And there is no plausible way to achieve that objective other than to ban the guns.

D

The upshot is that the District's objectives are compelling; its predictive judgments as to its law's tendency to achieve those objectives are adequately supported; the law does impose a burden upon any self-defense interest that the Amendment seeks to secure; and there is no clear less restrictive alternative. I turn now to the final portion of the "permissible regulation" question: Does the District's law disproportionately burden Amendment-protected interests? Several considerations, taken together, convince me that it does not.

First, the District law is tailored to the life-threatening problems it attempts to address. The law concerns one class of weapons, handguns, leaving residents free to possess shotguns and rifles, along with ammunition. The area that falls within its scope is totally urban. That urban area suffers from a serious hand-gun-fatality problem. The District's law directly aims at that compelling problem. And there is no less restrictive way to achieve the problem-related benefits that it seeks.

Second, the self-defense interest in maintaining loaded handguns in the home to shoot intruders is not the primary interest, but at most a subsidiary interest, that the Second Amendment seeks to serve. The Second Amendment's language, while speaking of a "Militia," says nothing of "self-defense."

Further, any self-defense interest at the time of the Framing could not have focused exclusively upon urban-crime related dangers. Two hundred years ago, most Americans, many living on the frontier, would likely have thought of self-defense primarily in terms of outbreaks of fighting with Indian tribes, rebellions such as Shays' Rebellion, marauders, and crime-related dangers to travelers on the roads, on footpaths, or along waterways. Insofar as the Framers focused at all on the tiny fraction of the population living in large cities, they would have been aware that these city dwellers were subject to firearm restrictions that their rural counterparts were not. They are unlikely then to have thought of a right to keep loaded handguns in homes to confront intruders in urban settings as central. And the subsequent development of modern urban police departments, by diminishing the need to keep loaded guns nearby in case of intruders, would have moved any such right even further away from the heart of the amendment's more basic protective ends.

Nor, for that matter, am I aware of any evidence that handguns in particular were central to the Framers' conception of the Second Amendment. The lists of militia-related weapons in the late 18th-century state statutes appear primarily to refer to other sorts of weapons, muskets in particular.

Third, irrespective of what the Framers could have thought, we know what they did think. Samuel Adams, who lived in Boston, advocated a constitutional amendment that would have precluded the Constitution from ever being "construed" to "prevent the people of the United States, who are peaceable citizens, from keeping their own arms." And he doubtless knew that Massachusetts law prohibited Bostonians from keeping loaded guns in the house. So how could Samuel Adams have advocated such protection unless he thought that the protection was consistent with local regulation that seriously impeded urban residents from using their arms against intruders? It seems unlikely that he meant to deprive the Federal Government of power (to enact Boston-type weapons regulation) that he know Boston had and (as far as we know) he would have thought constitutional under the Massachusetts Constitution.

Fourth, a contrary view, as embodied in today's decision, will have unfortunate consequences. The decision will encourage legal challenges to gun regulation throughout the Nation. Because it says little about the standards used to evaluate regulatory decisions, it will leave the Nation without clear standards for resolving those challenges. And litigation over the course of many years, or the mere specter of such litigation, threatens to leave cities without effective protection against gun violence and accidents during that time. As important, the majority's decision threatens severely to limit the ability of more knowledgeable, democratically elected officials to deal with gun-related problems. But I cannot understand how one can take from the elected branches of government the right to decide whether to insist upon a handgun-free urban populace in a city now facing a serious crime problem and which, in the future, could well face environmental or other emergencies that threaten the breakdown of law and order.

For these reasons, I conclude that the District's measure is a proportionate, not a disproportionate, response to the compelling concerns that led the District to adopt it.

3. Justiciability Limits

b. Standing

i. Constitutional Standing Requirements

In *Massachusetts v. Environmental Protection Agency*, below, the Court applied the constitutional requirements for standing in an unusual context: whether a state government has standing to sue a federal agency for its failure to promulgate regulations to deal with the problem of global warming. It is notable that the Court applied the traditional standing requirements—injury, causation, and redressability—and found that they were met here.

MASSACHUSETTS v. ENVIRONMENTAL PROTECTION AGENCY
127 S.Ct. 1438 (2007)

Justice STEVENS delivered the opinion of the Court.

A well-documented rise in global temperatures has coincided with a significant increase in the concentration of carbon dioxide in the atmosphere. Respected scientists believe the two trends are related. For when carbon dioxide is released into the atmosphere, it acts like the ceiling of a greenhouse, trapping solar energy and retarding the escape of reflected heat. It is therefore a species—the most important species—of a "greenhouse gas."

Calling global warming "the most pressing environmental challenge of our time," a group of States, local governments, and private organizations, alleged in a petition for certiorari that the Environmental Protection Agency (EPA) has abdicated its responsibility under the Clean Air Act to regulate the emissions of four greenhouse gases, including carbon dioxide. Specifically, petitioners asked us to answer two questions concerning the meaning of § 202(a)(1) of the Act: whether EPA has the statutory authority to regulate greenhouse gas emissions from new motor vehicles; and if so, whether its stated reasons for refusing to do so are consistent with the statute.

In response, EPA, supported by 10 intervening States and six trade associations, correctly argued that we may not address those two questions unless at least one petitioner has standing to invoke our jurisdiction under Article III of the Constitution.

Article III of the Constitution limits federal-court jurisdiction to "Cases" and "Controversies." Those two words confine "the business of federal courts to questions presented in an adversary context and in a form historically viewed as capable of resolution through the judicial process." The parties' dispute turns on the proper construction of a congressional statute, a question eminently suitable to resolution in federal court. Congress has moreover authorized this type of challenge to EPA action. See 42 U.S.C. § 7607(b)(1). That authorization is of critical importance to the standing inquiry: "Congress has the power to define injuries and articulate chains of causation that will give rise to a case or controversy where none existed before." "In exercising this power, however, Congress must at the very least identify the injury it seeks to vindicate and relate the injury to the class of persons entitled to bring suit." Ibid. We will not, therefore, "entertain citizen suits to vindicate the public's nonconcrete interest in the proper administration of the laws."

EPA maintains that because greenhouse gas emissions inflict widespread harm, the doctrine of standing presents an insuperable jurisdictional obstacle. We do not agree. At bottom, "the gist of the question of standing" is whether petitioners have "such a personal stake in the outcome of the controversy as to assure that concrete adverseness which sharpens the presentation of issues upon which the court so largely depends for illumination." *Baker v. Carr*, (1962).

To ensure the proper adversarial presentation, *Lujan v. Defenders of Wildlife* (1992), holds that a litigant must demonstrate that it has suffered a concrete and particularized injury that is either actual or imminent, that the injury is fairly traceable to the defendant, and that it is likely that a favorable decision will redress that injury. However, a litigant to whom Congress has "accorded a procedural right to protect his concrete interests,"—here, the right to challenge agency action unlawfully withheld, § 7607(b)(1)—"can assert that right without meeting all the normal standards for redressability and immediacy." When a litigant is vested with a procedural right, that litigant has standing if there is some possibility that the requested relief will prompt the injury-causing party to reconsider the decision that allegedly harmed the litigant.

Only one of the petitioners needs to have standing to permit us to consider the petition for review. We stress here, the special position and interest of Massachusetts. It is of considerable relevance that the party seeking review here is a sovereign State and not, as it was in *Lujan*, a private individual.

Well before the creation of the modern administrative state, we recognized that States are not normal litigants for the purposes of invoking federal jurisdiction. That Massachusetts does in fact own a great deal of the "territory alleged to be affected" only reinforces the conclusion that its stake in the outcome of this case is sufficiently concrete to warrant the exercise of federal judicial power.

When a State enters the Union, it surrenders certain sovereign prerogatives. Massachusetts cannot invade Rhode Island to force reductions in greenhouse gas emissions, it cannot negotiate an emissions treaty with China or India, and in some circumstances the exercise of its police powers to reduce in-state motor-vehicle emissions might well be pre-empted.

These sovereign prerogatives are now lodged in the Federal Government, and Congress has ordered EPA to protect Massachusetts (among others) by prescribing standards applicable to the "emission of any air pollutant from any class or classes of new motor vehicle engines, which in [the Administrator's] judgment cause, or contribute to, air pollution which may reasonably be anticipated to endanger public health or welfare." Congress has moreover recognized a concomitant procedural right to challenge the rejection of its rulemaking petition as arbitrary and capricious. Given that procedural right and Massachusetts' stake in protecting its quasi-sovereign interests, the Commonwealth is entitled to special solicitude in our standing analysis.

With that in mind, it is clear that petitioners' submissions as they pertain to Massachusetts have satisfied the most demanding standards of the adversarial process. EPA's steadfast refusal to regulate greenhouse gas emissions presents a risk of harm to Massachusetts that is both "actual" and "imminent." There is, moreover, a "substantial likelihood that the judicial relief requested" will prompt EPA to take steps to reduce that risk.

The Injury

The harms associated with climate change are serious and well recognized. Indeed, the NRC Report itself—which EPA regards as an "objective and independent assessment of the relevant science," identifies a number of environmental changes that have already inflicted significant harms, including "the global retreat of mountain glaciers, reduction in snow-cover extent, the earlier spring melting of rivers and lakes, [and] the accelerated rate of rise of sea levels during the 20th century relative to the past few thousand years. . . ."

Petitioners allege that this only hints at the environmental damage yet to come. According to the climate scientist Michael MacCracken, "qualified scientific experts involved in climate change research" have reached a "strong consensus" that global warming threatens (among other things) a precipitate rise in sea levels by the end of the century, "severe and irreversible changes to natural ecosystems," a "significant reduction in water storage in winter snowpack in mountainous regions with direct and important economic consequences," ibid., and an increase in the spread of disease. He also observes that rising ocean temperatures may contribute to the ferocity of hurricanes.

That these climate-change risks are "widely shared" does not minimize Massachusetts' interest in the outcome of this litigation. The severity of that injury will only increase over the course of the next century: If sea levels continue to rise as predicted, one Massachusetts official believes that a significant fraction of coastal property will be "either permanently lost through inundation or temporarily lost through periodic storm surge and flooding events." Remediation costs alone, petitioners allege, could run well into the hundreds of millions of dollars.

Causation

EPA does not dispute the existence of a causal connection between man-made greenhouse gas emissions and global warming. At a minimum, therefore, EPA's refusal to regulate such emissions "contributes" to Massachusetts' injuries.

EPA nevertheless maintains that its decision not to regulate greenhouse gas emissions from new motor vehicles contributes so insignificantly to petitioners' injuries that the agency cannot be haled into federal court to answer for them. For the same reason, EPA does not believe that any realistic possibility exists that the relief petitioners seek would mitigate global climate change and remedy their injuries. That is especially so because predicted increases in greenhouse gas emissions from developing nations, particularly China and India, are likely to offset any marginal domestic decrease.

But EPA overstates its case. Its argument rests on the erroneous assumption that a small incremental step, because it is incremental, can never be attacked in a federal judicial forum. Yet accepting that premise would doom most challenges to regulatory action. Agencies, like legislatures, do not generally resolve massive problems in one fell regulatory swoop. They instead whittle away at them over time, refining their preferred approach as circumstances change and as they develop a more-nuanced understanding of how best to proceed. That a first step might be tentative does not by itself support the notion that federal courts lack jurisdiction to determine whether that step conforms to law.

And reducing domestic automobile emissions is hardly a tentative step. Even leaving aside the other greenhouse gases, the United States transportation sector emits an enormous quantity of carbon dioxide into the atmosphere—according to the MacCracken affidavit, more than 1.7 billion metric tons in 1999 alone. That accounts for more than 6% of worldwide carbon dioxide emissions. To put this in perspective: Considering just emissions from the transportation sector, which represent less than one-third of this country's total carbon dioxide emissions, the United States would still rank as the third-largest emitter of carbon dioxide in the world, outpaced only by the European Union and China. Judged by any standard, U.S. motor-vehicle emissions make a meaningful contribution to greenhouse gas concentrations and hence, according to petitioners, to global warming.

The Remedy

While it may be true that regulating motor-vehicle emissions will not by itself reverse global warming, it by no means follows that we lack jurisdiction to decide whether EPA has a duty to take steps to slow or reduce it. Because of the enormity of the potential consequences associated with man-made climate change, the fact that the effectiveness of a remedy might be delayed during the (relatively short) time it takes for a new motor-vehicle fleet to replace an older one is essentially irrelevant. Nor is it dispositive that developing countries such as China and India are poised to increase greenhouse gas emissions substantially over the next century: A reduction in domestic emissions would slow the pace of global emissions increases, no matter what happens elsewhere.

[Justice Stevens then went on to hold that the EPA had statutory authority to promulgate regulations dealing with global warming and either had to do so or justify not doing so.]

Chief Justice ROBERTS, with whom Justice SCALIA, Justice THOMAS, and Justice ALITO join, dissenting.

Global warming may be a "crisis," even "the most pressing environmental problem of our time." Indeed, it may ultimately affect nearly everyone on the planet in some potentially adverse way, and it may be that governments have done too little to address it. It is not a problem, however, that has escaped the attention of policymakers in the Executive and Legislative Branches of our Government, who continue to consider regulatory, legislative, and treaty-based means of addressing global climate change.

Apparently dissatisfied with the pace of progress on this issue in the elected branches, petitioners have come to the courts claiming broad-ranging injury, and attempting to tie that injury to the Government's alleged failure to comply with a rather narrow statutory provision. I would reject these challenges as nonjusticiable. Such a conclusion involves no judgment on whether global warming exists, what causes it, or the extent of the problem. Nor does it render petitioners without recourse. This Court's standing jurisprudence simply recognizes that redress of grievances of the sort at issue here "is the function of Congress and the Chief Executive," not the federal courts.

I

Our modern framework for addressing standing is familiar: "A plaintiff must allege personal injury fairly traceable to the defendant's allegedly unlawful conduct and likely to be redressed by the requested relief." Applying that standard here, petitioners bear the burden of alleging an injury that is fairly traceable to the Environmental Protection Agency's failure to promulgate new motor vehicle greenhouse gas emission standards, and that is likely to be redressed by the prospective issuance of such standards.

Before determining whether petitioners can meet this familiar test, however, the Court changes the rules. It asserts that "States are not normal litigants for the purposes of invoking federal jurisdiction," and that given "Massachusetts' stake in protecting its quasi-sovereign interests, the Commonwealth is entitled to special solicitude in our standing analysis."

Relaxing Article III standing requirements because asserted injuries are pressed by a State, however, has no basis in our jurisprudence, and support for any such "special solicitude" is conspicuously absent from the Court's opinion. The general judicial review provision cited by the Court, 42 U.S.C. § 7607(b)(1), affords States no special rights or status. The Court states that "Congress has ordered EPA to protect Massachusetts (among others)" through the statutory provision at issue, and that "Congress has . . . recognized a concomitant procedural right to challenge the rejection of its rulemaking petition as arbitrary and capricious." The reader might think from this unfortunate phrasing that Congress said something about the rights of States in this particular provision of the statute. Congress knows how to do that when it wants to, see, e.g., § 7426(b) (affording States the right to petition EPA to directly regulate certain sources of pollution), but it has done nothing of the sort here. Under the law on which petitioners rely, Congress treated public and private litigants exactly the same.

Nor does the case law cited by the Court provide any support for the notion that Article III somehow implicitly treats public and private litigants differently. What is more, the Court's reasoning falters on its own terms. The Court asserts that Massachusetts is entitled to "special solicitude" due to its "quasi-sovereign interests," but then applies our Article III standing test to the asserted injury of the State's loss of coastal property. In the context of parens patriae standing, however, we have characterized state ownership of land as a "nonsovereign interes[t]" because a State "is likely to have the same interests as other similarly situated proprietors."

II

It is not at all clear how the Court's "special solicitude" for Massachusetts plays out in the standing analysis, except as an implicit concession that petitioners cannot establish standing on traditional terms. But the status of Massachusetts as a State cannot compensate for petitioners' failure to demonstrate injury in fact, causation, and redressability.

When the Court actually applies the three-part test, it focuses on the State's asserted loss of coastal land as the injury in fact. If petitioners rely on loss of land as the Article III injury, however, they must ground the rest of the standing analysis in that specific injury. That alleged injury must be "concrete and particularized," and "distinct and palpable." Central to this concept of "particularized" injury is the requirement that a plaintiff be affected in a "personal and individual way," and seek relief that "directly and tangibly benefits him" in a manner distinct from its impact on "the public at large."

The very concept of global warming seems inconsistent with this particularization requirement. Global warming is a phenomenon "harmful to humanity at large," and the redress petitioners seek is focused no more on them than on the public generally—it is literally to change the atmosphere around the world.

If petitioners' particularized injury is loss of coastal land, it is also that injury that must be "actual or imminent, not conjectural or hypothetical," "real and immediate," and "certainly impending."

As to "actual" injury, the Court observes that "global sea levels rose somewhere between 10 and 20 centimeters over the 20th century as a result of global warming" and that "[t]hese rising seas have already begun to swallow Massachusetts' coastal land." But none of petitioners' declarations supports that connection. One declaration states that "a rise in sea level due to climate change is occurring on the coast of Massachusetts, in the metropolitan Boston area," but there is no elaboration. And the declarant goes on to identify a "significan[t]" non-global-warming cause of Boston's rising sea level: land subsidence. Thus, aside from a single conclusory statement, there is nothing in petitioners' 43 standing declarations and accompanying exhibits to support an inference of actual loss of Massachusetts coastal land from 20th century global sea level increases. It is pure conjecture.

The Court's attempts to identify "imminent" or "certainly impending" loss of Massachusetts coastal land fares no better. One of petitioners' declarants predicts global warming will cause sea level to rise by 20 to 70 centimeters by the year 2100. Another uses a computer modeling program to map the Commonwealth's coastal land and its current elevation, and calculates that the high-end estimate of sea level rise would result in the loss of significant state-owned coastal land. But the computer modeling program has a conceded average error of about 30 centimeters and a maximum observed error of 70 centimeters. As an initial matter, if it is possible that the model underrepresents the elevation of coastal land to an extent equal to or in excess of the projected sea level rise, it is difficult to put much stock in the predicted loss of land. But even placing that problem to the side, accepting a century-long time horizon and a series of compounded estimates renders requirements of imminence and immediacy utterly toothless. "Allegations of possible future injury do not satisfy the requirements of Art. III. A threatened injury must be certainly impending to constitute injury in fact."

III

Petitioners' reliance on Massachusetts's loss of coastal land as their injury in fact for standing purposes creates insurmountable problems for them with respect to causation and redressability. To establish standing, petitioners must show a causal connection between that specific injury and the lack of new motor vehicle greenhouse gas emission standards, and that the promulgation of such standards would likely redress that injury. As is often the case, the questions of causation and redressability overlap. And importantly, when a party is challenging the Government's allegedly unlawful regulation, or lack of regulation, of a third party, satisfying the causation and redressability requirements becomes "substantially more difficult."

Petitioners view the relationship between their injuries and EPA's failure to promulgate new motor vehicle greenhouse gas emission standards as simple and direct: Domestic motor vehicles emit carbon dioxide and other greenhouse gases. Worldwide emissions of greenhouse gases contribute to global warming and therefore also to petitioners' alleged injuries. Without the new vehicle standards, greenhouse gas emissions—and therefore global warming and its attendant harms—have been higher than they otherwise would have been; once EPA changes course, the trend will be reversed.

The Court ignores the complexities of global warming, and does so by now disregarding the "particularized" injury it relied on in step one, and using the dire nature of global warming itself as a bootstrap for finding causation and redressability. First, it is important to recognize the extent of the emissions at issue here. Because local greenhouse gas emissions disperse throughout the atmosphere and remain there for anywhere from 50 to 200 years, it is global emissions data that are relevant. According to one of petitioners' declarations, domestic motor vehicles contribute about 6 percent of global carbon dioxide emissions and 4 percent of global greenhouse gas emissions. The amount of global emissions at issue here is smaller still; § 202(a)(1) of the Clean Air Act covers only new motor vehicles and new motor vehicle engines, so petitioners' desired emission standards might reduce only a fraction of 4 percent of global emissions.

This gets us only to the relevant greenhouse gas emissions; linking them to global warming and ultimately to petitioners' alleged injuries next requires consideration of further complexities. As EPA explained in its denial of petitioners' request for rulemaking, "predicting future climate change necessarily involves a complex web of economic and physical factors including: our ability to predict future global anthropogenic emissions of [greenhouse gases] and aerosols; the fate of these emissions once they enter the atmosphere (e.g., what percentage are absorbed by vegetation or are taken up by the oceans); the impact of those emissions that remain in the atmosphere on the radiative properties of the atmosphere; changes in critically important climate feedbacks (e.g., changes in cloud cover and ocean circulation); changes in temperature characteristics (e.g., average temperatures, shifts in daytime and evening temperatures); changes in other climatic parameters (e.g., shifts in precipitation, storms); and ultimately the impact of such changes on human health and welfare (e.g., increases or decreases in agricultural productivity, human health impacts)."

Petitioners are never able to trace their alleged injuries back through this complex web to the fractional amount of global emissions that might have been limited with EPA standards. In light of the bit-part domestic new motor vehicle greenhouse gas emissions have played in what petitioners describe as a 150-year global phenomenon, and the myriad additional factors bearing on petitioners' alleged injury—the loss of Massachusetts coastal land—the connection is far too speculative to establish causation.

IV

Redressability is even more problematic. To the tenuous link between petitioners' alleged injury and the indeterminate fractional domestic emissions at issue here, add the fact that petitioners cannot meaningfully predict what will come of the 80 percent of global greenhouse gas emissions that originate outside the United States. As the Court acknowledges, "developing countries such as China and India are poised to increase greenhouse gas emissions substantially over the next century," so the domestic emissions at issue here may become an increasingly marginal portion of global emissions, and any decreases produced by petitioners' desired standards are likely to be overwhelmed many times over by emissions increases elsewhere in the world.

The Court's sleight-of-hand is in failing to link up the different elements of the three-part standing test. What must be likely to be redressed is the particular injury in fact. The injury the Court looks to is the asserted loss of land. The Court contends that regulating domestic motor vehicle emissions will reduce carbon dioxide in the atmosphere, and therefore redress Massachusetts's injury. But even if regulation does reduce emissions—to some indeterminate degree, given events elsewhere in the world—the Court never explains why that makes it likely that the injury in fact—the loss of land—will be redressed. Schoolchildren know that a kingdom might be lost "all for the want of a horseshoe nail," but "likely" redressability is a different matter. The realities make it pure conjecture to suppose that EPA regulation of new automobile emissions will likely prevent the loss of Massachusetts coastal land.

The good news is that the Court's "special solicitude" for Massachusetts limits the future applicability of the diluted standing requirements applied in this case. The bad news is that the Court's self-professed relaxation of those Article III requirements has caused us to transgress "the proper—and properly limited—role of the courts in a democratic society."

I respectfully dissent.

ii. Prudential Standing Limits

The Prohibition of Generalized Grievances (*casebook, p. 58*)

In the last two years, there have been two cases about taxpayer standing, though in very different contexts. In *Hein v. Freedom from Religion*, the Court considered whether taxpayers have standing to challenge government expenditures from executive funds that aid religion. The Court returned to *Flast v. Cohen* (casebook p. 61) and *Valley Forge Christian College v. Americans United for Separation of Church and State* (casebook p. 64) and held that under these cases taxpayers have standing to challenge government expenditures pursuant to a federal statute, but not pursuant to executive spending.

In *Daimler Chrysler Corp. v. Cuno*, the Court applied the prohibition of taxpayer standing to prevent a challenge under the dormant commerce clause to a state and local government giving tax benefits to a company to move into an area.[2]

HEIN v. FREEDOM FROM RELIGION FOUNDATION
127 S.Ct. 2553 (2007)

Justice ALITO announced the judgment of the Court and delivered an opinion in which THE CHIEF JUSTICE and Justice KENNEDY join.

This is a lawsuit in which it was claimed that conferences held as part of the President's Faith-Based and Community Initiatives program violated the Establishment Clause of the First Amendment because, among other things, President Bush and former Secretary of Education Paige gave speeches that used "religious imagery" and praised the efficacy of faith-based programs in delivering social services. The plaintiffs contend that they meet the standing requirements of Article III of the Constitution because they pay federal taxes.

It has long been established, however, that the payment of taxes is generally not enough to establish standing to challenge an action taken by the Federal Government. In light of the size of the federal budget, it is a complete fiction to argue that an unconstitutional federal expenditure causes an individual federal taxpayer any measurable economic harm. And if every federal taxpayer could

---

2. The dormant commerce clause is the principle that state and local governments act unconstitutionally if they place an undue burden on interstate commerce. The dormant commerce clause is discussed in Chapter 4.

sue to challenge any Government expenditure, the federal courts would cease to function as courts of law and would be cast in the role of general complaint bureaus.

In *Flast v. Cohen* (1968), we recognized a narrow exception to the general rule against federal taxpayer standing. Under *Flast*, a plaintiff asserting an Establishment Clause claim has standing to challenge a law authorizing the use of federal funds in a way that allegedly violates the Establishment Clause. In the present case, Congress did not specifically authorize the use of federal funds to pay for the conferences or speeches that the plaintiffs challenged. Instead, the conferences and speeches were paid for out of general Executive Branch appropriations. The Court of Appeals, however, held that the plaintiffs have standing as taxpayers because the conferences were paid for with money appropriated by Congress.

The question that is presented here is whether this broad reading of *Flast* is correct. We hold that it is not.

I

In 2001, the President issued an executive order creating the White House Office of Faith-Based and Community Initiatives within the Executive Office of the President. The purpose of this new office was to ensure that "private and charitable community groups, including religious ones ... have the fullest opportunity permitted by law to compete on a level playing field, so long as they achieve valid public purposes" and adhere to "the bedrock principles of pluralism, nondiscrimination, evenhandedness, and neutrality." The office was specifically charged with the task of eliminating unnecessary bureaucratic, legislative, and regulatory barriers that could impede such organizations' effectiveness and ability to compete equally for federal assistance.

By separate executive orders, the President also created Executive Department Centers for Faith-Based and Community Initiatives within several federal agencies and departments. These centers were given the job of ensuring that faith-based community groups would be eligible to compete for federal financial support without impairing their independence or autonomy, as long as they did "not use direct Federal financial assistance to support any inherently religious activities, such as worship, religious instruction, or proselytization." To this end, the President directed that "[n]o organization should be discriminated against on the basis of religion or religious belief in the administration or distribution of Federal financial assistance under social service programs," and that "[a]ll organizations that receive Federal financial assistance under social services programs should be prohibited from discriminating against beneficiaries or potential beneficiaries of the social services programs on the basis of religion or religious belief."

No congressional legislation specifically authorized the creation of the White House Office or the Executive Department Centers. Rather, they were "created entirely within the executive branch ... by Presidential executive order." Nor has Congress enacted any law specifically appropriating money for these entities' activities. Instead, their activities are funded through general Executive Branch appropriations.

The respondents are Freedom From Religion Foundation, Inc., a nonstock corporation "opposed to government endorsement of religion," and three of its members. Respondents brought suit in the United States District Court for the Western District of Wisconsin, alleging that petitioners violated the Establishment Clause by organizing conferences at which faith-based organizations allegedly "are singled out as being particularly worthy of federal funding . . . , and the belief in God is extolled as distinguishing the claimed effectiveness of faith-based social services." Respondents further alleged that the content of these conferences sent a message to religious believers "that they are insiders and favored members of the political community" and that the conferences sent the message to nonbelievers "that they are outsiders" and "not full members of the political community." In short, respondents alleged that the conferences were designed to promote, and had the effect of promoting, religious community groups over secular ones.

The only asserted basis for standing was that the individual respondents are federal taxpayers who are "opposed to the use of Congressional taxpayer appropriations to advance and promote religion." In their capacity as federal taxpayers, respondents sought to challenge Executive Branch expenditures for these conferences, which, they contended, violated the Establishment Clause.

II

Article III of the Constitution limits the judicial power of the United States to the resolution of "Cases" and "Controversies," and " 'Article III standing . . . enforces the Constitution's case-or-controversy requirement.' " " 'No principle is more fundamental to the judiciary's proper role in our system of government than the constitutional limitation of federal-court jurisdiction to actual cases or controversies.' "

The constitutionally mandated standing inquiry is especially important in a case like this one, in which taxpayers seek "to challenge laws of general application where their own injury is not distinct from that suffered in general by other taxpayers or citizens." This is because "[t]he judicial power of the United States defined by Art. III is not an unconditioned authority to determine the constitutionality of legislative or executive acts." The federal courts are not empowered to seek out and strike down any governmental act that they deem to be repugnant to the Constitution. Rather, federal courts sit "solely, to decide on the rights of individuals," *Marbury v. Madison* (1803), and must " 'refrai[n] from passing upon the constitutionality of an act . . . unless obliged to do so in the proper performance of our judicial function, when the question is raised by a party whose interests entitle him to raise it.' "

As a general matter, the interest of a federal taxpayer in seeing that Treasury funds are spent in accordance with the Constitution does not give rise to the kind of redressable "personal injury" required for Article III standing. Of course, a taxpayer has standing to challenge the collection of a specific tax assessment as unconstitutional; being forced to pay such a tax causes a real and immediate economic injury to the individual taxpayer. But that is not the interest on which respondents assert standing here. Rather, their claim is that, having paid lawfully collected taxes into the Federal Treasury at some point, they have a continuing, legally cognizable interest in ensuring that those funds are not used by the Government in a way that violates the Constitution.

We have consistently held that this type of interest is too generalized and attenuated to support Article III standing. Because the interests of the taxpayer are, in essence, the interests of the public-at-large, deciding a constitutional claim based solely on taxpayer standing "would be[,] not to decide a judicial controversy, but to assume a position of authority over the governmental acts of another and co-equal department, an authority which plainly we do not possess."

In *Flast v. Cohen*, the Court carved out a narrow exception to the general constitutional prohibition against taxpayer standing. The taxpayer-plaintiff in that case challenged the distribution of federal funds to religious schools under the Elementary and Secondary Education Act of 1965, alleging that such aid violated the Establishment Clause. The Court set out a two-part test for determining whether a federal taxpayer has standing to challenge an allegedly unconstitutional expenditure:

> "First, the taxpayer must establish a logical link between that status and the type of legislative enactment attacked. Thus, a taxpayer will be a proper party to allege the unconstitutionality only of exercises of congressional power under the taxing and spending clause of Art. I, § 8, of the Constitution. It will not be sufficient to allege an incidental expenditure of tax funds in the administration of an essentially regulatory statute. . . . Secondly, the taxpayer must establish a nexus between that status and the precise nature of the constitutional infringement alleged. Under this requirement, the taxpayer must show that the challenged enactment exceeds specific constitutional limitations imposed upon the exercise of the congressional taxing and spending power and not simply that the enactment is generally beyond the powers delegated to Congress by Art. I, § 8."

III

Respondents argue that this case falls within the *Flast* exception, which they read to cover any "expenditure of government funds in violation of the Establishment Clause." But this broad reading fails to observe "the rigor with which the Flast exception to the Frothingham principle ought to be applied."

The expenditures at issue in *Flast* were made pursuant to an express congressional mandate and a specific congressional appropriation. The plaintiff in that case challenged disbursements made under the Elementary and Secondary Education Act of 1965. That Act expressly appropriated the sum of $100 million for fiscal year 1966, and authorized the disbursement of those funds to local educational agencies for the education of low-income students. The expenditures challenged in Flast, then, were funded by a specific congressional appropriation and were disbursed to private schools (including religiously affiliated schools) pursuant to a direct and unambiguous congressional mandate.

Given that the alleged Establishment Clause violation in *Flast* was funded by a specific congressional appropriation and was undertaken pursuant to an express congressional mandate, the Court concluded that the taxpayer-plaintiffs had established the requisite "logical link between [their taxpayer] status and the type of legislative enactment attacked." But as this Court later noted, *Flast* "limited taxpayer standing to challenges directed 'only [at] exercises of congressional power'" under the Taxing and Spending Clause.

The link between congressional action and constitutional violation that supported taxpayer standing in *Flast* is missing here. Respondents do not challenge any specific congressional action or appropriation; nor do they ask the Court to invalidate any congressional enactment or legislatively created program as unconstitutional. That is because the expenditures at issue here were not made pursuant to any Act of Congress. Rather, Congress provided general appropriations to the Executive Branch to fund its day-to-day activities. These appropriations did not expressly authorize, direct, or even mention the expenditures of which respondents complain. Those expenditures resulted from executive discretion, not congressional action.

We have never found taxpayer standing under such circumstances. In *Valley Forge [Christian College v. Americans United for Separation of Church and State* (1981)], we held that a taxpayer lacked standing to challenge "a decision by [the federal Department of Health, Education and Welfare] to transfer a parcel of federal property" to a religious college because this transfer was "not a congressional action." In fact, the connection to congressional action was closer in *Valley Forge* than it is here, because in that case, the "particular Executive Branch action" being challenged was at least "arguably authorized" by the Federal Property and Administrative Services Act of 1949, which permitted federal agencies to transfer surplus property to private entities. Nevertheless, we found that the plaintiffs lacked standing because *Flast* "limited taxpayer standing to challenges directed 'only [at] exercises of congressional power'" under the Taxing and Spending Clause.

Because the expenditures that respondents challenge were not expressly authorized or mandated by any specific congressional enactment, respondents' lawsuit is not directed at an exercise of congressional power, and thus lacks the requisite "logical nexus" between taxpayer status "and the type of legislative enactment attacked."

IV

Respondents argue that it is "arbitrary" to distinguish between money spent pursuant to congressional mandate and expenditures made in the course of executive discretion, because "the injury to taxpayers in both situations is the very injury targeted by the Establishment Clause and *Flast*—the expenditure for the support of religion of funds exacted from taxpayers." But *Flast* focused on congressional action, and we must decline this invitation to extend its holding to encompass discretionary Executive Branch expenditures.

It is significant that, in the four decades since its creation, the *Flast* exception has largely been confined to its facts. We have declined to lower the taxpayer standing bar in suits alleging violations of any constitutional provision apart from the Establishment Clause.

Because almost all Executive Branch activity is ultimately funded by some congressional appropriation, extending the *Flast* exception to purely executive expenditures would effectively subject every federal action—be it a conference, proclamation or speech—to Establishment Clause challenge by any taxpayer in federal court. To see the wide swathe of activity that respondents' proposed rule would cover, one need look no further than the amended complaint in this action, which focuses largely on speeches and presentations made by Executive Branch officials. Such a broad reading would ignore the first prong of *Flast*'s standing test, which requires "a logical link between [taxpayer] status and the type of legislative enactment attacked."

It would also raise serious separation-of-powers concerns. As we have recognized, *Flast* itself gave too little weight to these concerns. By framing the standing question solely in terms of whether the dispute would be presented in an adversary context and in a form traditionally viewed as capable of judicial resolution, *Flast* "failed to recognize that this doctrine has a separation-of-powers component, which keeps courts within certain traditional bounds vis-à-vis the other branches, concrete adverseness or not." Respondents' position, if adopted, would repeat and compound this mistake.

Respondents set out a parade of horribles that they claim could occur if *Flast* is not extended to discretionary Executive Branch expenditures. For example, they say, a federal agency could use its discretionary funds to build a house of worship or to hire clergy of one denomination and send them out to spread their faith. Or an agency could use its funds to make bulk purchases of Stars of David, crucifixes, or depictions of the star and crescent for use in its offices or for distribution to the employees or the general public. Of course, none of these things has happened, even though *Flast* has not previously been expanded in the way that respondents urge. In the unlikely event that any of these executive actions did take place, Congress could quickly step in. And respondents make no effort to show that these improbable abuses could not be challenged in federal court by plaintiffs who would possess standing based on grounds other than taxpayer standing.

Over the years, *Flast* has been defended by some and criticized by others. But the present case does not require us to reconsider that precedent. The Court of Appeals did not apply *Flast*; it extended *Flast*. It is a necessary concomitant of the doctrine of stare decisis that a precedent is not always expanded to the limit of its logic. That was the approach that then—Justice Rehnquist took in his opinion for the Court in *Valley Forge*, and it is the approach we take here. We do not extend *Flast*, but we also do not overrule it. We leave Flast as we found it.

Justice SCALIA, with whom Justice THOMAS joins, concurring in the judgment.

Today's opinion is, in one significant respect, entirely consistent with our previous cases addressing taxpayer standing to raise Establishment Clause challenges to government expenditures. Unfortunately, the consistency lies in the creation of utterly meaningless distinctions which separate the case at hand from the precedents that have come out differently, but which cannot possibly be (in any sane world) the reason it comes out differently. If this Court is to decide cases by rule of law rather than show of hands, we must surrender to logic and choose sides: Either *Flast v. Cohen* (1968), should be applied to (at a minimum) all challenges to the governmental expenditure of general tax revenues in a manner alleged to violate a constitutional provision specifically limiting the taxing and spending power, or *Flast* should be repudiated. For me, the choice is easy. *Flast* is wholly irreconcilable with the Article III restrictions on federal-court jurisdiction that this Court has repeatedly confirmed are embodied in the doctrine of standing.

There is a simple reason why our taxpayer-standing cases involving Establishment Clause challenges to government expenditures are notoriously inconsistent: We have inconsistently described the first element of the "irreducible constitutional minimum of standing," which minimum consists of (1) a "concrete and particularized" "'injury in fact'" that is (2) fairly traceable to the defendant's alleged unlawful conduct and (3) likely to be redressed by a favorable decision. We have alternately relied on two entirely distinct conceptions of injury in fact, which for convenience I will call "Wallet Injury" and "Psychic Injury."

Wallet Injury is the type of concrete and particularized injury one would expect to be asserted in a taxpayer suit, namely, a claim that the plaintiff's tax liability is higher than it would be, but for the allegedly unlawful government action. The stumbling block for suits challenging government expenditures based on this conventional type of injury is quite predictable. The plaintiff cannot satisfy the traceability and redressability prongs of standing. It is uncertain what the plaintiff's tax bill would have been had the allegedly forbidden expenditure not been made, and it is even more speculative whether the government will, in response to an adverse court decision, lower taxes rather than spend the funds in some other manner.

Psychic Injury, on the other hand, has nothing to do with the plaintiff's tax liability. Instead, the injury consists of the taxpayer's mental displeasure that money extracted from him is being spent in an unlawful manner. This shift in focus eliminates traceability and redressability problems. Psychic Injury is directly traceable to the improper use of taxpayer funds, and it is redressed when the improper use is enjoined, regardless of whether that injunction affects the taxpayer's purse. *Flast* and the cases following its teaching have invoked a peculiarly restricted version of Psychic Injury, permitting taxpayer displeasure over unconstitutional spending to support standing only if the constitutional provision allegedly violated is a specific limitation on the taxing and spending power. Restricted or not, this conceptualizing of injury in fact in purely mental terms conflicts squarely with the familiar proposition that a plaintiff lacks a concrete and particularized injury when his only complaint is the generalized grievance that the law is being violated.

The basic logical flaw in our cases is thus twofold: We have never explained why Psychic Injury was insufficient in the cases in which standing was denied, and we have never explained why Psychic Injury, however limited, is cognizable under Article III.

We must initially decide whether Psychic Injury is consistent with Article III. If it is, we should apply *Flast* to all challenges to government expenditures in violation of constitutional provisions that specifically limit the taxing and spending power; if it is not, we should overturn *Flast*.

The plurality today avails itself of neither principled option. Instead, essentially accepting the Solicitor General's primary submission, it limits *Flast* to challenges to expenditures that are "expressly authorized or mandated by . . . specific congressional enactment." It offers no intellectual justification for this limitation, except that "[i]t is a necessary concomitant of the doctrine of stare decisis that a precedent is not always expanded to the limit of its logic." That is true enough, but since courts purport to be engaged in reasoned decisionmaking, it is only true when (1) the precedent's logic is seen to require narrowing or readjustment in light of relevant distinctions that the new fact situation brings to the fore; or (2) its logic is fundamentally flawed, and so deserves to be limited to the facts that begot it. Today's plurality claims neither of these justifications. As to the first, the plurality offers no explanation of why the factual differences between this case and *Flast* are material. It virtually admits that express congressional allocation vel non has nothing to do with whether the plaintiffs have alleged an injury in fact that is fairly traceable and likely to be redressed. Whether the challenged government expenditure is expressly allocated by a specific congressional enactment has absolutely no relevance to the Article III criteria of injury in fact, traceability, and redressability.

Ultimately, the arguments by the parties in this case and the opinions of my colleagues serve only to confirm that *Flast*'s adoption of Psychic Injury has to be addressed head-on. Minimalism is an admirable judicial trait, but not when it comes at the cost of meaningless and disingenuous distinctions that hold the sure promise of engendering further meaningless and disingenuous distinctions in the future. The rule of law is ill served by forcing lawyers and judges to make arguments that deaden the soul of the law, which is logic and reason. Either *Flast* was correct, and must be accorded the wide application that it logically dictates, or it was not, and must be abandoned in its entirety.

Is a taxpayer's purely psychological displeasure that his funds are being spent in an allegedly unlawful manner ever sufficiently concrete and particularized to support Article III standing? The answer is plainly no.

My call for the imposition of logic and order upon this chaotic set of precedents will perhaps be met with the snappy epigram that "[t]he life of the law has not been logic: it has been experience." O. Holmes, The Common Law 1 (1881). But what experience has shown is that *Flast*'s lack of a logical theoretical underpinning has rendered our taxpayer-standing doctrine such a jurisprudential disaster that our appellate judges do not know what to make of it. And of course the case has engendered no reliance interests, not only because one does not arrange his affairs with an eye to standing, but also because there is no relying on the random and irrational. I can think of few cases less warranting of stare decisis respect. It is time—it is past time—to call an end. *Flast* should be overruled.

Justice SOUTER, with whom Justice STEVENS, Justice GINSBURG, and Justice BREYER join, dissenting.

Flast v. Cohen (1968), held that plaintiffs with an Establishment Clause claim could "demonstrate the necessary stake as taxpayers in the outcome of the litigation to satisfy Article III requirements." Here, the controlling, plurality opinion declares that *Flast* does not apply, but a search of that opinion for a suggestion that these taxpayers have any less stake in the outcome than the taxpayers in *Flast* will come up empty: the plurality makes no such finding, nor could it. Instead, the controlling opinion closes the door on these taxpayers because the Executive Branch, and not the Legislative Branch, caused their injury. I see no basis for this distinction in either logic or precedent, and respectfully dissent.

We held in *Flast*, and repeated just last Term, that the "'injury' alleged in Establishment Clause challenges to federal spending" is "the very 'extract[ion] and spen[ding]' of 'tax money' in aid of religion." *DaimlerChrysler Corp. v. Cuno* (2006). As the Court said in *Flast*, the importance of that type of injury has deep historical roots going back to the ideal of religious liberty in James Madison's Memorial and Remonstrance Against Religious Assessments, that the government in a free society may not "force a citizen to contribute three pence only of his property for the support of any one establishment" of religion. Madison thus translated into practical terms the right of conscience described when he wrote that "[t]he Religion . . . of every man must be left to the conviction and conscience of every man; and it is the right of every man to exercise it as these may dictate."

Here, there is no dispute that taxpayer money in identifiable amounts is funding conferences, and these are alleged to have the purpose of promoting religion. The taxpayers therefore seek not to "extend" *Flast*, but merely to apply it. When executive agencies spend identifiable sums of tax money for religious purposes, no less than when Congress authorizes the same thing, taxpayers suffer injury. And once we recognize the injury as sufficient for Article III, there can be no serious question about the other elements of the standing enquiry: the injury is indisputably "traceable" to the spending, and "likely to be redressed by" an injunction prohibiting it.

The plurality points to the separation of powers to explain its distinction between legislative and executive spending decisions, but there is no difference on that point of view between a Judicial Branch review of an executive decision and a judicial evaluation of a congressional one. We owe respect to each of the other branches, no more to the former than to the latter, and no one has suggested that the Establishment Clause lacks applicability to executive uses of money. It would surely violate the Establishment Clause for the Department of Health and Human Services to draw on a general appropriation to build a chapel for weekly church services (no less than if a statute required it), and for good reason: if the Executive could accomplish through the exercise of discretion exactly what Congress cannot do through legislation, Establishment Clause protection would melt away.

Thus, *Flast* speaks for this Court's recognition (shared by a majority of the Court today) that when the Government spends money for religious purposes a taxpayer's injury is serious and concrete enough to be "judicially cognizable." The judgment of sufficient injury takes account of the Madisonian relationship of tax money and conscience, but it equally reflects the Founders' pragmatic "conviction that individual religious liberty could be achieved best under a government which was stripped of all power to tax, to support, or otherwise to assist any or all religions," and the realization continuing to the modern day that favoritism for religion " 'sends the . . . message to . . . nonadherents that they are outsiders, not full members of the political community.' "

Because the taxpayers in this case have alleged the type of injury this Court has seen as sufficient for standing, I would affirm.

DAIMLERCHRYSLER CORP. v. CUNO
126 S.Ct. 1854 (2006)

Chief Justice ROBERTS delivered the opinion of the Court.

Jeeps were first mass-produced in 1941 for the U.S. Army by the Willys-Overland Motor Company in Toledo, Ohio. Nearly 60 years later, the city of Toledo and State of Ohio sought to encourage the current manufacturer of Jeeps—DaimlerChrysler—to expand its Jeep operation in Toledo, by offering local and state tax benefits for new investment. Taxpayers in Toledo sued, alleging that their local and state tax burdens were increased by the tax breaks for DaimlerChrysler, tax breaks that they asserted violated the Commerce Clause. The Court of Appeals agreed that a state tax credit offered under Ohio law violated the Commerce Clause, and state and local officials and DaimlerChrysler sought review in this Court. We are obligated before reaching this Commerce Clause question to determine whether the taxpayers who objected to the credit have standing to press their complaint in federal court. We conclude that they do not, and we therefore can proceed no further.

Plaintiffs principally claim standing by virtue of their status as Ohio taxpayers, alleging that the franchise tax credit "depletes the funds of the State of Ohio to which the Plaintiffs contribute through their tax payments" and thus "diminish[es] the total funds available for lawful uses and impos[es] disproportionate burdens on" them. On several occasions, this Court has denied federal taxpayers standing under Article III to object to a particular expenditure of federal funds simply because they are taxpayers.

The animating principle behind these cases was announced in their progenitor, *Frothingham v. Mellon* (1923). In rejecting a claim that improper federal appropriations would "increase the burden of future taxation and thereby take [the plaintiff's] property without due process of law," the Court observed that a federal taxpayer's "interest in the moneys of the Treasury is shared with millions of others; is comparatively minute and indeterminable; and the effect upon future taxation, of any payment out of the funds, so remote, fluctuating and uncertain, that no basis is afforded for an appeal to the preventive powers of a court of equity."

This logic is equally applicable to taxpayer challenges to expenditures that deplete the treasury, and to taxpayer challenges to so-called "tax expenditures," which reduce amounts available to the treasury by granting tax credits or exemptions. In either case, the alleged injury is based on the asserted effect of the allegedly illegal activity on public revenues, to which the taxpayer contributes. Standing has been rejected in such cases because the alleged injury is not "concrete and particularized," but instead a grievance the taxpayer "suffers in some indefinite way in common with people generally." In addition, the injury is not "actual or imminent," but instead "conjectural or hypothetical." As an initial matter, it is unclear that tax breaks of the sort at issue here do in fact deplete the treasury: The very point of the tax benefits is to spur economic activity, which in turn increases government revenues. In this very action, the Michigan plaintiffs claimed that they were injured because they lost out on the added revenues that would have accompanied DaimlerChrysler's decision to expand facilities in Michigan.

Plaintiffs' alleged injury is also "conjectural or hypothetical" in that it depends on how legislators respond to a reduction in revenue, if that is the consequence of the credit. Establishing injury requires speculating that elected officials will increase a taxpayer-plaintiff's tax bill to make up a deficit; establishing redressability requires speculating that abolishing the challenged credit will redound to the benefit of the taxpayer because legislators will pass along the supposed increased revenue in the form of tax reductions. Neither sort of speculation suffices to support standing.

A taxpayer-plaintiff has no right to insist that the government dispose of any increased revenue it might experience as a result of his suit by decreasing his tax liability or bolstering programs that benefit him. To the contrary, the decision of how to allocate any such savings is the very epitome of a policy judgment committed to the "broad and legitimate discretion" of lawmakers, which "the courts cannot presume either to control or to predict." Under such circumstances, we have no assurance that the asserted injury is "imminent"— that it is "certainly impending."

The foregoing rationale for rejecting federal taxpayer standing applies with undiminished force to state taxpayers. We indicated as much in *Doremus v. Board of Ed. of Hawthorne* (1952). In that case, we noted our earlier holdings that "the interests of a taxpayer in the moneys of the federal treasury are too indeterminable, remote, uncertain and indirect" to support standing to challenge "their manner of expenditure." We then "reiterate[d]" what we had said in rejecting a federal taxpayer challenge to a federal statute "as equally true when a state Act is assailed: 'The [taxpayer] must be able to show . . . that he has sustained . . . some direct injury . . . and not merely that he suffers in some indefinite way in common with people generally.'" The allegations of injury that plaintiffs make in their complaint furnish no better basis for finding standing than those made in the cases where federal taxpayer standing was denied. Plaintiffs claim that DaimlerChrysler's tax credit depletes the Ohio fisc and "impos[es] disproportionate burdens on [them]." This is no different from similar claims by federal taxpayers we have already rejected under Article III as insufficient to establish standing. For the foregoing reasons, we hold that state taxpayers have no standing under Article III to challenge state tax or spending decisions simply by virtue of their status as taxpayers.

Plaintiffs argue that an exception to the general prohibition on taxpayer standing should exist for Commerce Clause challenges to state tax or spending decisions, analogizing their Commerce Clause claim to the Establishment Clause challenge we permitted in *Flast v. Cohen* (1968). *Flast* held that because "the Establishment Clause . . . specifically limit[s] the taxing and spending power conferred by Art. I, § 8, "a taxpayer will have standing consistent with Article III to invoke federal judicial power when he alleges that congressional action under the taxing and spending clause is in derogation of" the Establishment Clause. But as plaintiffs candidly concede, "only the Establishment Clause" has supported federal taxpayer suits since *Flast*. Quite apart from whether the franchise tax credit is analogous to an exercise of congressional power under Art. I, § 8, plaintiffs' reliance on *Flast* is misguided: Whatever rights plaintiffs have under the Commerce Clause, they are fundamentally unlike the right not to "contribute three pence . . . for the support of any one [religious] establishment." (2 Writings of James Madison 186 (G. Hunt ed.1901)). Indeed, plaintiffs compare the Establishment Clause to the Commerce Clause at such a high level of generality that almost any constitutional constraint on government power would "specifically limit" a State's taxing and spending power for *Flast* purposes. And even if the two clauses are similar in that they often implicate governments' fiscal decisions, a finding that the Commerce Clause satisfies the *Flast* test would leave no principled way of distinguishing those other constitutional provisions that we have recognized constrain governments' taxing and spending decisions. Yet such a broad application of *Flast's* exception to the general prohibition on taxpayer standing would be quite at odds with its narrow application in our precedent and *Flast's* own promise that it would not transform federal courts into forums for taxpayers' "generalized grievances." Plaintiffs thus do not have state taxpayer standing on the ground that their Commerce Clause challenge is just like the Establishment Clause challenge in *Flast*.

All the theories plaintiffs have offered to support their standing to challenge the franchise tax credit are unavailing. Because plaintiffs have no standing to challenge that credit, the lower courts erred by considering their claims against it on the merits.

d. Mootness (casebook p. 72)

As explained in the casebook, an exception to the mootness doctrine is for "wrongs capable of repetition but evading review." In *Federal Election Commission v. Wisconsin Right to Life, Inc.*, 127 S.Ct. ___ (2007), the Court held that a challenge to a provision of the Bipartisan Campaign Finance Reform Act was not moot because it presented a wrong capable of repetition but evading review. Chief Justice Roberts explained: "Article III's 'case-or-controversy' requirement subsists through all stages of federal judicial proceedings. . . . [I]t is not enough that a dispute was very much alive when suit was filed." Based on these principles, the FEC argues (though the intervenors do not) that these cases are moot because the 2004 election has passed and WRTL "does not assert any continuing interest in running [its three] advertisements, nor does it identify any reason to believe that a significant dispute over Senate filibusters of judicial nominees will occur in the foreseeable future."

As the District Court concluded, however, these cases fit comfortably within the established exception to mootness for disputes capable of repetition, yet evading review. The exception applies where "(1) the challenged action is in its duration too short to be fully litigated prior to cessation or expiration; and (2) there is a reasonable expectation that the same complaining party will be subject to the same action again."

As the District Court found, it would be "entirely unreasonable . . . to expect that [WRTL] could have obtained complete judicial review of its claims in time for it to air its ads" during the BCRA blackout periods. The FEC contends that the 2-year window between elections provides ample time for parties to litigate their rights before each BCRA blackout period. But groups like WRTL cannot predict what issues will be matters of public concern during a future blackout period. In these cases, WRTL had no way of knowing well in advance that it would want to run ads on judicial filibusters during the BCRA blackout period. In any event, despite BCRA's command that the cases be expedited "to the greatest possible extent," two BCRA blackout periods have come and gone during the pendency of this action.

The second prong of the "capable of repetition" exception requires a "'reasonable expectation'" or a "'demonstrated probability'" that "the same controversy will recur involving the same complaining party." Our cases find the same controversy sufficiently likely to recur when a party has a reasonable expectation that it "will again be subjected to the alleged illegality," or "will be subject to the threat of prosecution" under the challenged law, Bellotti. The FEC argues that in order to prove likely recurrence of the same controversy,

WRTL must establish that it will run ads in the future sharing all "the characteristics that the district court deemed legally relevant."

The FEC asks for too much. We have recognized that the "'capable of repetition, yet evading review' doctrine, in the context of election cases, is appropriate when there are 'as applied' challenges as well as in the more typical case involving only facial attacks." Requiring repetition of every "legally relevant" characteristic of an as-applied challenge—down to the last detail— would effectively overrule this statement by making this exception unavailable for virtually all as-applied challenges. History repeats itself, but not at the level of specificity demanded by the FEC. Here, WRTL credibly claimed that it planned on running "'materially similar'" future targeted broadcast ads mentioning a candidate within the blackout period, and there is no reason to believe that the FEC will "refrain from prosecuting violations" of BCRA. Under the circumstances, particularly where WRTL sought another preliminary injunction based on an ad it planned to run during the 2006 blackout period, we hold that there exists a reasonable expectation that the same controversy involving the same party will recur. We have jurisdiction to decide these cases.

e.   The Political Question Doctrine

i.   The Political Question Doctrine Defined

WHAT IS A POLITICAL QUESTION: THE ISSUES OF PARTISAN GERRYMANDERING AND PARTISAN GERRYMANDERING

In *Vieth v. Jubelirer* (2004) (casebook p. 81), the Supreme Court, by a 5-4 margin and without a majority opinion, held that challenges to partisan gerrymandering are non-justiciable political questions. Justice Scalia, writing for himself and three other Justices, concluded that such challenges are always non-justiciable political questions because there inherently are not judicially discoverable or manageable standards. Justice Kennedy, concurring in the judgment, said that no such standards could be identified at this time, but that in the future standards might be found and then such challenges would be justiciable.

In *League of United Latin American Citizens v. Perry* (2006), the Court again dismissed a challenge to partisan gerrymandering. After Republicans gained control of the Texas legislature in 2002, they redrew districts for Congress so as to maximize likely seats for Republicans. This replaced a plan that was drawn by a federal district court in 2001. The redistricting was very successful. The Texas congressional delegation went from 17 Democrats and 15 Republicans in the 2002 election to 11 Democrats and 21 Republicans in the 2004 election.

Many lawsuits were brought and raised three major issues:

1) Is partisan gerrymandering a non-justiciable political question and if it is justiciable, does it violate equal protection?
2) Is the mid-decade redistricting unconstitutional?
3) Did Texas violate the Voting Rights Act by diluting the voting strength of minority voters?

LEAGUE OF UNITED LATIN AMERICAN CITIZENS v. PERRY
548 U.S. 399 (2006)

Justice KENNEDY announced the judgment of the Court.

In Davis v. Bandemer (1986), the Court held that an equal protection challenge to a political gerrymander presents a justiciable case or controversy, but there was disagreement over what substantive standard to apply. That disagreement persists. A plurality of the Court in *Vieth v. Jubelirer* [2004] would have held such challenges to be nonjusticiable political questions, but a majority declined to do so. We do not revisit the justiciability holding but do proceed to examine whether appellants' claims offer the Court a manageable, reliable measure of fairness for determining whether a partisan gerrymander violates the Constitution.

Appellants claim that Plan 1374C, enacted by the Texas Legislature in 2003, is an unconstitutional political gerrymander. A decision, they claim, to effect mid-decennial redistricting, when solely motivated by partisan objectives, violates equal protection and the First Amendment because it serves no legitimate public purpose and burdens one group because of its political opinions and affiliation. The mid-decennial nature of the redistricting, appellants say, reveals the legislature's sole motivation. Unlike *Vieth*, where the legislature acted in the context of a required decennial redistricting, the Texas Legislature voluntarily replaced a plan that itself was designed to comply with new census data. Because Texas had "no constitutional obligation to act at all" in 2003, it is hardly surprising, according to appellants, that the District Court found "[t]here is little question but that the single-minded purpose of the Texas Legislature in enacting Plan 1374C was to gain partisan advantage" for the Republican majority over the Democratic minority.

A rule, or perhaps a presumption, of invalidity when a mid-decade redistricting plan is adopted solely for partisan motivations is a salutary one, in appellants' view, for then courts need not inquire about, nor parties prove, the discriminatory effects of partisan gerrymandering—a matter that has proved elusive since *Bandemer*. Adding to the test's simplicity is that it does not quibble with the drawing of individual district lines but challenges the decision to redistrict at all.

For a number of reasons, appellants' case for adopting their test is not convincing. To begin with, the state appellees dispute the assertion that partisan gain was the "sole" motivation for the decision to replace Plan 1151C. There is some merit to that criticism, for the pejorative label overlooks indications that partisan motives did not dictate the plan in its entirety. The legislature does seem to have decided to redistrict with the sole purpose of achieving a Republican congressional majority, but partisan aims did not guide every line it drew. As the District Court found, the contours of some contested district lines were drawn based on more mundane and local interests. The state appellees also contend, and appellants do not contest, that a number of line-drawing requests by Democratic state legislators were honored.

Evaluating the legality of acts arising out of mixed motives can be complex, and affixing a single label to those acts can be hazardous, even when the actor is an individual performing a discrete act. When the actor is a legislature and the act is a composite of manifold choices, the task can be even more daunting. Even setting this skepticism aside, a successful claim attempting to identify unconstitutional acts of partisan gerrymandering must do what appellants' sole-motivation theory explicitly disavows: show a burden, as measured by a reliable standard, on the complainants' representational rights. For this reason, a majority of the Court rejected a test proposed in *Vieth* that is markedly similar to the one appellants present today.

The sole-intent standard offered here is no more compelling when it is linked to the circumstance that Plan 1374C is mid-decennial legislation. The text and structure of the Constitution and our case law indicate there is nothing inherently suspect about a legislature's decision to replace mid-decade a court-ordered plan with one of its own. And even if there were, the fact of mid-decade redistricting alone is no sure indication of unlawful political gerrymanders. Under appellants' theory, a highly effective partisan gerrymander that coincided with decennial redistricting would receive less scrutiny than a bumbling, yet solely partisan, mid-decade redistricting. More concretely, the test would leave untouched the 1991 Texas redistricting, which entrenched a party on the verge of minority status, while striking down the 2003 redistricting plan, which resulted in the majority Republican Party capturing a larger share of the seats. A test that treats these two similarly effective power plays in such different ways does not have the reliability appellants ascribe to it.

Furthermore, compared to the map challenged in *Vieth*, which led to a Republican majority in the congressional delegation despite a Democratic majority in the statewide vote, Plan 1374C can be seen as making the party balance more congruent to statewide party power. To be sure, there is no constitutional requirement of proportional representation, and equating a party's statewide share of the vote with its portion of the congressional delegation is a rough measure at best. Nevertheless, a congressional plan that more closely reflects the distribution of state party power seems a less likely vehicle for partisan discrimination than one that entrenches an electoral minority. By this measure, Plan 1374C can be seen as fairer than the plan that survived in *Vieth* and the two previous Texas plans—all three of which would pass the modified sole-intent test that Plan 1374C would fail.

In the absence of any other workable test for judging partisan gerrymanders, one effect of appellants' focus on mid-decade redistricting could be to encourage partisan excess at the outset of the decade, when a legislature redistricts pursuant to its decennial constitutional duty and is then immune from the charge of sole-motivation. If mid-decade redistricting were barred or at least subject to close judicial oversight, opposition legislators would also have every incentive to prevent passage of a legislative plan and try their luck with a court that might give them a better deal than negotiation with their political rivals.

In sum, we disagree with appellants' view that a legislature's decision to override a valid, court-drawn plan mid-decade is sufficiently suspect to give shape to a reliable standard for identifying unconstitutional political gerrymanders. We conclude that appellants have established no legally impermissible use of political classifications. For this reason, they state no claim on which relief may be granted for their statewide challenge.

[Justice Kennedy's opinion went on to conclude that the drawing of one district did violate the Voting Rights Act by diluting the voting strength of Latino voters].

Justice STEVENS, with whom Justice BREYER joins concurring in part and dissenting in part.

This is a suit in which it is perfectly clear that judicially manageable standards enable us to decide the merits of a statewide challenge to a political gerrymander. Applying such standards, I shall explain why the wholly unnecessary replacement of the neutral plan fashioned by the three-judge court (Plan 1151C or Balderas Plan) with Plan 1374C, which creates districts with less compact shapes, violates the Voting Rights Act, and fragments communities of interest—all for purely partisan purposes—violated the State's constitutional duty to govern impartially. Prior misconduct by the Texas Legislature neither excuses nor justifies that violation.

The maintenance of existing district boundaries is advantageous to both voters and candidates. Changes, of course, must be made after every census to equalize the population of each district or to accommodate changes in the size of a State's congressional delegation. Similarly, changes must be made in response to a finding that a districting plan violates § 2 or § 5 of the Voting Rights Act. But the interests in orderly campaigning and voting, as well as in maintaining communication between representatives and their constituents, underscore the importance of requiring that any decision to redraw district boundaries—like any other state action that affects the electoral process—must, at the very least, serve some legitimate governmental purpose. A purely partisan desire "to minimize or cancel out the voting strength of racial or political elements of the voting population," is not such a purpose. Because a desire to minimize the strength of Texas Democrats was the sole motivation for the adoption of Plan 1374C, the plan cannot withstand constitutional scrutiny.

The districting map that Plan 1374C replaced, Plan 1151C, was not only manifestly fair and neutral, it may legitimately be described as a milestone in

Texas' political history because it put an end to a long history of Democratic misuse of power in that State. For decades after the Civil War, the political party associated with the former Commander in Chief of the Union Army attracted the support of former slaves and a handful of "carpetbaggers," but had no significant political influence in Texas. The Democrats maintained their political power by excluding black voters from participating in primary elections, by the artful management of multimember electoral schemes, and, most recently, by outrageously partisan gerrymandering. Unfortunately, some of these tactics are not unique to Texas Democrats; the apportionment scheme they devised in the 1990's is only one example of the excessively gerrymandered districting plans that parties with control of their States' governing bodies have implemented in recent years.

Despite the Texas Democratic Party's sordid history of manipulating the electoral process to perpetuate its stranglehold on political power, the Texas Republican Party managed to become the State's majority party by 2002. If, after finally achieving political strength in Texas, the Republicans had adopted a new plan in order to remove the excessively partisan Democratic gerrymander of the 1990's, the decision to do so would unquestionably have been supported by a neutral justification. But that is not what happened. Instead, Texas Republicans abandoned a neutral apportionment map for the sole purpose of manipulating district boundaries to maximize their electoral advantage and thus create their own impermissible stranglehold on political power.

The unique question of law that is raised in this appeal is one that the Court has not previously addressed. That narrow question is whether it was unconstitutional for Texas to replace a lawful districting plan "in the middle of a decade, for the sole purpose of maximizing partisan advantage." This question is both different from, and simpler than, the principal question presented in *Vieth v. Jubelirer*, in which the " 'lack of judicially discoverable and manageable standards' " prevented the plurality from deciding the merits of a statewide challenge to a political gerrymander.

The legislature's decision to redistrict at issue in this litigation was entirely inconsistent with these principles. By taking an action for the sole purpose of advantaging Republicans and disadvantaging Democrats, the State of Texas violated its constitutional obligation to govern impartially.

[Justice Stevens then went on to conclude that there was a violation of the Voting Rights Act.]

Justice SOUTER, with whom Justice GINSBURG joins, concurring in part and dissenting in part.

I join the principal opinion, rejecting the one-person, one-vote challenge to Plan 1374C based simply on its mid-decade timing, and I also join [the part of the opinion], in which the Court preserves the principle that partisan gerrymandering can be recognized as a violation of equal protection. I see nothing to be gained by working through these cases on the standard I would have applied in

Vieth, because here as in *Vieth* we have no majority for any single criterion of impermissible gerrymander (and none for a conclusion that Plan 1374C is unconstitutional across the board). I therefore treat the broad issue of gerrymander much as the subject of an improvident grant of certiorari.

[Justice Souter then went on to conclude that there was a violation of the Voting Rights Act.]

Chief Justice ROBERTS, with whom Justice ALITO joins, concurring in part, concurring in the judgment in part, and dissenting in part.

I agree with the determination that appellants have not provided "a reliable standard for identifying unconstitutional political gerrymanders." The question whether any such standard exists—that is, whether a challenge to a political gerrymander presents a justiciable case or controversy—has not been argued in these cases. I therefore take no position on that question, which has divided the Court, see *Vieth v. Jubelirer* (2004), and I join the Court's disposition without specifying whether appellants have failed to state a claim on which relief can be granted, or have failed to present a justiciable controversy.

[Chief Justice Roberts then dissented as to whether there was a violation of the Voting Rights Act.]

Justice SCALIA, with whom Justice THOMAS joins, and with whom THE CHIEF JUSTICE and Justice ALITO join [in part], concurring in the judgment in part and dissenting in part.

As I have previously expressed, claims of unconstitutional partisan gerrymandering do not present a justiciable case or controversy. See *Vieth v. Jubelirer* (2004) (plurality opinion). Justice Kennedy's discussion of appellants' political-gerrymandering claims ably demonstrates that, yet again, no party or judge has put forth a judicially discernable standard by which to evaluate them. Unfortunately, the opinion then concludes that the appellants have failed to state a claim as to political gerrymandering, without ever articulating what the elements of such a claim consist of. That is not an available disposition of this appeal. We must either conclude that the claim is nonjusticiable and dismiss it, or else set forth a standard and measure appellant's claim against it. Instead, we again dispose of this claim in a way that provides no guidance to lower-court judges and perpetuates a cause of action with no discernible content. We should simply dismiss appellants' claims as nonjusticiable.

[Justice Scalia then went on to dissent as to whether there was a violation of the Voting Rights Act.]

Chapter 2

The Federal Legislative Power

B. The Commerce Power

4. 1990s-???: Narrowing of the Commerce Power and Revival of the Tenth Amendment as a Constraint on Congress

a. What Is Congress's Authority to Regulate "Commerce Among the States"? (casebook, p. 153)

In *Gonzales v. Raich,* excerpted below, the Supreme Court considered the constitutionality of whether Congress, pursuant to its commerce power, can criminally prohibit and punish cultivation and possession of small amounts of marijuana for medical purposes. In upholding the law at issue here, Justice Stevens's majority opinion argues that the ruling is consistent with earlier decisions such as *Wickard v. Filburn, United States v. Lopez,* and *United States v. Morrison.* In appraising *Gonzales v. Raich,* it is important to consider whether this decision is consistent with these precedents, or whether there is tension between it and especially *Lopez* and *Morrison,* which narrowed the scope of Congress's commerce power.

GONZALES v. RAICH
545 U.S. 1 (2005)

Justice STEVENS delivered the opinion of the Court.

California is one of at least nine States that authorize the use of marijuana for medicinal purposes. The question presented in this case is whether the power vested in Congress by Article I, § 8, of the Constitution "[t]o make all Laws which shall be necessary and proper for carrying into Execution" its authority to "regulate Commerce with foreign Nations, and among the several States" includes the power to prohibit the local cultivation and use of marijuana in compliance with California law.

I

California has been a pioneer in the regulation of marijuana. In 1913, California was one of the first States to prohibit the sale and possession of marijuana, and at the end of the century, California became the first State to authorize limited use of the drug for medicinal purposes. In 1996, California voters passed Proposition 215, now codified as the Compassionate Use Act of 1996. The proposition was designed to ensure that "seriously ill" residents of the State have access to marijuana for medical purposes, and to encourage Federal and State Governments to take steps towards ensuring the safe and affordable distribution of the drug to patients in need. The Act creates an exemption from criminal prosecution for physicians, as well as for patients and primary caregivers who possess or cultivate marijuana for medicinal purposes with the recommendation or approval of a physician.

Respondents Angel Raich and Diane Monson are California residents who suffer from a variety of serious medical conditions and have sought to avail themselves of medical marijuana pursuant to the terms of the Compassionate Use Act. They are being treated by licensed, board-certified family practitioners, who have concluded, after prescribing a host of conventional medicines to treat respondents' conditions and to alleviate their associated symptoms, that marijuana is the only drug available that provides effective treatment. Both women have been using marijuana as a medication for several years pursuant to their doctors' recommendation, and both rely heavily on cannabis to function on a daily basis. Indeed, Raich's physician believes that forgoing cannabis treatments would certainly cause Raich excruciating pain and could very well prove fatal.

On August 15, 2002, county deputy sheriffs and agents from the federal Drug Enforcement Administration (DEA) came to Monson's home. After a thorough investigation, the county officials concluded that her use of marijuana was entirely lawful as a matter of California law. Nevertheless, after a 3-hour standoff, the federal agents seized and destroyed all six of her cannabis plants. Respondents thereafter brought this action against the Attorney General of the United States and the head of the DEA seeking injunctive and declaratory relief prohibiting the enforcement of the federal Controlled Substances Act (CSA) to the extent it prevents them from possessing, obtaining, or manufacturing cannabis for their personal medical use.

The case is made difficult by respondents' strong arguments that they will suffer irreparable harm because, despite a congressional finding to the contrary, marijuana does have valid therapeutic purposes. The question before us, however, is not whether it is wise to enforce the statute in these circumstances; rather, it is whether Congress' power to regulate interstate markets for medicinal substances encompasses the portions of those markets that are supplied with drugs produced and consumed locally. Well-settled law controls our answer. The CSA is a valid exercise of federal power, even as applied to the troubling facts of this case. We accordingly vacate the judgment of the Court of Appeals.

II

Shortly after taking office in 1969, President Nixon declared a national "war on drugs." As the first campaign of that war, Congress set out to enact legislation that would consolidate various drug laws on the books into a comprehensive statute, provide meaningful regulation over legitimate sources of drugs to prevent diversion into illegal channels, and strengthen law enforcement tools against the traffic in illicit drugs. That effort culminated in the passage of the Comprehensive Drug Abuse Prevention and Control Act of 1970.

[Subsequently, Congress enacted the CSA and] Congress devised a closed regulatory system making it unlawful to manufacture, distribute, dispense, or possess any controlled substance except in a manner authorized by the CSA. The CSA categorizes all controlled substances into five schedules. The drugs are grouped together based on their accepted medical uses, the potential for abuse, and their psychological and physical effects on the body. Each schedule is associated with a distinct set of controls regarding the manufacture, distribution, and use of the substances listed therein. The CSA and its implementing regulations set forth strict requirements regarding registration, labeling and packaging, production quotas, drug security, and recordkeeping.

In enacting the CSA, Congress classified marijuana as a Schedule I drug. Schedule I drugs are categorized as such because of their high potential for abuse, lack of any accepted medical use, and absence of any accepted safety for use in medically supervised treatment.

III

Respondents in this case do not dispute that passage of the CSA, as part of the Comprehensive Drug Abuse Prevention and Control Act, was well within Congress' commerce power. Nor do they contend that any provision or section of the CSA amounts to an unconstitutional exercise of congressional authority. Rather, respondents' challenge is actually quite limited; they argue that the CSA's categorical prohibition of the manufacture and possession of marijuana as applied to the intrastate manufacture and possession of marijuana for medical purposes pursuant to California law exceeds Congress' authority under the Commerce Clause.

In assessing the validity of congressional regulation, none of our Commerce Clause cases can be viewed in isolation. As charted in considerable detail in *United States v. Lopez*, our understanding of the reach of the Commerce Clause, as well as Congress' assertion of authority thereunder, has evolved over time. Cases decided during that "new era," which now spans more than a century, have identified three general categories of regulation in which Congress is authorized to engage under its commerce power. First, Congress can regulate the channels of interstate commerce. Second, Congress has authority to regulate and protect the instrumentalities of interstate commerce, and persons or things in interstate commerce. Third, Congress has the power to regulate activities that substantially affect interstate commerce. Only the third category is implicated in the case at hand.

Our case law firmly establishes Congress' power to regulate purely local activities that are part of an economic "class of activities" that have a substantial effect on interstate commerce. See, e.g., *Wickard v. Filburn* (1942). As we stated in *Wickard*, "even if appellee's activity be local and though it may not be regarded as commerce, it may still, whatever its nature, be reached by Congress if it exerts a substantial economic effect on interstate commerce." We have never required Congress to legislate with scientific exactitude. When Congress decides that the "'total incidence'" of a practice poses a threat to a national market, it may regulate the entire class. In this vein, we have reiterated that when "'a general regulatory statute bears a substantial relation to commerce, the de minimis character of individual instances arising under that statute is of no consequence.'"

Our decision in *Wickard* is of particular relevance. In *Wickard*, we upheld the application of regulations promulgated under the Agricultural Adjustment Act of 1938, which were designed to control the volume of wheat moving in interstate and foreign commerce in order to avoid surpluses and consequent abnormally low prices. *Wickard* thus establishes that Congress can regulate purely intrastate activity that is not itself "commercial," in that it is not produced for sale, if it concludes that failure to regulate that class of activity would undercut the regulation of the interstate market in that commodity.

The similarities between this case and *Wickard* are striking. Like the farmer in *Wickard*, respondents are cultivating, for home consumption, a fungible commodity for which there is an established, albeit illegal, interstate market. Just as the Agricultural Adjustment Act was designed "to control the volume [of wheat] moving in interstate and foreign commerce in order to avoid surpluses . . ." and consequently control the market price, a primary purpose of the CSA is to control the supply and demand of controlled substances in both lawful and unlawful drug markets. In *Wickard*, we had no difficulty concluding that Congress had a rational basis for believing that, when viewed in the aggregate, leaving homeconsumed wheat outside the regulatory scheme would have a substantial influence on price and market conditions. Here too, Congress had a rational basis for concluding that leaving home-consumed marijuana outside federal control would similarly affect price and market conditions.

More concretely, one concern prompting inclusion of wheat grown for home consumption in the 1938 Act was that rising market prices could draw such wheat into the interstate market, resulting in lower market prices. The parallel concern making it appropriate to include marijuana grown for home consumption in the CSA is the likelihood that the high demand in the interstate market will draw such marijuana into that market. While the diversion of homegrown wheat tended to frustrate the federal interest in stabilizing prices by regulating the volume of commercial transactions in the interstate market, the diversion of homegrown marijuana tends to frustrate the federal interest in eliminating commercial transactions in the interstate market in their entirety. In both cases, the regulation is squarely within Congress' commerce power because production of the commodity meant for home consumption, be it wheat or marijuana, has a substantial effect on supply and demand in the national market for that commodity.[1]

Nonetheless, respondents suggest that *Wickard* differs from this case in three respects: (1) the Agricultural Adjustment Act, unlike the CSA, exempted small farming operations; (2) *Wickard* involved a "quintessential economic activity"— a commercial farm—whereas respondents do not sell marijuana; and (3) the *Wickard* record made it clear that the aggregate production of wheat for use on farms had a significant impact on market prices. Those differences, though factually accurate, do not diminish the precedential force of this Court's reasoning. The fact that Wickard's own impact on the market was "trivial by itself" was not a sufficient reason for removing him from the scope of federal regulation. That the Secretary of Agriculture elected to exempt even smaller farms from regulation does not speak to his power to regulate all those whose aggregated production was significant, nor did that fact play any role in the Court's analysis. Moreover, even though Wickard was indeed a commercial farmer, the activity he was engaged in—the cultivation of wheat for home consumption—was not treated by the Court as part of his commercial farming operation. And while it is true that the record in the *Wickard* case itself established the causal connection between the production for local use and the national market, we have before us findings by Congress to the same effect.

In assessing the scope of Congress' authority under the Commerce Clause, we stress that the task before us is a modest one. We need not determine whether respondents' activities, taken in the aggregate, substantially affect interstate commerce in fact, but only whether a "rational basis" exists for so concluding. Given the enforcement difficulties that attend distinguishing between marijuana cultivated locally and marijuana grown elsewhere, 21 U.S.C. § 801(5), and concerns about diversion into illicit channels, we have no difficulty concluding that Congress had a rational basis for believing that failure to regulate the intrastate manufacture and possession of marijuana would leave a gaping hole in the CSA. Thus, as in *Wickard*, when it enacted comprehensive legislation to regulate the interstate market in a fungible commodity, Congress was acting well within its authority to "make all Laws which shall be necessary and proper" to "regulate Commerce . . . among the several States." U.S. Const., Art. I, § 8. That the regulation ensnares some purely intrastate activity is of no moment. As we have done many times before, we refuse to excise individual components of that larger scheme.

---

1. To be sure, the wheat market is a lawful market that Congress sought to protect and stabilize, whereas the marijuana market is an unlawful market that Congress sought to eradicate. This difference, however, is of no constitutional import. It has long been settled that Congress' power to regulate commerce includes the power to prohibit commerce in a particular commodity. [Footnote by the Court.]

IV

To support their contrary submission, respondents rely heavily on two of our more recent Commerce Clause cases. In their myopic focus, they overlook the larger context of modern-era Commerce Clause jurisprudence preserved by those cases. Moreover, even in the narrow prism of respondents' creation, they read those cases far too broadly. Those two cases, of course, are United States v. Lopez (1995) and *United States v. Morrison* (2000). As an initial matter, the statutory challenges at issue in those cases were markedly different from the challenge respondents pursue in the case at hand. Here, respondents ask us to excise individual applications of a concededly valid statutory scheme. In contrast, in both *Lopez* and *Morrison*, the parties asserted that a particular statute or provision fell outside Congress' commerce power in its entirety. This distinction is pivotal for we have often reiterated that "[w]here the class of activities is regulated and that class is within the reach of federal power, the courts have no power 'to excise, as trivial, individual instances' of the class."

Unlike those at issue in *Lopez* and *Morrison*, the activities regulated by the CSA are quintessentially economic. "Economics" refers to "the production, distribution, and consumption of commodities." Webster's Third New International Dictionary (1966). The CSA is a statute that regulates the production, distribution, and consumption of commodities for which there is an established, and lucrative, interstate market. Prohibiting the intrastate possession or manufacture of an article of commerce is a rational (and commonly utilized) means of regulating commerce in that product. Such prohibitions include specific decisions requiring that a drug be withdrawn from the market as a result of the failure to comply with regulatory requirements as well as decisions excluding Schedule I drugs entirely from the market. Because the CSA is a statute that directly regulates economic, commercial activity, our opinion in *Morrison* casts no doubt on its constitutionality.

V

Respondents also raise a substantive due process claim and seek to avail themselves of the medical necessity defense. These theories of relief were set forth in their complaint but were not reached by the Court of Appeals. We therefore do not address the question whether judicial relief is available to respondents on these alternative bases. We do note, however, the presence of another avenue of relief. As the Solicitor General confirmed during oral argument, the statute authorizes procedures for the reclassification of Schedule I drugs. But perhaps even more important than these legal avenues is the democratic process, in which the voices of voters allied with these respondents may one day be heard in the halls of Congress.

Justice SCALIA, concurring in the judgment.

I agree with the Court's holding that the Controlled Substances Act (CSA) may validly be applied to respondents' cultivation, distribution, and possession of marijuana for personal, medicinal use. I write separately because my understanding of the doctrinal foundation on which that holding rests is, if not inconsistent with that of the Court, at least more nuanced.

Since *Perez v. United States* (1971), our cases have mechanically recited that the Commerce Clause permits congressional regulation of three categories: (1) the channels of interstate commerce; (2) the instrumentalities of interstate commerce, and persons or things in interstate commerce; and (3) activities that "substantially affect" interstate commerce. The first two categories are self-evident, since they are the ingredients of interstate commerce itself. The third category, however, is different in kind, and its recitation without explanation is misleading and incomplete.

It is misleading because, unlike the channels, instrumentalities, and agents of interstate commerce, activities that substantially affect interstate commerce are not themselves part of interstate commerce, and thus the power to regulate them cannot come from the Commerce Clause alone. Rather, Congress's regulatory authority over intrastate activities that are not themselves part of interstate commerce (including activities that have a substantial effect on interstate commerce) derives from the Necessary and Proper Clause. And the category of "activities that substantially affect interstate commerce" is incomplete because the authority to enact laws necessary and proper for the regulation of interstate commerce is not limited to laws governing intrastate activities that substantially affect interstate commerce. Where necessary to make a regulation of interstate commerce effective, Congress may regulate even those intrastate activities that do not themselves substantially affect interstate commerce.

Today's principal dissent objects that, by permitting Congress to regulate activities necessary to effective interstate regulation, the Court reduces *Lopez* and *Morrison* to "little more than a drafting guide." I think that criticism unjustified. Unlike the power to regulate activities that have a substantial effect on interstate commerce, the power to enact laws enabling effective regulation of interstate commerce can only be exercised in conjunction with congressional regulation of an interstate market, and it extends only to tho measures necessary to make the interstate regulation effective. As *Lopez* itself states, and the Court affirms today, Congress may regulate noneconomic intrastate activities only where the failure to do so "could . . . undercut" its regulation of interstate commerce. This is not a power that threatens to obliterate the line between "what is truly national and what is truly local."

Lopez and *Morrison* affirm that Congress may not regulate certain "purely local" activity within the States based solely on the attenuated effect that such activity may have in the interstate market. But those decisions do not declare noneconomic intrastate activities to be categorically beyond the reach of the

Federal Government. Neither case involved the power of Congress to exert control over intrastate activities in connection with a more comprehensive scheme of regulation.

To dismiss this distinction as "superficial and formalistic," (O'Connor, J., dissenting), is to misunderstand the nature of the Necessary and Proper Clause, which empowers Congress to enact laws in effectuation of its enumerated powers that are not within its authority to enact in isolation. See McCulloch v. Maryland (1819). And there are other restraints upon the Necessary and Proper Clause authority. As Chief Justice Marshall wrote in McCulloch v. Maryland, even when the end is constitutional and legitimate, the means must be "appropriate" and "plainly adapted" to that end. Moreover, they may not be otherwise "prohibited" and must be "consistent with the letter and spirit of the constitution." These phrases are not merely hortatory.

III

The application of these principles to the case before us is straightforward. In the CSA, Congress has undertaken to extinguish the interstate market in Schedule I controlled substances, including marijuana. The Commerce Clause unquestionably permits this. The power to regulate interstate commerce "extends not only to those regulations which aid, foster and protect the commerce, but embraces those which prohibit it." To effectuate its objective, Congress has prohibited almost all intrastate activities related to Schedule I substances—both economic activities (manufacture, distribution, possession with the intent to distribute) and noneconomic activities (simple possession). That simple possession is a noneconomic activity is immaterial to whether it can be prohibited as a necessary part of a larger regulation. Rather, Congress's authority to enact all of these prohibitions of intrastate controlled-substance activities depends only upon whether they are appropriate means of achieving the legitimate end of eradicating Schedule I substances from interstate commerce.

By this measure, I think the regulation must be sustained. Not only is it impossible to distinguish "controlled substances manufactured and distributed intrastate" from "controlled substances manufactured and distributed interstate," but it hardly makes sense to speak in such terms. Drugs like marijuana are fungible commodities. As the Court explains, marijuana that is grown at home and possessed for personal use is never more than an instant from the interstate market— and this is so whether or not the possession is for medicinal use or lawful use under the laws of a particular State. Congress need not accept on faith that state law will be effective in maintaining a strict division between a lawful market for "medical" marijuana and the more general marijuana market.

I thus agree with the Court that, however the class of regulated activities is subdivided, Congress could reasonably conclude that its objective of prohibiting marijuana from the interstate market "could be undercut" if those activities were excepted from its general scheme of regulation. That is sufficient to authorize the application of the CSA to respondents.

Justice O'CONNOR, with whom THE CHIEF JUSTICE and Justice THOMAS join as to all but Part III, dissenting.

We enforce the "outer limits" of Congress' Commerce Clause authority not for their own sake, but to protect historic spheres of state sovereignty from excessive federal encroachment and thereby to maintain the distribution of power fundamental to our federalist system of government. *United States v. Lopez* (1995). One of federalism's chief virtues, of course, is that it promotes innovation by allowing for the possibility that "a single courageous State may, if its citizens choose, serve as a laboratory; and try novel social and economic experiments without risk to the rest of the country." *New State Ice Co. v. Liebmann* (1932) (Brandeis, J., dissenting).

This case exemplifies the role of States as laboratories. The States' core police powers have always included authority to define criminal law and to protect the health, safety, and welfare of their citizens. Exercising those powers, California (by ballot initiative and then by legislative codification) has come to its own conclusion about the difficult and sensitive question of whether marijuana should be available to relieve severe pain and suffering. Today the Court sanctions an application of the federal Controlled Substances Act that extinguishes that experiment, without any proof that the personal cultivation, possession, and use of marijuana for medicinal purposes, if economic activity in the first place, has a substantial effect on interstate commerce and is therefore an appropriate subject of federal regulation. In so doing, the Court announces a rule that gives Congress a perverse incentive to legislate broadly pursuant to the Commerce Clause—nestling questionable assertions of its authority into comprehensive regulatory schemes—rather than with precision. That rule and the result it produces in this case are irreconcilable with our decisions in *Lopez* and *Morrison*. Accordingly I dissent.

The Court's principal means of distinguishing *Lopez* from this case is to observe that the Gun-Free School Zones Act of 1990 was a "brief, single-subject statute," whereas the CSA is "a lengthy and detailed statute creating a comprehensive framework for regulating the production, distribution, and possession of five classes of 'controlled substances.'" Thus, according to the Court, it was possible in *Lopez* to evaluate in isolation the constitutionality of criminalizing local activity (there gun possession in school zones), whereas the local activity that the CSA targets (in this case cultivation and possession of marijuana for personal medicinal use) cannot be separated from the general drug control scheme of which it is a part.

Today's decision allows Congress to regulate intrastate activity without check, so long as there is some implication by legislative design that regulating intrastate activity is essential (and the Court appears to equate "essential" with "necessary") to the interstate regulatory scheme. Seizing upon our language in *Lopez* that the statute prohibiting gun possession in school zones was "not an essential part of a larger regulation of economic activity, in which the regulatory scheme could be undercut unless the intrastate activity were regulated," the Court appears to reason that the placement of local activity in a comprehensive scheme confirms that it is essential to that scheme. If the Court is right, then *Lopez* stands for nothing more than a drafting guide: Congress should have described the relevant crime as "transfer or possession of a firearm anywhere in the nation"—thus including commercial and noncommercial activity, and clearly encompassing some activity with assuredly substantial effect on interstate commerce. Had it done so, the majority hints, we would have sustained its authority to regulate possession of firearms in school zones. Furthermore, today's decision suggests we would readily sustain a congressional decision to attach the regulation of intrastate activity to a pre-existing comprehensive (or even not-so-comprehensive) scheme. If so, the Court invites increased federal regulation of local activity even if, as it suggests, Congress would not enact a new interstate scheme exclusively for the sake of reaching intrastate activity. I cannot agree that our decision in *Lopez* contemplated such evasive or overbroad legislative strategies with approval. Until today, such arguments have been made only in dissent.

Lopez and *Morrison* did not indicate that the constitutionality of federal regulation depends on superficial and formalistic distinctions. Likewise I did not understand our discussion of the role of courts in enforcing outer limits of the Commerce Clause for the sake of maintaining the federalist balance our Constitution requires as a signal to Congress to enact legislation that is more extensive and more intrusive into the domain of state power. If the Court always defers to Congress as it does today, little may be left to the notion of enumerated powers.

The hard work for courts, then, is to identify objective markers for confining the analysis in Commerce Clause cases. Here, respondents challenge the constitutionality of the CSA as applied to them and those similarly situated. I agree with the Court that we must look beyond respondents' own activities. Otherwise, individual litigants could always exempt themselves from Commerce Clause regulation merely by pointing to the obvious—that their personal activities do not have a substantial effect on interstate commerce. The task is to identify a mode of analysis that allows Congress to regulate more than nothing (by declining to reduce each case to its litigants) and less than everything (by declining to let Congress set the terms of analysis). The analysis may not be the same in every case, for it depends on the regulatory scheme at issue and the federalism concerns implicated.

A number of objective markers are available to confine the scope of constitutional review here. Both federal and state legislation—including the CSA itself, the California Compassionate Use Act, and other state medical marijuana legislation—recognize that medical and nonmedical (i.e., recreational) uses of drugs are realistically distinct and can be segregated, and regulate them differently. Respondents challenge only the application of the CSA to medicinal use of marijuana. Moreover, because fundamental structural concerns about dual sovereignty animate our Commerce Clause cases, it is relevant that this case involves the interplay of federal and state regulation in areas of criminal law and social policy, where "States lay claim by right of history and expertise." Under our precedents, the conduct is economic and, in the aggregate, substantially affects interstate commerce. Even if intrastate cultivation and possession of marijuana for one's own medicinal use can properly be characterized as economic, and I question whether it can, it has not been shown that such activity substantially affects interstate commerce. Similarly, it is neither self-evident nor demonstrated that regulating such activity is necessary to the interstate drug control scheme.

The Court's definition of economic activity is breathtaking. It defines as economic any activity involving the production, distribution, and consumption of commodities. And it appears to reason that when an interstate market for a commodity exists, regulating the intrastate manufacture or possession of that commodity is constitutional either because that intrastate activity is itself economic, or because regulating it is a rational part of regulating its market. Putting to one side the problem endemic to the Court's opinion—the shift in focus from the activity at issue in this case to the entirety of what the CSA regulates—the Court's definition of economic activity for purposes of Commerce Clause jurisprudence threatens to sweep all of productive human activity into federal regulatory reach.

Even assuming that economic activity is at issue in this case, the Government has made no showing in fact that the possession and use of homegrown marijuana for medical purposes, in California or elsewhere, has a substantial effect on interstate commerce. Similarly, the Government has not shown that regulating such activity is necessary to an interstate regulatory scheme. Whatever the specific theory of "substantial effects" at issue (i.e., whether the activity substantially affects interstate commerce, whether its regulation is necessary to an interstate regulatory scheme, or both), a concern for dual sovereignty requires that Congress' excursion into the traditional domain of States be justified.

That is why characterizing this as a case about the Necessary and Proper Clause does not change the analysis significantly. Congress must exercise its authority under the Necessary and Proper Clause in a manner consistent with basic constitutional principles. Likewise, that authority must be used in a manner consistent with the notion of enumerated powers—a structural principle that is as much part of the Constitution as the Tenth Amendment's explicit textual command. Accordingly, something more than mere assertion is required when Congress purports to have power over local activity whose connection to an intrastate market is not self-evident. Otherwise, the Necessary and Proper Clause will always be a back door for unconstitutional federal regulation. Indeed, if it were enough in "substantial effects" cases for the Court to supply conceivable justifications for intrastate regulation related to an interstate market, then we could have surmised in *Lopez* that guns in school zones are "never more than an instant from the interstate market" in guns already subject to extensive federal regulation, recast *Lopez* as a Necessary and Proper Clause case, and thereby upheld the Gun-Free School Zones Act of 1990.

There is simply no evidence that homegrown medicinal marijuana users constitute, in the aggregate, a sizable enough class to have a discernable, let alone substantial, impact on the national illicit drug market—or otherwise to threaten the CSA regime.

The Government has not overcome empirical doubt that the number of Californians engaged in personal cultivation, possession, and use of medical marijuana, or the amount of marijuana they produce, is enough to threaten the federal regime. Nor has it shown that Compassionate Use Act marijuana users have been or are realistically likely to be responsible for the drug's seeping into the market in a significant way. The Government does cite one estimate that there were over 100,000 Compassionate Use Act users in California in 2004, but does not explain, in terms of proportions, what their presence means for the national illicit drug market.

Relying on Congress' abstract assertions, the Court has endorsed making it a federal crime to grow small amounts of marijuana in one's own home for one's own medicinal use. This overreaching stifles an express choice by some States, concerned for the lives and liberties of their people, to regulate medical marijuana differently. If I were a California citizen, I would not have voted for the medical marijuana ballot initiative; if I were a California legislator I would not have supported the Compassionate Use Act. But whatever the wisdom of California's experiment with medical marijuana, the federalism principles that have driven our Commerce Clause cases require that room for experiment be protected in this case. For these reasons I dissent.

Justice THOMAS, dissenting.

Respondents Diane Monson and Angel Raich use marijuana that has never been bought or sold, that has never crossed state lines, and that has had no demonstrable effect on the national market for marijuana. If Congress can regulate this under the Commerce Clause, then it can regulate virtually anything—and the Federal Government is no longer one of limited and enumerated powers.

I

Respondents' local cultivation and consumption of marijuana is not "Commerce . . . among the several States." By holding that Congress may regulate activity that is neither interstate nor commerce under the Interstate Commerce Clause, the Court abandons any attempt to enforce the Constitution's limits on federal power. The majority supports this conclusion by invoking, without explanation, the Necessary and Proper Clause. Regulating respondents' conduct, however, is not "necessary and proper for carrying into Execution" Congress' restrictions on the interstate drug trade. Thus, neither the Commerce Clause nor the Necessary and Proper Clause grants Congress the power to regulate respondents' conduct.

As I explained at length in *United States v. Lopez* (1995), the Commerce Clause empowers Congress to regulate the buying and selling of goods and services trafficked across state lines. The Clause's text, structure, and history all indicate that, at the time of the founding, the term "'commerce' consisted of selling, buying, and bartering, as well as transporting for these purposes." Commerce, or trade, stood in contrast to productive activities like manufacturing and agriculture.

Even the majority does not argue that respondents' conduct is itself "Commerce among the several States." Monson and Raich neither buy nor sell the marijuana that they consume. They cultivate their cannabis entirely in the State of California—it never crosses state lines, much less as part of a commercial transaction. Certainly no evidence from the founding suggests that "commerce" included the mere possession of a good or some purely personal activity that did not involve trade or exchange for value. In the early days of the Republic, it would have been unthinkable that Congress could prohibit the local cultivation, possession, and consumption of marijuana.

More difficult, however, is whether the CSA is a valid exercise of Congress' power to enact laws that are "necessary and proper for carrying into Execution" its power to regulate interstate commerce. The Necessary and Proper Clause is not a warrant to Congress to enact any law that bears some conceivable connection to the exercise of an enumerated power. Nor is it, however, a command to Congress to enact only laws that are absolutely indispensable to the exercise of an enumerated power.

On its face, a ban on the intrastate cultivation, possession and distribution of marijuana may be plainly adapted to stopping the interstate flow of marijuana. Unregulated local growers and users could swell both the supply and the demand sides of the interstate marijuana market, making the market more difficult to regulate. But respondents do not challenge the CSA on its face. Instead, they challenge it as applied to their conduct. The question is thus whether the intrastate ban is "necessary and proper" as applied to medical marijuana users like respondents.

Respondents are not regulable simply because they belong to a large class (local growers and users of marijuana) that Congress might need to reach, if they also belong to a distinct and separable subclass (local growers and users of state-authorized, medical marijuana) that does not undermine the CSA's interstate ban. California's Compassionate Use Act sets respondents' conduct apart from other intrastate producers and users of marijuana.

In sum, neither in enacting the CSA nor in defending its application to respondents has the Government offered any obvious reason why banning medical marijuana use is necessary to stem the tide of interstate drug trafficking. Congress' goal of curtailing the interstate drug trade would not plainly be thwarted if it could not apply the CSA to patients like Monson and Raich. That is, unless Congress' aim is really to exercise police power of the sort reserved to the States in order to eliminate even the intrastate possession and use of marijuana.

The majority prevents States like California from devising drug policies that they have concluded provide much-needed respite to the seriously ill. It does so without any serious inquiry into the necessity for federal regulation or the propriety of "displac[ing] state regulation in areas of traditional state concern." The majority's rush to embrace federal power "is especially unfortunate given the importance of showing respect for the sovereign States that comprise our Federal Union." Our federalist system, properly understood, allows California and a growing number of other States to decide for themselves how to safeguard the health and welfare of their citizens. I would affirm the judgment of the Court of Appeals.

Two high profile cases raised potentially important issues concerning the scope of Congress's commerce clause authority, but each was decided on statutory interpretation grounds without reaching the constitutional issues. In *Gonzales v. Oregon*, 126 S. Ct. 904 (2006), the Court considered the legality of an interpretive rule issued by Attorney General John Ashcroft that physicians who assist with suicide of terminally ill patients pursuant to the Oregon Death With Dignity Act would be violating the federal Controlled Substances Act and could thereby lose the ability to issue prescriptions. The Court, in a 6-3 decision with Justice Kennedy writing for the majority, held that the interpretive rule did not fit within the scope of the Attorney General's authority under the Controlled Substances Act and thus was invalid.

There was no discussion of the Constitution or federalism, except for the following paragraph: "Just as the conventions of expression indicate that Congress is unlikely to alter a statute's obvious scope and division of authority through muffled hints, the background principles of our federal system also belie the notion that Congress would use such an obscure grant of authority to regulate areas traditionally supervised by the States' police power. It is unnecessary even to consider the application of clear statement requirements, or presumptions against pre-emption, to reach this commonsense conclusion. For all these reasons, we conclude the CSA's prescription requirement does not authorize the Attorney General to bar dispensing controlled substances for assisted suicide in the face of a state medical regime permitting such conduct."

The other case that potentially raised commerce clause issues was *Rapanos v. United States*, 126 S.Ct. 2208 (2006), in which the Court considered whether the federal Clean Water Act (CWA) could be applied to intrastate wetlands. Justice Scalia, writing for a plurality of four, gave a narrow construction to the statute and said that the term "navigable waters," under CWA, includes only relatively permanent, standing or flowing bodies of water, not intermittent or ephemeral flows of water, and only those wetlands with a continuous surface connection to bodies that are waters of the United States in their own right are adjacent to such waters and covered by the CWA. Again, the plurality opinion was based on statutory interpretation and not on the commerce clause.

However, at the conclusion of the plurality opinion, Justice Scalia invoked the Constitution: "Even if the phrase 'the waters of the United States' were ambiguous as applied to intermittent flows, our own canons of construction would establish that the Corps' interpretation of the statute is impermissible. As we noted in [*Solid Waste Agency of Northern Cook County v. United States Army*

Corps of Engineers (SWANCC)], the Government's expansive interpretation would "result in a significant impingement of the States' traditional and primary power over land and water use." Regulation of land use, as through the issuance of the development permits sought by petitioners in both of these cases, is a quintessential state and local power. The extensive federal jurisdiction urged by the Government would authorize the Corps to function as a de facto regulator of immense stretches of intrastate land—an authority the agency has shown its willingness to exercise with the scope of discretion that would befit a local zoning board. We ordinarily expect a "clear and manifest" statement from Congress to authorize an unprecedented intrusion into traditional state authority. The phrase "the waters of the United States" hardly qualifies.

Likewise, just as we noted in *SWANCC*, the Corps' interpretation stretches the outer limits of Congress's commerce power and raises difficult questions about the ultimate scope of that power. Even if the term "the waters of the United States" were ambiguous as applied to channels that sometimes host ephemeral flows of water (which it is not), we would expect a clearer statement from Congress to authorize an agency theory of jurisdiction that presses the envelope of constitutional validity.

Justice Kennedy concurred in the judgment, and said that the Water Pollution Control Act applies to intrastate waters that have a "significant nexus" to interstate waters. He disagreed with the plurality's approach and said its that reading of the Act "is inconsistent with its text, structure, and purpose." Justice Kennedy said that the significant nexus test he urged also would meet the requirements under the commerce clause.

Justices Stevens, Souter, Ginsburg, and Breyer would have upheld that federal regulation of the intrastate wetlands. As a result, since Justice Kennedy's vote was the narrowest ground upon which a majority agreed, his "significant nexus" test is now to be followed for the application of the CWA.

E. Congress's Power to Authorize Suits Against State Governments

1. Background on the Eleventh Amendment and Sovereign Immunity (casebook, p. 222)

In *Central Virginia Community College v. Katz*, 546 U.S. 346 (2006), the Court ruled that sovereign immunity does not apply in bankruptcy courts. Justice Stevens, writing for the Court in a 5-4 decision, stated: "Bankruptcy jurisdiction, as understood today and at the time of the framing, is principally in rem jurisdiction. In bankruptcy, 'the court's jurisdiction is premised on the debtor and his estate, and not on the creditors.' As such, its exercise does not, in the usual case, interfere with state sovereignty even when States' interests are affected.

The text of Article I, § 8, cl. 4, of the Constitution, however, provides that Congress shall have the power to establish 'uniform Laws on the subject of Bankruptcies throughout the United States.' Although the interest in avoiding unjust imprisonment for debt and making federal discharges in bankruptcy enforceable in every State was a primary motivation for the adoption of that provision, its coverage encompasses the entire 'subject of Bankruptcies.' The power granted to Congress by that Clause is a unitary concept rather than an amalgam of discrete segments.

The ineluctable conclusion, then, is that States agreed in the plan of the Convention not to assert any sovereign immunity defense they might have had in proceedings brought pursuant to 'Laws on the subject of Bankruptcies.'

It is interesting to note that this was a 5-4 decision, with Justice O'Connor in the majority. Perhaps the result would have been different with Justice Alito on the Court, and perhaps it will be revisited by the Court in the future.

2. Congress's Power to Authorize Suits Against State Governments

c. Congress's Greater Authority to Legislate Concerning Types of Discrimination and Rights that Receive Heightened Scrutiny (casebook, p. 246)

As the casebook indicates, based on the most recent Supreme Court decisions concerning sovereign immunity, *Nevada Department of Human Resources v. Hibbs* and *Tennessee v. Lane,* Congress has greater authority to legislate under section five of the Fourteenth Amendment when it is dealing with a type of discrimination or a right that receives heightened scrutiny. In *United States v. Georgia,* below, the Court considered, as it did in *Lane,* whether a state government could be sued for violating Title II of the Americans with Disabilities Act. Title II prohibits state and local governments from discriminating against people with disabilities in government programs, services, and activities. In *Lane,* the Court held that state governments can be sued for violating Title II when the fundamental right of access to the courts is implicated.

In *United States v. Georgia,* the Court held that a prisoner who alleged unconstitutional state behavior could sue the state because Congress under section five of the Fourteenth Amendment can provide a remedy for unconstitutional state conduct. Thus, it appears after *United States v. Georgia,* in considering whether a state government can be sued for violating a federal law that authorizes such suits, the initial question is whether the plaintiff alleges a constitutional violation. If so, a state can be sued. If not, the question becomes whether the statute is dealing with a type of discrimination that receives heightened scrutiny or a fundamental right, in which case the lawsuit against the state likely can go forward. But if the plaintiff is not alleging a constitutional violation and the case does not involve a type of discrimination or a right receiving heightened scrutiny, the state can be sued only if Congress finds pervasive unconstitutional state conduct.

UNITED STATES v. GEORGIA
126 S.Ct. 877 (2006)

Justice SCALIA delivered the opinion of the Court.

We consider whether a disabled inmate in a state prison may sue the State for money damages under Title II of the Americans with Disabilities Act of 1990.

Tony Goodman is a paraplegic inmate in the Georgia prison system who, at all relevant times, was housed at the Georgia State Prison in Reidsville. Goodman's pro se complaint and subsequent filings in the District Court included many allegations, both grave and trivial, regarding the conditions of his confinement in the Reidsville prison. Among his more serious allegations, he claimed that he was confined for 23-to-24 hours per day in a 12-by-3-foot cell in which he could not turn his wheelchair around. He alleged that the lack of accessible facilities rendered him unable to use the toilet and shower without assistance, which was often denied. On multiple occasions, he asserted, he had injured himself in attempting to transfer from his wheelchair to the shower or toilet on his own, and, on several other occasions, he had been forced to sit in his own feces and urine while prison officials refused to assist him in cleaning up the waste. He also claimed that he had been denied physical therapy and medical treatment, and denied access to virtually all prison programs and services on account of his disability.

While the Members of this Court have disagreed regarding the scope of Congress's "prophylactic" enforcement powers under § 5 of the Fourteenth Amendment, no one doubts that § 5 grants Congress the power to "enforce . . . the provisions" of the Amendment by creating private remedies against the States for actual violations of those provisions. "Section 5 authorizes Congress to create a cause of action through which the citizen may vindicate his Fourteenth Amendment rights." This enforcement power includes the power to abrogate state sovereign immunity by authorizing private suits for damages against the States. Thus, insofar as Title II creates a private cause of action for damages against the States for conduct that actually violates the Fourteenth Amendment, Title II validly abrogates state sovereign immunity. The Eleventh Circuit erred in dismissing those of Goodman's Title II claims that were based on such unconstitutional conduct.

From the many allegations in Goodman's pro se complaint and his subsequent filings in the District Court, it is not clear precisely what conduct he intended to allege in support of his Title II claims. Because the Eleventh Circuit did not address the issue, it is likewise unclear to what extent the conduct underlying Goodman's constitutional claims also violated Title II. It is therefore unclear whether Goodman's amended complaint will assert Title II claims premised on conduct that does not independently violate the Fourteenth Amendment. Once Goodman's complaint is amended, the lower courts will be best situated to determine in the first instance, on a claim-by-claim basis, (1) which aspects of the State's alleged conduct violated Title II; (2) to what extent such misconduct also violated the Fourteenth Amendment; and (3) insofar as such misconduct violated Title II but did not violate the Fourteenth Amendment, whether Congress's purported abrogation of sovereign immunity as to that class of conduct is nevertheless valid.

Chapter 3

The Federal Executive Power

E. Presidential Power and the War on Terrorism

2. Military Tribunals (casebook, p. 342)

Perhaps the most important decision in October Term 2005 was the Supreme Court's decision in *Hamdan v. Rumsfeld*, below. The case concerned the legality of the military tribunals created by Presidential Executive Order (casebook, p. 343). The United States military captured Yemeni citizen Salim Ahmed Hamdan during its invasion of Afghanistan. There seems no dispute that he was the driver for Bin Laden, although Hamdan does deny any involvement in terrorist activity. The United States detained Hamdan at its naval base in Guantanamo Bay, Cuba. Hamdan was one of the first individuals to be designated for trial in a military tribunal created by Presidential Executive Order.

Hamdan brought a habeas corpus petition arguing that the military tribunal violated his rights under due process and international law. The United States District Court for the District of Columbia granted his habeas petition. The United States Court of Appeals for the District of Columbia Circuit reversed, with then-Judge John Roberts participating.

Subsequent to the grant of certiorari, Congress enacted the Detainee Treatment Act, which said that those in Guantanamo did not have access to habeas corpus and could gain review only in the D.C. Circuit of decisions of the military tribunals.

The Court, in what was essentially a 5-3 ruling, reversed the D.C. Circuit decision and held that the military tribunals created by executive order violated the Geneva Accords and the Uniform Code of Military Justice. (Chief Justice Roberts did not participate because he had been on the panel that decided the case in the D.C. Circuit.) Several aspects of the decision, although important, do not relate to constitutional issues and are not included in the excerpt below. First, the Court held that despite Congress's passage of the Detainee Treatment Act of 2005, the Court had jurisdiction. The Court found that Congress had not clearly indicated that it wanted the restriction on jurisdiction to apply retroactively to cases pending at the time it was adopted. The Court, as a matter of statutory construction, said that Congress did not provide that the provisions restricting jurisdiction would apply retroactively to cases such as this that were already pending in the courts.

Second, the Court rejected the government's argument that abstention was appropriate because the matter was pending in a military tribunal. The Court read *Ex parte Quirin* (casebook, p. 347), which upheld the use of a military tribunal during World War II, as precedent for judicial review.

The core constitutional issue involved whether there was adequate congressional authorization for the Executive Order providing for military tribunals. The Court also considered whether the military tribunals as constituted by the Executive Order met the requirements of international law or the Uniform Code of Military Justice. These aspects of the decision are below.

HAMDAN v. RUMSFELD
548 U.S. 557 (2006)

Justice STEVENS announced the judgment of the Court.

Petitioner Salim Ahmed Hamdan, a Yemeni national, is in custody at an American prison in Guantanamo Bay, Cuba. In November 2001, during hostilities between the United States and the Taliban (which then governed Afghanistan), Hamdan was captured by militia forces and turned over to the U.S. military. In June 2002, he was transported to Guantanamo Bay. Over a year later, the President deemed him eligible for trial by military commission for then-unspecified crimes. After another year had passed, Hamdan was charged with one count of conspiracy "to commit . . . offenses triable by military commission."

Hamdan filed petitions for writs of habeas corpus and mandamus to challenge the Executive Branch's intended means of prosecuting this charge. He concedes that a court-martial constituted in accordance with the Uniform Code of Military Justice (UCMJ) would have authority to try him. His objection is that the military commission the President has convened lacks such authority, for two principal reasons: First, neither congressional Act nor the common law of war supports trial by this commission for the crime of conspiracy—an offense that, Hamdan says, is not a violation of the law of war. Second, Hamdan contends, the procedures that the President has adopted to try him violate the most basic tenets of military and international law, including the principle that a defendant must be permitted to see and hear the evidence against him.

For the reasons that follow, we conclude that the military commission convened to try Hamdan lacks power to proceed because its structure and procedures violate both the UCMJ and the Geneva Conventions. Four of us also conclude, see Part V, infra, that the offense with which Hamdan has been charged is not an "offens[e] that by . . . the law of war may be tried by military commissions."

I

On September 11, 2001, agents of the al Qaeda terrorist organization hijacked commercial airplanes and attacked the World Trade Center in New York City and the national headquarters of the Department of Defense in Arlington, Virginia. Americans will never forget the devastation wrought by these acts. Nearly 3,000 civilians were killed.

Congress responded by adopting a Joint Resolution authorizing the President to "use all necessary and appropriate force against those nations, organizations, or persons he determines planned, authorized, committed, or aided the terrorist attacks . . . in order to prevent any future acts of international terrorism against the United States by such nations, organizations or persons." Authorization for Use of Military Force (AUMF). Acting pursuant to the AUMF, and having determined that the Taliban regime had supported al Qaeda, the President ordered the Armed Forces of the United States to invade Afghanistan. In the ensuing hostilities, hundreds of individuals, Hamdan among them, were captured and eventually detained at Guantanamo Bay.

On November 13, 2001, while the United States was still engaged in active combat with the Taliban, the President issued a comprehensive military order intended to govern the "Detention, Treatment, and Trial of Certain Non-Citizens in the War Against Terrorism." [The Executive Order is found in the casebook at p. 343.]

[II]

The military commission, a tribunal neither mentioned in the Constitution nor created by statute, was born of military necessity. Exigency alone, of course, will not justify the establishment and use of penal tribunals not contemplated by Article I, § 8 and Article III, § 1 of the Constitution unless some other part of that document authorizes a response to the felt need.

Whether the President may constitutionally convene military commissions "without the sanction of Congress" in cases of "controlling necessity" is a question this Court has not answered definitively, and need not answer today. For we held in *Quirin* that Congress had, through Article of War 15, sanctioned the use of military commissions in such circumstances. Article 21 of the UCMJ, the language of which is substantially identical to the old Article 15 and was preserved by Congress after World War II, reads as follows:

> "Jurisdiction of courts-martial not exclusive.
> The provisions of this code conferring jurisdiction upon courts-martial shall not be construed as depriving military commissions, provost courts, or other military tribunals of concurrent jurisdiction in respect of offenders or offenses that by statute or by the law of war may be tried by such military commissions, provost courts, or other military tribunals."

We have no occasion to revisit *Quirin's* controversial characterization of Article of War 15 as congressional authorization for military commissions. Contrary to the Government's assertion, however, even *Quirin* did not view the authorization as a sweeping mandate for the President to "invoke military commissions when he deems them necessary." Rather, the *Quirin* Court recognized that Congress had simply preserved what power, under the Constitution and the common law of war, the President had had before 1916 to convene military commissions—with the express condition that the President and those under his command comply with the law of war.[1] That much is evidenced by the Court's inquiry, following its conclusion that Congress had authorized military commissions, into whether the law of war had indeed been complied with in that case.

The Government would have us dispense with the inquiry that the *Quirin* Court undertook and find in either the AUMF or the [Detainee Treatment Act (DTA)] specific, overriding authorization for the very commission that has been convened to try Hamdan. Neither of these congressional Acts, however, expands the President's authority to convene military commissions. First, while we assume that the AUMF activated the President's war powers, see *Hamdi v. Rumsfeld* (2004) (plurality opinion), and that those powers include the authority to convene military commissions in appropriate circumstances, there is nothing in the text or legislative history of the AUMF even hinting that Congress intended to expand or alter the authorization set forth in Article 21 of the UCMJ.

Likewise, the DTA cannot be read to authorize this commission. Although the DTA, unlike either Article 21 or the AUMF, was enacted after the President had convened Hamdan's commission, it contains no language authorizing that tribunal or any other at Guantanamo Bay. The DTA obviously "recognize[s]" the existence of the Guantanamo Bay commissions in the weakest sense, because it references some of the military orders governing them and creates limited judicial review of their "final decision[s]." But the statute also pointedly reserves judgment on whether "the Constitution and laws of the United States are applicable" in reviewing such decisions and whether, if they are, the "standards and procedures" used to try Hamdan and other detainees actually violate the "Constitution and laws."

Together, the UCMJ, the AUMF, and the DTA at most acknowledge a general Presidential authority to convene military commissions in circumstances where justified under the "Constitution and laws," including the law of war. Absent a more specific congressional authorization, the task of this Court is, as it was in *Quirin*, to decide whether Hamdan's military commission is so justified. It is to that inquiry we now turn.

[III]

The common law governing military commissions may be gleaned from past practice and what sparse legal precedent exists. Commissions historically have been used in three situations. First, they have substituted for civilian courts at times and in places where martial law has been declared. Their use in these

---

1. Whether or not the President has independent power, absent congressional authorization, to convene military commissions, he may not disregard limitations that Congress had, in proper exercise of its own war powers, placed on his powers. See *Youngstown Sheet & Tube Co. v. Sawyer* (1952) (Jackson, J., concurring). The Government does not argue otherwise. [Footnote by Justice Stevens]

circumstances has raised constitutional questions. Second, commissions have been established to try civilians "as part of a temporary military government over occupied enemy territory or territory regained from an enemy where civilian government cannot and does not function." Illustrative of this second kind of commission is the one that was established, with jurisdiction to apply the German Criminal Code, in occupied Germany following the end of World War II.

The third type of commission, convened as an "incident to the conduct of war" when there is a need "to seize and subject to disciplinary measures those enemies who in their attempt to thwart or impede our military effort have violated the law of war," has been described as "utterly different" from the other two. Not only is its jurisdiction limited to offenses cognizable during time of war, but its role is primarily a factfinding one—to determine, typically on the battlefield itself, whether the defendant has violated the law of war. The last time the U.S. Armed Forces used the law-of-war military commission was during World War II. In *Quirin*, this Court sanctioned President Roosevelt's use of such a tribunal to try Nazi saboteurs captured on American soil during the War. And in Yamashita, we held that a military commission had jurisdiction to try a Japanese commander for failing to prevent troops under his command from committing atrocities in the Philippines.

Quirin is the model the Government invokes most frequently to defend the commission convened to try Hamdan. That is both appropriate and unsurprising. Since Guantanamo Bay is neither enemy-occupied territory nor under martial law, the law-of-war commission is the only model available. At the same time, no more robust model of executive power exists; *Quirin* represents the high-water mark of military power to try enemy combatants for war crimes.

The charge against Hamdan alleges a conspiracy extending over a number of years, from 1996 to November 2001. All but two months of that more than 5-year-long period preceded the attacks of September 11, 2001, and the enactment of the AUMF—the Act of Congress on which the Government relies for exercise of its war powers and thus for its authority to convene military commissions. Neither the purported agreement with Osama bin Laden and others to commit war crimes, nor a single overt act, is alleged to have occurred in a theater of war or on any specified date after September 11, 2001. None of the overt acts that Hamdan is alleged to have committed violates the law of war.

These facts alone cast doubt on the legality of the charge and, hence, the commission; the offense alleged must have been committed both in a theater of war and during, not before, the relevant conflict. But the deficiencies in the time and place allegations also underscore—indeed are symptomatic of—the most serious defect of this charge: The offense it alleges is not triable by law-of-war military commission. There is no suggestion that Congress has, in exercise of its constitutional authority to "define and punish . . . Offences against the Law of Nations," U.S. Const., Art. I, § 8, cl. 10, positively identified "conspiracy" as a war crime. As we explained in *Quirin*, that is not necessarily fatal to the Government's claim of authority to try the alleged offense by military commission; Congress, through Article 21 of the UCMJ, has "incorporated by reference" the common law of war, which may render triable by military commission certain offenses not defined by statute. When, however, neither the elements of the offense nor the range of permissible punishments is defined by statute or treaty, the precedent must be plain and unambiguous. To demand any less would be to risk concentrating in military hands a degree of adjudicative and punitive power in excess of that contemplated either by statute or by the Constitution. This high standard was met in *Quirin*; the violation there alleged was, by "universal agreement and practice" both in this country and internationally, recognized as an offense against the law of war.

At a minimum, the Government must make a substantial showing that the crime for which it seeks to try a defendant by military commission is acknowledged to be an offense against the law of war. That burden is far from satisfied here. The crime of "conspiracy" has rarely if ever been tried as such in this country by any law-of-war military commission not exercising some other form of jurisdiction, and does not appear in either the Geneva Conventions or the Hague Conventions-the major treaties on the law of war.

[V]

Whether or not the Government has charged Hamdan with an offense against the law of war cognizable by military commission, the commission lacks power to proceed. The UCMJ conditions the President's use of military commissions on compliance not only with the American common law of war, but also with the rest of the UCMJ itself, insofar as applicable, and with the "rules and precepts of the law of nations," including the four Geneva Conventions signed in 1949. The procedures that the Government has decreed will govern Hamdan's trial by commission violate these laws.

These rights [provided by the Presidential Executive Order] are subject, however, to one glaring condition: The accused and his civilian counsel may be excluded from, and precluded from ever learning what evidence was presented during, any part of the proceeding that either the Appointing Authority or the presiding officer decides to "close." Grounds for such closure "include the protection of information classified or classifiable . . . ; information protected by law or rule from unauthorized disclosure; the physical safety of participants in Commission proceedings, including prospective witnesses; intelligence and law enforcement sources, methods, or activities; and other national security interests." Appointed military defense counsel must be privy to these closed sessions, but may, at the presiding officer's discretion, be forbidden to reveal to his or her client what took place therein.

Another striking feature of the rules governing Hamdan's commission is that they permit the admission of any evidence that, in the opinion of the presiding officer, "would have probative value to a reasonable person." Under this test, not only is testimonial hearsay and evidence obtained through coercion fully admissible, but neither live testimony nor witnesses' written statements need be sworn. Moreover, the accused and his civilian counsel may be denied access to evidence in the form of "protected information" (which includes classified information as well as "information protected by law or rule from unauthorized disclosure" and "information concerning other national security interests," so long as the presiding officer concludes that the evidence is "probative" and that its admission without the accused's knowledge would not "result in the denial of a full and fair trial." Finally, a presiding officer's determination that evidence "would not have probative value to a reasonable person" may be overridden by a majority of the other commission members.

Once all the evidence is in, the commission members (not including the presiding officer) must vote on the accused's guilt. A two-thirds vote will suffice for both a verdict of guilty and for imposition of any sentence not including death (the imposition of which requires a unanimous vote). Any appeal is taken to a three-member review panel composed of military officers and designated by the Secretary of Defense, only one member of which need have experience as a judge. The review panel is directed to "disregard any variance from procedures specified in this Order or elsewhere that would not materially have affected the outcome of the trial before the Commission." Once the panel makes its recommendation to the Secretary of Defense, the Secretary can either remand for further proceedings or forward the record to the President with his recommendation as to final disposition. The President then, unless he has delegated the task to the Secretary, makes the "final decision." He may change the commission's findings or sentence only in a manner favorable to the accused.

Hamdan raises both general and particular objections to the procedures set forth in Commission Order No. 1. His general objection is that the procedures' admitted deviation from those governing courts-martial itself renders the commission illegal. Chief among his particular objections are that he may, under the Commission Order, be convicted based on evidence he has not seen or heard, and that any evidence admitted against him need not comply with the admissibility or relevance rules typically applicable in criminal trials and court-martial proceedings.

In part because the difference between military commissions and courts-martial originally was a difference of jurisdiction alone, and in part to protect against abuse and ensure evenhandedness under the pressures of war, the procedures governing trials by military commission historically have been the same as those governing courts-martial. The uniformity principle is not an inflexible one; it does not preclude all departures from the procedures dictated for use by courts-martial. But any departure must be tailored to the exigency that necessitates it. That understanding is reflected in Article 36 of the UCMJ, which provides:

"(a) The procedure, including modes of proof, in cases before courts-martial, courts of inquiry, military commissions, and other military tribunals may be prescribed by the President by regulations which shall, so far as he considers practicable, apply the principles of law and the rules of evidence generally recognized in the trial of criminal cases in the United States district courts, but which may not be contrary to or inconsistent with this chapter.

(b) All rules and regulations made under this article shall be uniform insofar as practicable and shall be reported to Congress."

Article 36 places two restrictions on the President's power to promulgate rules of procedure for courts-martial and military commissions alike. First, no procedural rule he adopts may be "contrary to or inconsistent with" the UCMJ—however practical it may seem. Second, the rules adopted must be "uniform insofar as practicable." That is, the rules applied to military commissions must be the same as those applied to courts-martial unless such uniformity proves impracticable.

Hamdan argues that Commission Order No. 1 violates both of these restrictions; he maintains that the procedures described in the Commission Order are inconsistent with the UCMJ and that the Government has offered no explanation for their deviation from the procedures governing courts-martial, which are set forth in the Manual for Courts-Martial. Among the inconsistencies Hamdan identifies is that between § 6 of the Commission Order, which permits exclusion of the accused from proceedings and denial of his access to evidence in certain circumstances, and the UCMJ's requirement that "[a]ll . . . proceedings" other than votes and deliberations by courts-martial "shall be made a part of the record and shall be in the presence of the accused." Hamdan also observes that the Commission Order dispenses with virtually all evidentiary rules applicable in courts-martial.

Without reaching the question whether any provision of Commission Order No. 1 is strictly "contrary to or inconsistent with" other provisions of the UCMJ, we conclude that the "practicability" determination the President has made is insufficient to justify variances from the procedures governing courts-martial. Subsection (b) of Article 36 was added after World War II, and requires a different showing of impracticability from the one required by subsection (a). Subsection (a) requires that the rules the President promulgates for courts-martial, provost courts, and military commissions alike conform to those that govern procedures in Article III courts,"so far as he considers practicable." Subsection (b), by contrast, demands that the rules applied in courts-martial, provost courts, and military commissions—whether or not they conform with the Federal Rules of Evidence—be "uniform insofar as practicable." Under the latter provision, then, the rules set forth in the Manual for Courts-Martial must apply to military commissions unless impracticable.

The President here has determined, pursuant to subsection (a), that it is impracticable to apply the rules and principles of law that govern "the trial of criminal cases in the United States district courts," to Hamdan's commission. We assume that complete deference is owed that determination. The President has not, however, made a similar official determination that it is impracticable to apply the rules for courts-martial. And even if subsection (b)'s requirements may be satisfied without such an official determination, the requirements of that subsection are not satisfied here.

Nothing in the record before us demonstrates that it would be impracticable to apply court-martial rules in this case. There is no suggestion, for example, of any logistical difficulty in securing properly sworn and authenticated evidence or in applying the usual principles of relevance and admissibility. Assuming arguendo that the reasons articulated in the President's Article 36(a) determination ought to be considered in evaluating the impracticability of applying court-martial rules, the only reason offered in support of that determination is the danger posed by international terrorism. Without for one moment underestimating that danger, it is not evident to us why it should require, in the case of Hamdan's trial, any variance from the rules that govern courts-martial.

The absence of any showing of impracticability is particularly disturbing when considered in light of the clear and admitted failure to apply one of the most fundamental protections afforded not just by the Manual for Courts-Martial but also by the UCMJ itself: the right to be present. Whether or not that departure technically is "contrary to or inconsistent with" the terms of the UCMJ, the jettisoning of so basic a right cannot lightly be excused as "practicable." Under the circumstances, then, the rules applicable in courts-martial must apply. Since it is undisputed that Commission Order No. 1 deviates in many significant respects from those rules, it necessarily violates Article 36(b).

The procedures adopted to try Hamdan also violate the Geneva Conventions. The conflict with al Qaeda is not, according to the Government, a conflict to which the full protections afforded detainees under the 1949 Geneva Conventions apply because Article 2 of those Conventions (which appears in all four Conventions) renders the full protections applicable only to "all cases of declared war or of any other armed conflict which may arise between two or more of the High Contracting Parties." Since Hamdan was captured and detained incident to the conflict with al Qaeda and not the conflict with the Taliban, and since al Qaeda, unlike Afghanistan, is not a "High Contracting Party"— i.e., a signatory of the Conventions, the protections of those Conventions are not, it is argued, applicable to Hamdan.

We need not decide the merits of this argument because there is at least one provision of the Geneva Conventions that applies here even if the relevant conflict is not one between signatories. Article 3, often referred to as Common Article 3 because, like Article 2, it appears in all four Geneva Conventions, provides that in a "conflict not of an international character occurring in the territory of one of the High Contracting Parties, each Party to the conflict shall be bound to apply, as a minimum," certain provisions protecting "[p]ersons taking no active part in the hostilities, including members of armed forces who have laid down their arms and those placed hors de combat by . . . detention." One such provision prohibits "the passing of sentences and the carrying out of executions without previous judgment pronounced by a regularly constituted court affording all the judicial guarantees which are recognized as indispensable by civilized peoples."

Common Article 3, then, is applicable here and, as indicated above, requires that Hamdan be tried by a "regularly constituted court affording all the judicial guarantees which are recognized as indispensable by civilized peoples." While the term "regularly constituted court" is not specifically defined in either Common Article 3 or its accompanying commentary, other sources disclose its core meaning. The commentary accompanying a provision of the Fourth Geneva Convention, for example, defines "'regularly constituted' tribunals" to include "ordinary military courts" and "definitely exclud[e] all special tribunals." And one of the Red Cross' own treatises defines "regularly constituted court" as used in Common Article 3 to mean "established and organized in accordance with the laws and procedures already in force in a country."

Inextricably intertwined with the question of regular constitution is the evaluation of the procedures governing the tribunal and whether they afford "all the judicial guarantees which are recognized as indispensable by civilized peoples." Like the phrase "regularly constituted court," this phrase is not defined in the text of the Geneva Conventions. But it must be understood to incorporate at least the barest of those trial protections that have been recognized by customary international law. Many of these are described in Article 75 of Protocol I to the Geneva Conventions of 1949, adopted in 1977 (Protocol I). Among the rights set forth in Article 75 is the "right to be tried in [one's] presence."

Common Article 3 obviously tolerates a great degree of flexibility in trying individuals captured during armed conflict; its requirements are general ones, crafted to accommodate a wide variety of legal systems. But requirements they are nonetheless. The commission that the President has convened to try Hamdan does not meet those requirements.

We have assumed, as we must, that the allegations made in the Government's charge against Hamdan are true. We have assumed, moreover, the truth of the message implicit in that charge—viz., that Hamdan is a dangerous individual whose beliefs, if acted upon, would cause great harm and even death to innocent civilians, and who would act upon those beliefs if given the opportunity. It bears emphasizing that Hamdan does not challenge, and we do not today address, the Government's power to detain him for the duration of active hostilities in order to prevent such harm. But in undertaking to try Hamdan and subject him to criminal punishment, the Executive is bound to comply with the Rule of Law that prevails in this jurisdiction.

Justice BREYER, with whom Justice KENNEDY, Justice SOUTER, and Justice GINSBURG join, concurring.

The dissenters say that today's decision would "sorely hamper the President's ability to confront and defeat a new and deadly enemy." They suggest that it undermines our Nation's ability to "preven[t] future attacks" of the grievous sort that we have already suffered. That claim leads me to state briefly what I believe the majority sets forth both explicitly and implicitly at greater length. The Court's conclusion ultimately rests upon a single ground: Congress has not issued the Executive a "blank check." Indeed, Congress has denied the President the legislative authority to create military commissions of the kind at issue here. Nothing prevents the President from returning to Congress to seek the authority he believes necessary.

Where, as here, no emergency prevents consultation with Congress, judicial insistence upon that consultation does not weaken our Nation's ability to deal with danger. To the contrary, that insistence strengthens the Nation's ability to determine—through democratic means—how best to do so. The Constitution places its faith in those democratic means. Our Court today simply does the same.

Justice KENNEDY concurring in part.

Military Commission Order No. 1, which governs the military commission established to try petitioner Salim Hamdan for war crimes, exceeds limits that certain statutes, duly enacted by Congress, have placed on the President's authority to convene military courts. This is not a case, then, where the Executive can assert some unilateral authority to fill a void left by congressional inaction. It is a case where Congress, in the proper exercise of its powers as an independent branch of government, and as part of a long tradition of legislative involvement in matters of military justice, has considered the subject of military tribunals and set limits on the President's authority. Where a statute provides the conditions for the exercise of governmental power, its requirements are the result of a deliberative and reflective process engaging both of the political branches. Respect for laws derived from the customary operation of the Executive and Legislative Branches gives some assurance of stability in time of crisis. The Constitution is best preserved by reliance on standards tested over time and insulated from the pressures of the moment.

These principles seem vindicated here, for a case that may be of extraordinary importance is resolved by ordinary rules. The rules of most relevance here are those pertaining to the authority of Congress and the interpretation of its enactments.

It seems appropriate to recite these rather fundamental points because the Court refers, as it should in its exposition of the case, to the requirement of the Geneva Conventions of 1949 that military tribunals be "regularly constituted"—a requirement that controls here, if for no other reason, because Congress requires that military commissions like the ones at issue conform to the "law of war." Whatever the substance and content of the term "regularly constituted" as interpreted in this and any later cases, there seems little doubt that it relies upon the importance of standards deliberated upon and chosen in advance of crisis, under a system where the single power of the Executive is checked by other constitutional mechanisms. All of which returns us to the point of beginning—that domestic statutes control this case. If Congress, after due consideration, deems it appropriate to change the controlling statutes, in conformance with the Constitution and other laws, it has the power and prerogative to do so.

Justice SCALIA, with whom Justice THOMAS and Justice ALITO join, dissenting.

On December 30, 2005, Congress enacted the Detainee Treatment Act (DTA). It unambiguously provides that, as of that date, "no court, justice, or judge" shall have jurisdiction to consider the habeas application of a Guantanamo Bay detainee. Notwithstanding this plain directive, the Court today concludes that, on what it calls the statute's most natural reading, every "court, justice, or judge" before whom such a habeas application was pending on December 30 has jurisdiction to hear, consider, and render judgment on it. This conclusion is patently erroneous. And even if it were not, the jurisdiction supposedly retained should, in an exercise of sound equitable discretion, not be exercised. [Justice Scalia then elaborated his argument that the Detainee Treatment Act should be seen as precluding the Court from having jurisdiction or reaching the merits of the case.]

Even if Congress had not clearly and constitutionally eliminated jurisdiction over this case, neither this Court nor the lower courts ought to exercise it. Traditionally, equitable principles govern both the exercise of habeas jurisdiction and the granting of the injunctive relief sought by petitioner. In light of Congress's provision of an alternate avenue for petitioner's claims in [the Detainee Treatment Act] those equitable principles counsel that we abstain from exercising jurisdiction in this case.

Justice THOMAS dissenting.

For the reasons set forth in Justice Scalia's dissent, it is clear that this Court lacks jurisdiction to entertain petitioner's claims. The Court having concluded otherwise, it is appropriate to respond to the Court's resolution of the merits of petitioner's claims because its opinion openly flouts our well-established duty to respect the Executive's judgment in matters of military operations and foreign affairs. The Court's evident belief that it is qualified to pass on the "[m]ilitary necessity," of the Commander in Chief's decision to employ a particular form of force against our enemies is so antithetical to our constitutional structure that it simply cannot go unanswered. I respectfully dissent.

Our review of petitioner's claims arises in the context of the President's wartime exercise of his commander-in-chief authority in conjunction with the complete support of Congress. Accordingly, it is important to take measure of the respective roles the Constitution assigns to the three branches of our Government in the conduct of war.

As I explained in *Hamdi v. Rumsfeld* (2004), the structural advantages attendant to the Executive Branch—namely, the decisiveness, "activity, secrecy, and dispatch" that flow from the Executive's "unity," (quoting The Federalist No. 70, p. 472 (J. Cooke ed. 1961) (A.Hamilton)) led the Founders to conclude that the "President ha[s] primary responsibility—along with the necessary power—to protect the national security and to conduct the Nation's foreign relations." Consistent with this conclusion, the Constitution vests in the President "[t]he executive Power," Art. II, § 1, provides that he "shall be Commander in Chief" of the Armed Forces, § 2, and places in him the power to recognize foreign governments, § 3. This Court has observed that these provisions confer upon the President broad constitutional authority to protect the Nation's security in the manner he deems fit.

Congress, to be sure, has a substantial and essential role in both foreign affairs and national security. But "Congress cannot anticipate and legislate with regard to every possible action the President may find it necessary to take or every possible situation in which he might act," and "[s]uch failure of Congress . . . does not, 'especially . . . in the areas of foreign policy and national security,' imply 'congressional disapproval' of action taken by the Executive." Rather, in these domains, the fact that Congress has provided the President with broad authorities does not imply—and the Judicial Branch should not infer—that Congress intended to deprive him of particular powers not specifically enumerated.

When "the President acts pursuant to an express or implied authorization from Congress," his actions are "'supported by the strongest of presumptions and the widest latitude of judicial interpretation, and the burden of persuasion . . . rest[s] heavily upon any who might attack it.'" Accordingly, in the very context that we address today, this Court has concluded that "the detention and trial of petitioners—ordered by the President in the declared exercise of his powers as Commander in Chief of the Army in time of war and of grave public danger—are not to be set aside by the courts without the clear conviction that they are in conflict with the Constitution or laws of Congress constitutionally enacted." *Ex parte Quirin* (1942).

Under this framework, the President's decision to try Hamdan before a military commission for his involvement with al Qaeda is entitled to a heavy measure of deference. In the present conflict, Congress has authorized the President "to use all necessary and appropriate force against those nations, organizations, or persons he determines planned, authorized, committed, or aided the terrorist attacks that occurred on September 11, 2001 . . . in order to prevent any future acts of international terrorism against the United States by such nations, organizations or persons." As a plurality of the Court observed in Hamdi, the "capture, detention, and trial of unlawful combatants, by 'universal agreement and practice,' are 'important incident[s] of war,'" and are therefore "an exercise of the 'necessary and appropriate force' Congress has authorized the President to use." Hamdi's observation that military commissions are included within the AUMF's authorization is supported by this Court's previous recognition that "[a]n important incident to the conduct of war is the adoption of measures by the military commander, not only to repel and defeat the enemy, but to seize and subject to disciplinary measures those enemies who, in their attempt to thwart or impede our military effort, have violated the law of war."

Ultimately, the plurality's determination that Hamdan has not been charged with an offense triable before a military commission rests not upon any historical example or authority, but upon the plurality's raw judgment of the "inability on the Executive's part here to satisfy the most basic precondition . . . for establishment of military commissions: military necessity." This judgment starkly confirms that the plurality has appointed itself the ultimate arbiter of what is quintessentially a policy and military judgment, namely, the appropriate military measures to take against those who "aided the terrorist attacks that occurred on September 11, 2001." The plurality's suggestion that Hamdan's commission is illegitimate because it is not dispensing swift justice on the battlefield is unsupportable. Even a cursory review of the authorities confirms that law-of-war military commissions have wide-ranging jurisdiction to try offenses against the law of war in exigent and nonexigent circumstances alike.

Today a plurality of this Court would hold that conspiracy to massacre innocent civilians does not violate the laws of war. This determination is unsustainable. The judgment of the political branches that Hamdan, and others like him, must be held accountable before military commissions for their involvement with and membership in an unlawful organization dedicated to inflicting massive civilian casualties is supported by virtually every relevant authority, including all of the authorities invoked by the plurality today. It is also supported by the nature of the present conflict. We are not engaged in a traditional battle with a nation-state, but with a worldwide, hydra-headed enemy, who lurks in the shadows conspiring to reproduce the atrocities of September 11, 2001, and who has boasted of sending suicide bombers into civilian gatherings, has proudly distributed videotapes of beheadings of civilian workers, and has tortured and dismembered captured American soldiers. But according to the plurality, when our Armed Forces capture those who are plotting terrorist atrocities like the bombing of the Khobar Towers, the bombing of the U.S.S. Cole, and the attacks of September 11—even if their plots are advanced to the very brink of fulfillment—our military cannot charge those criminals with any offense against the laws of war. Instead, our troops must catch the terrorists "redhanded," ante, at 48, in the midst of the attack itself, in order to bring them to justice. Not only is this conclusion fundamentally inconsistent with the cardinal principal of the law of war, namely protecting non-combatants, but it would sorely hamper the President's ability to confront and defeat a new and deadly enemy.

Justice ALITO dissenting.

The holding of the Court, as I understand it, rests on the following reasoning. A military commission is lawful only if it is authorized by 10 U.S.C. § 821; this provision permits the use of a commission to try "offenders or offenses" that "by statute or by the law of war may be tried by" such a commission; because no statute provides that an offender such as petitioner or an offense such as the one with which he is charged may be tried by a military commission, he may be tried by military commission only if the trial is authorized by "the law of war"; the Geneva Conventions are part of the law of war; and Common Article 3 of the Conventions prohibits petitioner's trial because the commission before which he would be tried is not "a regularly constituted court." Third Geneva Convention, Art. 3, ¶ 1 (d) , Relative to the Treatment of Prisoners of War, Aug.

12, 1949. I disagree with this holding because petitioner's commission is "a regularly constituted court."

In sum, I believe that Common Article 3 is satisfied here because the military commissions (1) qualify as courts, (2) that were appointed and established in accordance with domestic law, and (3) any procedural improprieties that might occur in particular cases can be reviewed in those cases. [Justice Alito developed each of these points at length.]

3. Habeas Corpus and the War on Terrorism

Following *Hamdan*, Congress passed and President Bush signed the Military Commission Act of 2006. Pub.L. No. 109-366, 120 Stat. 2600 (2006). Among other things, the Act provides that non-citizens held as enemy combatants shall not have access to federal court via a writ of habeas corpus. Instead, they must go through military proceedings and then seek review in the United States Court of Appeals for the District of Columbia Circuit. The D.C. Circuit is limited to hearing claims under the Constitution and federal statutes, it cannot hear claims under treaties such as the Geneva Accords. The Military Commission Act creates express statutory authority for military commissions and defines their procedures.

In February 2007, the United States Court of Appeals for the District of Columbia Circuit upheld the constitutionality of Military Commission Act, rejecting a challenge that it was an unconstitutional suspension of the writ of habeas corpus. *Boumediene v. Bush*, 476 F.3d 981 (D.C. Cir. 2007).

In June 2008, the Supreme Court reversed the D.C. Circuit. The decision focuses on what the Constitution requires in terms of the availability of habeas corpus; specifically, what is an unconstitutional suspension of the writ? Underlying the majority and the dissenting are very different views about the appropriate role of the judiciary in the war on terror.

BOUMEDIENE v. BUSH
128 S.Ct. 2229 (2008)

Justice KENNEDY delivered the opinion of the Court.

Petitioners are aliens designated as enemy combatants and detained at the United States Naval Station at Guantanamo Bay, Cuba. There are others detained there, also aliens, who are not parties to this suit.

Petitioners present a question not resolved by our earlier cases relating to the detention of aliens at Guantanamo: whether they have the constitutional privilege of habeas corpus, a privilege not to be withdrawn except in conformance with the Suspension Clause, Art. I, § 9, cl. 2. We hold these petitioners do have the habeas corpus privilege. Congress has enacted a statute, the Detainee Treatment Act of 2005(DTA), that provides certain procedures for review of the detainees' status. We hold that those procedures are not an adequate and effective substitute for habeas corpus. Therefore § 7 of the Military Commissions Act of 2006(MCA), operates as an unconstitutional suspension of the writ. We do not address whether the President has authority to detain these petitioners nor do we hold that the writ must issue. These and other questions regarding the legality of the detention are to be resolved in the first instance by the District Court.

I

Under the Authorization for Use of Military Force (AUMF), the President is authorized "to use all necessary and appropriate force against those nations, organizations, or persons he determines planned, authorized, committed, or aided the terrorist attacks that occurred on September 11, 2001, or harbored such organizations or persons, in order to prevent any future acts of international terrorism against the United States by such nations, organizations or persons."

In Hamdi v. Rumsfeld (2004), five Members of the Court recognized that detention of individuals who fought against the United States in Afghanistan "for the duration of the particular conflict in which they were captured, is so fundamental and accepted an incident to war as to be an exercise of the 'necessary and appropriate force' Congress has authorized the President to use." After Hamdi, the Deputy Secretary of Defense established Combatant Status Review Tribunals (CSRTs) to determine whether individuals detained at Guantanamo were "enemy combatants," as the Department defines that term. A later memorandum established procedures to implement the CSRTs. The Government maintains these procedures were designed to comply with the due process requirements identified by the plurality in Hamdi.

Interpreting the AUMF, the Department of Defense ordered the detention of these petitioners, and they were transferred to Guantanamo. Some of these individuals were apprehended on the battlefield in Afghanistan, others in places as far away from there as Bosnia and Gambia. All are foreign nationals, but none is a citizen of a nation now at war with the United States. Each denies he is a member of the al Qaeda terrorist network that carried out the September 11 attacks or of the Taliban regime that provided sanctuary for al Qaeda. Each petitioner appeared before a separate CSRT; was determined to be an enemy combatant; and has sought a writ of habeas corpus in the United States District Court for the District of Columbia.

The first actions commenced in February 2002. We granted certiorari and reversed, holding that 28 U.S.C. § 2241 extended statutory habeas corpus jurisdiction to Guantanamo. See Rasul v. Bush (2004). After Rasul, petitioners' cases were consolidated and entertained in two separate proceedings. In the first set of cases, Judge Richard J. Leon granted the Government's motion to dismiss, holding that the detainees had no rights that could be vindicated in a habeas corpus action. In the second set of cases Judge Joyce Hens Green reached the opposite conclusion, holding the detainees had rights under the Due Process Clause of the Fifth Amendment.

While appeals were pending from the District Court decisions, Congress passed the DTA. Subsection (e) of § 1005 of the DTA amended 28 U.S.C. § 2241 to provide that "no court, justice, or judge shall have jurisdiction to hear or consider . . . an application for a writ of habeas corpus filed by or on behalf of an alien detained by the Department of Defense at Guantanamo Bay, Cuba." Section 1005 further provides that the Court of Appeals for the District of Columbia Circuit shall have "exclusive" jurisdiction to review decisions of the CSRTs. Ibid.

In Hamdan v. Rumsfeld (2006), the Court held this provision did *2242 not apply to cases (like petitioners') pending when the DTA was enacted. Congress responded by passing the MCA.

II

As a threshold matter, we must decide whether MCA § 7 denies the federal courts jurisdiction to hear habeas corpus actions pending at the time of its enactment. We hold the statute does deny that jurisdiction, so that, if the statute is valid, petitioners' cases must be dismissed.

As amended by the terms of the MCA, 28 U.S.C.A. § 2241(e) now provides: "(1) No court, justice, or judge shall have jurisdiction to hear or consider an application for a writ of habeas corpus filed by or on behalf of an alien detained by the United States who has been determined by the United States to have been properly detained as an enemy combatant or is awaiting such determination. "(2) Except as provided in [§§ 1005(e)(2) and (e)(3) of the DTA] no court, justice, or judge shall have jurisdiction to hear or consider any other action against the United States or its agents relating to any aspect of the detention, transfer, treatment, trial, or conditions of confinement of an alien who is or was detained by the United States and has been determined by the United States to have been properly detained as an enemy combatant or is awaiting such determination."

Section 7(b) of the MCA provides the effective date for the amendment of § 2241(e). It states: "The amendment made by [MCA § 7(a)] shall take effect on the date of the enactment of this Act, and shall apply to all cases, without exception, pending on or after the date of the enactment of this Act which relate to any aspect of the detention, transfer, treatment, trial, or conditions of detention of an alien detained by the United States since September 11, 2001."

If this ongoing dialogue between and among the branches of Government is to be respected, we cannot ignore that the MCA was a direct response to Hamdan's holding that the DTA's jurisdiction-stripping provision had no application to pending cases. The Court of Appeals was correct to take note of the legislative history when construing the statute, and we agree with its conclusion that the MCA deprives the federal courts of jurisdiction to entertain the habeas corpus actions now before us.

III

In deciding the constitutional questions now presented we must determine whether petitioners are barred from seeking the writ or invoking the protections of the Suspension Clause either because of their status, i.e., petitioners' designation by the Executive Branch as enemy combatants, or their physical location, i.e., their presence at Guantanamo Bay. The Government contends that noncitizens designated as enemy combatants and detained in territory located outside our Nation's borders have no constitutional rights and no privilege of habeas corpus. Petitioners contend they do have cognizable constitutional rights and that Congress, in seeking to eliminate recourse to habeas corpus as a means to assert those rights, acted in violation of the Suspension Clause.

A

The Framers viewed freedom from unlawful restraint as a fundamental precept of liberty, and they understood the writ of habeas corpus as a vital instrument to secure that freedom. Experience taught, however, that the common-law writ all too often had been insufficient to guard against the abuse of monarchial power. That history counseled the necessity for specific language in the Constitution to secure the writ and ensure its place in our legal system.

That the Framers considered the writ a vital instrument for the protection of individual liberty is evident from the care taken to specify the limited grounds for its suspension: "The Privilege of the Writ of Habeas Corpus shall not be suspended, unless when in Cases of Rebellion or Invasion the public Safety may require it." Art. I, § 9, cl. 2. The word "privilege" was used, perhaps, to avoid mentioning some rights to the exclusion of others. (Indeed, the only mention of the term "right" in the Constitution, as ratified, is in its clause giving Congress the power to protect the rights of authors and inventors. See Art. I, § 8, cl. 8.) Surviving accounts of the ratification debates provide additional evidence that the Framers deemed the writ to be an essential mechanism in the separation-of-powers scheme.

In our own system the Suspension Clause is designed to protect against these cyclical abuses. The Clause protects the rights of the detained by a means consistent with the essential design of the Constitution. It ensures that, except during periods of formal suspension, the Judiciary will have a time-tested device, the writ, to maintain the "delicate balance of governance" that is itself the surest safeguard of liberty. The Clause protects the rights of the detained by affirming the duty and authority of the Judiciary to call the jailer to account.

B

The broad historical narrative of the writ and its function is central to our analysis, but we seek guidance as well from founding-era authorities addressing the specific question before us: whether foreign nationals, apprehended and detained in distant countries during a time of serious threats to our Nation's security, may assert the privilege of the writ and seek its protection. The Court has been careful not to foreclose the possibility that the protections of the Suspension Clause have expanded along with post-1789 developments that define the present scope of the writ. But the analysis may begin with precedents as of 1789, for the Court has said that "at the absolute minimum" the Clause protects the writ as it existed when the Constitution was drafted and ratified.

To support their arguments, the parties in these cases have examined historical sources to construct a view of the common-law writ as it existed in 1789—as have amici whose expertise in legal history the Court has relied upon in the past. Diligent search by all parties reveals no certain conclusions. In none of the cases cited do we find that a common-law court would or would not have granted, or refused to hear for lack of jurisdiction, a petition for a writ of habeas corpus brought by a prisoner deemed an enemy combatant, under a standard like the one the Department of Defense has used in these cases, and when held in a territory, like Guantanamo, over which the Government has total military and civil control.

Both arguments are premised, however, upon the assumption that the historical record is complete and that the common law, if properly understood, yields a definite answer to the questions before us. There are reasons to doubt both assumptions. Recent scholarship points to the inherent shortcomings in the historical record. And given the unique status of Guantanamo Bay and the particular dangers of terrorism in the modern age, the common-law courts simply may not have confronted cases with close parallels to this one. We decline, therefore, to infer too much, one way or the other, from the lack of historical evidence on point. Cf. Brown v. Board of Education (1954) (noting evidence concerning the circumstances surrounding the adoption of the Fourteenth Amendment, discussed in the parties' briefs and uncovered through the Court's own investigation, "convince us that, although these sources cast some light, it is not enough to resolve the problem with which we are faced. At best, they are inconclusive").

IV

Drawing from its position that at common law the writ ran only to territories over which the Crown was sovereign, the Government says the Suspension Clause affords petitioners no rights because the United States does not claim sovereignty over the place of detention.

Guantanamo Bay is not formally part of the United States. And under the terms of the lease between the United States and Cuba, Cuba retains "ultimate sovereignty" over the territory while the United States exercises "complete jurisdiction and control." Under the terms of the 1934 Treaty, however, Cuba effectively has no rights as a sovereign until the parties agree to modification of the 1903 Lease Agreement or the United States abandons the base.

The United States contends, nevertheless, that Guantanamo is not within its sovereign control. This was the Government's position well before the events of September 11, 2001. And in other contexts the Court has held that questions of sovereignty are for the political branches to decide. Even if this were a treaty interpretation case that did not involve a political question, the President's construction of the lease agreement would be entitled to great respect.

We therefore do not question the Government's position that Cuba, not the United States, maintains sovereignty, in the legal and technical sense of the term, over Guantanamo Bay. But this does not end the analysis. Our cases do not hold it is improper for us to inquire into the objective degree of control the Nation asserts over foreign territory. Accordingly, for purposes of our analysis, we accept the Government's position that Cuba, and not the United States, retains de jure sovereignty over Guantanamo Bay. As we did in Rasul, however, we take notice of the obvious and uncontested fact that the United States, by virtue of its complete jurisdiction and control over the base, maintains de facto sovereignty over this territory.

Were we to hold that the present cases turn on the political question doctrine, we would be required first to accept the Government's premise that de jure sovereignty is the touchstone of habeas corpus jurisdiction. This premise, however, is unfounded. For the reasons indicated above, the history of common-law habeas corpus provides scant support for this proposition; and, for the reasons indicated below, that position would be inconsistent with our precedents and contrary to fundamental separation-of-powers principles.

A

The Court has discussed the issue of the Constitution's extraterritorial application on many occasions. These decisions undermine the Government's argument that, at least as applied to noncitizens, the Constitution necessarily stops where de jure sovereignty ends.

Practical considerations weighed heavily as well in Johnson v. Eisentrager (1950), where the Court addressed whether habeas corpus jurisdiction extended to enemy aliens who had been convicted of violating the laws of war. The prisoners were detained at Landsberg Prison in Germany during the Allied Powers' postwar occupation. The Court stressed the difficulties of ordering the Government to produce the prisoners in a habeas corpus proceeding. It "would require allocation of shipping space, guarding personnel, billeting and rations" and would damage the prestige of military commanders at a sensitive time.

True, the Court in Eisentrager denied access to the writ, and it noted the prisoners "at no relevant time were within any territory over which the United

States is sovereign, and [that] the scenes of their offense, their capture, their trial and their punishment were all beyond the territorial jurisdiction of any court of the United States." The Government seizes upon this language as proof positive that the Eisentrager Court adopted a formalistic, sovereignty-based test for determining the reach of the Suspension Clause. We reject this reading for three reasons.

First, we do not accept the idea that the above-quoted passage from Eisentrager is the only authoritative language in the opinion and that all the rest is dicta. The Court's further determinations, based on practical considerations, were integral to Part II of its opinion and came before the decision announced its holding.

Second, because the United States lacked both de jure sovereignty and plenary control over Landsberg Prison, it is far from clear that the Eisentrager Court used the term sovereignty only in the narrow technical sense and not to connote the degree of control the military asserted over the facility. The Justices who decided Eisentrager would have understood sovereignty as a multifaceted concept. That the Court devoted a significant portion of Part II to a discussion of practical barriers to the running of the writ suggests that the Court was not concerned exclusively with the formal legal status of Landsberg Prison but also with the objective degree of control the United States asserted over it. Even if we assume the Eisentrager Court considered the United States' lack of formal legal sovereignty over Landsberg Prison as the decisive factor in that case, its holding is not inconsistent with a functional approach to questions of extraterritoriality. The formal legal status of a given territory affects, at least to some extent, the political branches' control over that territory. De jure sovereignty is a factor that bears upon which constitutional guarantees apply there.

Third, if the Government's reading of Eisentrager were correct, the opinion would have marked not only a change in, but a complete repudiation of, the Insular Cases' functional approach to questions of extraterritoriality. We cannot accept the Government's view. Nothing in Eisentrager says that de jure sovereignty is or has ever been the only relevant consideration in determining the geographic reach of the Constitution or of habeas corpus.

B

The Government's formal sovereignty-based test raises troubling separation-of-powers concerns as well. The political history of Guantanamo illustrates the deficiencies of this approach. The United States has maintained complete and uninterrupted control of the bay for over 100 years. Yet the Government's view is that the Constitution had no effect there, at least as to noncitizens, because the United States disclaimed sovereignty in the formal sense of the term. The necessary implication of the argument is that by surrendering formal sovereignty over any unincorporated territory to a third party, while at the same time entering into a lease that grants total control over the territory back to the United

States, it would be possible for the political branches to govern without legal constraint.

Our basic charter cannot be contracted away like this. Even when the United States acts outside its borders, its powers are not "absolute and unlimited" but are subject "to such restrictions as are expressed in the Constitution." Abstaining from questions involving formal sovereignty and territorial governance is one thing. To hold the political branches have the power to switch the Constitution on or off at will is quite another. The former position reflects this Court's recognition that certain matters requiring political judgments are best left to the political branches. The latter would permit a striking anomaly in our tripartite system of government, leading to a regime in which Congress and the President, not this Court, say "what the law is." Marbury v. Madison (1803).

These concerns have particular bearing upon the Suspension Clause question in the cases now before us, for the writ of habeas corpus is itself an indispensable mechanism for monitoring the separation of powers. The test for determining the scope of this provision must not be subject to manipulation by those whose power it is designed to restrain.

c

In addition to the practical concerns discussed above, the Eisentrager Court found relevant that each petitioner:

"(a) is an enemy alien; (b) has never been or resided in the United States; (c) was captured outside of our territory and there held in military custody as a prisoner of war; (d) was tried and convicted by a Military Commission sitting outside the United States; (e) for offenses against laws of war committed outside the United States; (f) and is at all times imprisoned outside the United States."

Based on this language from Eisentrager, and the reasoning in our other extraterritoriality opinions, we conclude that at least three factors are relevant in determining the reach of the Suspension Clause: (1) the citizenship and status of the detainee and the adequacy of the process through which that status determination was made; (2) the nature of the sites where apprehension and then detention took place; and (3) the practical obstacles inherent in resolving the prisoner's entitlement to the writ.

Applying this framework, we note at the onset that the status of these detainees is a matter of dispute. The petitioners, like those in Eisentrager, are not American citizens. But the petitioners in Eisentrager did not contest, it seems, the Court's assertion that they were "enemy alien[s]." In the instant cases, by contrast, the detainees deny they are enemy combatants. They have been afforded some process in CSRT proceedings to determine their status; but, unlike in Eisentrager, there has been no trial by military commission for violations of the laws of war. The difference is not trivial. The records from the Eisentrager trials suggest that, well before the petitioners brought their case to this Court, there had been a rigorous adversarial process to test the legality of their detention. The Eisentrager petitioners were charged by a bill of particulars that made detailed factual allegations against them. To rebut the accusations, they were entitled to representation by counsel, allowed to introduce evidence on their own behalf, and permitted to cross-examine the prosecution's witnesses.

In comparison the procedural protections afforded to the detainees in the CSRT hearings are far more limited, and, we conclude, fall well short of the procedures and adversarial mechanisms that would eliminate the need for habeas corpus review. Although the detainee is assigned a "Personal Representative" to assist him during CSRT proceedings, the Secretary of the Navy's memorandum makes clear that person is not the detainee's lawyer or even his "advocate." The Government's evidence is accorded a presumption of validity. The detainee is allowed to present "reasonably available" evidence, but his ability to rebut the Government's evidence against him is limited by the circumstances of his confinement and his lack of counsel at this stage. And although the detainee can seek review of his status determination in the Court of Appeals, that review process cannot cure all defects in the earlier proceedings.

As to the second factor relevant to this analysis, the detainees here are similarly situated to the Eisentrager petitioners in that the sites of their apprehension and detention are technically outside the sovereign territory of the United States. As noted earlier, this is a factor that weighs against finding they have rights under the Suspension Clause. But there are critical differences between Landsberg Prison, circa 1950, and the United States Naval Station at Guantanamo Bay in 2008. Unlike its present control over the naval station, the United States' control over the prison in Germany was neither absolute nor indefinite. Like all parts of occupied Germany, the prison was under the jurisdiction of the combined Allied Forces. Guantanamo Bay, on the other hand, is no transient possession. In every practical sense Guantanamo is not abroad; it is within the constant jurisdiction of the United States.

As to the third factor, we recognize, as the Court did in Eisentrager, that there are costs to holding the Suspension Clause applicable in a case of military detention abroad. Habeas corpus proceedings may require expenditure of funds by the Government and may divert the attention of military personnel from other pressing tasks. While we are sensitive to these concerns, we do not find them dispositive. Compliance with any judicial process requires some incremental expenditure of resources. Yet civilian courts and the Armed Forces have functioned along side each other at various points in our history. The Government presents no credible arguments that the military mission at Guantanamo would be compromised if habeas corpus courts had jurisdiction to hear the detainees' claims. And in light of the plenary control the United States asserts over the base, none are apparent to us.

The situation in Eisentrager was far different, given the historical context and nature of the military's mission in post-War Germany. When hostilities in the European Theater came to an end, the United States became responsible for an occupation zone encompassing over 57,000 square miles with a population of 18 million. In addition to supervising massive reconstruction and aid efforts the American forces stationed in Germany faced potential security threats from a defeated enemy. In retrospect the post-War occupation may seem uneventful. But at the time Eisentrager was decided, the Court was right to be concerned about judicial interference with the military's efforts to contain "enemy elements, guerilla fighters, and 'were-wolves.'"

Similar threats are not apparent here; nor does the Government argue that they are. The United States Naval Station at Guantanamo Bay consists of 45 square miles of land and water. The base has been used, at various points, to house migrants and refugees temporarily. At present, however, other than the detainees themselves, the only long-term residents are American military personnel, their families, and a small number of workers. The detainees have been deemed enemies of the United States. At present, dangerous as they may be if released, they are contained in a secure prison facility located on an isolated and heavily fortified military base.

There is no indication, furthermore, that adjudicating a habeas corpus petition would cause friction with the host government. No Cuban court has jurisdiction over American military personnel at Guantanamo or the enemy combatants detained there. While obligated to abide by the terms of the lease, the United States is, for all practical purposes, answerable to no other sovereign for its acts on the base. Were that not the case, or if the detention facility were located in an active theater of war, arguments that issuing the writ would be "impracticable or anomalous" would have more weight. Under the facts presented here, however, there are few practical barriers to the running of the writ. To the extent barriers arise, habeas corpus procedures likely can be modified to address them.

We hold that Art. I, § 9, cl. 2, of the Constitution has full effect at Guantanamo Bay. If the privilege of habeas corpus is to be denied to the detainees now before us, Congress must act in accordance with the requirements of the Suspension Clause.

V

In light of this holding the question becomes whether the statute stripping jurisdiction to issue the writ avoids the Suspension Clause mandate because Congress has provided adequate substitute procedures for habeas corpus.

The gravity of the separation-of-powers issues raised by these cases and the fact that these detainees have been denied meaningful access to a judicial forum for a period of years render these cases exceptional.

Our case law does not contain extensive discussion of standards defining suspension of the writ or of circumstances under which suspension has occurred. This simply confirms the care Congress has taken throughout our Nation's history to preserve the writ and its function. Indeed, most of the major legislative enactments pertaining to habeas corpus have acted not to contract the writ's protection but to expand it or to hasten resolution of prisoners' claims.

We do not endeavor to offer a comprehensive summary of the requisites for an adequate substitute for habeas corpus. We do consider it uncontroversial, however, that the privilege of habeas corpus entitles the prisoner to a meaningful opportunity to demonstrate that he is being held pursuant to "the erroneous application or interpretation" of relevant law. And the habeas court must have the power to order the conditional release of an individual unlawfully detained-though release need not be the exclusive remedy and is not the appropriate one in every case in which the writ is granted.

Where a person is detained by executive order, rather than, say, after being tried and convicted in a court, the need for collateral review is most pressing. A criminal conviction in the usual course occurs after a judicial hearing before a tribunal disinterested in the outcome and committed to procedures designed to ensure its own independence. These dynamics are not inherent in executive detention orders or executive review procedures. In this context the need for habeas corpus is more urgent. The intended duration of the detention and the reasons for it bear upon the precise scope of the inquiry. Habeas corpus proceedings need not resemble a criminal trial, even when the detention is by executive order. But the writ must be effective. The habeas court must have sufficient authority to conduct a meaningful review of both the cause for detention and the Executive's power to detain.

To determine the necessary scope of habeas corpus review, therefore, we must assess the CSRT process, the mechanism through which petitioners' designation as enemy combatants became final. Whether one characterizes the CSRT process as direct review of the Executive's battlefield determination that the detainee is an enemy combatant-as the parties have and as we do-or as the first step in the collateral review of a battlefield determination makes no difference in a proper analysis of whether the procedures Congress put in place are an adequate substitute for habeas corpus. What matters is the sum total of procedural protections afforded to the detainee at all stages, direct and collateral.

Petitioners identify what they see as myriad deficiencies in the CSRTs. The most relevant for our purposes are the constraints upon the detainee's ability to rebut the factual basis for the Government's assertion that he is an enemy combatant. As already noted, at the CSRT stage the detainee has limited means to find or present evidence to challenge the Government's case against him. He does not have the assistance of counsel and may not be aware of the most critical allegations that the Government relied upon to order his detention. The detainee can confront witnesses that testify during the CSRT proceedings. But given that there are in effect no limits on the admission of hearsay evidence-the only requirement is that the tribunal deem the evidence "relevant and helpful," the detainee's opportunity to question witnesses is likely to be more theoretical than real.

Even if we were to assume that the CSRTs satisfy due process standards, it would not end our inquiry. Habeas corpus is a collateral process that exists, in Justice Holmes' words, to "cu[t] through all forms and g[o] to the very tissue of the structure. It comes in from the outside, not in subordination to the proceedings, and although every form may have been preserved opens the inquiry whether they have been more than an empty shell." Even when the procedures authorizing detention are structurally sound, the Suspension Clause remains applicable and the writ relevant.

Although we make no judgment as to whether the CSRTs, as currently constituted, satisfy due process standards, we agree with petitioners that, even when all the parties involved in this process act with diligence and in good faith, there is considerable risk of error in the tribunal's findings of fact. And given that the consequence of error may be detention of persons for the duration of hostilities that may last a generation or more, this is a risk too significant to ignore.

For the writ of habeas corpus, or its substitute, to function as an effective and proper remedy in this context, the court that conducts the habeas proceeding must have the means to correct errors that occurred during the CSRT proceedings. This includes some authority to assess the sufficiency of the Government's evidence against the detainee. It also must have the authority to admit and consider relevant exculpatory evidence that was not introduced during the earlier proceeding. Federal habeas petitioners long have had the means to supplement the record on review, even in the postconviction habeas setting. Here that opportunity is constitutionally required.

The extent of the showing required of the Government in these cases is a matter to be determined. We need not explore it further at this stage. We do hold that when the judicial power to issue habeas corpus properly is invoked the judicial officer must have adequate authority to make a determination in light of the relevant law and facts and to formulate and issue appropriate orders for relief, including, if necessary, an order directing the prisoner's release.

C

We now consider whether the DTA allows the Court of Appeals to conduct a proceeding meeting these standards. The DTA does not explicitly empower the Court of Appeals to order the applicant in a DTA review proceeding released should the court find that the standards and procedures used at his CSRT hearing were insufficient to justify detention. This is troubling. Yet, for present purposes, we can assume congressional silence permits a constitutionally required remedy. The absence of a release remedy and specific language allowing AUMF challenges are not the only constitutional infirmities from which the statute potentially suffers, however. The more difficult question is whether the DTA permits the Court of Appeals to make requisite findings of fact. Assuming the DTA can be construed to allow the Court of Appeals to review or correct the CSRT's factual determinations, as opposed to merely certifying that the tribunal applied the correct standard of proof, we see no way to construe the statute to allow what is also constitutionally required in this context: an opportunity for the detainee to present relevant exculpatory evidence that was not made part of the record in the earlier proceedings.

On its face the statute allows the Court of Appeals to consider no evidence outside the CSRT record. Under the DTA the Court of Appeals has the power to review CSRT determinations by assessing the legality of standards and procedures. This implies the power to inquire into what happened at the CSRT hearing and, perhaps, to remedy certain deficiencies in that proceeding. But should the Court of Appeals determine that the CSRT followed appropriate and lawful standards and procedures, it will have reached the limits of its jurisdiction. There is no language in the DTA that can be construed to allow the Court of Appeals to admit and consider newly discovered evidence that could not have been made part of the CSRT record because it was unavailable to either the Government or the detainee when the CSRT made its findings. This evidence, however, may be critical to the detainee's argument that he is not an enemy combatant and there is no cause to detain him.

By foreclosing consideration of evidence not presented or reasonably available to the detainee at the CSRT proceedings, the DTA disadvantages the detainee by limiting the scope of collateral review to a record that may not be accurate or complete.

Although we do not hold that an adequate substitute must duplicate § 2241 in all respects, it suffices that the Government has not established that the detainees' access to the statutory review provisions at issue is an adequate substitute for the writ of habeas corpus. MCA § 7 thus effects an unconstitutional suspension of the writ. In view of our holding we need not discuss the reach of the writ with respect to claims of unlawful conditions of treatment or confinement.

VI

The real risks, the real threats, of terrorist attacks are constant and not likely soon to abate. The ways to disrupt our life and laws are so many and unforeseen that the Court should not attempt even some general catalogue of crises that might occur. Certain principles are apparent, however. Practical considerations and exigent circumstances inform the definition and reach of the law's writs, including habeas corpus. The cases and our tradition reflect this precept.

In cases involving foreign citizens detained abroad by the Executive, it likely would be both an impractical and unprecedented extension of judicial power to assume that habeas corpus would be available at the moment the prisoner is taken into custody. If and when habeas corpus jurisdiction applies, as it does in these cases, then proper deference can be accorded to reasonable procedures for screening and initial detention under lawful and proper conditions of confinement and treatment for a reasonable period of time. Domestic exigencies, furthermore, might also impose such onerous burdens on the Government that here, too, the Judicial Branch would be required to devise sensible rules for staying habeas corpus proceedings until the Government can comply with its requirements in a responsible way. Here, as is true with detainees apprehended abroad, a relevant consideration in determining the courts' role is whether there are suitable alternative processes in place to protect against the arbitrary exercise of governmental power.

The cases before us, however, do not involve detainees who have been held for a short period of time while awaiting their CSRT determinations. Were that the case, or were it probable that the Court of Appeals could complete a prompt review of their applications, the case for requiring temporary abstention or exhaustion of alternative remedies would be much stronger. These qualifications no longer pertain here. In some of these cases six years have elapsed without the judicial oversight that habeas corpus or an adequate substitute demands. And there has been no showing that the Executive faces such onerous burdens that it cannot respond to habeas corpus actions. To require these detainees to complete DTA review before proceeding with their habeas corpus actions would be to require additional months, if not years, of delay. The detainees in these cases are entitled to a prompt habeas corpus hearing.

Our decision today holds only that the petitioners before us are entitled to seek the writ; that the DTA review procedures are an inadequate substitute for habeas corpus; and that the petitioners in these cases need not exhaust the review procedures in the Court of Appeals before proceeding with their habeas actions in the District Court. The only law we identify as unconstitutional is MCA § 7. Accordingly, both the DTA and the CSRT process remain intact. Our holding with regard to exhaustion should not be read to imply that a habeas court should intervene the moment an enemy combatant steps foot in a territory where the writ runs. The Executive is entitled to a reasonable period of time to determine a detainee's status before a court entertains that detainee's habeas corpus petition.

In considering both the procedural and substantive standards used to impose detention to prevent acts of terrorism, proper deference must be accorded to the political branches. There are further considerations, however. Security subsists, too, in fidelity to freedom's first principles. Chief among these are freedom from arbitrary and unlawful restraint and the personal liberty that is secured by adherence to the separation of powers. It is from these principles that the judicial authority to consider petitions for habeas corpus relief derives.

Our opinion does not undermine the Executive's powers as Commander in Chief. On the contrary, the exercise of those powers is vindicated, not eroded, when confirmed by the Judicial Branch. Within the Constitution's separation-of-powers structure, few exercises of judicial power are as legitimate or as necessary as the responsibility to hear challenges to the authority of the Executive to imprison a person. Some of these petitioners have been in custody for six years with no definitive judicial determination as to the legality of their detention. Their access to the writ is a necessity to determine the lawfulness of their status, even if, in the end, they do not obtain the relief they seek.

Because our Nation's past military conflicts have been of limited duration, it has been possible to leave the outer boundaries of war powers undefined. If, as some fear, terrorism continues to pose dangerous threats to us for years to come, the Court might not have this luxury. This result is not inevitable, however. The political branches, consistent with their independent obligations to interpret and uphold the Constitution, can engage in a genuine debate about how best to preserve constitutional values while protecting the Nation from terrorism.

It bears repeating that our opinion does not address the content of the law that governs petitioners' detention. That is a matter yet to be determined. We hold that petitioners may invoke the fundamental procedural protections of habeas corpus. The laws and Constitution are designed to survive, and remain in force, in extraordinary times. Liberty and security can be reconciled; and in our system they are reconciled within the framework of the law. The Framers decided that habeas corpus, a right of first importance, must be a part of that framework, a part of that law.

Justice SOUTER, with whom Justice GINSBURG and Justice BREYER join, concurring.

I join the Court's opinion in its entirety and add this afterword only to emphasize two things one might overlook after reading the dissents.

Four years ago, this Court in Rasul v. Bush (2004) held that statutory habeas jurisdiction extended to claims of foreign nationals imprisoned by the United States at Guantanamo Bay, "to determine the legality of the Executive's potentially indefinite detention" of them. Subsequent legislation eliminated the statutory habeas jurisdiction over these claims, so that now there must be constitutionally based jurisdiction or none at all. But no one who reads the Court's opinion in Rasul could seriously doubt that the jurisdictional question must be answered the same way in purely constitutional cases, given the Court's reliance on the historical background of habeas generally in answering the statutory question.

A second fact insufficiently appreciated by the dissents is the length of the disputed imprisonments, some of the prisoners represented here today having been locked up for six years. Hence the hollow ring when the dissenters suggest that the Court is somehow precipitating the judiciary into reviewing claims that the military (subject to appeal to the Court of Appeals for the District of Columbia Circuit) could handle within some reasonable period of time. These suggestions of judicial haste are all the more out of place given the Court's realistic acknowledgment that in periods of exigency the tempo of any habeas review must reflect the immediate peril facing the country. After six years of sustained executive detentions in Guantanamo, subject to habeas jurisdiction but without any actual habeas scrutiny, today's decision is no judicial victory, but an act of perseverance in trying to make habeas review, and the obligation of the courts to provide it, mean something of value both to prisoners and to the Nation.

Chief Justice ROBERTS, with whom Justice SCALIA, Justice THOMAS, and Justice ALITO join, dissenting.

Today the Court strikes down as inadequate the most generous set of procedural protections ever afforded aliens detained by this country as enemy combatants. The political branches crafted these procedures amidst an ongoing military conflict, after much careful investigation and thorough debate. The Court rejects them today out of hand, without bothering to say what due process rights the detainees possess, without explaining how the statute fails to vindicate those rights, and before a single petitioner has even attempted to avail himself of the law's operation. And to what effect? The majority merely replaces a review system designed by the people's representatives with a set of shapeless procedures to be defined by federal courts at some future date. One cannot help but think, after surveying the modest practical results of the majority's ambitious opinion, that this decision is not really about the detainees at all, but about control of federal policy regarding enemy combatants.

The majority is adamant that the Guantanamo detainees are entitled to the protections of habeas corpus—its opinion begins by deciding that question. I regard the issue as a difficult one, primarily because of the unique and unusual jurisdictional status of Guantanamo Bay. I nonetheless agree with Justice Scalia's analysis of our precedents and the pertinent history of the writ, and accordingly join his dissent. The important point for me, however, is that the Court should have resolved these cases on other grounds. Habeas is most fundamentally a procedural right, a mechanism for contesting the legality of executive detention. The critical threshold question in these cases, prior to any inquiry about the writ's scope, is whether the system the political branches designed protects whatever rights the detainees may possess. If so, there is no need for any additional process, whether called "habeas" or something else.

Congress entrusted that threshold question in the first instance to the Court of Appeals for the District of Columbia Circuit, as the Constitution surely allows Congress to do. But before the D.C. Circuit has addressed the issue, the Court cashiers the statute, and without answering this critical threshold question itself. The Court does eventually get around to asking whether review under the DTA is, as the Court frames it, an "adequate substitute" for habeas, but even then its opinion fails to determine what rights the detainees possess and whether the DTA system satisfies them. The majority instead compares the undefined DTA process to an equally undefined habeas right—one that is to be given shape only in the future by district courts on a case-by-case basis. This whole approach is misguided.

It is also fruitless. How the detainees' claims will be decided now that the DTA is gone is anybody's guess. But the habeas process the Court mandates will most likely end up looking a lot like the DTA system it replaces, as the district court judges shaping it will have to reconcile review of the prisoners' detention with the undoubted need to protect the American people from the terrorist threat-precisely the challenge Congress undertook in drafting the DTA. All that today's opinion has done is shift responsibility for those sensitive foreign policy and national security decisions from the elected branches to the Federal Judiciary.

I believe the system the political branches constructed adequately protects any constitutional rights aliens captured abroad and detained as enemy combatants may enjoy. I therefore would dismiss these cases on that ground. With all respect for the contrary views of the majority, I must dissent.

The majority's overreaching is particularly egregious given the weakness of its objections to the DTA. Simply put, the Court's opinion fails on its own terms. The majority strikes down the statute because it is not an "adequate substitute" for habeas review, but fails to show what rights the detainees have that cannot be vindicated by the DTA system.

Because the central purpose of habeas corpus is to test the legality of executive detention, the writ requires most fundamentally an Article III court able to hear the prisoner's claims and, when necessary, order release. Beyond that, the process a given prisoner is entitled to receive depends on the circumstances and the rights of the prisoner. After much hemming and hawing, the majority appears to concede that the DTA provides an Article III court competent to order release. The only issue in dispute is the process the Guantanamo prisoners are entitled to use to test the legality of their detention. Hamdi concluded that American citizens detained as enemy combatants are entitled to only limited process, and that much of that process could be supplied by a military tribunal, with review to follow in an Article III court. That is precisely the system we have here. It is adequate to vindicate whatever due process rights petitioners may have.

The Court reaches the opposite conclusion partly because it misreads the statute. The majority appears not to understand how the review system it invalidates actually works-specifically, how CSRT review and review by the D.C. Circuit fit together. After briefly acknowledging in its recitation of the facts that the Government designed the CSRTs "to comply with the due process requirements identified by the plurality in Hamdi," the Court proceeds to dismiss the tribunal proceedings as no more than a suspect method used by the Executive for determining the status of the detainees in the first instance.

The majority is equally wrong to characterize the CSRTs as part of that initial determination process. They are instead a means for detainees to challenge the Government's determination. The Executive designed the CSRTs to mirror Army Regulation 190-8, the very procedural model the plurality in Hamdi said provided the type of process an enemy combatant could expect from a habeas cour. The CSRTs operate much as habeas courts would if hearing the detainee's collateral challenge for the first time: They gather evidence, call witnesses, take testimony, and render a decision on the legality of the Government's detention. If the CSRT finds a particular detainee has been improperly held, it can order release.

The majority insists that even if "the CSRTs satisf[ied] due process standards," full habeas review would still be necessary, because habeas is a collateral remedy available even to prisoners "detained pursuant to the most rigorous proceedings imaginable." This comment makes sense only if the CSRTs are incorrectly viewed as a method used by the Executive for determining the prisoners' status, and not as themselves part of the collateral review to test the validity of that determination. The majority can deprecate the importance of the CSRTs only by treating them as something they are not.

In short, the Hamdi plurality concluded that this type of review would be enough to satisfy due process, even for citizens. Congress followed the Court's lead, only to find itself the victim of a constitutional bait and switch.

Given the statutory scheme the political branches adopted, and given Hamdi, it simply will not do for the majority to dismiss the CSRT procedures as "far more limited" than those used in military trials, and therefore beneath the level of process "that would eliminate the need for habeas corpus review." The question is not how much process the CSRTs provide in comparison to other modes of adjudication. The question is whether the CSRT procedures—coupled with the judicial review specified by the DTA—provide the "basic process" Hamdi said the Constitution affords American citizens detained as enemy combatants.

To what basic process are these detainees due as habeas petitioners? We have said that "at the absolute minimum," the Suspension Clause protects the writ "'as it existed in 1789.'" The majority admits that a number of historical authorities suggest that at the time of the Constitution's ratification, "common-law courts abstained altogether from matters involving prisoners of war." If this is accurate, the process provided prisoners under the DTA is plainly more than sufficient—it allows alleged combatants to challenge both the factual and legal bases of their detentions.

Assuming the constitutional baseline is more robust, the DTA still provides adequate process, and by the majority's own standards. The DTA system— CSRT review of the Executive's determination followed by D.C. Circuit review for sufficiency of the evidence and the constitutionality of the CSRT process— meets these criteria.

All told, the DTA provides the prisoners held at Guantanamo Bay adequate opportunity to contest the bases of their detentions, which is all habeas corpus need allow. The DTA provides more opportunity and more process, in fact, than that afforded prisoners of war or any other alleged enemy combatants in history.

Despite these guarantees, the Court finds the DTA system an inadequate habeas substitute, for one central reason: Detainees are unable to introduce at the appeal stage exculpatory evidence discovered after the conclusion of their CSRT proceedings. The Court hints darkly that the DTA may suffer from other infirmities, but it does not bother to name them, making a response a bit difficult. As it stands, I can only assume the Court regards the supposed defect it did identify as the gravest of the lot.

If this is the most the Court can muster, the ice beneath its feet is thin indeed. As noted, the CSRT procedures provide ample opportunity for detainees to introduce exculpatory evidence—whether documentary in nature or from live witnesses—before the military tribunals. And if their ability to introduce such evidence is denied contrary to the Constitution or laws of the United States, the D.C. Circuit has the authority to say so on review.

For all its eloquence about the detainees' right to the writ, the Court makes no effort to elaborate how exactly the remedy it prescribes will differ from the procedural protections detainees enjoy under the DTA. The Court objects to the detainees' limited access to witnesses and classified material, but proposes no alternatives of its own. Indeed, it simply ignores the many difficult questions its holding presents. What, for example, will become of the CSRT process? The majority says federal courts should generally refrain from entertaining detainee challenges until after the petitioner's CSRT proceeding has finished. But to what deference, if any, is that CSRT determination entitled?

There are other problems. Take witness availability. What makes the majority think witnesses will become magically available when the review procedure is labeled "habeas"? Will the location of most of these witnesses change—will they suddenly become easily susceptible to service of process? Or will subpoenas issued by American habeas courts run to Basra? And if they did, how would they be enforced? Speaking of witnesses, will detainees be able to call active-duty military officers as witnesses? If not, why not?

The majority has no answers for these difficulties. What it does say leaves open the distinct possibility that its "habeas" remedy will, when all is said and done, end up looking a great deal like the DTA review it rejects.

The majority rests its decision on abstract and hypothetical concerns. Step back and consider what, in the real world, Congress and the Executive have actually granted aliens captured by our Armed Forces overseas and found to be enemy combatants:

- The right to hear the bases of the charges against them, including a summary of any classified evidence.
- The ability to challenge the bases of their detention before military tribunals modeled after Geneva Convention procedures. Some 38 detainees have been released as a result of this process.
- The right, before the CSRT, to testify, introduce evidence, call witnesses, question those the Government calls, and secure release, if and when appropriate.
- The right to the aid of a personal representative in arranging and presenting their cases before a CSRT.
- Before the D.C. Circuit, the right to employ counsel, challenge the factual record, contest the lower tribunal's legal determinations, ensure compliance with the Constitution and laws, and secure release, if any errors below establish their entitlement to such relief.

In sum, the DTA satisfies the majority's own criteria for assessing adequacy. This statutory scheme provides the combatants held at Guantanamo greater procedural protections than have ever been afforded alleged enemy detainees—whether citizens or aliens—in our national history.

So who has won? Not the detainees. The Court's analysis leaves them with only the prospect of further litigation to determine the content of their new habeas right, followed by further litigation to resolve their particular cases, followed by further litigation before the D.C. Circuit—where they could have started had they invoked the DTA procedure. Not Congress, whose attempt to "determine—through democratic means—how best" to balance the security of the American people with the detainees' liberty interests, has been unceremoniously brushed aside. Not the Great Writ, whose majesty is hardly enhanced by its extension to a jurisdictionally quirky outpost, with no tangible benefit to anyone. Not the rule of law, unless by that is meant the rule of lawyers, who will now arguably have a greater role than military and intelligence officials in shaping policy for alien enemy combatants. And certainly not the American people, who today lose a bit more control over the conduct of this Nation's foreign policy to unelected, politically unaccountable judges.

Justice SCALIA, with whom THE CHIEF JUSTICE, Justice THOMAS, and Justice ALITO join, dissenting.

Today, for the first time in our Nation's history, the Court confers a constitutional right to habeas corpus on alien enemies detained abroad by our military forces in the course of an ongoing war. The Chief Justice's dissent, which I join, shows that the procedures prescribed by Congress in the Detainee Treatment Act provide the essential protections that habeas corpus guarantees; there has thus been no suspension of the writ, and no basis exists for judicial intervention beyond what the Act allows. My problem with today's opinion is more fundamental still: The writ of habeas corpus does not, and never has, run in favor of aliens abroad; the Suspension Clause thus has no application, and the Court's intervention in this military matter is entirely ultra vires.

I shall devote most of what will be a lengthy opinion to the legal errors contained in the opinion of the Court. Contrary to my usual practice, however, I think it appropriate to begin with a description of the disastrous consequences of what the Court has done today.

America is at war with radical Islamists. The enemy began by killing Americans and American allies abroad: 241 at the Marine barracks in Lebanon, 19 at the Khobar Towers in Dhahran, 224 at our embassies in Dar es Salaam and Nairobi, and 17 on the USS Cole in Yemen. On September 11, 2001, the enemy brought the battle to American soil, killing 2,749 at the Twin Towers in New York City, 184 at the Pentagon in Washington, D. C., and 40 in Pennsylvania. It has threatened further attacks against our homeland; one need only walk about buttressed and barricaded Washington, or board a plane anywhere in the country, to know that the threat is a serious one. Our Armed Forces are now in the field against the enemy, in Afghanistan and Iraq. Last week, 13 of our countrymen in arms were killed.

The game of bait-and-switch that today's opinion plays upon the Nation's Commander in Chief will make the war harder on us. It will almost certainly cause more Americans to be killed. That consequence would be tolerable if necessary to preserve a time-honored legal principle vital to our constitutional Republic. But it is this Court's blatant abandonment of such a principle that produces the decision today. The President relied on our settled precedent in Johnson v. Eisentrager (1950), when he established the prison at Guantanamo Bay for enemy aliens. Citing that case, the President's Office of Legal Counsel advised him "that the great weight of legal authority indicates that a federal district court could not properly exercise habeas jurisdiction over an alien detained at [Guantanamo Bay]." Memorandum from Patrick F. Philbin and John C. Yoo, Deputy Assistant Attorneys General, Office of Legal Counsel, to William J. Haynes II, General Counsel, Dept. of Defense (Dec. 28, 2001). Had the law been otherwise, the military surely would not have transported prisoners there, but would have kept them in Afghanistan, transferred them to another of our foreign military bases, or turned them over to allies for detention. Those other facilities might well have been worse for the detainees themselves.

In the long term, then, the Court's decision today accomplishes little, except perhaps to reduce the well-being of enemy combatants that the Court ostensibly seeks to protect. In the short term, however, the decision is devastating. At least 30 of those prisoners hitherto released from Guantanamo Bay have returned to the battlefield. See S.Rep. No. 110-90, pt. 7, p. 13 (2007) (Minority Views of Sens. Kyl, Sessions, Graham, Cornyn, and Coburn) (hereinafter Minority Report). Some have been captured or killed. See also Mintz, Released Detainees Rejoining the Fight, Washington Post, Oct. 22, 2004, pp. A1, A12. But others have succeeded in carrying on their atrocities against innocent civilians. In one case, a detainee released from Guantanamo Bay masterminded the kidnapping of two Chinese dam workers, one of whom was later shot to death when used as a human shield against Pakistani commandoes. Another former detainee promptly resumed his post as a senior Taliban commander and murdered a United Nations engineer and three Afghan soldiers. Mintz, supra. Still another murdered an Afghan judge. It was reported only last month that a released detainee carried out a suicide bombing against Iraqi soldiers in Mosul, Iraq. See White, Ex-Guantanamo Detainee Joined Iraq Suicide Attack, Washington Post, May 8, 2008, p. A18.

These, mind you, were detainees whom the military had concluded were not enemy combatants. Their return to the kill illustrates the incredible difficulty of assessing who is and who is not an enemy combatant in a foreign theater of operations where the environment does not lend itself to rigorous evidence collection. Astoundingly, the Court today raises the bar, requiring military officials to appear before civilian courts and defend their decisions under procedural and evidentiary rules that go beyond what Congress has specified. As The Chief Justice's dissent makes clear, we have no idea what those procedural and evidentiary rules are, but they will be determined by civil courts and (in the Court's contemplation at least) will be more detainee-friendly than those now applied, since otherwise there would no reason to hold the congressionally prescribed procedures unconstitutional. If they impose a higher standard of proof (from foreign battlefields) than the current procedures require, the number of the enemy returned to combat will obviously increase.

But even when the military has evidence that it can bring forward, it is often foolhardy to release that evidence to the attorneys representing our enemies. And one escalation of procedures that the Court is clear about is affording the detainees increased access to witnesses (perhaps troops serving in Afghanistan?) and to classified information. During the 1995 prosecution of Omar Abdel Rahman, federal prosecutors gave the names of 200 unindicted co-conspirators to the "Blind Sheik's" defense lawyers; that information was in the hands of Osama Bin Laden within two weeks. In another case, trial testimony revealed to the enemy that the United States had been monitoring their cellular network, whereupon they promptly stopped using it, enabling more of them to evade capture and continue their atrocities.

And today it is not just the military that the Court elbows aside. A mere two Terms ago in Hamdan v. Rumsfeld (2006), when the Court held (quite amazingly) that the Detainee Treatment Act of 2005 had not stripped habeas jurisdiction over Guantanamo petitioners' claims, four Members of today's five-Justice majority joined an opinion saying the following: "Nothing prevents the President from returning to Congress to seek the authority [for trial by military commission] he believes necessary."

Turns out they were just kidding. For in response, Congress, at the President's request, quickly enacted the Military Commissions Act, emphatically reasserting that it did not want these prisoners filing habeas petitions. It is therefore clear that Congress and the Executive—both political branches—have determined that limiting the role of civilian courts in adjudicating whether prisoners captured abroad are properly detained is important to success in the war that some 190,000 of our men and women are now fighting. As the Solicitor General argued, "the Military Commissions Act and the Detainee Treatment Act . . . represent an effort by the political branches to strike an appropriate balance between the need to preserve liberty and the need to accommodate the weighty and sensitive governmental interests in ensuring that those who have in fact fought with the enemy during a war do not return to battle against the United States."

But it does not matter. The Court today decrees that no good reason to accept the judgment of the other two branches is "apparent." "The Government," it declares, "presents no credible arguments that the military mission at Guantanamo would be compromised if habeas corpus courts had jurisdiction to hear the detainees' claims." What competence does the Court have to second-guess the judgment of Congress and the President on such a point? None whatever. But the Court blunders in nonetheless. Henceforth, as today's opinion makes unnervingly clear, how to handle enemy prisoners in this war will ultimately lie with the branch that knows least about the national security concerns that the subject entails.

Today the Court warps our Constitution in a way that goes beyond the narrow issue of the reach of the Suspension Clause, invoking judicially brainstormed separation-of-powers principles to establish a manipulable "functional" test for the extraterritorial reach of habeas corpus (and, no doubt, for the extraterritorial reach of other constitutional protections as well). It blatantly misdescribes important precedents, most conspicuously Justice Jackson's opinion for the Court in Johnson v. Eisentrager. It breaks a chain of precedent as old as the common law that prohibits judicial inquiry into detentions of aliens abroad absent statutory authorization. And, most tragically, it sets our military commanders the impossible task of proving to a civilian court, under whatever standards this Court devises in the future, that evidence supports the confinement of each and every enemy prisoner.

The Nation will live to regret what the Court has done today. I dissent.

Chapter 4

Limits on State Regulatory and Taxing Power

A. Preemption of State and Local Laws

1. Express Preemption

The book makes the key point that even when there is a federal statute with an express preemption provision, courts still must construe its scope. This is illustrated by a recent Supreme Court case, *Riegel v. Medtronic.*

RIEGEL v. MEDTRONIC
128 S.Ct. 999 (2008)

Justice SCALIA delivered the opinion of the Court.

We consider whether the pre-emption clause enacted in the Medical Device Amendments of 1976, 21 U.S.C. § 360k, bars common-law claims challenging the safety and effectiveness of a medical device given premarket approval by the Food and Drug Administration (FDA).

I

A

The Federal Food, Drug, and Cosmetic Act (FDCA), has long required FDA approval for the introduction of new drugs into the market. Until the statutory enactment at issue here, however, the introduction of new medical devices was left largely for the States to supervise as they saw fit.

The regulatory landscape changed in the 1960's and 1970's, as complex devices proliferated and some failed. Most notably, the Dalkon Shield intrauterine device, introduced in 1970, was linked to serious infections and several deaths, not to mention a large number of pregnancies. Thousands of tort claims followed. In the view of many, the Dalkon Shield failure and its aftermath demonstrated the inability of the common-law tort system to manage the risks associated with dangerous devices.

Congress stepped in with passage of the Medical Device Amendments of 1976(MDA), which swept back some state obligations and imposed a regime of detailed federal oversight. The MDA includes an express pre-emption provision that states:

"Except as provided in subsection (b) of this section, no State or political subdivision of a State may establish or continue in effect with respect to a device intended for human use any requirement–

(1) which is different from, or in addition to, any requirement applicable under this chapter to the device, and

(2) which relates to the safety or effectiveness of the device or to any other matter included in a requirement applicable to the device under this chapter."

The devices receiving the most federal oversight are those in Class III, which include replacement heart valves, implanted cerebella stimulators, and pacemaker pulse generators. Premarket approval is a "rigorous" process. A manufacturer must submit what is typically a multivolume application. The FDA spends an average of 1,200 hours reviewing each application, and grants premarket approval only if it finds there is a "reasonable assurance" of the device's "safety and effectiveness." The agency must "weig[h] any probable benefit to health from the use of the device against any probable risk of injury or illness from such use." It may thus approve devices that present great risks if they nonetheless offer great benefits in light of available alternatives. It approved, for example, under its Humanitarian Device Exemption procedures, a ventricular assist device for children with failing hearts, even though the survival rate of children using the device was less than 50 percent. After completing its review, the FDA may grant or deny premarket approval. It may also condition approval on adherence to performance standards, restrictions upon sale or distribution, or compliance with other requirements. The agency is also free to impose device-specific restrictions by regulation.

Once a device has received premarket approval, the MDA forbids the manufacturer to make, without FDA permission, changes in design specifications, manufacturing processes, labeling, or any other attribute, that would affect safety or effectiveness. If the applicant wishes to make such a change, it must submit, and the FDA must approve, an application for supplemental premarket approval, to be evaluated under largely the same criteria as an initial application. After premarket approval, the devices are subject to reporting requirements. The FDA has the power to withdraw premarket approval based on newly reported data or existing information and must withdraw approval if it determines that a device is unsafe or ineffective under the conditions in its labeling.

B

Except as otherwise indicated, the facts set forth in this section appear in the opinion of the Court of Appeals. The device at issue is an Evergreen Balloon

Catheter marketed by defendant-respondent Medtronic, Inc. It is a Class III device that received premarket approval from the FDA in 1994; changes to its label received supplemental approvals in 1995 and 1996.

Charles Riegel underwent coronary angioplasty in 1996, shortly after suffering a myocardial infarction. His right coronary artery was diffusely diseased and heavily calcified. Riegel's doctor inserted the Evergreen Balloon Catheter into his patient's coronary artery in an attempt to dilate the artery, although the device's labeling stated that use was contraindicated for patients with diffuse or calcified stenoses. The label also warned that the catheter should not be inflated beyond its rated burst pressure of eight atmospheres. Riegel's doctor inflated the catheter five times, to a pressure of 10 atmospheres; on its fifth inflation, the catheter ruptured. Riegel developed a heart block, was placed on life support, and underwent emergency coronary bypass surgery.

Riegel and his wife Donna brought this lawsuit in April 1999, in the United States District Court for the Northern District of New York. Their complaint alleged that Medtronic's catheter was designed, labeled, and manufactured in a manner that violated New York common law, and that these defects caused Riegel to suffer severe and permanent injuries. The complaint raised a number of common-law claims.

[II]

We turn, then, to the question: whether the Riegels' common-law claims rely upon "any requirement" of New York law applicable to the catheter that is "different from, or in addition to" federal requirements and that "relates to the safety or effectiveness of the device or to any other matter included in a requirement applicable to the device." Safety and effectiveness are the very subjects of the Riegels' common-law claims, so the critical issue is whether New York's tort duties constitute "requirements" under the MDA.

Congress is entitled to know what meaning this Court will assign to terms regularly used in its enactments. Absent other indication, reference to a State's "requirements" includes its common-law duties. Common-law liability is "premised on the existence of a legal duty," and a tort judgment therefore establishes that the defendant has violated a state-law obligation. And while the common-law remedy is limited to damages, a liability award " 'can be, indeed is designed to be, a potent method of governing conduct and controlling policy.' "

In the present case, there is nothing to contradict this normal meaning. To the contrary, in the context of this legislation excluding common-law duties from the scope of pre-emption would make little sense. State tort law that requires a manufacturer's catheters to be safer, but hence less effective, than the model the FDA has approved disrupts the federal scheme no less than state regulatory law to the same effect. Indeed, one would think that tort law, applied by juries under a negligence or strict-liability standard, is less deserving of preservation. A state statute, or a regulation adopted by a state agency, could at least be expected to apply cost-benefit analysis similar to that applied by the experts at the FDA:

How many more lives will be saved by a device which, along with its greater effectiveness, brings a greater risk of harm? A jury, on the other hand, sees only the cost of a more dangerous design, and is not concerned with its benefits; the patients who reaped those benefits are not represented in court.

The dissent would narrow the pre-emptive scope of the term "requirement" on the grounds that it is "difficult to believe that Congress would, without comment, remove all means of judicial recourse" for consumers injured by FDA-approved devices. But, as we have explained, this is exactly what a pre-emption clause for medical devices does by its terms. It is not our job to speculate upon congressional motives. If we were to do so, however, the only indication available—the text of the statute—suggests that the solicitude for those injured by FDA-approved devices, which the dissent finds controlling, was overcome in Congress's estimation by solicitude for those who would suffer without new medical devices if juries were allowed to apply the tort law of 50 States to all innovations.

[III]

State requirements are pre-empted under the MDA only to the extent that they are "different from, or in addition to" the requirements imposed by federal law. Thus, § 360k does not prevent a State from providing a damages remedy for claims premised on a violation of FDA regulations; the state duties in such a case "parallel," rather than add to, federal requirements.

Justice GINSBURG, dissenting.

The Medical Device Amendments of 1976, as construed by the Court, cut deeply into a domain historically occupied by state law. The MDA's preemption clause, the Court holds, spares medical device manufacturers from personal injury claims alleging flaws in a design or label once the application for the design or label has gained premarket approval from the Food and Drug Administration (FDA); a state damages remedy, the Court instructs, persists only for claims "premised on a violation of FDA regulations." I dissent from today's constriction of state authority. Congress, in my view, did not intend § 360k(a) to effect a radical curtailment of state common-law suits seeking compensation for injuries caused by defectively designed or labeled medical devices.

Congress' reason for enacting § 360k(a) is evident. Until 1976, the Federal Government did not engage in premarket regulation of medical devices. Some States acted to fill the void by adopting their own regulatory systems for medical devices. Section 360k(a) responded to that state regulation, and particularly to California's system of premarket approval for medical devices, by preempting State initiatives absent FDA permission. See § 360k(b).

I

The "purpose of Congress is the ultimate touchstone of pre-emption analysis." Preemption analysis starts with the assumption that "the historic police powers of the States [a]re not to be superseded . . . unless that was the clear and manifest purpose of Congress." "This assumption provides assurance that 'the federal-state balance' will not be disturbed unintentionally by Congress or unnecessarily by the courts." The presumption against preemption is heightened "where federal law is said to bar state action in fields of traditional state regulation."

Federal laws containing a preemption clause do not automatically escape the presumption against preemption. A preemption clause tells us that Congress intended to supersede or modify state law to some extent. In the absence of legislative precision, however, courts may face the task of determining the substance and scope of Congress' displacement of state law. Where the text of a preemption clause is open to more than one plausible reading, courts ordinarily "accept the reading that disfavors pre-emption."

II

The MDA's preemption clause states:

> "[N]o State or political subdivision of a State may establish or continue in effect with respect to a device intended for human use any requirement–

(1) which is different from, or in addition to, any requirement applicable under this chapter to the device, and

(2) which relates to the safety or effectiveness of the device or to any other matter included in a requirement applicable to the device under this chapter."

The Court recognizes that "§ 360k does not prevent a State from providing a damages remedy for claims premised on a violation of FDA regulations." That remedy, although important, does not help consumers injured by devices that receive FDA approval but nevertheless prove unsafe. The MDA's failure to create any federal compensatory remedy for such consumers further suggests that Congress did not intend broadly to preempt state common-law suits grounded on allegations independent of FDA requirements. It is "difficult to believe that Congress would, without comment, remove all means of judicial recourse" for large numbers of consumers injured by defective medical devices.

In sum, state premarket regulation of medical devices, not any design to suppress tort suits, accounts for Congress' inclusion of a preemption clause in the MDA; no such clause figures in earlier federal laws regulating drugs and additives, for States had not installed comparable control regimes in those areas.

Congress' experience regulating drugs also casts doubt on Medtronic's policy arguments for reading § 360k(a) to preempt state tort claims. Section 360k(a) must preempt state common-law suits, Medtronic contends, because Congress would not have wanted state juries to second-guess the FDA's finding that a medical device is safe and effective when used as directed. The Court is similarly minded.

But the process for approving new drugs is at least as rigorous as the premarket approval process for medical devices. Courts that have considered the question have overwhelmingly held that FDA approval of a new drug application does not preempt state tort suits. Decades of drug regulation thus indicate, contrary to Medtronic's argument, that Congress did not regard FDA regulation and state tort claims as mutually exclusive.

III

The constriction of state authority ordered today was not mandated by Congress and is at odds with the MDA's central purpose: to protect consumer safety. For the reasons stated, I would hold that § 360k(a) does not preempt Riegel's suit.

B. *The Dormant Commerce Clause*

3. The Contemporary Test for the Dormant Commerce Clause

b. *Determining Whether a Law Is Discriminatory (casebook p. 394)*

In *C & A Carbone, Inc. v. Town of Clarkstown, New York* [casebook, p. 397], the Court held that an ordinance requiring reprocessing of waste within a city was not discriminatory. In *United Haulers Ass'n, Inc. v. Oneida-Herkimer Solid Waste Management Authority*, the Court distinguished the earlier case and found that the law was not discriminatory. The key question in reading these cases is whether there is a meaningful distinction between them.

UNITED HAULERS ASS'N, INC. v. ONEIDA-HERKIMER
SOLID WASTE MANAGEMENT AUTHORITY
127 S.Ct. 1786 (2007)

Chief Justice ROBERTS delivered the opinion of the Court, except as to Part II-D.
"Flow control" ordinances require trash haulers to deliver solid waste to a particular waste processing facility. In *C & A Carbone, Inc. v. Clarkstown* (1994), this Court struck down under the Commerce Clause a flow control ordinance that forced haulers to deliver waste to a particular private processing facility. In this case, we face flow control ordinances quite similar to the one invalidated in *Carbone*. The only salient difference is that the laws at issue here require haulers to bring waste to facilities owned and operated by a state-created public benefit corporation. We find this difference constitutionally significant. Disposing of

trash has been a traditional government activity for years, and laws that favor the government in such areas—but treat every private business, whether in-state or out-of-state, exactly the same—do not discriminate against interstate commerce for purposes of the Commerce Clause. Applying the Commerce Clause test reserved for regulations that do not discriminate against interstate commerce, we uphold these ordinances because any incidental burden they may have on interstate commerce does not outweigh the benefits they confer on the citizens of Oneida and Herkimer Counties.

I

Located in central New York, Oneida and Herkimer Counties span over 2,600 square miles and are home to about 306,000 residents. Traditionally, each city, town, or village within the Counties has been responsible for disposing of its own waste. Many had relied on local landfills, some in a more environmentally responsible fashion than others.

By the 1980's, the Counties confronted what they could credibly call a solid waste "crisis." Many local landfills were operating without permits and in violation of state regulations. Sixteen were ordered to close and remediate the surrounding environment, costing the public tens of millions of dollars. These environmental problems culminated in a federal clean-up action against a land-fill in Oneida County; the defendants in that case named over 600 local businesses and several municipalities and school districts as third-party defendants.

The "crisis" extended beyond health and safety concerns. The Counties had an uneasy relationship with local waste management companies, enduring price fixing, pervasive overcharging, and the influence of organized crime. Dramatic price hikes were not uncommon: In 1986, for example, a county contractor doubled its waste disposal rate on six weeks' notice.

Responding to these problems, the Counties requested and New York's Legislature and Governor created the Oneida-Herkimer Solid Waste Management Authority (Authority), a public benefit corporation. The Authority is empowered to collect, process, and dispose of solid waste generated in the Counties. To further the Authority's governmental and public purposes, the Counties may impose "appropriate and reasonable limitations on competition" by, for instance, adopting "local laws requiring that all solid waste . . . be delivered to a specified solid waste management-resource recovery facility."

In 1989, the Authority and the Counties entered into a Solid Waste Management Agreement, under which the Authority agreed to manage all solid waste within the Counties. Private haulers would remain free to pick up citizens' trash from the curb, but the Authority would take over the job of processing the trash, sorting it, and sending it off for disposal. To fulfill its part of the bargain, the Authority agreed to purchase and develop facilities for the processing and disposal of solid waste and recyclables generated in the Counties.

The Authority collected "tipping fees" to cover its operating and maintenance costs for these facilities.[1] The tipping fees significantly exceeded those
charged for waste removal on the open market, but they allowed the Authority
to do more than the average private waste disposer. In addition to landfill
transportation and solid waste disposal, the fees enabled the Authority to provide
recycling of 33 kinds of materials, as well as composting, household hazardous
waste disposal, and a number of other services. If the Authority's operating
costs and debt service were not recouped through tipping fees and other charges,
the agreement provided that the Counties would make up the difference.

As described, the agreement had a flaw: Citizens might opt to have their
waste hauled to facilities with lower tipping fees. To avoid being stuck with the
bill for facilities that citizens voted for but then chose not to use, the Counties
enacted "flow control" ordinances requiring that all solid waste generated
within the Counties be delivered to the Authority's processing sites. Private
haulers must obtain a permit from the Authority to collect waste in the Counties.
Penalties for noncompliance with the ordinances include permit revocation,
fines, and imprisonment.

Petitioners are United Haulers Association, Inc., a trade association made up
of solid waste management companies, and six haulers that operated in Oneida
and Herkimer Counties when this action was filed. In 1995, they sued the
Counties and the Authority alleging that the flow control laws violate the
Commerce Clause by discriminating against interstate commerce. They submitted evidence that without the flow control laws and the associated $86-per-ton
tipping fees, they could dispose of solid waste at out-of-state facilities for
between $37 and $55 per ton, including transportation.

II

A

The Commerce Clause provides that "Congress shall have Power . . . [t]o
regulate Commerce with foreign Nations, and among the several States."
Although the Constitution does not in terms limit the power of States to regulate
commerce, we have long interpreted the Commerce Clause as an implicit
restraint on state authority, even in the absence of a conflicting federal statute.

To determine whether a law violates this so-called "dormant" aspect of the
Commerce Clause, we first ask whether it discriminates on its face against
interstate commerce. In this context, " 'discrimination' simply means differential treatment of in-state and out-of-state economic interests that benefits the

---

1. Tipping fees are disposal charges levied against collectors who drop off waste at a processing
facility. They are called "tipping" fees because garbage trucks literally tip their back end to dump out
the carried waste. As of 1995, haulers in the Counties had to pay tipping fees of at least $86 per ton, a
price that ballooned to as much as $172 per ton if a particular load contained more than 25% recycl-
ables. [Footnote by Chief Justice Roberts]

former and burdens the latter." Discriminatory laws motivated by "simple economic protectionism" are subject to a "virtually per se rule of invalidity," which can only be overcome by a showing that the State has no other means to advance a legitimate local purpose, *Maine v. Taylor* (1986).

B

[T]he haulers argue vigorously that the Counties' ordinances discriminate against interstate commerce under *Carbone*. In *Carbone*, the town of Clarkstown, New York, hired a private contractor to build a waste transfer station. According to the terms of the deal, the contractor would operate the facility for five years, charging an above-market tipping fee of $81 per ton; after five years, the town would buy the facility for one dollar. The town guaranteed that the facility would receive a certain volume of trash per year. To make good on its promise, Clarkstown passed a flow control ordinance requiring that all nonhazardous solid waste within the town be deposited at the transfer facility. This Court struck down the ordinance, holding that it discriminated against interstate commerce by "hoard[ing] solid waste, and the demand to get rid of it, for the benefit of the preferred processing facility." The dissent pointed out that all of this Court's local processing cases involved laws that discriminated in favor of private entities, not public ones. According to the dissent, Clarkstown's ostensibly private transfer station was "essentially a municipal facility," and this distinction should have saved Clarkstown's ordinance because favoring local government is by its nature different from favoring a particular private company. The majority did not comment on the dissent's public-private distinction.

The parties in this case draw opposite inferences from the majority's silence. The haulers say it proves that the majority agreed with the dissent's characterization of the facility, but thought there was no difference under the dormant Commerce Clause between laws favoring private entities and those favoring public ones. The Counties disagree, arguing that the majority studiously avoided the issue because the facility in *Carbone* was private, and therefore the question whether public facilities may be favored was not properly before the Court.

We believe the latter interpretation of *Carbone* is correct. If the Court thought Clarkstown's processing facility was public, that additional distinction was not merely "conceivable"—it was conceived, and discussed at length, by three Justices in dissent. *Carbone* cannot be regarded as having decided the public-private question.

C

The flow control ordinances in this case benefit a clearly public facility, while treating all private companies exactly the same. Because the question is now squarely presented on the facts of the case before us, we decide that such flow control ordinances do not discriminate against interstate commerce for purposes of the dormant Commerce Clause.

Compelling reasons justify treating these laws differently from laws favoring particular private businesses over their competitors. States and municipalities are not private businesses—far from it. Unlike private enterprise, government is vested with the responsibility of protecting the health, safety, and welfare of its citizens. These important responsibilities set state and local government apart from a typical private business.

Given these differences, it does not make sense to regard laws favoring local government and laws favoring private industry with equal skepticism. As our local processing cases demonstrate, when a law favors in-state business over out-of-state competition, rigorous scrutiny is appropriate because the law is often the product of "simple economic protectionism." Laws favoring local government, by contrast, may be directed toward any number of legitimate goals unrelated to protectionism. Here the flow control ordinances enable the Counties to pursue particular policies with respect to the handling and treatment of waste generated in the Counties, while allocating the costs of those policies on citizens and businesses according to the volume of waste they generate.

The contrary approach of treating public and private entities the same under the dormant Commerce Clause would lead to unprecedented and unbounded interference by the courts with state and local government. The dormant Commerce Clause is not a roving license for federal courts to decide what activities are appropriate for state and local government to undertake, and what activities must be the province of private market competition. In this case, the citizens of Oneida and Herkimer Counties have chosen the government to provide waste management services, with a limited role for the private sector in arranging for transport of waste from the curb to the public facilities. The citizens could have left the entire matter for the private sector, in which case any regulation they undertook could not discriminate against interstate commerce. But it was also open to them to vest responsibility for the matter with their government, and to adopt flow control ordinances to support the government effort. It is not the office of the Commerce Clause to control the decision of the voters on whether government or the private sector should provide waste management services.

We should be particularly hesitant to interfere with the Counties' efforts under the guise of the Commerce Clause because "[w]aste disposal is both typically and traditionally a local government function." Finally, it bears mentioning that the most palpable harm imposed by the ordinances—more expensive trash removal—is likely to fall upon the very people who voted for the laws. Our dormant Commerce Clause cases often find discrimination when a State shifts the costs of regulation to other States, because when "the burden of state regulation falls on interests outside the state, it is unlikely to be alleviated by the operation of those political restraints normally exerted when interests within the state are affected." Here, the citizens and businesses of the Counties bear the costs of the ordinances. There is no reason to step in and hand local businesses a victory they could not obtain through the political process.

We hold that the Counties' flow control ordinances, which treat in-state private business interests exactly the same as out-of-state ones, do not "discriminate against interstate commerce" for purposes of the dormant Commerce Clause.[2]

D

The Counties' flow control ordinances are properly analyzed under the test set forth in *Pike v. Bruce Church, Inc.* (1970), which is reserved for laws "directed to legitimate local concerns, with effects upon interstate commerce that are only incidental." Under the *Pike* test, we will uphold a nondiscriminatory statute like this one "unless the burden imposed on [interstate] commerce is clearly excessive in relation to the putative local benefits."

After years of discovery, both the Magistrate Judge and the District Court could not detect any disparate impact on out-of-state as opposed to in-state businesses. We find it unnecessary to decide whether the ordinances impose any incidental burden on interstate commerce because any arguable burden does not exceed the public benefits of the ordinances.

The ordinances give the Counties a convenient and effective way to finance their integrated package of waste-disposal services. While "revenue generation is not a local interest that can justify discrimination against interstate commerce," we think it is a cognizable benefit for purposes of the *Pike* test.

At the same time, the ordinances are more than financing tools. They increase recycling in at least two ways, conferring significant health and environmental benefits upon the citizens of the Counties. First, they create enhanced incentives for recycling and proper disposal of other kinds of waste. Solid waste disposal is expensive in Oneida-Herkimer, but the Counties accept recyclables and many forms of hazardous waste for free, effectively encouraging their citizens to sort their own trash. Second, by requiring all waste to be deposited at Authority facilities, the Counties have markedly increased their ability to enforce recycling laws. If the haulers could take waste to any disposal site, achieving an equal level of enforcement would be much more costly, if not impossible. For these reasons, any arguable burden the ordinances impose on interstate commerce does not exceed their public benefits.

Justice SCALIA, concurring in part.

---

2. The Counties and their amicus were asked at oral argument if affirmance would lead to the "Oneida-Herkimer Hamburger Stand," accompanied by a "flow control" law requiring citizens to purchase their burgers only from the state-owned producer. We doubt it. "The existence of major in-state interests adversely affected by [a law] is a powerful safeguard against legislative abuse." Recognizing that local government may facilitate a customary and traditional government function such as waste disposal, without running afoul of the Commerce Clause, is hardly a prescription for state control of the economy. In any event, Congress retains authority under the Commerce Clause as written to regulate interstate commerce, whether engaged in by private or public entities. It can use this power, as it has in the past, to limit state use of exclusive franchises.

I join Part I and Parts II-A through II-C of the Court's opinion. I write separately to reaffirm my view that "the so-called 'negative' Commerce Clause is an unjustified judicial invention, not to be expanded beyond its existing domain." "The historical record provides no grounds for reading the Commerce Clause to be other than what it says—an authorization for Congress to regulate commerce."

I have been willing to enforce on stare decisis grounds a "negative" self-executing Commerce Clause in two situations: "(1) against a state law that facially discriminates against interstate commerce, and (2) against a state law that is indistinguishable from a type of law previously held unconstitutional by the Court." As today's opinion makes clear, the flow-control law at issue in this case meets neither condition. It benefits a public entity performing a traditional local-government function and treats all private entities precisely the same way. "Disparate treatment constitutes discrimination only if the objects of the disparate treatment are, for the relevant purposes, similarly situated." None of this Court's cases concludes that public entities and private entities are similarly situated for Commerce Clause purposes. To hold that they are "would broaden the negative Commerce Clause beyond its existing scope, and intrude on a regulatory sphere traditionally occupied by . . . the States."

I am unable to join Part II-D of the principal opinion, in which the plurality performs so-called "*Pike* balancing." Generally speaking, the balancing of various values is left to Congress—which is precisely what the Commerce Clause (the real Commerce Clause) envisions.

Justice THOMAS, concurring in the judgment.

I concur in the judgment. Although I joined *C & A Carbone, Inc. v. Clarkstown* (1994), I no longer believe it was correctly decided. The negative Commerce Clause has no basis in the Constitution and has proved unworkable in practice. As the debate between the majority and dissent shows, application of the negative Commerce Clause turns solely on policy considerations, not on the Constitution. Because this Court has no policy role in regulating interstate commerce, I would discard the Court's negative Commerce Clause jurisprudence.

Because I believe that the power to regulate interstate commerce is a power given to Congress and not the Court, I concur in the judgment of the Court.

Justice ALITO, with whom Justice STEVENS and Justice KENNEDY join, dissenting.

In *C & A Carbone, Inc. v. Clarkstown* (1994), we held that "a so-called flow control ordinance, which require[d] all solid waste to be processed at a designated transfer station before leaving the municipality," discriminated against interstate commerce and was invalid under the Commerce Clause because it "depriv[ed] competitors, including out-of-state firms, of access to a local market." Because the provisions challenged in this case are essentially identical to the ordinance invalidated in *Carbone*, I respectfully dissent.

This case cannot be meaningfully distinguished from *Carbone*. As the Court itself acknowledges, "[t]he only salient difference" between the cases is that the ordinance invalidated in *Carbone* discriminated in favor of a privately owned facility, whereas the laws at issue here discriminate in favor of "facilities owned and operated by a state-created public benefit corporation." The Court relies on the distinction between public and private ownership to uphold the flow-control laws, even though a straightforward application of *Carbone* would lead to the opposite result. The public-private distinction drawn by the Court is both illusory and without precedent.

The fact that the flow control laws at issue discriminate in favor of a government-owned enterprise does not meaningfully distinguish this case from *Carbone*. The only real difference between the facility at issue in *Carbone* and its counterpart in this case is that title to the former had not yet formally passed to the municipality. The Court exalts form over substance in adopting a test that turns on this technical distinction, particularly since, barring any obstacle presented by state law, the transaction in *Carbone* could have been restructured to provide for the passage of title at the beginning, rather than the end, of the 5-year period.

For this very reason, it is not surprising that in *Carbone* the Court did not dispute the dissent's observation that the preferred facility was for all practical purposes owned by the municipality. To the contrary, the Court repeatedly referred to the transfer station in terms suggesting that the transfer station did in fact belong to the town.

Today the Court dismisses those statements as "at best inconclusive." The Court, however, fails to offer any explanation as to what other meaning could possibly attach to *Carbone*'s repeated references to Clarkstown's transfer station as a municipal facility. It also ignores the fact that the ordinance itself, which was included in its entirety in an appendix to the Court's opinion, repeatedly referred to the station as "the Town of Clarkstown solid waste facility." The Court likewise fails to acknowledge that the parties in *Carbone* openly acknowledged the municipal character of the transfer station.

I see no ambiguities in those statements, much less any reason to dismiss them as "at best inconclusive"; they reflect a clear understanding that the station was, for all purposes relevant to the dormant Commerce Clause, a municipal facility.

In any event, we have never treated discriminatory legislation with greater deference simply because the entity favored by that legislation was a government-owned enterprise. The Court has long subjected discriminatory legislation to strict scrutiny, and has never, until today, recognized an exception for discrimination in favor of a state-owned entity.

Nor has this Court ever suggested that discriminatory legislation favoring a state-owned enterprise is entitled to favorable treatment. To be sure, state-owned entities are accorded special status under the market-participant doctrine. But that doctrine is not applicable here.

Under the market-participant doctrine, a State is permitted to exercise "'independent discretion as to parties with whom [it] will deal.'" The doctrine thus allows States to engage in certain otherwise-discriminatory practices (e.g., selling exclusively to, or buying exclusively from, the State's own residents), so long as the State is "acting as a market participant, rather than as a market regulator."

Respondents are doing exactly what the market-participant doctrine says they cannot: While acting as market participants by operating a fee-for-service business enterprise in an area in which there is an established interstate market, respondents are also regulating that market in a discriminatory manner and claiming that their special governmental status somehow insulates them from a dormant Commerce Clause challenge.

The fallacy in the Court's approach can be illustrated by comparing a law that discriminates in favor of an in-state facility, owned by a corporation whose shares are publicly held, and a law discriminating in favor of an otherwise identical facility that is owned by the State or municipality. Those who are favored and disfavored by these two laws are essentially the same with one major exception: The law favoring the corporate facility presumably benefits the corporation's shareholders, most of whom are probably not local residents, whereas the law favoring the government-owned facility presumably benefits the people of the enacting State or municipality. I cannot understand why only the former law, and not the latter, should be regarded as a tool of economic protectionism. Nor do I think it is realistic or consistent with our precedents to condemn some discriminatory laws as protectionist while upholding other, equally discriminatory laws as lawful measures designed to serve legitimate local interests unrelated to protectionism.

For these reasons, I cannot accept the proposition that laws discriminating in favor of state-owned enterprises are so unlikely to be the product of economic protectionism that they should be exempt from the usual dormant Commerce Clause standards.

Thus, if the legislative means are themselves discriminatory, then regardless of how legitimate and nonprotectionist the underlying legislative goals may be, the legislation is subject to strict scrutiny. Similarly, the fact that a discriminatory law "may [in some sense] be directed toward any number of legitimate goals unrelated to protectionism" does not make the law nondiscriminatory. The existence of such goals is relevant, not to whether the law is discriminatory, but to whether the law can be allowed to stand even though it discriminates against interstate commerce. And even then, the existence of legitimate goals is not enough; discriminatory legislation can be upheld only where such goals cannot adequately be achieved through nondiscriminatory means.

Equally unpersuasive is the Court's suggestion that the flow-control laws do not discriminate against interstate commerce because they "treat in-state private business interests exactly the same as out-of-state ones." Again, the critical issue is whether the challenged legislation discriminates against interstate commerce. If it does, then regardless of whether those harmed by it reside entirely outside the State in question, the law is subject to strict scrutiny. Indeed, this Court has long recognized that "'a burden imposed by a State upon interstate commerce is not to be sustained simply because the statute imposing it applies alike to the people of all the States, including the people of the State enacting such statute.'"

The dormant Commerce Clause has long been understood to prohibit the kind of discriminatory legislation upheld by the Court in this case.

c. Analysis if a Law Is Deemed Discriminatory (casebook, p. 411)

GRANHOLM v. HEALD
544 U.S. 460 (2005)

Justice KENNEDY delivered the opinion of the Court.

These consolidated cases present challenges to state laws regulating the sale of wine from out-of-state wineries to consumers in Michigan and New York. The details and mechanics of the two regulatory schemes differ, but the object and effect of the laws are the same: to allow in-state wineries to sell wine directly to consumers in that State but to prohibit out-of-state wineries from doing so, or, at the least, to make direct sales impractical from an economic standpoint. It is evident that the object and design of the Michigan and New York statutes is to grant in-state wineries a competitive advantage over wineries located beyond the States' borders.

We hold that the laws in both States discriminate against interstate commerce in violation of the Commerce Clause, Art. I, § 8, cl. 3, and that the discrimination is neither authorized nor permitted by the Twenty-first Amendment.

I

Like many other States, Michigan and New York regulate the sale and importation of alcoholic beverages, including wine, through a three-tier distribution system. Separate licenses are required for producers, wholesalers, and retailers. As relevant to today's cases, though, the three-tier system is, in broad terms and with refinements to be discussed, mandated by Michigan and New York only for sales from out-of-state wineries. In-state wineries, by contrast, can obtain a license for direct sales to consumers. The differential treatment between in-state and out-of-state wineries constitutes explicit discrimination against interstate commerce.

This discrimination substantially limits the direct sale of wine to consumers, an otherwise emerging and significant business. From 1994 to 1999, consumer spending on direct wine shipments doubled, reaching $500 million per year, or three percent of all wine sales. The expansion has been influenced by several related trends. First, the number of small wineries in the United States has significantly increased. By some estimates there are over 3,000 wineries in the country. At the same time, the wholesale market has consolidated. Between 1984 and 2002, the number of licensed wholesalers dropped from 1,600 to 600. The increasing winery-to-wholesaler ratio means that many small wineries do not produce enough wine or have sufficient consumer demand for their wine to make it economical for wholesalers to carry their products. This has led many small wineries to rely on direct shipping to reach new markets. Technological improvements, in particular the ability of wineries to sell wine over the Internet, have helped make direct shipments an attractive sales channel.

Approximately 26 States allow some direct shipping of wine, with various restrictions. Thirteen of these States have reciprocity laws, which allow direct shipment from wineries outside the State, provided the State of origin affords similar nondiscriminatory treatment. In many parts of the country, however, state laws that prohibit or severely restrict direct shipments deprive consumers of access to the direct market.

The wine producers in the cases before us are small wineries that rely on direct consumer sales as an important part of their businesses. Domaine Alfred, one of the plaintiffs in the Michigan suit, is a small winery located in San Luis Obispo, California. It produces 3,000 cases of wine per year. Domaine Alfred has received requests for its wine from Michigan consumers but cannot fill the orders because of the State's direct-shipment ban. Even if the winery could find a Michigan wholesaler to distribute its wine, the wholesaler's markup would render shipment through the three-tier system economically infeasible.

Under Michigan law, wine producers, as a general matter, must distribute their wine through wholesalers. There is, however, an exception for Michigan's approximately 40 in-state wineries, which are eligible for "wine maker" licenses that allow direct shipment to in-state consumers. Out-of-state wineries can apply for a $300 "outside seller of wine" license, but this license only allows them to sell to in-state wholesalers.

New York's licensing scheme is somewhat different. It channels most wine sales through the three-tier system, but it too makes exceptions for in-state wineries. As in Michigan, the result is to allow local wineries to make direct sales to consumers in New York on terms not available to out-of-state wineries.

We consolidated these cases and granted certiorari on the following question: " 'Does a State's regulatory scheme that permits in-state wineries directly to ship alcohol to consumers but restricts the ability of out-of-state wineries to do so violate the dormant Commerce Clause in light of § 2 of the Twenty-first Amendment?' "

II

A

Time and again this Court has held that, in all but the narrowest circumstances, state laws violate the Commerce Clause if they mandate "differential treatment of in-state and out-of-state economic interests that benefits the former and burdens the latter." This rule is essential to the foundations of the Union. The mere fact of nonresidence should not foreclose a producer in one State from access to markets in other States. States may not enact laws that burden out-of-state producers or shippers simply to give a competitive advantage to in-state businesses. This mandate "reflect[s] a central concern of the Framers that was an immediate reason for calling the Constitutional Convention: the conviction that in order to succeed, the new Union would have to avoid the tendencies toward economic Balkanization that had plagued relations among the Colonies and later among the States under the Articles of Confederation."

The rule prohibiting state discrimination against interstate commerce follows also from the principle that States should not be compelled to negotiate with each other regarding favored or disfavored status for their own citizens. States do not need, and may not attempt, to negotiate with other States regarding their mutual economic interests. Rivalries among the States are thus kept to a minimum, and a proliferation of trade zones is prevented.

Laws of the type at issue in the instant cases contradict these principles. They deprive citizens of their right to have access to the markets of other States on equal terms. The perceived necessity for reciprocal sale privileges risks generating the trade rivalries and animosities, the alliances and exclusivity, that the Constitution and, in particular, the Commerce Clause were designed to avoid. The current patchwork of laws—with some States banning direct shipments altogether, others doing so only for out-of-state wines, and still others requiring reciprocity—is essentially the product of an ongoing, low-level trade war. Allowing States to discriminate against out-of-state wine "invite[s] a multiplication of preferential trade areas destructive of the very purpose of the Commerce Clause."

B

The discriminatory character of the Michigan system is obvious. Michigan allows in-state wineries to ship directly to consumers, subject only to a licensing requirement. Out-of-state wineries, whether licensed or not, face a complete ban on direct shipment. The differential treatment requires all out-of-state wine, but not all in-state wine, to pass through an in-state wholesaler and retailer before reaching consumers. These two extra layers of overhead increase the cost of out-of-state wines to Michigan consumers. The cost differential, and in some cases the inability to secure a wholesaler for small shipments, can effectively bar small wineries from the Michigan market.

The New York regulatory scheme differs from Michigan's in that it does not ban direct shipments altogether. Out-of-state wineries are instead required to establish a distribution operation in New York in order to gain the privilege of direct shipment. The New York scheme grants in-state wineries access to the State's consumers on preferential terms. The suggestion of a limited exception for direct shipment from out-of-state wineries does nothing to eliminate the discriminatory nature of New York's regulations. In-state producers, with the applicable licenses, can ship directly to consumers from their wineries. Out-of-state wineries must open a branch office and warehouse in New York, additional steps that drive up the cost of their wine. For most wineries, the expense of establishing a bricks-and-mortar distribution operation in 1 State, let alone all 50, is prohibitive. It comes as no surprise that not a single out-of-state winery has availed itself of New

York's direct-shipping privilege. We have "viewed with particular suspicion state statutes requiring business operations to be performed in the home State that could more efficiently be performed elsewhere." New York's in-state presence requirement runs contrary to our admonition that States cannot require an out-of-state firm "to become a resident in order to compete on equal terms."

III

State laws that discriminate against interstate commerce face "a virtually per se rule of invalidity." Philadelphia v. New Jersey (1978). The Michigan and New York laws by their own terms violate this proscription. The two States, however, contend their statutes are saved by § 2 of the Twenty-first Amendment, which provides: "The transportation or importation into any State, Territory, or possession of the United States for delivery or use therein of intoxicating liquors, in violation of the laws thereof, is hereby prohibited."

The States' position is inconsistent with our precedents and with the Twenty-first Amendment's history. Section 2 does not allow States to regulate the direct shipment of wine on terms that discriminate in favor of in-state producers.

A

Before 1919, the temperance movement fought to curb the sale of alcoholic beverages one State at a time. The movement made progress, and many States passed laws restricting or prohibiting the sale of alcohol. This Court upheld state laws banning the production and sale of alcoholic beverages, Mugler v. Kansas (1887), but was less solicitous of laws aimed at imports. In a series of cases before ratification of the Eighteenth Amendment the Court, relying on the Commerce Clause, invalidated a number of state liquor regulations.

These cases advanced two distinct principles. First, the Court held that the Commerce Clause prevented States from discriminating against imported liquor. Second, the Court held that the Commerce Clause prevented States from passing facially neutral laws that placed an impermissible burden on interstate commerce.

B

The ratification of the Eighteenth Amendment in 1919 provided a brief respite from the legal battles over the validity of state liquor regulations. With the ratification of the Twenty-first Amendment 14 years later, however, nationwide Prohibition came to an end. Section 1 of the Twenty-first Amendment repealed the Eighteenth Amendment. Section 2 of the Twenty-first Amendment is at issue here. Michigan and New York say the provision grants to the States the authority to discriminate against out-of-state goods. The history we have recited does not support this position. To the contrary, it provides strong support for the view that

§ 2 restored to the States the powers they had. The aim of the Twenty-first Amendment was to allow States to maintain an effective and uniform system for controlling liquor by regulating its transportation, importation, and use. The Amendment did not give States the authority to pass nonuniform laws in order to discriminate against out-of-state goods, a privilege they had not enjoyed at any earlier time. Our more recent cases, furthermore, confirm that the Twenty-first Amendment does not supersede other provisions of the Constitution and, in particular, does not displace the rule that States may not give a discriminatory preference to their own producers.

C

The modern § 2 cases fall into three categories. First, the Court has held that state laws that violate other provisions of the Constitution are not saved by the Twenty-first Amendment. The Court has applied this rule in the context of the First Amendment, 44 Liquormart, Inc. v. Rhode Island (1996); the Establishment Clause, Larkin v. Grendel's Den, Inc. (1982); the Equal Protection Clause, Craig v. Boren (1976); the Due Process Clause, Wisconsin v. Constantineau (1971); and the Import-Export Clause, Department of Revenue v. James B. Beam Distilling Co. (1964).

Second, the Court has held that § 2 does not abrogate Congress' Commerce Clause powers with regard to liquor. The argument that "the Twenty-first Amendment has somehow operated to 'repeal' the Commerce Clause" for alcoholic beverages has been rejected.

Finally, and most relevant to the issue at hand, the Court has held that state regulation of alcohol is limited by the nondiscrimination principle of the Commerce Clause. "When a state statute directly regulates or discriminates against interstate commerce, or when its effect is to favor in-state economic interests over out-of-state interests, we have generally struck down the statute without further inquiry."

IV

Our determination that the Michigan and New York direct-shipment laws are not authorized by the Twenty-first Amendment does not end the inquiry. We still must consider whether either State regime "advances a legitimate local purpose that cannot be adequately served by reasonable nondiscriminatory alternatives." The States offer two primary justifications for restricting direct shipments from out-of-state wineries: keeping alcohol out of the hands of minors and facilitating tax collection. We consider each in turn.

The States, aided by several amici, claim that allowing direct shipment from out-of-state wineries undermines their ability to police underage drinking. Minors, the States argue, have easy access to credit cards and the Internet and are likely to take advantage of direct wine shipments as a means of obtaining alcohol illegally. The States provide little evidence that the purchase of wine over the Internet by minors is a problem. Indeed, there is some evidence to the contrary. A recent study by the staff of the FTC found that the 26 States currently allowing direct shipments report no problems with minors' increased access to wine. This is not surprising for several reasons. First, minors are less likely to consume wine, as opposed to beer, wine coolers, and hard liquor. Second, minors who decide to disobey the law have more direct means of doing so. Third, direct shipping is an imperfect avenue of obtaining alcohol for minors who, in the words of the past president of the National Conference of State Liquor Administrators, " 'want instant gratification.' " Without concrete evidence that direct shipping of wine is likely to increase alcohol consumption by minors, we are left with the States' unsupported assertions. Under our precedents, which require the "clearest showing" to justify discriminatory state regulation, this is not enough.

Even were we to credit the States' largely unsupported claim that direct shipping of wine increases the risk of underage drinking, this would not justify regulations limiting only out-of-state direct shipments. As the wineries point out, minors are just as likely to order wine from in-state producers as from out-of-state ones.

The States' tax-collection justification is also insufficient. Increased direct shipping, whether originating in state or out of state, brings with it the potential for tax evasion. With regard to Michigan, however, the tax-collection argument is a diversion. That is because Michigan, unlike many other States, does not rely on wholesalers to collect taxes on wines imported from out-of-state. Instead, Michigan collects taxes directly from out-of-state wineries on all wine shipped to in-state wholesalers. If licensing and self-reporting provide adequate safeguards for wine distributed through the three-tier system, there is no reason to believe they will not suffice for direct shipments.

New York and its supporting parties also advance a tax-collection justification for the State's direct-shipment laws. In particular, New York could protect itself against lost tax revenue by requiring a permit as a condition of direct shipping. This is the approach taken by New York for in-state wineries. The State offers no reason to believe the system would prove ineffective for out-of-state wineries. Licensees could be required to submit regular sales reports and to remit taxes. Indeed, various States use this approach for taxing direct interstate wine shipments, and report no problems with tax collection.

In summary, the States provide little concrete evidence for the sweeping assertion that they cannot police direct shipments by out-of-state wineries. Our Commerce Clause cases demand more than mere speculation to support discrimination against out-of-state goods. The "burden is on the State to show that 'the discrimination is demonstrably justified.' " The Court has upheld state regulations that discriminate against interstate commerce only after finding, based on concrete record evidence, that a State's nondiscriminatory alternatives will prove unworkable. See, e.g., Maine v. Taylor (1986). Michigan and New York have not satisfied this exacting standard.

V

States have broad power to regulate liquor under § 2 of the Twenty-first Amendment. This power, however, does not allow States to ban, or severely limit, the direct shipment of out-of-state wine while simultaneously authorizing direct shipment by in-state producers. If a State chooses to allow direct shipment of wine, it must do so on evenhanded terms. Without demonstrating the need for discrimination, New York and Michigan have enacted regulations that disadvantage out-of-state wine producers. Under our Commerce Clause jurisprudence, these regulations cannot stand.

Justice STEVENS, with whom Justice O'CONNOR joins, dissenting.

The New York and Michigan laws challenged in these cases would be patently invalid under well settled dormant Commerce Clause principles if they regulated sales of an ordinary article of commerce rather than wine. But ever since the adoption of the Eighteenth Amendment and the Twenty-first Amendment, our Constitution has placed commerce in alcoholic beverages in a special category. Section 2 of the Twenty-first Amendment expressly provides that "[t]he transportation or importation into any State, Territory, or possession of the United States for delivery or use therein of intoxicating liquors, in violation of the laws thereof, is hereby prohibited."

Today many Americans, particularly those members of the younger generations who make policy decisions, regard alcohol as an ordinary article of commerce, subject to substantially the same market and legal controls as other consumer products. That was definitely not the view of the generations that made policy in 1919 when the Eighteenth Amendment was ratified or in 1933 when it was repealed by the Twenty-first Amendment. On the contrary, the moral condemnation of the use of alcohol as a beverage represented not merely the convictions of our religious leaders, but the views of a sufficiently large majority of the population to warrant the rare exercise of the power to amend the Constitution on two occasions. The Eighteenth Amendment entirely prohibited commerce in "intoxicating liquors" for beverage purposes throughout the United States and the territories subject to its jurisdiction. While § 1 of the Twenty-first Amendment repealed the nationwide prohibition, § 2 gave the States the option to maintain equally comprehensive prohibitions in their respective jurisdictions.

In the years following the ratification of the Twenty-first Amendment, States adopted manifold laws regulating commerce in alcohol, and many of these laws were discriminatory. So-called "dry states" entirely prohibited such commerce; others prohibited the sale of alcohol on Sundays; others permitted the sale of beer and wine but not hard liquor; most created either state monopolies or distribution systems that gave discriminatory preferences to local retailers and distributors. The notion that discriminatory state laws violated the unwritten prohibition against balkanizing the American economy—while persuasive in contemporary times when alcohol is viewed as an ordinary article of commerce—would have seemed strange indeed to the millions of

Americans who condemned the use of the "demon rum" in the 1920's and 1930's. Indeed, they expressly authorized the "balkanization" that today's decision condemns. Today's decision may represent sound economic policy and may be consistent with the policy choices of the contemporaries of Adam Smith who drafted our original Constitution; it is not, however, consistent with the policy choices made by those who amended our Constitution in 1919 and 1933.

My understanding (and recollection) of the historical context reinforces my conviction that the text of § 2 should be "broadly and colloquially interpreted." Indeed, the fact that the Twenty-first Amendment was the only Amendment in our history to have been ratified by the people in state conventions, rather than by state legislatures, provides further reason to give its terms their ordinary meaning. Because the New York and Michigan laws regulate the "transportation or importation" of "intoxicating liquors" for "delivery or use therein," they are exempt from dormant Commerce Clause scrutiny.

Justice THOMAS, with whom THE CHIEF JUSTICE, Justice STEVENS, and Justice O'CONNOR join, dissenting.

A century ago, this Court repeatedly invalidated, as inconsistent with the negative Commerce Clause, state liquor legislation that prevented out-of-state businesses from shipping liquor directly to a State's residents. The Webb-Kenyon Act and the Twenty-first Amendment cut off this intrusive review, as their text and history make clear and as this Court's early cases on the Twenty-first Amendment recognized. The Court today seizes back this power, based primarily on a historical argument that this Court decisively rejected long ago in State Bd. of Equalization of Cal. v. Young's Market Co. (1936). Because I would follow *Young's Market* and the language of both the statute that Congress enacted and the Amendment that the Nation ratified, rather than the Court's questionable reading of history and the "negative implications" of the Commerce Clause, I respectfully dissent.

I

The Court devotes much attention to the Twenty-first Amendment, yet little to the terms of the Webb-Kenyon Act. This is a mistake, because that Act's language displaces any negative Commerce Clause barrier to state regulation of liquor sales to in-state consumers.

The Webb-Kenyon Act immunizes from negative Commerce Clause review the state liquor laws that the Court holds are unconstitutional. The Act "prohibit[s]" any "shipment or transportation" of alcoholic beverages "into any State" when those beverages are "intended, by any person interested therein, to be received, possessed, sold, or in any manner used . . . in violation of any law of such State." State laws that regulate liquor imports in the manner described by the Act are exempt from judicial scrutiny under the negative Commerce Clause, as this Court has long held. The Webb-Kenyon Act's language, in other words, "prevent

[s] the immunity characteristic of interstate commerce from being used to permit the receipt of liquor through such commerce in States contrary to their laws."

The Michigan and New York direct-shipment laws are within the Webb-Kenyon Act's terms and therefore do not run afoul of the negative Commerce Clause. Those laws restrict out-of-state wineries from shipping and selling wine directly to Michigan and New York consumers. Any winery that ships wine directly to a Michigan or New York consumer in violation of those state-law restrictions is a "person interested therein" "intend[ing]" to "s[ell]" wine "in violation of" Michigan and New York law, and thus comes within the terms of the Webb-Kenyon Act.

II

[T]he state laws the Court strikes down are lawful under the plain meaning of § 2 of the Twenty-first Amendment, as this Court's case law in the wake of the Amendment and the contemporaneous practice of the States reinforce.

The state laws at issue in these cases fall within § 2's broad terms. They prohibit wine manufacturers from "transport[ing] or import[ing]" wine directly to consumers in New York and Michigan "for delivery or use therein." Michigan law does so by requiring all out-of-state wine manufacturers to distribute wine through licensed in-state wholesalers. New York law does so by prohibiting out-of-state wineries from shipping wine directly to consumers unless they establish an in-state physical presence, something that in-state wineries naturally have. The Twenty-first Amendment prohibits out-of-state wineries from shipping wine into Michigan and New York in violation of these laws. In holding that the Constitution prohibits Michigan's and New York's laws, the majority turns the Amendment's text on its head.

Though the majority dismisses this Court's early Twenty-first Amendment case law, it relies on the reasoning, if not the holdings, of our more recent Twenty-first Amendment cases. But the Court's later cases do not require the result the majority reaches. Moreover, I would resolve any conflict in this Court's precedents in favor of those cases most contemporaneous with the ratification of the Twenty-first Amendment.

[M]y interpretation of the Twenty-first Amendment would not free States to regulate liquor unhampered by other constitutional restraints, like the First Amendment and the Equal Protection Clause. As this Court explained in Craig v. Boren (1976), the text and history of the Twenty-first Amendment demonstrate that it displaces liquor's negative Commerce Clause immunity, not other constitutional provisions.

The Twenty-first Amendment and the Webb-Kenyon Act displaced the negative Commerce Clause as applied to regulation of liquor imports into a State. They require sustaining the constitutionality of Michigan's and New York's direct-shipment laws.

d. Analysis if a Law Is Deemed Non-Discriminatory (casebook, p. 414)

AMERICAN TRUCKING ASSOCIATIONS, INC. v. MICHIGAN PUBLIC SERVICE COMMISSION
545 U.S. 429 (2005)

Justice BREYER delivered the opinion of the Court.

In this case, we consider whether a flat $100 fee that Michigan charges trucks engaging in intrastate commercial hauling violates the dormant Commerce Clause. We hold that it does not.

I

A subsection of Michigan's Motor Carrier Act imposes upon each motor carrier "for the administration of this act, an annual fee of $100.00 for each self-propelled motor vehicle operated by or on behalf of the motor carrier." The provision assesses the fee upon, and only upon, vehicles that engage in intrastate commercial operations—that is, on trucks that undertake point-to-point hauls between Michigan cities. Petitioners, USF Holland, Inc., a trucking company with trucks that engage in both interstate and intrastate hauling, and the American Trucking Associations, Inc. (ATA), asked the Michigan courts to invalidate the provision. Both petitioners told those courts that trucks that carry both interstate and intrastate loads engage in intrastate business less than trucks that confine their operations to the Great Lakes State. Hence, because Michigan's fee is flat, it discriminates against interstate carriers and imposes an unconstitutional burden upon interstate trade.

II

Our Constitution "was framed upon the theory that the peoples of the several states must sink or swim together." Thus, this Court has consistently held that the Constitution's express grant to Congress of the power to "regulate Commerce . . . among the several States," Art. I, § 8, cl. 3, contains "a further, negative command, known as the dormant Commerce Clause," that "create[s] an area of trade free from interference by the States." This negative command prevents a State from "jeopardizing the welfare of the Nation as a whole" by "plac[ing] burdens on the flow of commerce across its borders that commerce wholly within those borders would not bear."

Thus, we have found unconstitutional state regulations that unjustifiably discriminate on their face against out-of-state entities, see Philadelphia v. New Jersey (1978), or that impose burdens on interstate trade that are "clearly excessive in relation to the putative local benefits," Pike v. Bruce Church, Inc. (1970). We have held that States may not impose taxes that facially discriminate against interstate business and offer commercial advantage to local enterprises, that improperly apportion state assessments on transactions with out-of-state components, or that have the "inevitable effect [of] threaten[ing] the free movement of commerce by placing a financial barrier around the State."

Applying these principles and precedents, we find nothing in [the Michigan law] that offends the Commerce Clause. To begin with, Michigan imposes the flat $100 fee only upon intrastate transactions—that is, upon activities taking place exclusively within the State's borders. Section 478.2(1) does not facially discriminate against interstate or out-of-state activities or enterprises. The statute applies evenhandedly to all carriers that make domestic journeys. It does not reflect an effort to tax activity that takes place, in whole or in part, outside the State. Nothing in our case law suggests that such a neutral, locally focused fee or tax is inconsistent with the dormant Commerce Clause.

This legal vacuum is not surprising. States impose numerous flat fees upon local businesses and service providers, including, for example, upon insurers, auctioneers, ambulance operators, and hosts of others. The record, moreover, shows no special circumstance suggesting that Michigan's fee operates in practice as anything other than an unobjectionable exercise of the State's police power. To the contrary, as the Michigan Court of Appeals pointed out, the record contains little, if any, evidence that the $100 fee imposes any significant practical burden upon interstate trade.

Neither does the record show that the flat assessment unfairly discriminates against interstate truckers. The fee seeks to defray costs such as those of regulating "vehicular size and weight," of administering "insurance requirements," and of applying "safety standards." The bulk of such costs would seem more likely to vary per truck or per carrier than to vary per-mile traveled. And that fact means that a per-truck, rather than a per-mile, assessment is likely fair. Nothing in the record suggests the contrary.

Nor would an effort to switch the manner of fee assessment—from lump sum to, for example, miles traveled—be burden free. The record contains an affidavit, sworn by a Michigan Public Service Commission official, that states that to obtain the same revenue (about $3.5 million) through a per-mile fee would require the State to create a "data accumulation system" capable of separating out intrastate hauls and determining their length, and to develop related liability, billing, and auditing mechanisms. This affidavit, on its face, suggests that the game is unlikely to be worth the candle. While petitioners argue the contrary, they do not provide the details of their preferred alternative administrative system nor point to record evidence showing its practicality.

Justice THOMAS, concurring in the judgment.

I would affirm the judgment of the Michigan Court of Appeals because " '[t]he negative Commerce Clause has no basis in the text of the Constitution, makes little sense, and has proved virtually unworkable in application,' Camps Newfound/Owatonna, Inc. v. Town of Harrison (1997) (Thomas, J., dissenting), and, consequently, cannot serve as a basis for striking down a state statute."

Chapter 6

Economic Liberties

B. Economic Substantive Due Process

4. Economic substantive due process since 1937 (casebook p. 558)

In *BMW of North America v. Gore* [casebook p. 547] and *State Farm Automobile Insurance Co. v. Campbell* [casebook p. 551], the Supreme Court imposed due process limits on punitive damage awards. In *Philip Morris USA v. Williams*, the Court returned to this issue. The crucial issue after this case will be whether and to what extent juries may consider harms to third parties in awarding punitive damages.

PHILIP MORRIS U.S.A. v. WILLIAMS
127 S.Ct. 1057 (2007)

Justice BREYER delivered the opinion of the Court.

The question we address today concerns a large state-court punitive damages award. We are asked whether the Constitution's Due Process Clause permits a jury to base that award in part upon its desire to punish the defendant for harming persons who are not before the court (e.g., victims whom the parties do not represent). We hold that such an award would amount to a taking of "property" from the defendant without due process.

I

This lawsuit arises out of the death of Jesse Williams, a heavy cigarette smoker. Respondent, Williams' widow, represents his estate in this state lawsuit for negligence and deceit against Philip Morris, the manufacturer of Marlboro, the brand that Williams favored. A jury found that Williams' death was caused by smoking; that Williams smoked in significant part because he thought it was safe to do so; and that Philip Morris knowingly and falsely led him to believe that this was so. The jury ultimately found that Philip Morris was negligent (as was Williams) and that Philip Morris had engaged in deceit. In respect to deceit, the claim at issue here, it awarded compensatory damages of about $821,000 (about $21,000 economic and $800,000 noneconomic) along with $79.5 million in punitive damages.

Philip Morris made two arguments [on appeal to the Oregon Supreme Court] relevant here. First, it said that the trial court should have accepted, but did not accept, a proposed "punitive damages" instruction that specified the jury could not seek to punish Philip Morris for injury to other persons not before the court. In particular, Philip Morris pointed out that the plaintiff's attorney had told the jury to "think about how many other Jesse Williams in the last 40 years in the State of Oregon there have been. . . . In Oregon, how many people do we see outside, driving home . . . smoking cigarettes? . . . [C]igarettes . . . are going to kill ten [of every hundred]. [And] the market share of Marlboros [i.e., Philip Morris] is one-third [i.e., one of every three killed]." In light of this argument, Philip Morris asked the trial court to tell the jury that "you may consider the extent of harm suffered by others in determining what [the] reasonable relationship is" between any punitive award and "the harm caused to Jesse Williams" by Philip Morris' misconduct, "[but] you are not to punish the defendant for the impact of its alleged misconduct on other persons, who may bring lawsuits of their own in which other juries can resolve their claims. . . . " The judge rejected this proposal and instead told the jury that "[p]unitive damages are awarded against a defendant to punish misconduct and to deter misconduct," and "are not intended to compensate the plaintiff or anyone else for damages caused by the defendant's conduct." In Philip Morris' view, the result was a significant likelihood that a portion of the $79.5 million award represented punishment for its having harmed others, a punishment that the Due Process Clause would here forbid. Second, Philip Morris pointed to the roughly 100-to-1 ratio the $79.5 million punitive damages award bears to $821,000 in compensatory damages.

The Oregon Supreme Court rejected these and other Philip Morris arguments.

For reasons we shall set forth, we consider only the first of these questions. We vacate the Oregon Supreme Court's judgment, and we remand the case for further proceedings.

[II]

In our view, the Constitution's Due Process Clause forbids a State to use a punitive damages award to punish a defendant for injury that it inflicts upon nonparties or those whom they directly represent, i.e., injury that it inflicts upon those who are, essentially, strangers to the litigation. For one thing, the Due Process Clause prohibits a State from punishing an individual without first providing that individual with "an opportunity to present every available defense." Yet a defendant threatened with punishment for injuring a nonparty victim has no opportunity to defend against the charge, by showing, for example in a case such as this, that the other victim was not entitled to damages because he or she knew that smoking was dangerous or did not rely upon the defendant's statements to the contrary.

For another, to permit punishment for injuring a nonparty victim would add a near standardless dimension to the punitive damages equation. How many such victims are there? How seriously were they injured? Under what circumstances did injury occur? The trial will not likely answer such questions as to nonparty victims. The jury will be left to speculate. And the fundamental due process concerns to which our punitive damages cases refer—risks of arbitrariness, uncertainty and lack of notice—will be magnified.

Finally, we can find no authority supporting the use of punitive damages awards for the purpose of punishing a defendant for harming others. We have said that it may be appropriate to consider the reasonableness of a punitive damages award in light of the potential harm the defendant's conduct could have caused. But we have made clear that the potential harm at issue was harm potentially caused the plaintiff.

Respondent argues that she is free to show harm to other victims because it is relevant to a different part of the punitive damages constitutional equation, namely, reprehensibility. That is to say, harm to others shows more reprehensible conduct. Philip Morris, in turn, does not deny that a plaintiff may show harm to others in order to demonstrate reprehensibility. Nor do we. Evidence of actual harm to nonparties can help to show that the conduct that harmed the plaintiff also posed a substantial risk of harm to the general public, and so was particularly reprehensible—although counsel may argue in a particular case that conduct resulting in no harm to others nonetheless posed a grave risk to the public, or the converse. Yet for the reasons given above, a jury may not go further than this and use a punitive damages verdict to punish a defendant directly on account of harms it is alleged to have visited on nonparties.

Given the risks of unfairness that we have mentioned, it is constitutionally important for a court to provide assurance that the jury will ask the right question, not the wrong one. And given the risks of arbitrariness, the concern for adequate notice, and the risk that punitive damages awards can, in practice, impose one State's (or one jury's) policies (e.g., banning cigarettes) upon other States—all of which accompany awards that, today, may be many times the size of such awards in the 18th and 19th centuries, it is particularly important that States avoid procedure that unnecessarily deprives juries of proper legal guidance. We therefore conclude that the Due Process Clause requires States to provide assurance that juries are not asking the wrong question, i.e., seeking, not simply to determine reprehensibility, but also to punish for harm caused strangers.

[III]

As the preceding discussion makes clear, we believe that the Oregon Supreme Court applied the wrong constitutional standard when considering Philip Morris' appeal. We remand this case so that the Oregon Supreme Court can apply the standard we have set forth. Because the application of this standard may lead to the need for a new trial, or a change in the level of the punitive damages award, we shall not consider whether the award is constitutionally "grossly excessive." We vacate the Oregon Supreme Court's judgment and remand the case for further proceedings not inconsistent with this opinion.

Justice STEVENS, dissenting.

Unlike the Court, I see no reason why an interest in punishing a wrongdoer "for harming persons who are not before the court," should not be taken into consideration when assessing the appropriate sanction for reprehensible conduct. Whereas compensatory damages are measured by the harm the defendant has caused the plaintiff, punitive damages are a sanction for the public harm the defendant's conduct has caused or threatened. There is little difference between the justification for a criminal sanction, such as a fine or a term of imprisonment, and an award of punitive damages. In our early history either type of sanction might have been imposed in litigation prosecuted by a private citizen. And while in neither context would the sanction typically include a pecuniary award measured by the harm that the conduct had caused to any third parties, in both contexts the harm to third parties would surely be a relevant factor to consider in evaluating the reprehensibility of the defendant's wrongdoing. We have never held otherwise.

In the case before us, evidence attesting to the possible harm the defendant's extensive deceitful conduct caused other Oregonians was properly presented to the jury. No evidence was offered to establish an appropriate measure of damages to compensate such third parties for their injuries, and no one argued that the punitive damages award would serve any such purpose. To award compensatory damages to remedy such third-party harm might well constitute a taking of property from the defendant without due process. But a punitive damages award, instead of serving a compensatory purpose, serves the entirely different purposes of retribution and deterrence that underlie every criminal sanction. This justification for punitive damages has even greater salience when, as in this case, the award is payable in whole or in part to the State rather than to the private litigant.

While apparently recognizing the novelty of its holding, ante, at 1065, the majority relies on a distinction between taking third-party harm into account in order to assess the reprehensibility of the defendant's conduct—which is permitted—from doing so in order to punish the defendant "directly"—which is forbidden. This nuance eludes me. When a jury increases a punitive damages award because injuries to third parties enhanced the reprehensibility of the defendant's conduct, the jury is by definition punishing the defendant—directly—for third-party harm. A murderer who kills his victim by throwing a bomb that injures dozens of bystanders should be punished more severely than one who harms no one other than his intended victim. Similarly, there is no reason why the measure of the appropriate punishment for engaging in a campaign of deceit in distributing a poisonous and addictive substance to thousands of cigarette smokers statewide should not include consideration of the harm to those "bystanders" as well as the harm to the individual plaintiff. The Court endorses a contrary conclusion without providing us with any reasoned justification.

It is far too late in the day to argue that the Due Process Clause merely guarantees fair procedure and imposes no substantive limits on a State's lawmaking power. It remains true, however, that the Court should be "reluctant to expand the concept of substantive due process because guideposts for responsible decisionmaking in this unchartered area are scarce and open-ended." Judicial restraint counsels us to "exercise the utmost care whenever we are asked to break new ground in this field." Today the majority ignores that sound advice when it announces its new rule of substantive law.

Justice THOMAS, dissenting.

I join Justice Ginsburg's dissent in full. I write separately to reiterate my view that " 'the Constitution does not constrain the size of punitive damages awards.' " It matters not that the Court styles today's holding as "procedural" because the "procedural" rule is simply a confusing implementation of the substantive due process regime this Court has created for punitive damages. Today's opinion proves once again that this Court's punitive damages jurisprudence is "insusceptible of principled application."

Justice GINSBURG, with whom Justice SCALIA and Justice THOMAS join, dissenting.

The purpose of punitive damages, it can hardly be denied, is not to compensate, but to punish. Punish for what? Not for harm actually caused "strangers to the litigation," the Court states, but for the reprehensibility of defendant's conduct. "[C]onduct that risks harm to many," the Court observes, "is likely more reprehensible than conduct that risks harm to only a few." The Court thus conveys that, when punitive damages are at issue, a jury is properly instructed to consider the extent of harm suffered by others as a measure of reprehensibility, but not to mete out punishment for injuries in fact sustained by nonparties. The Oregon courts did not rule otherwise. They have endeavored to follow our decisions.

The right question regarding reprehensibility, the Court acknowledges, would train on "the harm that Philip Morris was prepared to inflict on the smoking public at large." The Court identifies no evidence introduced and no charge delivered inconsistent with that inquiry.

The Court's order vacating the Oregon Supreme Court's judgment is all the more inexplicable considering that Philip Morris did not preserve any objection to the charges in fact delivered to the jury, to the evidence introduced at trial, or to opposing counsel's argument. The sole objection Philip Morris preserved was to the trial court's refusal to give defendant's requested charge number 34. Under that charge, just what use could the jury properly make of "the extent of harm suffered by others"? The answer slips from my grasp. A judge seeking to enlighten rather than confuse surely would resist delivering the requested charge.

The Court ventures no opinion on the propriety of the charge proposed by Philip Morris, though Philip Morris preserved no other objection to the trial proceedings. Rather than addressing the one objection Philip Morris properly preserved, the Court reaches outside the bounds of the case as postured when the trial court entered its judgment. I would accord more respectful treatment to the proceedings and dispositions of state courts that sought diligently to adhere to our changing, less than crystalline precedent.

In Exxon Shipping v. Baker, 128 S.Ct. 2605 (2008), the Court held that under the common law of maritime, punitive damages should be in a 1:1 relationship with compensatory damages. The Court reduced a punitive damage award resulting from the Exxon Valdez oil spill from $2.5 billion to $507 million. The Court expressly did not rely on the Constitution or due process. Justice Souter, writing for the majority in a 5-3 decision, expressed great concern that juries vary widely and said that a fixed ratio is the best solution to create more consistency in punitive damage awards.

D. The Takings Clause

There were two important takings decisions during October Term 2004. First, in Lingle v. Chevron, U.S.A. Inc., the Court considered the test for regulatory takings and whether a government action must substantially advance a legitimate purpose in order to avoid being a taking. Second, in Kelo v. City of New London, the Court considered what is "public use" and whether a taking for purposes of economic development is for public use.

2. Is There a "Taking"? (casebook, p. 575)

The Court long has held that there are two types of takings: possessory and regulatory takings. As to regulatory takings, must the government's action "substantially advance" a legitimate government purpose in order to avoid being a taking?

LINGLE v. CHEVRON U.S.A. INC.
544 U.S. 528 (2005)

Justice O'CONNOR delivered the opinion of the Court.

On occasion, a would-be doctrinal rule or test finds its way into our case law through simple repetition of a phrase—however fortuitously coined. A quarter century ago, in Agins v. City of Tiburon (1980), the Court declared that government regulation of private property "effects a taking if [such regulation] does not substantially advance legitimate state interests. . . ." Through reiteration in a half dozen or so decisions since *Agins*, this language has been ensconced in our Fifth Amendment takings jurisprudence.

In the case before us, the lower courts applied *Agins'* "substantially advances" formula to strike down a Hawaii statute that limits the rent that oil companies may charge to dealers who lease service stations owned by the companies. The lower courts held that the rent cap effects an uncompensated taking of private property in violation of the Fifth and Fourteenth Amendments because it does not substantially advance Hawaii's asserted interest in controlling retail gasoline prices. This case requires us to decide whether the "substantially advances" formula announced in *Agins* is an appropriate test for determining whether a regulation effects a Fifth Amendment taking. We conclude that it is not.

I

Gasoline is sold at retail in Hawaii from about 300 different service stations. About half of these stations are leased from oil companies by independent lessee-dealers, another 75 or so are owned and operated by "open" dealers, and the remainder are owned and operated by the oil companies. Chevron sells most of its product through 64 independent lessee-dealer stations. In a typical lessee-dealer arrangement, Chevron buys or leases land from a third party, builds a service station, and then leases the station to a dealer on a turnkey basis. Chevron charges the lessee-dealer a monthly rent, defined as a percentage of the dealer's margin on retail sales of gasoline and other goods. In addition, Chevron requires the lessee-dealer to enter into a supply contract, under which the dealer agrees to purchase from Chevron whatever is necessary to satisfy demand at the station for Chevron's product. Chevron unilaterally sets the wholesale price of its product.

The Hawaii Legislature enacted Act 257 in June 1997, apparently in response to concerns about the effects of market concentration on retail gasoline prices. The statute seeks to protect independent dealers by imposing certain restrictions on the ownership and leasing of service stations by oil companies. It prohibits oil companies from converting existing lessee-dealer stations to company-operated stations and from locating new company-operated stations in close proximity to existing dealer-operated stations. More importantly for present purposes, Act 257 limits the amount of rent that an oil company may charge a lessee-dealer to 15 percent of the dealer's gross profits from gasoline sales plus 15 percent of gross sales of products other than gasoline.

II

A

The Takings Clause of the Fifth Amendment, made applicable to the States through the Fourteenth, provides that private property shall not "be taken for public use, without just compensation." As its text makes plain, the Takings Clause "does not prohibit the taking of private property, but instead places a condition on the exercise of that power." In other words, it "is designed not to limit the governmental interference with property rights per se, but rather to secure compensation in the event of otherwise proper interference amounting to a taking."

Beginning with Pennsylvania Coal Co. v. Mahon (1922), the Court recognized that government regulation of private property may, in some instances, be so onerous that its effect is tantamount to a direct appropriation or ouster—and that such "regulatory takings" may be compensable under the Fifth Amendment.

Our precedents stake out two categories of regulatory action that generally will be deemed per se takings for Fifth Amendment purposes. First, where government requires an owner to suffer a permanent physical invasion of her property— however minor—it must provide just compensation. A second categorical rule applies to regulations that completely deprive an owner of "all economically beneficial us[e]" of her property.

Outside these two relatively narrow categories, regulatory takings challenges are governed by the standards set forth in Penn Central Transp. Co. v. New York City (1978). The Court in *Penn Central* acknowledged that it had hitherto been "unable to develop any 'set formula'" for evaluating regulatory takings claims, but identified "several factors that have particular significance." Primary among those factors are "[t]he economic impact of the regulation on the claimant and, particularly, the extent to which the regulation has interfered with distinct investment-backed expectations." In addition, the "character of the governmental action"—for instance whether it amounts to a physical invasion or instead merely affects property interests through "some public program adjusting the benefits and burdens of economic life to promote the common good"—may be relevant in discerning whether a taking has occurred. The *Penn Central* factors—though each has given rise to vexing subsidiary questions— have served as the principal guidelines for resolving regulatory takings claims that do not fall within the physical takings or *Lucas* rules.

B

In Agins v. City of Tiburon, a case involving a facial takings challenge to certain municipal zoning ordinances, the Court declared that "[t]he application of a general zoning law to particular property effects a taking if the ordinance does not substantially advance legitimate state interests or denies an owner economically viable use of his land." Because this statement is phrased in the disjunctive, *Agins*' "substantially advances" language has been read to announce a standalone regulatory takings test that is wholly independent of *Penn Central* or any other test. Indeed, the lower courts in this case struck down Hawaii's rent control statute as an "unconstitutional regulatory taking," based solely upon a finding that it does not substantially advance the State's asserted interest in controlling retail gasoline prices. Although a number of our takings precedents have recited the "substantially advances" formula minted in *Agins*, this is our first opportunity to consider its validity as a freestanding takings test. We conclude that this formula prescribes an inquiry in the nature of a due process, not a takings, test, and that it has no proper place in our takings jurisprudence.

There is no question that the "substantially advances" formula was derived from due process, not takings, precedents. Although *Agins'* reliance on due process precedents is understandable, the language the Court selected was regrettably imprecise. The "substantially advances" formula suggests a means-ends test: It asks, in essence, whether a regulation of private property is effective in achieving some legitimate public purpose. An inquiry of this nature has some logic in the context of a due process challenge, for a regulation that fails to serve any legitimate governmental objective may be so arbitrary or irrational that it runs afoul of the Due Process Clause. But such a test is not a valid method of discerning whether private property has been "taken" for purposes of the Fifth Amendment.

In stark contrast to the three regulatory takings tests discussed above, the "substantially advances" inquiry reveals nothing about the magnitude or character of the burden a particular regulation imposes upon private property rights. Nor does it provide any information about how any regulatory burden is distributed among property owners. In consequence, this test does not help to identify those regulations whose effects are functionally comparable to government appropriation or invasion of private property; it is tethered neither to the text of the Takings Clause nor to the basic justification for allowing regulatory actions to be challenged under the Clause.

Chevron appeals to the general principle that the Takings Clause is meant " 'to bar Government from forcing some people alone to bear public burdens which, in all fairness and justice, should be borne by the public as a whole.' " But that appeal is clearly misplaced, for the reasons just indicated. A test that tells us nothing about the actual burden imposed on property rights, or how that burden is allocated cannot tell us when justice might require that the burden be spread among taxpayers through the payment of compensation. The owner of a property subject to a regulation that effectively serves a legitimate state interest may be just as singled out and just as burdened as the owner of a property subject to an ineffective regulation. It would make little sense to say that the second owner has suffered a taking while the first has not. Likewise, an ineffective regulation may not significantly burden property rights at all, and it may distribute any burden broadly and evenly among property owners. The notion that such a regulation nevertheless "takes" private property for public use merely by virtue of its ineffectiveness or foolishness is untenable.

Instead of addressing a challenged regulation's effect on private property, the "substantially advances" inquiry probes the regulation's underlying validity. But such an inquiry is logically prior to and distinct from the question whether a regulation effects a taking, for the Takings Clause presupposes that the government has acted in pursuit of a valid public purpose. The Clause expressly requires compensation where government takes private property "for public use." It does not bar government from interfering with property rights, but rather requires compensation "in the event of otherwise proper interference amounting to a taking." Conversely, if a government action is found to be impermissible— for instance because it fails to meet the "public use" requirement or is so arbitrary as to violate due process—that is the end of the inquiry. No amount of compensation can authorize such action.

Chevron's challenge to the Hawaii statute in this case illustrates the flaws in the "substantially advances" theory. To begin with, it is unclear how significantly Hawaii's rent cap actually burdens Chevron's property rights. The parties stipulated below that the cap would reduce Chevron's aggregate rental income on 11 of its 64 lessee-dealer stations by about $207,000 per year, but that Chevron nevertheless expects to receive a return on its investment in these stations that satisfies any constitutional standard. Moreover, Chevron asserted below, and the District Court found, that Chevron would recoup any reductions in its rental income by raising wholesale gasoline prices. In short, Chevron has not clearly argued—let alone established—that it has been singled out to bear any particularly severe regulatory burden. Rather, the gravamen of Chevron's claim is simply that Hawaii's rent cap will not actually serve the State's legitimate interest in protecting consumers against high gasoline prices. Whatever the merits of that claim, it does not sound under the Takings Clause. Chevron plainly does not seek compensation for a taking of its property for a legitimate public use, but rather an injunction against the enforcement of a regulation that it alleges to be fundamentally arbitrary and irrational.

Finally, the "substantially advances" formula is not only doctrinally untenable as a takings test—its application as such would also present serious practical difficulties. The *Agins* formula can be read to demand heightened means-ends review of virtually any regulation of private property. If so interpreted, it would require courts to scrutinize the efficacy of a vast array of state and federal regulations—a task for which courts are not well suited. Moreover, it would empower—and might often require—courts to substitute their predictive judgments for those of elected legislatures and expert agencies.

For the foregoing reasons, we conclude that the "substantially advances" formula announced in *Agins* is not a valid method of identifying regulatory takings for which the Fifth Amendment requires just compensation. Since Chevron argued only a "substantially advances" theory in support of its takings claim, it was not entitled to summary judgment on that claim.

III

We emphasize that our holding today—that the "substantially advances" formula is not a valid takings test—does not require us to disturb any of our prior holdings. To be sure, we applied a "substantially advances" inquiry in *Agins* itself. But in no case have we found a compensable taking based on such an inquiry. Indeed, in most of the cases reciting the "substantially advances" formula, the Court has merely assumed its validity when referring to it in dicta.

We hold that the "substantially advances" formula is not a valid takings test, and indeed conclude that it has no proper place in our takings jurisprudence. In so doing, we reaffirm that a plaintiff seeking to challenge a government regulation as an uncompensated taking of private property may proceed under one of the other theories discussed above—by alleging a "physical" taking, a

Lucas-type "total regulatory taking," a *Penn Central* taking, or a land-use exaction violating the standards set forth in *Nollan* and *Dolan*. Because Chevron argued only a "substantially advances" theory in support of its takings claim, it was not entitled to summary judgment on that claim.

Justice KENNEDY, concurring.

This separate writing is to note that today's decision does not foreclose the possibility that a regulation might be so arbitrary or irrational as to violate due process. The failure of a regulation to accomplish a stated or obvious objective would be relevant to that inquiry. Chevron voluntarily dismissed its due process claim without prejudice, however, and we have no occasion to consider whether Act 257 of the 1997 Hawaii Session Laws "represents one of the rare instances in which even such a permissive standard has been violated." With these observations, I join the opinion of the Court.

3. Is It for "Public Use"? (casebook, p. 609)

The Court's decision in Kelo v. City of New London was among the most controversial of the year. In reading the decision, it is important to focus on whether the ruling changes the law concerning what is "public use" (and, if so, how).

KELO v. CITY OF NEW LONDON
545 U.S. 469 (2005)

Justice STEVENS delivered the opinion of the Court.

In 2000, the city of New London approved a development plan that, in the words of the Supreme Court of Connecticut, was "projected to create in excess of 1,000 jobs, to increase tax and other revenues, and to revitalize an economic-ally distressed city, including its downtown and waterfront areas." In assembling the land needed for this project, the city's development agent has purchased property from willing sellers and proposes to use the power of eminent domain to acquire the remainder of the property from unwilling owners in exchange for just compensation. The question presented is whether the city's proposed disposition of this property qualifies as a "public use" within the meaning of the Takings Clause of the Fifth Amendment to the Constitution.

I

The city of New London (hereinafter City) sits at the junction of the Thames River and the Long Island Sound in southeastern Connecticut. Decades of economic decline led a state agency in 1990 to designate the City a "distressed municipality." In 1996, the Federal Government closed the Naval Undersea

Warfare Center, which had been located in the Fort Trumbull area of the City and had employed over 1,500 people. In 1998, the City's unemployment rate was nearly double that of the State, and its population of just under 24,000 residents was at its lowest since 1920.

These conditions prompted state and local officials to target New London, and particularly its Fort Trumbull area, for economic revitalization. To this end, respondent New London Development Corporation (NLDC), a private nonprofit entity established some years earlier to assist the City in planning economic development, was reactivated. In January 1998, the State authorized a $5.35 million bond issue to support the NLDC's planning activities and a $10 million bond issue toward the creation of a Fort Trumbull State Park. In February, the pharmaceutical company Pfizer Inc. announced that it would build a $300 million research facility on a site immediately adjacent to Fort Trumbull; local planners hoped that Pfizer would draw new business to the area, thereby serving as a catalyst to the area's rejuvenation. After receiving initial approval from the city council, the NLDC continued its planning activities and held a series of neighborhood meetings to educate the public about the process.

The city council approved the plan in January 2000, and designated the NLDC as its development agent in charge of implementation. The city council also authorized the NLDC to purchase property or to acquire property by exercising eminent domain in the City's name. The NLDC successfully negotiated the purchase of most of the real estate in the 90-acre area, but its negotiations with petitioners failed. As a consequence, in November 2000, the NLDC initiated the condemnation proceedings that gave rise to this case.

II

Petitioner Susette Kelo has lived in the Fort Trumbull area since 1997. She has made extensive improvements to her house, which she prizes for its water view. Petitioner Wilhelmina Dery was born in her Fort Trumbull house in 1918 and has lived there her entire life. Her husband Charles (also a petitioner) has lived in the house since they married some 60 years ago. In all, the nine petitioners own 15 properties in Fort Trumbull. There is no allegation that any of these properties is blighted or otherwise in poor condition; rather, they were condemned only because they happen to be located in the development area.

III

Two polar propositions are perfectly clear. On the one hand, it has long been accepted that the sovereign may not take the property of A for the sole purpose of transferring it to another private party B, even though A is paid just compensation. On the other hand, it is equally clear that a State may transfer property from one private party to another if future "use by the public" is the purpose of the taking; the condemnation of land for a railroad with common-carrier duties is a familiar example. Neither of these propositions, however, determines the disposition of this case.

As for the first proposition, the City would no doubt be forbidden from taking petitioners' land for the purpose of conferring a private benefit on a particular private party. Nor would the City be allowed to take property under the mere pretext of a public purpose, when its actual purpose was to bestow a private benefit. The takings before us, however, would be executed pursuant to a "carefully considered" development plan. The trial judge and all the members of the Supreme Court of Connecticut agreed that there was no evidence of an illegitimate purpose in this case.

On the other hand, this is not a case in which the City is planning to open the condemned land—at least not in its entirety—to use by the general public. Nor will the private lessees of the land in any sense be required to operate like common carriers, making their services available to all comers. But although such a projected use would be sufficient to satisfy the public use requirement, this "Court long ago rejected any literal requirement that condemned property be put into use for the general public." Indeed, while many state courts in the mid-19th century endorsed "use by the public" as the proper definition of public use, that narrow view steadily eroded over time. Not only was the "use by the public" test difficult to administer (e.g., what proportion of the public need have access to the property? at what price?), but it proved to be impractical given the diverse and always evolving needs of society. Accordingly, when this Court began applying the Fifth Amendment to the States at the close of the 19th century, it embraced the broader and more natural interpretation of public use as "public purpose." Thus, in a case upholding a mining company's use of an aerial bucket line to transport ore over property it did not own, Justice Holmes' opinion for the Court stressed "the inadequacy of use by the general public as a universal test." Strickley v. Highland Boy Gold Mining Co. (1906). We have repeatedly and consistently rejected that narrow test ever since.

The disposition of this case therefore turns on the question whether the City's development plan serves a "public purpose." Without exception, our cases have defined that concept broadly, reflecting our longstanding policy of deference to legislative judgments in this field.

In Berman v. Parker (1954), this Court upheld a redevelopment plan targeting a blighted area of Washington, D.C., in which most of the housing for the area's 5,000 inhabitants was beyond repair. Under the plan, the area would be condemned and part of it utilized for the construction of streets, schools, and other public facilities. The remainder of the land would be leased or sold to private parties for the purpose of redevelopment, including the construction of low-cost housing. The owner of a department store located in the area challenged the condemnation, pointing out that his store was not itself blighted and arguing that the creation of a "better balanced, more attractive community" was not a valid public use. Writing for a unanimous Court, Justice Douglas refused to evaluate this claim in isolation, deferring instead to the legislative and agency judgment that the area "must be planned as a whole" for the plan to be successful. The Court explained that "community redevelopment programs need not, by force of the Constitution, be on a piecemeal basis—lot by lot, building by building." The public use underlying the taking was unequivocally affirmed.

In Hawaii Housing Authority v. Midkiff (1984), the Court considered a Hawaii statute whereby fee title was taken from lessors and transferred to lessees (for just compensation) in order to reduce the concentration of land ownership. We unanimously upheld the statute and rejected the Ninth Circuit's view that it was "a naked attempt on the part of the state of Hawaii to take the property of A and transfer it to B solely for B's private use and benefit." Reaffirming *Berman*'s deferential approach to legislative judgments in this field, we concluded that the State's purpose of eliminating the "social and economic evils of a land oligopoly" qualified as a valid public use. Our opinion also rejected the contention that the mere fact that the State immediately transferred the properties to private individuals upon condemnation somehow diminished the public character of the taking. "[I]t is only the taking's purpose, and not its mechanics," we explained, that matters in determining public use.

In that same Term we decided another public use case that arose in a purely economic context. In Ruckelshaus v. Monsanto Co. (1984), the Court dealt with provisions of the Federal Insecticide, Fungicide, and Rodenticide Act under which the Environmental Protection Agency could consider the data (including trade secrets) submitted by a prior pesticide applicant in evaluating a subsequent application, so long as the second applicant paid just compensation for the data. We acknowledged that the "most direct beneficiaries" of these provisions were the subsequent applicants, but we nevertheless upheld the statute under Berman and *Midkiff*. We found sufficient Congress' belief that sparing applicants the cost of time-consuming research eliminated a significant barrier to entry in the pesticide market and thereby enhanced competition.

Viewed as a whole, our jurisprudence has recognized that the needs of society have varied between different parts of the Nation, just as they have evolved over time in response to changed circumstances. Our earliest cases in particular embodied a strong theme of federalism, emphasizing the "great respect" that we owe to state legislatures and state courts in discerning local public needs. For more than a century, our public use jurisprudence has wisely eschewed rigid formulas and intrusive scrutiny in favor of affording legislatures broad latitude in determining what public needs justify the use of the takings power.

IV

Those who govern the City were not confronted with the need to remove blight in the Fort Trumbull area, but their determination that the area was sufficiently distressed to justify a program of economic rejuvenation is entitled to our deference. The City has carefully formulated an economic development plan that it believes will provide appreciable benefits to the community, including—but by no means limited to—new jobs and increased tax revenue. As with other exercises in urban planning and development, the City is endeavoring to coordinate a variety of commercial, residential, and recreational uses of land, with the hope that they will form a whole greater than the sum of its parts. To effectuate this plan, the City has invoked a state statute that specifically authorizes the use of eminent domain to promote economic development. Given the comprehensive character of the plan, the thorough deliberation that preceded its adoption, and the limited scope of our review, it is appropriate for us, as it was in *Berman*, to resolve the challenges of the individual owners, not on a piecemeal basis, but rather in light of the entire plan. Because that plan unquestionably serves a public purpose, the takings challenged here satisfy the public use requirement of the Fifth Amendment.

To avoid this result, petitioners urge us to adopt a new bright-line rule that economic development does not qualify as a public use. Putting aside the unpersuasive suggestion that the City's plan will provide only purely economic benefits, neither precedent nor logic supports petitioners' proposal. Promoting economic development is a traditional and long accepted function of government. There is, moreover, no principled way of distinguishing economic development from the other public purposes that we have recognized. In our cases upholding takings that facilitated agriculture and mining, for example, we emphasized the importance of those industries to the welfare of the States in question. It would be incongruous to hold that the City's interest in the economic benefits to be derived from the development of the Fort Trumbull area has less of a public character than any of those other interests. Clearly, there is no basis for exempting economic development from our traditionally broad understanding of public purpose.

Petitioners contend that using eminent domain for economic development impermissibly blurs the boundary between public and private takings. Again, our cases foreclose this objection. Quite simply, the government's pursuit of a public purpose will often benefit individual private parties.

It is further argued that without a bright-line rule nothing would stop a city from transferring citizen A's property to citizen B for the sole reason that citizen B will put the property to a more productive use and thus pay more taxes. Such a one-to-one transfer of property, executed outside the confines of an integrated development plan, is not presented in this case. While such an unusual exercise of government power would certainly raise a suspicion that a private purpose was afoot, the hypothetical cases posited by petitioners can be confronted if and when they arise. They do not warrant the crafting of an artificial restriction on the concept of public use.

Alternatively, petitioners maintain that for takings of this kind we should require a "reasonable certainty" that the expected public benefits will actually accrue. Such a rule, however, would represent an even greater departure from our precedent. "When the legislature's purpose is legitimate and its means are not irrational, our cases make clear that empirical debates over the wisdom of takings—no less than debates over the wisdom of other kinds of socioeconomic legislation—are not to be carried out in the federal courts."

In affirming the City's authority to take petitioners' properties, we do not minimize the hardship that condemnations may entail, notwithstanding the payment of just compensation. We emphasize that nothing in our opinion precludes any State from placing further restrictions on its exercise of the takings power. Indeed, many States already impose "public use" requirements that are stricter than the federal baseline. Some of these requirements have been established as a matter of state constitutional law, while others are expressed in state eminent domain statutes that carefully limit the grounds upon which takings may be exercised. As the submissions of the parties and their amici make clear, the necessity and wisdom of using eminent domain to promote economic development are certainly matters of legitimate public debate. This Court's authority, however, extends only to determining whether the City's proposed condemnations are for a "public use" within the meaning of the Fifth Amendment to the Federal Constitution. Because over a century of our case law interpreting that provision dictates an affirmative answer to that question, we may not grant petitioners the relief that they seek.

Justice KENNEDY, concurring.

I join the opinion for the Court and add these further observations. This Court has declared that a taking should be upheld as consistent with the Public Use Clause, U.S. Const., Amdt. 5., as long as it is "rationally related to a conceivable public purpose." Hawaii Housing Authority v. Midkiff (1984); see also Berman v. Parker (1954). This deferential standard of review echoes the rational-basis test used to review economic regulation under the Due Process and Equal Protection Clauses. The determination that a rational-basis standard of review is appropriate does not, however, alter the fact that transfers intended to confer benefits on particular, favored private entities, and with only incidental or pretextual public benefits, are forbidden by the Public Use Clause.

A court applying rational-basis review under the Public Use Clause should strike down a taking that, by a clear showing, is intended to favor a particular private party, with only incidental or pretextual public benefits, just as a court applying rational-basis review under the Equal Protection Clause must strike down a government classification that is clearly intended to injure a particular class of private parties, with only incidental or pretextual public justifications.

A court confronted with a plausible accusation of impermissible favoritism to private parties should treat the objection as a serious one and review the record to see if it has merit, though with the presumption that the government's actions were reasonable and intended to serve a public purpose. Here, the trial court conducted a careful and extensive inquiry.

Petitioners and their amici argue that any taking justified by the promotion of economic development must be treated by the courts as per se invalid, or at least presumptively invalid. Petitioners overstate the need for such a rule, however, by making the incorrect assumption that review under Berman and Midkiff imposes no meaningful judicial limits on the government's power to condemn any property it likes. A broad per se rule or a strong presumption of invalidity, furthermore, would prohibit a large number of government takings that have the purpose and expected effect of conferring substantial benefits on the public at large and so do not offend the Public Use Clause.

My agreement with the Court that a presumption of invalidity is not warranted for economic development takings in general, or for the particular takings at issue in this case, does not foreclose the possibility that a more stringent standard of review than that announced in *Berman* and *Midkiff* might be appropriate for a more narrowly drawn category of takings. There may be private transfers in which the risk of undetected impermissible favoritism of private parties is so acute that a presumption (rebuttable or otherwise) of invalidity is warranted under the Public Use Clause. This demanding level of scrutiny, however, is not required simply because the purpose of the taking is economic development.

This is not the occasion for conjecture as to what sort of cases might justify a more demanding standard, but it is appropriate to underscore aspects of the instant case that convince me no departure from *Berman* and *Midkiff* is appropriate here. This taking occurred in the context of a comprehensive development plan meant to address a serious city-wide depression, and the projected economic benefits of the project cannot be characterized as de minimus. The identity of most of the private beneficiaries were unknown at the time the city formulated its plans. The city complied with elaborate procedural requirements that facilitate review of the record and inquiry into the city's purposes. In sum, while there may be categories of cases in which the transfers are so suspicious, or the procedures employed so prone to abuse, or the purported benefits are so trivial or implausible, that courts should presume an impermissible private purpose, no such circumstances are present in this case.

Justice O'CONNOR, with whom THE CHIEF JUSTICE, Justice SCALIA, and Justice THOMAS join, dissenting.

Over two centuries ago, just after the Bill of Rights was ratified, Justice Chase wrote: "An ACT of the Legislature (for I cannot call it a law) contrary to the great first principles of the social compact, cannot be considered a rightful exercise of legislative authority. . . . A few instances will suffice to explain what I mean. . . . [A] law that takes property from A. and gives it to B: It is against all reason and justice, for a people to entrust a Legislature with SUCH powers; and, therefore, it cannot be presumed that they have done it." Calder v. Bull (1798).

Today the Court abandons this long-held, basic limitation on government power. Under the banner of economic development, all private property is now vulnerable to being taken and transferred to another private owner, so long as it might be upgraded—i.e., given to an owner who will use it in a way that the legislature deems more beneficial to the public—in the process. To reason, as the Court does, that the incidental public benefits resulting from the subsequent ordinary use of private property render economic development takings "for public use" is to wash out any distinction between private and public use of property— and thereby effectively to delete the words "for public use" from the Takings Clause of the Fifth Amendment. Accordingly I respectfully dissent.

The public use requirement, in turn, imposes a more basic limitation, circumscribing the very scope of the eminent domain power: Government may compel an individual to forfeit her property for the public's use, but not for the benefit of another private person. This requirement promotes fairness as well as security. Where is the line between "public" and "private" property use? We give considerable deference to legislatures' determinations about what governmental activities will advantage the public. But were the political branches the sole arbiters of the public-private distinction, the Public Use Clause would amount to little more than hortatory fluff. An external, judicial check on how the public use requirement is interpreted, however limited, is necessary if this constraint on government power is to retain any meaning.

Our cases have generally identified three categories of takings that comply with the public use requirement, though it is in the nature of things that the boundaries between these categories are not always firm. Two are relatively straightforward and uncontroversial. First, the sovereign may transfer private property to public ownership—such as for a road, a hospital, or a military base. Second, the sovereign may transfer private property to private parties, often common carriers, who make the property available for the public's use—such as with a railroad, a public utility, or a stadium. But "public ownership" and "use-by-the-public" are sometimes too constricting and impractical ways to define the scope of the Public Use Clause. Thus we have allowed that, in certain circumstances and to meet certain exigencies, takings that serve a public purpose also satisfy the Constitution even if the property is destined for subsequent private use. See, e.g., Berman v. Parker (1954); Hawaii Housing Authority v. Midkiff (1984).

This case returns us for the first time in over 20 years to the hard question of when a purportedly "public purpose" taking meets the public use requirement. It presents an issue of first impression: Are economic development takings constitutional? I would hold that they are not.

Here New London does not claim that Susette Kelo's and Wilhelmina Dery's well-maintained homes are the source of any social harm. Indeed, it could not so claim without adopting the absurd argument that any single-family home that might be razed to make way for an apartment building, or any church that might be replaced with a retail store, or any small business that might be more lucrative if it were instead part of a national franchise, is inherently harmful to society and thus within the government's power to condemn.

In moving away from our decisions sanctioning the condemnation of harmful property use, the Court today significantly expands the meaning of public use. It holds that the sovereign may take private property currently put to ordinary private use, and give it over for new, ordinary private use, so long as the new use is predicted to generate some secondary benefit for the public—such as increased tax revenue, more jobs, maybe even aesthetic pleasure. But nearly any lawful use of real private property can be said to generate some incidental benefit to the public. Thus, if predicted (or even guaranteed) positive side-effects are enough to render transfer from one private party to another constitutional, then the words "for public use" do not realistically exclude any takings, and thus do not exert any constraint on the eminent domain power.

Even if there were a practical way to isolate the motives behind a given taking, the gesture toward a purpose test is theoretically flawed. If it is true that incidental public benefits from new private use are enough to ensure the "public purpose" in a taking, why should it matter, as far as the Fifth Amendment is concerned, what inspired the taking in the first place? How much the government does or does not desire to benefit a favored private party has no bearing on whether an economic development taking will or will not generate secondary benefit for the public. And whatever the reason for a given condemnation, the effect is the same from the constitutional perspective—private property is forcibly relinquished to new private ownership.

A second proposed limitation is implicit in the Court's opinion. The logic of today's decision is that eminent domain may only be used to upgrade—not downgrade—property. At best this makes the Public Use Clause redundant with the Due Process Clause, which already prohibits irrational government action. The Court rightfully admits, however, that the judiciary cannot get bogged down in predictive judgments about whether the public will actually be better off after a property transfer. In any event, this constraint has no realistic import. For who among us can say she already makes the most productive or attractive possible use of her property? The specter of condemnation hangs over all property. Nothing is to prevent the State from replacing any Motel 6 with a Ritz-Carlton, any home with a shopping mall, or any farm with a factory.

Any property may now be taken for the benefit of another private party, but the fallout from this decision will not be random. The beneficiaries are likely to be those citizens with disproportionate influence and power in the political process, including large corporations and development firms. As for the victims, the government now has license to transfer property from those with fewer resources to those with more. The Founders cannot have intended this perverse result. "[T]hat alone is a just government," wrote James Madison, "which impartially secures to every man, whatever is his own."

Justice THOMAS, dissenting.

Long ago, William Blackstone wrote that "the law of the land . . . postpone[s] even public necessity to the sacred and inviolable rights of private property." The Framers embodied that principle in the Constitution, allowing the government to take property not for "public necessity," but instead for "public use." Defying this understanding, the Court replaces the Public Use Clause with a " '[P]ublic [P]urpose' " Clause (or perhaps the "Diverse and Always Evolving Needs of Society" Clause), a restriction that is satisfied, the Court instructs, so long as the purpose is "legitimate" and the means "not irrational." This deferential shift in phraseology enables the Court to hold, against all common sense, that a costly urban-renewal project whose stated purpose is a vague promise of new jobs and increased tax revenue, but which is also suspiciously agreeable to the Pfizer Corporation, is for a "public use."

I cannot agree. If such "economic development" takings are for a "public use," any taking is, and the Court has erased the Public Use Clause from our Constitution, as Justice O'Connor powerfully argues in dissent. I do not believe that this Court can eliminate liberties expressly enumerated in the Constitution and therefore join her dissenting opinion.

Regrettably, however, the Court's error runs deeper than this. Today's decision is simply the latest in a string of our cases construing the Public Use Clause to be a virtual nullity, without the slightest nod to its original meaning. In my view, the Public Use Clause, originally understood, is a meaningful limit on the government's eminent domain power. Our cases have strayed from the Clause's original meaning, and I would reconsider them.

There is no justification, however, for affording almost insurmountable deference to legislative conclusions that a use serves a "public use." To begin with, a court owes no deference to a legislature's judgment concerning the quintessentially legal question of whether the government owns, or the public has a legal right to use, the taken property. Even under the "public purpose" interpretation, moreover, it is most implausible that the Framers intended to defer to legislatures as to what satisfies the Public Use Clause, uniquely among all the express provisions of the Bill of Rights. We would not defer to a legislature's determination of the various circumstances that establish, for example, when a search of a home would be reasonable, or when a convicted double-murderer may be shackled during a sentencing proceeding without on-the-record findings, or when state law creates a property interest protected by the Due Process Clause.

Still worse, it is backwards to adopt a searching standard of constitutional review for nontraditional property interests, such as welfare benefits, while deferring to the legislature's determination as to what constitutes a public use when it exercises the power of eminent domain, and thereby invades individuals' traditional rights in real property.

The consequences of today's decision are not difficult to predict, and promise to be harmful. So-called "urban renewal" programs provide some compensation for the properties they take, but no compensation is possible for the subjective value of these lands to the individuals displaced and the indignity inflicted by uprooting them from their homes. Allowing the government to take property solely for public purposes is bad enough, but extending the concept of public purpose to encompass any economically beneficial goal guarantees that these losses will fall disproportionately on poor communities. Those communities are not only systematically less likely to put their lands to the highest and best social use, but are also the least politically powerful. If ever there were justification for intrusive judicial review of constitutional provisions that protect "discrete and insular minorities," United States v. Carolene Products Co. (1938), surely that principle would apply with great force to the powerless groups and individuals the Public Use Clause protects. The deferential standard this Court has adopted for the Public Use Clause is therefore deeply perverse. It encourages "those citizens with disproportionate influence and power in the political process, including large corporations and development firms" to victimize the weak.

The Court relies almost exclusively on this Court's prior cases to derive today's far-reaching, and dangerous, result. But the principles this Court should employ to dispose of this case are found in the Public Use Clause itself, not in Justice Peckham's high opinion of reclamation laws. When faced with a clash of constitutional principle and a line of unreasoned cases wholly divorced from the text, history, and structure of our founding document, we should not hesitate to resolve the tension in favor of the Constitution's original meaning. For the reasons I have given, and for the reasons given in Justice O'Connor's dissent, the conflict of principle raised by this boundless use of the eminent domain power should be resolved in petitioners' favor. I would reverse the judgment of the Connecticut Supreme Court.

Chapter 7

Equal Protection

C. Classifications Based on Race and National Origin

3. Proving the Existence of a Race or National Origin Classification (casebook, p. 653)

The Supreme Court long has held that laws requiring separation of the races are a form of race discrimination that must meet strict scrutiny. Is this also so in prisons? That is the focus of Johnson v. California. It is important to note that the Court does not decide the constitutionality of the California prison regulation, but only announces the legal test and then remands the case for its application.

JOHNSON v. CALIFORNIA
543 U.S. 499 (2005)

Justice O'CONNOR delivered the opinion of the Court.

The California Department of Corrections (CDC) has an unwritten policy of racially segregating prisoners in double cells in reception centers for up to 60 days each time they enter a new correctional facility. We consider whether strict scrutiny is the proper standard of review for an equal protection challenge to that policy.

I

A

CDC institutions house all new male inmates and all male inmates transferred from other state facilities in reception centers for up to 60 days upon their arrival. During that time, prison officials evaluate the inmates to determine their ultimate placement. Double-cell assignments in the reception centers are based on a number of factors, predominantly race. In fact, the CDC has admitted that the chances of an inmate being assigned a cellmate of another race are " '[p]retty close' " to zero percent. The CDC further subdivides prisoners within each racial group. Thus, Japanese-Americans are housed separately from Chinese-Americans, and Northern California Hispanics are separated from Southern California Hispanics.

The CDC's asserted rationale for this practice is that it is necessary to prevent violence caused by racial gangs. It cites numerous incidents of racial violence in CDC facilities and identifies five major prison gangs in the State: Mexican Mafia, Nuestra Familia, Black Guerrilla Family, Aryan Brotherhood, and Nazi Low Riders. The CDC also notes that prison-gang culture is violent and murderous. An associate warden testified that if race were not considered in making initial housing assignments, she is certain there would be racial conflict in the cells and in the yard. Other prison officials also expressed their belief that violence and conflict would result if prisoners were not segregated. The CDC claims that it must therefore segregate all inmates while it determines whether they pose a danger to others.

With the exception of the double cells in reception areas, the rest of the state prison facilities—dining areas, yards, and cells—are fully integrated. After the initial 60-day period, prisoners are allowed to choose their own cellmates. The CDC usually grants inmate requests to be housed together, unless there are security reasons for denying them.

B

Garrison Johnson is an African-American inmate in the custody of the CDC. He has been incarcerated since 1987 and, during that time, has been housed at a number of California prison facilities. Upon his arrival at Folsom prison in 1987, and each time he was transferred to a new facility thereafter, Johnson was double-celled with another African-American inmate.

Johnson filed a complaint pro se in the United States District Court for the Central District of California on February 24, 1995, alleging that the CDC's reception-center housing policy violated his right to equal protection under the Fourteenth Amendment by assigning him cellmates on the basis of his race.

II

A

We have held that "*all* racial classifications [imposed by government] . . . must be analyzed by a reviewing court under strict scrutiny." Adarand Constructors, Inc. v. Peña (1995) (emphasis added). Under strict scrutiny, the government has the burden of proving that racial classifications "are narrowly tailored measures that further compelling governmental interests." We have insisted on strict scrutiny in every context, even for so-called "benign" racial classifications, such as race-conscious university admissions policies, see Grutter v. Bollinger (2003), race-based preferences in government contracts, and race-based district-ing intended to improve minority representation, Shaw v. Reno (1993).

The reasons for strict scrutiny are familiar. Racial classifications raise special fears that they are motivated by an invidious purpose. Thus, we have admonished time and again that, "[a]bsent searching judicial inquiry into the justification for such race-based measures, there is simply no way of determining . . . what classifications are in fact motivated by illegitimate notions of racial inferiority or simple racial politics." Richmond v. J. A. Croson Co. (1989) (plurality opinion). We therefore apply strict scrutiny to all racial classifications to "'smoke out' illegitimate uses of race by assuring that [government] is pursuing a goal important enough to warrant use of a highly suspect tool."

The CDC claims that its policy should be exempt from our categorical rule because it is "neutral"—that is, it "neither benefits nor burdens one group or individual more than any other group or individual." In other words, strict scrutiny should not apply because all prisoners are "equally" segregated. The CDC's argument ignores our repeated command that "racial classifications receive close scrutiny even when they may be said to burden or benefit the races equally." Indeed, we rejected the notion that separate can ever be equal— or "neutral"—50 years ago in Brown v. Board of Education (1954), and we refuse to resurrect it today.

We have previously applied a heightened standard of review in evaluating racial segregation in prisons. In Lee v. Washington (1968) (per curiam), we upheld a three-judge court's decision striking down Alabama's policy of segregation in its prisons.

The need for strict scrutiny is no less important here, where prison officials cite racial violence as the reason for their policy. As we have recognized in the past, racial classifications "threaten to stigmatize individuals by reason of their membership in a racial group and to incite racial hostility." Indeed, by insisting that inmates be housed only with other inmates of the same race, it is possible that prison officials will breed further hostility among prisoners and reinforce racial and ethnic divisions. By perpetuating the notion that race matters most, racial segregation of inmates "may exacerbate the very patterns of [violence that it is] said to counteract."

The CDC's policy is unwritten. Although California claimed at oral argument that two other States follow a similar policy, this assertion was unsubstantiated, and we are unable to confirm or deny its accuracy. Virtually all other States and the Federal Government manage their prison systems without reliance on racial segregation. Federal regulations governing the Federal Bureau of Prisons (BOP) expressly prohibit racial segregation. The United States contends that racial integration actually "leads to less violence in BOP's institutions and better prepares inmates for re-entry into society." Indeed, the United States argues, based on its experience with the BOP, that it is possible to address "concerns of prison security through individualized consideration without the use of racial segregation, unless warranted as a necessary and temporary response to a race riot or other serious threat of race-related violence." As to transferees, in particular, whom the CDC has already evaluated at least once, it is not clear why more individualized determinations are not possible.

Because the CDC's policy is an express racial classification, it is "immediately suspect." We therefore hold that the Court of Appeals erred when it failed to apply strict scrutiny to the CDC's policy and to require the CDC to demonstrate that its policy is narrowly tailored to serve a compelling state interest.

B

The CDC invites us to make an exception to the rule that strict scrutiny applies to all racial classifications, and instead to apply the deferential standard of review articulated in Turner v. Safley (1987), because its segregation policy applies only in the prison context. We decline the invitation. In *Turner*, we considered a claim by Missouri prisoners that regulations restricting inmate marriages and inmate-to-inmate correspondence were unconstitutional. We rejected the prisoners' argument that the regulations should be subject to strict scrutiny, asking instead whether the regulation that burdened the prisoners' fundamental rights was "reasonably related" to "legitimate penological interests."

We have never applied *Turner* to racial classifications. *Turner* itself did not involve any racial classification, and it cast no doubt on *Lee*. We think this unsurprising, as we have applied *Turner*'s reasonable-relationship test only to rights that are "inconsistent with proper incarceration." This is because certain privileges and rights must necessarily be limited in the prison context. Thus, for example, we have relied on *Turner* in addressing First Amendment challenges to prison regulations, including restrictions on freedom of association; limits on inmate correspondence; restrictions on inmates' access to courts; restrictions on receipt of subscription publications; and work rules limiting prisoners' attendance at religious services. We have also applied *Turner* to some due process claims, such as involuntary medication of mentally ill prisoners, and restrictions on the right to marry.

The right not to be discriminated against based on one's race is not susceptible to the logic of *Turner*. It is not a right that need necessarily be compromised for the sake of proper prison administration. On the contrary, compliance with the Fourteenth Amendment's ban on racial discrimination is not only consistent with proper prison administration, but also bolsters the legitimacy of the entire criminal justice system. Race discrimination is "especially pernicious in the administration of justice." And public respect for our system of justice is undermined when the system discriminates based on race. When government officials are permitted to use race as a proxy for gang membership and violence without demonstrating a compelling government interest and proving that their means are narrowly tailored, society as a whole suffers.

In the prison context, when the government's power is at its apex, we think that searching judicial review of racial classifications is necessary to guard against invidious discrimination. Granting the CDC an exemption from the rule that strict scrutiny applies to all racial classifications would undermine our "unceasing efforts to eradicate racial prejudice from our criminal justice system." McCleskey v. Kemp (1987).

The CDC argues that "[d]eference to the particular expertise of prison officials in the difficult task of managing daily prison operations" requires a more relaxed standard of review for its segregation policy. But we have refused to defer to state officials' judgments on race in other areas where those officials traditionally exer-cise substantial discretion. For example, we have held that, despite the broad dis-cretion given to prosecutors when they use their peremptory challenges, using those challenges to strike jurors on the basis of their race is impermissible. Similarly, in the redistricting context, despite the traditional deference given to States when they design their electoral districts, we have subjected redistricting plans to strict scrutiny when States draw district lines based predominantly on race.

We did not relax the standard of review for racial classifications in prison in *Lee*, and we refuse to do so today. Rather, we explicitly reaffirm what we implicitly held in *Lee*: The "necessities of prison security and discipline" are a compelling government interest justifying only those uses of race that are narrowly tailored to address those necessities.

Justice Thomas would subject race-based policies in prisons to *Turner*'s deferential standard of review because, in his view, judgments about whether race-based policies are necessary "are better left in the first instance to the officials who run our Nation's prisons." But *Turner* is too lenient a standard to ferret out invidious uses of race. *Turner* requires only that the policy be "reasonably related" to "legitimate penological interests." *Turner* would allow prison officials to use race-based policies even when there are race-neutral means to accomplish the same goal, and even when the race-based policy does not in practice advance that goal.

For example, in Justice Thomas' world, prison officials could segregate visiting areas on the ground that racial mixing would cause unrest in the racially charged prison atmosphere. Indeed, under Justice Thomas' view, there is no obvious limit to permissible segregation in prisons. It is not readily apparent why, if segregation in reception centers is justified, segregation in the dining halls, yards, and general housing areas is not also permissible. Any of these areas could be the potential site of racial violence. If Justice Thomas' approach were to carry the day, even the blanket segregation policy struck down in *Lee* might stand a chance of survival if prison officials simply asserted that it was necessary to prison management. We therefore reject the *Turner* standard for racial classifications in prisons because it would make rank discrimination too easy to defend.

The CDC protests that strict scrutiny will handcuff prison administrators and render them unable to address legitimate problems of race-based violence in prisons. Not so. Strict scrutiny is not "strict in theory, but fatal in fact." Strict scrutiny does not preclude the ability of prison officials to address the compelling interest in prison safety. Prison administrators, however, will have to demonstrate that any race-based policies are narrowly tailored to that end.

The fact that strict scrutiny applies "says nothing about the ultimate validity of any particular law; that determination is the job of the court applying strict scrutiny." At this juncture, no such determination has been made. On remand, the CDC will have the burden of demonstrating that its policy is narrowly tailored with regard to new inmates as well as transferees. Prisons are dangerous places, and the special circumstances they present may justify racial classifications in some contexts. Such circumstances can be considered in applying strict scrutiny, which is designed to take relevant differences into account.

We do not decide whether the CDC's policy violates the Equal Protection Clause. We hold only that strict scrutiny is the proper standard of review and remand the case to allow the Court of Appeals for the Ninth Circuit, or the District Court, to apply it in the first instance.

Justice STEVENS, dissenting.

In my judgment a state policy of segregating prisoners by race during the first 60 days of their incarceration, as well as the first 60 days after their transfer from one facility to another, violates the Equal Protection Clause of the Fourteenth Amendment. The California Department of Corrections (CDC) has had an ample opportunity to justify its policy during the course of this litigation, but has utterly failed to do so whether judged under strict scrutiny or the more deferential standard set out in Turner v. Safley (1987). The CDC had no incentive in the proceedings below to withhold evidence supporting its policy; nor has the CDC made any offer of proof to suggest that a remand for further factual development would serve any purpose other than to postpone the inevitable. I therefore agree with the submission of the United States as amicus curiae that the Court should hold the policy unconstitutional on the current record.

The CDC's segregation policy is based on a conclusive presumption that housing inmates of different races together creates an unacceptable risk of racial violence. Under the policy's logic, an inmate's race is a proxy for gang membership, and gang membership is a proxy for violence. The CDC, however, has offered scant empirical evidence or expert opinion to justify this use of race under even a minimal level of constitutional scrutiny. The presumption underlying the policy is undoubtedly overbroad. The CDC has made no effort to prove what fraction of new or transferred inmates are members of race-based gangs, nor has it shown more generally that interracial violence is disproportionately greater than intraracial violence in its prisons. Proclivity toward racial violence unquestionably varies from inmate to inmate, yet the CDC applies its blunderbuss policy to all new and transferred inmates housed in double cells regardless of their criminal histories or records of previous incarceration. Under the CDC's policy, for example, two car thieves of different races—neither of whom has any history of gang involvement, or of violence, for that matter— would be barred from being housed together during their first two months of prison. This result derives from the CDC's inflexible judgment that such integrated living conditions are simply too dangerous. This Court has never countenanced such racial prophylaxis.

Given the inherent indignity of segregation and its shameful historical connotations, one might assume that the CDC came to its policy only as a last resort. Distressingly, this is not so: There is no evidence that the CDC has ever experimented with, or even carefully considered, race-neutral methods of achieving its goals. That the policy is unwritten reflects, I think, the evident lack of deliberation that preceded its creation.

Specifically, the CDC has failed to explain why it could not, as an alternative to automatic segregation, rely on an individualized assessment of each inmate's risk of violence when assigning him to a cell in a reception center. The Federal Bureau of Prisons and other state systems do so without any apparent difficulty. For inmates who are being transferred from one facility to another—who represent approximately 85% of those subject to the segregation policy—the CDC can simply examine their prison records to determine if they have any known gang affiliations or if they have ever engaged in or threatened racial violence. For example, the CDC has had an opportunity to observe the petitioner for almost 20 years; surely the CDC could have determined his placement without subjecting him to a period of segregation. For new inmates, assignments can be based on their presentence reports, which contain information about offense conduct, criminal record, and personal history—including any available information about gang affiliations.

Justice THOMAS, with whom Justice SCALIA joins, dissenting.

The questions presented in this case require us to resolve two conflicting lines of precedent. On the one hand, as the Court stresses, this Court has said that "'all racial classifications reviewable under the Equal Protection Clause must be strictly scrutinized.'" Gratz v. Bollinger (2003). On the other, this Court has no less categorically said that "the [relaxed] standard of review we adopted in Turner [v. Safley (1987)] applies to *all* circumstances in which the needs of prison administration implicate constitutional rights." Washington v. Harper (1990) (emphasis added).

Emphasizing the former line of cases, the majority resolves the conflict in favor of strict scrutiny. I disagree. The Constitution has always demanded less within the prison walls. Time and again, even when faced with constitutional rights no less "fundamental" than the right to be free from state-sponsored racial discrimination, we have deferred to the reasonable judgments of officials experienced in running this Nation's prisons. There is good reason for such deference in this case. California oversees roughly 160,000 inmates, in prisons that have been a breeding ground for some of the most violent prison gangs in America—all of them organized along racial lines. In that atmosphere, California racially segregates a portion of its inmates, in a part of its prisons, for brief periods of up to 60 days, until the State can arrange permanent housing. The majority is concerned with sparing inmates the indignity and stigma of racial discrimination. California is concerned with their safety and saving their lives. I respectfully dissent.

The majority decides this case without addressing the problems that racial violence poses for wardens, guards, and inmates throughout the federal and state prison systems. But that is the core of California's justification for its policy: It maintains that, if it does not racially separate new cellmates thrown together in close confines during their initial admission or transfer, violence will erupt. The dangers California seeks to prevent are real.

The problem of prison gangs is not unique to California, but California has a history like no other. There are at least five major gangs in this country—the Aryan Brotherhood, the Black Guerrilla Family, the Mexican Mafia, La Nuestra Familia, and the Texas Syndicate—all of which originated in California's prisons. Unsurprisingly, then, California has the largest number of gang-related inmates of any correctional system in the country, including the Federal Government.

As their very names suggest, prison gangs like the Aryan Brotherhood and the Black Guerrilla Family organize themselves along racial lines, and these gangs perpetuate hate and violence. Interracial murders and assaults among inmates perpetrated by these gangs are common. And, again, that brutality is particularly severe in California's prisons.

It is against this backdrop of pervasive racial violence that California racially segregates inmates in the reception centers' double cells, for brief periods of up to 60 days, until such time as the State can assign permanent housing. Viewed in that context and in light of the four factors enunciated in *Turner*, California's policy is constitutional: The CDC's policy is reasonably related to a legitimate penological interest; alternative means of exercising the restricted right remain open to inmates; racially integrating double cells might negatively impact prison inmates, staff, and administrators; and there are no obvious, easy alternatives to the CDC's policy.

In place of the Court's usual deference, the majority gives conclusive force to its own guesswork about "proper" prison administration. It hypothesizes that California's policy might incite, rather than diminish, racial hostility. The majority's speculations are implausible. New arrivals have a strong interest in promptly convincing other inmates of their willingness to use violent force. In any event, the majority's guesswork falls far short of the compelling showing needed to overcome the deference we owe to prison administrators.

4. Remedies: The Problem of School Segregation (casebook, p. 692)

In *Parents Involved in Community Schools v. Seattle School Dist. No. 1*, the Court considered whether school systems may use race as a factor in assigning students to schools for desegregation purposes. In reading the case, it is important to note that most of Chief Justice Roberts' opinion is for the majority, but for part Justice Kennedy disagreed and concurred in the judgment. The key question after this case is how, if at all, may school systems use race as a factor in formulating remedies for segregation. It also is worth considering the implications of the case for the ability of the government to use race to benefit minorities and the likely future of *Grutter v. Bollinger* [casebook p. 722], which is discussed by all of the opinions in this case.

PARENTS INVOLVED IN COMMUNITY SCHOOLS v.
SEATTLE SCHOOL DIST. NO. 1
127 S.Ct. 2738 (2007)

Chief Justice ROBERTS announced the judgment of the Court, and delivered the opinion of the Court with respect to Parts I, II, III-A, and III-C, and an opinion with respect to Parts III-B and IV, in which Justices SCALIA, THOMAS, and ALITO join.

The school districts in these cases voluntarily adopted student assignment plans that rely upon race to determine which public schools certain children may attend. The Seattle school district classifies children as white or nonwhite; the Jefferson County school district as black or "other." In Seattle, this racial classification is used to allocate slots in oversubscribed high schools. In Jefferson County, it is used to make certain elementary school assignments and to rule on transfer requests. In each case, the school district relies upon an individual student's race in assigning that student to a particular school, so that the racial balance at the school falls within a predetermined range based on the racial composition of the school district as a whole. Parents of students denied assignment to particular schools under these plans solely because of their race brought suit, contending that allocating children to different public schools on the basis of race violated the Fourteenth Amendment guarantee of equal protection. The Courts of Appeals below upheld the plans. We granted certiorari, and now reverse.

I

Both cases present the same underlying legal question—whether a public school that had not operated legally segregated schools or has been found to be unitary may choose to classify students by race and rely upon that classification in making school assignments. Although we examine the plans under the same legal framework, the specifics of the two plans, and the circumstances surrounding their adoption, are in some respects quite different.

A

Seattle School District No. 1 operates 10 regular public high schools. In 1998, it adopted the plan at issue in this case for assigning students to these schools. The plan allows incoming ninth graders to choose from among any of the district's high schools, ranking however many schools they wish in order of preference.

Some schools are more popular than others. If too many students list the same school as their first choice, the district employs a series of "tiebreakers" to determine who will fill the open slots at the oversubscribed school. The first tiebreaker selects for admission students who have a sibling currently enrolled in the chosen school. The next tiebreaker depends upon the racial composition of the particular school and the race of the individual student. In the district's public schools approximately 41 percent of enrolled students are white; the remaining 59 percent, comprising all other racial groups, are classified by Seattle for assignment purposes as nonwhite. If an oversubscribed school is not within 10 percentage points of the district's overall white/nonwhite racial balance, it is what the district calls "integration positive," and the district employs a tiebreaker that selects for assignment students whose race "will serve to bring the school into balance." If it is still necessary to select students for the school after using the racial tiebreaker, the next tiebreaker is the geographic proximity of the school to the student's residence.

Seattle has never operated segregated schools—legally separate schools for students of different races—nor has it ever been subject to court-ordered desegregation. It nonetheless employs the racial tiebreaker in an attempt to address the effects of racially identifiable housing patterns on school assignments. Most white students live in the northern part of Seattle, most students of other racial backgrounds in the southern part.

B

Jefferson County Public Schools operates the public school system in metropolitan Louisville, Kentucky. In 1973 a federal court found that Jefferson County had maintained a segregated school system, and in 1975 the District Court entered a desegregation decree. Jefferson County operated under this decree until 2000, when the District Court dissolved the decree after finding that the district had achieved unitary status by eliminating "[t]o the greatest extent practicable" the vestiges of its prior policy of segregation.

In 2001, after the decree had been dissolved, Jefferson County adopted the voluntary student assignment plan at issue in this case. Approximately 34 percent of the district's 97,000 students are black; most of the remaining 66 percent are white. The plan requires all nonmagnet schools to maintain a minimum black enrollment of 15 percent, and a maximum black enrollment of 50 percent.

At the elementary school level, based on his or her address, each student is designated a "resides" school to which students within a specific geographic area are assigned; elementary resides schools are "grouped into clusters in order to facilitate integration." The district assigns students to nonmagnet schools in one of two ways: Parents of kindergartners, first-graders, and students new to the district may submit an application indicating a first and second choice among the schools within their cluster; students who do not submit such an application are assigned within the cluster by the district. "Decisions to assign students to schools within each cluster are based on available space within the schools and the racial guidelines in the District's current student assignment plan." If a school has reached the "extremes of the racial guidelines," a student whose race would contribute to the school's racial imbalance will not be assigned there. After assignment, students at all grade levels are permitted to apply to transfer between nonmagnet schools in the district. Transfers may be requested for any number of reasons, and may be denied because of lack of available space or on the basis of the racial guidelines.

II

[The Court found that the plaintiffs had standing because they alleged that individuals had been denied being able to attend schools because of their race. Chief Justice Roberts explained: "As we have held, one form of injury under the Equal Protection Clause is being forced to compete in a race-based system that may prejudice the plaintiff, an injury that the members of Parents Involved can validly claim on behalf of their children."]

III

A

It is well established that when the government distributes burdens or benefits on the basis of individual racial classifications, that action is reviewed under strict scrutiny. In order to satisfy this searching standard of review, the school districts must demonstrate that the use of individual racial classifications in the assignment plans here under review is "narrowly tailored" to achieve a "compelling" government interest.

Without attempting in these cases to set forth all the interests a school district might assert, it suffices to note that our prior cases, in evaluating the use of racial classifications in the school context, have recognized two interests that qualify as compelling. The first is the compelling interest of remedying the effects of past intentional discrimination. Yet the Seattle public schools have not shown that they were ever segregated by law, and were not subject to court-ordered desegregation decrees. The Jefferson County public schools were previously segregated by law and were subject to a desegregation decree entered in 1975. In 2000, the District Court that entered that decree dissolved it, finding that Jefferson County had "eliminated the vestiges associated with the former policy of segregation and its pernicious effects," and thus had achieved "unitary" status. Jefferson County accordingly does not rely upon an interest in remedying the effects of past intentional discrimination in defending its present use of race in assigning students.

Nor could it. We have emphasized that the harm being remedied by mandatory desegregation plans is the harm that is traceable to segregation, and that "the Constitution is not violated by racial imbalance in the schools, without more." Once Jefferson County achieved unitary status, it had remedied the constitutional wrong that allowed race-based assignments. Any continued use of race must be justified on some other basis.

The second government interest we have recognized as compelling for purposes of strict scrutiny is the interest in diversity in higher education upheld in *Grutter* [*v. Bollinger* (2003)]. The specific interest found compelling in *Grutter* was student body diversity "in the context of higher education." The diversity interest was not focused on race alone but encompassed "all factors that may contribute to student body diversity." The entire gist of the analysis in *Grutter* was that the admissions program at issue there focused on each applicant as an individual, and not simply as a member of a particular racial group. The classification of applicants by race upheld in *Grutter* was only as part of a highly individualized, holistic review.

In the present cases, by contrast, race is not considered as part of a broader effort to achieve "exposure to widely diverse people, cultures, ideas, and viewpoints"; race, for some students, is determinative standing alone. The districts argue that other factors, such as student preferences, affect assignment decisions under their plans, but under each plan when race comes into play, it is decisive by itself. It is not simply one factor weighed with others in reaching a decision, as in *Grutter*; it is the factor. Like the University of Michigan undergraduate plan struck down in *Gratz* [*v. Bollinger* (2003)], the plans here "do not provide for a meaningful individualized review of applicants" but instead rely on racial classifications in a "nonindividualized, mechanical" way.

Even when it comes to race, the plans here employ only a limited notion of diversity, viewing race exclusively in white/nonwhite terms in Seattle and black/ "other" terms in Jefferson County. The Seattle "Board Statement Reaffirming Diversity Rationale" speaks of the "inherent educational value" in "[p]roviding students the opportunity to attend schools with diverse student enrollment." But under the Seattle plan, a school with 50 percent Asian-American students and 50 percent white students but no African-American, Native-American, or Latino students would qualify as balanced, while a school with 30 percent Asian-American, 25 percent African-American, 25 percent Latino, and 20 percent white students would not. It is hard to understand how a plan that could allow these results can be viewed as being concerned with achieving enrollment that is " 'broadly diverse.' "

In upholding the admissions plan in *Grutter*, though, this Court relied upon considerations unique to institutions of higher education, noting that in light of "the expansive freedoms of speech and thought associated with the university environment, universities occupy a special niche in our constitutional tradition." The Court explained that "[c]ontext matters" in applying strict scrutiny, and repeatedly noted that it was addressing the use of race "in the context of higher education." The Court in *Grutter* expressly articulated key limitations on its holding—defining a specific type of broad-based diversity and noting the unique context of higher education-but these limitations were largely disregarded by the lower courts in extending *Grutter* to uphold race-based assignments in elementary and secondary schools. The present cases are not governed by *Grutter*.

B

Perhaps recognizing that reliance on *Grutter* cannot sustain their plans, both school districts assert additional interests, distinct from the interest upheld in *Grutter*, to justify their race-based assignments. In briefing and argument before this Court, Seattle contends that its use of race helps to reduce racial concentration in schools and to ensure that racially concentrated housing patterns do not prevent nonwhite students from having access to the most desirable schools. Jefferson County has articulated a similar goal, phrasing its interest in terms of educating its students "in a racially integrated environment." Each school district argues that educational and broader socialization benefits flow from a racially diverse learning environment, and each contends that because the diversity they seek is racial diversity—not the broader diversity at issue in *Grutter*—it makes sense to promote that interest directly by relying on race alone.

The parties and their amici dispute whether racial diversity in schools in fact has a marked impact on test scores and other objective yardsticks or achieves intangible socialization benefits. The debate is not one we need to resolve, however, because it is clear that the racial classifications employed by the districts are not narrowly tailored to the goal of achieving the educational and social benefits asserted to flow from racial diversity. In design and operation, the plans are directed only to racial balance, pure and simple, an objective this Court has repeatedly condemned as illegitimate.

The districts offer no evidence that the level of racial diversity necessary to achieve the asserted educational benefits happens to coincide with the racial demographics of the respective school districts—or rather the white/nonwhite or black/"other" balance of the districts, since that is the only diversity addressed by the plans. Indeed, in its brief Seattle simply assumes that the educational benefits track the racial breakdown of the district.

This working backward to achieve a particular type of racial balance, rather than working forward from some demonstration of the level of diversity that provides the purported benefits, is a fatal flaw under our existing precedent. We have many times over reaffirmed that "[r]acial balance is not to be achieved for its own sake."

Accepting racial balancing as a compelling state interest would justify the imposition of racial proportionality throughout American society, contrary to our repeated recognition that "[a]t the heart of the Constitution's guarantee of equal protection lies the simple command that the Government must treat citizens as individuals, not as simply components of a racial, religious, sexual or national class." Allowing racial balancing as a compelling end in itself would "effectively assur[e] that race will always be relevant in American life, and that the 'ultimate goal' of 'eliminating entirely from governmental decisionmaking such irrelevant factors as a human being's race' will never be achieved."

The principle that racial balancing is not permitted is one of substance, not semantics. Racial balancing is not transformed from "patently unconstitutional" to a compelling state interest simply by relabeling it "racial diversity." While the school districts use various verbal formulations to describe the interest they seek to promote—racial diversity, avoidance of racial isolation, racial integration—they offer no definition of the interest that suggests it differs from racial balance.

C

The districts assert, as they must, that the way in which they have employed individual racial classifications is necessary to achieve their stated ends. The minimal effect these classifications have on student assignments, however, suggests that other means would be effective. Seattle's racial tiebreaker results, in the end, only in shifting a small number of students between schools. Approximately 307 student assignments were affected by the racial tiebreaker in 2000-2001. In over one-third of the assignments affected by the racial tiebreaker the use of race in the end made no difference, and the district could identify only 52 students who were ultimately affected adversely by the racial tiebreaker in that it resulted in assignment to a school they had not listed as a preference and to which they would not otherwise have been assigned. Similarly, Jefferson County's use of racial classifications has only a minimal effect on the assignment of students.

While we do not suggest that greater use of race would be preferable, the minimal impact of the districts' racial classifications on school enrollment casts doubt on the necessity of using racial classifications. Classifying and assigning schoolchildren according to a binary conception of race is an extreme approach in light of our precedents and our Nation's history of using race in public schools, and requires more than such an amorphous end to justify it.

The districts have also failed to show that they considered methods other than explicit racial classifications to achieve their stated goals. Narrow tailoring requires "serious, good faith consideration of workable race-neutral alternatives," and yet in Seattle several alternative assignment plans—many of which would not have used express racial classifications—were rejected with little or no consideration. Jefferson County has failed to present any evidence that it considered alternatives, even though the district already claims that its goals are achieved primarily through means other than the racial classifications.

IV

Justice Breyer's dissent takes a different approach to these cases, one that fails to ground the result it would reach in law. Instead, it selectively relies on inapplicable precedent and even dicta while dismissing contrary holdings, alters and misapplies our well-established legal framework for assessing equal protection challenges to express racial classifications, and greatly exaggerates the consequences of today's decision.

To begin with, Justice Breyer seeks to justify the plans at issue under our precedents recognizing the compelling interest in remedying past intentional discrimination. Not even the school districts go this far, and for good reason. The distinction between segregation by state action and racial imbalance caused by other factors has been central to our jurisprudence in this area for generations. The dissent elides this distinction between de jure and de facto segregation, casually intimates that Seattle's school attendance patterns reflect illegal segregation, and fails to credit the judicial determination—under the most rigorous standard—that Jefferson County had eliminated the vestiges of prior segregation. The dissent thus alters in fundamental ways not only the facts presented here but the established law.

Justice Breyer's position comes down to a familiar claim: The end justifies the means. He admits that "there is a cost in applying 'a state-mandated racial label,'" but he is confident that the cost is worth paying. Our established strict scrutiny test for racial classifications, however, insists on "detailed examination, both as to ends and as to means." Simply because the school districts may seek a worthy goal does not mean they are free to discriminate on the basis of race to achieve it, or that their racial classifications should be subject to less exacting scrutiny.

In keeping with his view that strict scrutiny should not apply, Justice Breyer repeatedly urges deference to local school boards on these issues. Such deference "is fundamentally at odds with our equal protection jurisprudence. We put the burden on state actors to demonstrate that their race-based policies are justified."

* * *

If the need for the racial classifications embraced by the school districts is unclear, even on the districts' own terms, the costs are undeniable. "[D]istinctions between citizens solely because of their ancestry are by their very nature odious to a free people whose institutions are founded upon the doctrine of equality." Government action dividing us by race is inherently suspect because such classifications promote "notions of racial inferiority and lead to a politics of racial hostility," "reinforce the belief, held by too many for too much of our history, that individuals should be judged by the color of their skin," and "endorse race-based reasoning and the conception of a Nation divided into racial blocs, thus contributing to an escalation of racial hostility and conflict."

All this is true enough in the contexts in which these statements were made-government contracting, voting districts, allocation of broadcast licenses, and electing state officers—but when it comes to using race to assign children to schools, history will be heard. In *Brown v. Board of Education* (1954) (*Brown I*), we held that segregation deprived black children of equal educational opportunities regardless of whether school facilities and other tangible factors were equal, because government classification and separation on grounds of race themselves denoted inferiority. The next Term, we accordingly stated that "full compliance" with *Brown I* required school districts "to achieve a system of determining admission to the public schools on a nonracial basis."

The parties and their amici debate which side is more faithful to the heritage of *Brown*, but the position of the plaintiffs in *Brown* was spelled out in their brief and could not have been clearer: "[T]he Fourteenth Amendment prevents states from according differential treatment to American children on the basis of their color or race." Brief for Appellants in Nos. 1, 2, and 4 and for Respondents in No. 10 on Reargument in *Brown I*, O.T.1953, p. 15 (Summary of Argument). What do the racial classifications at issue here do, if not accord differential treatment on the basis of race? As counsel who appeared before this Court for the plaintiffs in *Brown* put it: "We have one fundamental contention which we will seek to develop in the course of this argument, and that contention is that no State has any authority under the equal-protection clause of the Fourteenth Amendment to use race as a factor in affording educational opportunities among its citizens." Tr. of Oral Arg. in *Brown I*, p. 7 (Robert L. Carter, Dec. 9, 1952). There is no ambiguity in that statement. And it was that position that prevailed in this Court, which emphasized in its remedial opinion that what was "[a]t stake is the personal interest of the plaintiffs in admission to public schools as soon as practicable on a nondiscriminatory basis," and what was required was "determining admission to the public schools on a nonracial basis." *Brown II*. What do the racial classifications do in these cases, if not determine admission to a public school on a racial basis?

Before *Brown*, schoolchildren were told where they could and could not go to school based on the color of their skin. The school districts in these cases have not carried the heavy burden of demonstrating that we should allow this once again—even for very different reasons. For schools that never segregated on the basis of race, such as Seattle, or that have removed the vestiges of past segregation, such as Jefferson County, the way "to achieve a system of determining admission to the public schools on a nonracial basis," is to stop assigning students on a racial basis. The way to stop discrimination on the basis of race is to stop discriminating on the basis of race.

Justice THOMAS, concurring.

Today, the Court holds that state entities may not experiment with race-based means to achieve ends they deem socially desirable. I wholly concur in the Chief Justice's opinion. I write separately to address several of the contentions in Justice BREYER's dissent. Contrary to the dissent's arguments, resegregation is not occurring in Seattle or Louisville; these school boards have no present interest in remedying past segregation; and these race-based student-assignment programs do not serve any compelling state interest. Accordingly, the plans are unconstitutional. Disfavoring a color-blind interpretation of the Constitution, the dissent would give school boards a free hand to make decisions on the basis of race—an approach reminiscent of that advocated by the segregationists in *Brown v. Board of Education* (1954). This approach is just as wrong today as it was a half-century ago. The Constitution and our cases require us to be much more demanding before permitting local school boards to make decisions based on race.

The dissent repeatedly claims that the school districts are threatened with resegregation and that they will succumb to that threat if these plans are declared unconstitutional. It also argues that these plans can be justified as part of the school boards' attempts to "eradicat[e] earlier school segregation." Contrary to the dissent's rhetoric, neither of these school districts is threatened with resegregation, and neither is constitutionally compelled or permitted to undertake race-based remediation. Racial imbalance is not segregation, and the mere incantation of terms like resegregation and remediation cannot make up the difference.

Although there is arguably a danger of racial imbalance in schools in Seattle and Louisville, there is no danger of resegregation. No one contends that Seattle has established or that Louisville has reestablished a dual school system that separates students on the basis of race. The statistics cited in the dissent are not to the contrary. At most, those statistics show a national trend toward classroom racial imbalance. However, racial imbalance without intentional state action to separate the races does not amount to segregation. To raise the specter of resegregation to defend these programs is to ignore the meaning of the word and the nature of the cases before us.

Lacking a cognizable interest in remediation, neither of these plans can survive strict scrutiny because neither plan serves a genuinely compelling state interest. The dissent avoids reaching that conclusion by unquestioningly accepting the assertions of selected social scientists while completely ignoring the fact that those assertions are the subject of fervent debate. Ultimately, the dissent's entire analysis is corrupted by the considerations that lead it initially to question whether strict scrutiny should apply at all. What emerges is a version of "strict scrutiny" that combines hollow assurances of harmlessness with reflexive acceptance of conventional wisdom. When it comes to government race-based decisionmaking, the Constitution demands more.

Though the dissent admits to discomfort in applying strict scrutiny to these plans, it claims to have nonetheless applied that exacting standard. But in its search for a compelling interest, the dissent casually accepts even the most tenuous interests asserted on behalf of the plans, grouping them all under the term "'integration.'"

The dissent asserts that racially balanced schools improve educational outcomes for black children. In support, the dissent unquestioningly cites certain social science research to support propositions that are hotly disputed among social scientists. In reality, it is far from apparent that coerced racial mixing has any educational benefits, much less that integration is necessary to black achievement.

Scholars have differing opinions as to whether educational benefits arise from racial balancing. Some have concluded that black students receive genuine educational benefits. Add to the inconclusive social science the fact of black achievement in "racially isolated" environments. Before *Brown*, the most prominent example of an exemplary black school was Dunbar High School. Dunbar is by no means an isolated example. Given this tenuous relationship between forced racial mixing and improved educational results for black children, the dissent cannot plausibly maintain that an educational element supports the integration interest, let alone makes it compelling.

It should escape no one that behind Justice Breyer's veil of judicial modesty hides an inflated role for the Federal Judiciary. The dissent's approach confers on judges the power to say what sorts of discrimination are benign and which are invidious. Having made that determination (based on no objective measure that I can detect), a judge following the dissent's approach will set the level of scrutiny to achieve the desired result. Only then must the judge defer to a democratic majority. In my view, to defer to one's preferred result is not to defer at all.

Most of the dissent's criticisms of today's result can be traced to its rejection of the color-blind Constitution. The dissent attempts to marginalize the notion of a color-blind Constitution by consigning it to me and Members of today's plurality. But I am quite comfortable in the company I keep. My view of the Constitution is Justice Harlan's view in *Plessy*: "Our Constitution is color-blind, and neither knows nor tolerates classes among citizens." And my view was the rallying cry for the lawyers who litigated *Brown*.

The plans before us base school assignment decisions on students' race. Because "[o]ur Constitution is color-blind, and neither knows nor tolerates classes among citizens," such race-based decisionmaking is unconstitutional. *Plessy* [*v. Ferguson* (1896)].

Justice KENNEDY, concurring in part and concurring in the judgment.

The Nation's schools strive to teach that our strength comes from people of different races, creeds, and cultures uniting in commitment to the freedom of all. In these cases two school districts in different parts of the country seek to teach that principle by having classrooms that reflect the racial makeup of the surrounding community. That the school districts consider these plans to be necessary should remind us our highest aspirations are yet unfulfilled. But the solutions mandated by these school districts must themselves be lawful. To make race matter now so that it might not matter later may entrench the very prejudices we seek to overcome. In my view the state-mandated racial classifications at issue, official labels proclaiming the race of all persons in a broad class of citizens—elementary school students in one case, high school students in another—are unconstitutional as the cases now come to us.

I

The dissent finds that the school districts have identified a compelling interest in increasing diversity, including for the purpose of avoiding racial isolation. The plurality, by contrast, does not acknowledge that the school districts have identified a compelling interest here. For this reason, among others, I do not join Parts III-B and IV. Diversity, depending on its meaning and definition, is a compelling educational goal a school district may pursue.

Our Nation from the inception has sought to preserve and expand the promise of liberty and equality on which it was founded. Today we enjoy a society that is remarkable in its openness and opportunity. Yet our tradition is to go beyond present achievements, however significant, and to recognize and confront the flaws and injustices that remain. This is especially true when we seek assurance that opportunity is not denied on account of race. The enduring hope is that race should not matter; the reality is that too often it does.

This is by way of preface to my respectful submission that parts of the opinion by the Chief Justice imply an all-too-unyielding insistence that race cannot be a factor in instances when, in my view, it may be taken into account. The plurality opinion is too dismissive of the legitimate interest government has in ensuring all people have equal opportunity regardless of their race. The plurality's postulate that "[t]he way to stop discrimination on the basis of race is to stop discriminating on the basis of race," is not sufficient to decide these cases. Fifty years of experience since *Brown v. Board of Education* (1954), should teach us that the problem before us defies so easy a solution. School districts can seek to reach *Brown's* objective of equal educational opportunity. The plurality opinion is at least open to the interpretation that the Constitution requires school districts to ignore the problem of de facto resegregation in schooling. I cannot endorse that conclusion. To the extent the plurality opinion suggests the Constitution mandates that state and local school authorities must accept the status quo of racial isolation in schools, it is, in my view, profoundly mistaken.

The statement by Justice Harlan that "[o]ur Constitution is color-blind" was most certainly justified in the context of his dissent in *Plessy v. Ferguson* (1896). The Court's decision in that case was a grievous error it took far too long to overrule. *Plessy*, of course, concerned official classification by race applicable to all persons who sought to use railway carriages. And, as an aspiration, Justice Harlan's axiom must command our assent. In the real world, it is regrettable to say, it cannot be a universal constitutional principle.

In the administration of public schools by the state and local authorities it is permissible to consider the racial makeup of schools and to adopt general policies to encourage a diverse student body, one aspect of which is its racial composition. If school authorities are concerned that the student-body compositions of certain schools interfere with the objective of offering an equal educational opportunity to all of their students, they are free to devise race-conscious measures to address the problem in a general way and without treating each student in different fashion solely on the basis of a systematic, individual typing by race.

School boards may pursue the goal of bringing together students of diverse backgrounds and races through other means, including strategic site selection of new schools; drawing attendance zones with general recognition of the demographics of neighborhoods; allocating resources for special programs; recruiting students and faculty in a targeted fashion; and tracking enrollments, performance, and other statistics by race. These mechanisms are race conscious but do not lead to different treatment based on a classification that tells each student he or she is to be defined by race, so it is unlikely any of them would demand strict scrutiny to be found permissible. Executive and legislative branches, which for generations now have considered these types of policies and procedures, should be permitted to employ them with candor and with confidence that a constitutional violation does not occur whenever a decision-maker considers the impact a given approach might have on students of different races. Assigning to each student a personal designation according to a crude system of individual racial classifications is quite a different matter; and the legal analysis changes accordingly.

[II]

The dissent rests on the assumptions that these sweeping race-based classifications of persons are permitted by existing precedents; that its confident endorsement of race categories for each child in a large segment of the community presents no danger to individual freedom in other, prospective realms of governmental regulation; and that the racial classifications used here cause no hurt or anger of the type the Constitution prevents. Each of these premises is, in my respectful view, incorrect.

As to the dissent, the general conclusions upon which it relies have no principled limit and would result in the broad acceptance of governmental racial classifications in areas far afield from schooling. The dissent's permissive strict scrutiny (which bears more than a passing resemblance to rational-basis review) could invite widespread governmental deployment of racial classifications. There is every reason to think that, if the dissent's rationale were accepted, Congress, assuming an otherwise proper exercise of its spending authority or commerce power, could mandate either the Seattle or the Jefferson County plans nationwide. There seems to be no principled rule, moreover, to limit the dissent's rationale to the context of public schools.

To uphold these programs the Court is asked to brush aside two concepts of central importance for determining the validity of laws and decrees designed to alleviate the hurt and adverse consequences resulting from race discrimination. The first is the difference between de jure and de facto segregation; the second, the presumptive invalidity of a State's use of racial classifications to differentiate its treatment of individuals.

Though this may oversimplify the matter a bit, one of the main concerns underlying those opinions was this: If it is legitimate for school authorities to work to avoid racial isolation in their schools, must they do so only by indirection and general policies? Does the Constitution mandate this inefficient result? Why may the authorities not recognize the problem in candid fashion and solve it altogether through resort to direct assignments based on student racial classifications? So, the argument proceeds, if race is the problem, then perhaps race is the solution.

The argument ignores the dangers presented by individual classifications, dangers that are not as pressing when the same ends are achieved by more indirect means. When the government classifies an individual by race, it must first define what it means to be of a race. Who exactly is white and who is nonwhite? To be forced to live under a state-mandated racial label is inconsistent with the dignity of individuals in our society. And it is a label that an individual is powerless to change. Governmental classifications that command people to march in different directions based on racial typologies can cause a new divisiveness. The practice can lead to corrosive discourse, where race serves not as an element of our diverse heritage but instead as a bargaining chip in the political process. On the other hand race-conscious measures that do not rely on differential treatment based on individual classifications present these problems to a lesser degree.

The idea that if race is the problem, race is the instrument with which to solve it cannot be accepted as an analytical leap forward. And if this is a frustrating duality of the Equal Protection Clause it simply reflects the duality of our history and our attempts to promote freedom in a world that sometimes seems set against it. Under our Constitution the individual, child or adult, can find his own identity, can define her own persona, without state intervention that classifies on the basis of his race or the color of her skin.

This Nation has a moral and ethical obligation to fulfill its historic commitment to creating an integrated society that ensures equal opportunity for all of its children. A compelling interest exists in avoiding racial isolation, an interest that a school district, in its discretion and expertise, may choose to pursue. Likewise, a district may consider it a compelling interest to achieve a diverse student population. Race may be one component of that diversity, but other demographic factors, plus special talents and needs, should also be considered. What the government is not permitted to do, absent a showing of necessity not made here, is to classify every student on the basis of race and to assign each of them to schools based on that classification. Crude measures of this sort threaten to reduce children to racial chits valued and traded according to one school's supply and another's demand.

The decision today should not prevent school districts from continuing the important work of bringing together students of different racial, ethnic, and economic backgrounds. Due to a variety of factors—some influenced by government, some not—neighborhoods in our communities do not reflect the diversity of our Nation as a whole. Those entrusted with directing our public schools can bring to bear the creativity of experts, parents, administrators, and other concerned citizens to find a way to achieve the compelling interests they face without resorting to widespread governmental allocation of benefits and burdens on the basis of racial classifications.

Justice STEVENS, dissenting.

There is a cruel irony in the Chief Justice's reliance on our decision in *Brown v. Board of Education* (1955). The first sentence in the concluding paragraph of his opinion states: "Before *Brown*, schoolchildren were told where they could and could not go to school based on the color of their skin." This sentence reminds me of Anatole France's observation: "[T]he majestic equality of the la[w], forbid[s] rich and poor alike to sleep under bridges, to beg in the streets, and to steal their bread." The Chief Justuce fails to note that it was only black schoolchildren who were so ordered; indeed, the history books do not tell stories of white children struggling to attend black schools. In this and other ways, the Chief Justice rewrites the history of one of this Court's most important decisions.

Justice BREYER, with whom Justice STEVENS, Justice SOUTER, and Justice GINSBURG join, dissenting.

These cases consider the longstanding efforts of two local school boards to integrate their public schools. The school board plans before us resemble many others adopted in the last 50 years by primary and secondary schools throughout the Nation. All of those plans represent local efforts to bring about the kind of racially integrated education that *Brown v. Board of Education* (1954), long ago promised—efforts that this Court has repeatedly required, permitted, and encouraged local authorities to undertake. This Court has recognized that the public interests at stake in such cases are "compelling." We have approved of "narrowly tailored" plans that are no less race-conscious than the plans before us. And we have understood that the Constitution permits local communities to adopt desegregation plans even where it does not require them to do so.

The plurality pays inadequate attention to this law, to past opinions' rationales, their language, and the contexts in which they arise. As a result, it reverses course and reaches the wrong conclusion. In doing so, it distorts precedent, it misapplies the relevant constitutional principles, it announces legal rules that will obstruct efforts by state and local governments to deal effectively with the growing resegregation of public schools, it threatens to substitute for present calm a disruptive round of race-related litigation, and it undermines *Brown's* promise of integrated primary and secondary education that local communities have sought to make a reality. This cannot be justified in the name of the Equal Protection Clause.

I

Overall these efforts brought about considerable racial integration. More recently, however, progress has stalled. Between 1968 and 1980, the number of black children attending a school where minority children constituted more than half of the school fell from 77% to 63% in the Nation (from 81% to 57% in the South) but then reversed direction by the year 2000, rising from 63% to 72% in the Nation (from 57% to 69% in the South). Similarly, between 1968 and 1980, the number of black children attending schools that were more than 90% minority fell from 64% to 33% in the Nation (from 78% to 23% in the South), but that too reversed direction, rising by the year 2000 from 33% to 37% in the Nation (from 23% to 31% in the South). As of 2002, almost 2.4 million students, or over 5% of all public school enrollment, attended schools with a white population of less than 1%. Of these, 2.3 million were black and Latino students, and only 72,000 were white. Today, more than one in six black children attend a school that is 99-100% minority. In light of the evident risk of a return to school systems that are in fact (though not in law) resegregated, many school districts have felt a need to maintain or to extend their integration efforts.

The upshot is that myriad school districts operating in myriad circumstances have devised myriad plans, often with race-conscious elements, all for the sake of eradicating earlier school segregation, bringing about integration, or preventing retrogression. Seattle and Louisville are two such districts, and the histories of their present plans set forth typical school integration stories.

First, the school districts' plans serve "compelling interests" and are "narrowly tailored" on any reasonable definition of those terms. Second, the distinction between de jure segregation (caused by school systems) and de facto segregation (caused, e.g., by housing patterns or generalized societal discrimination) is meaningless in the present context, thereby dooming the plurality's endeavor to find support for its views in that distinction. Third, real-world efforts to substitute racially diverse for racially segregated schools (however caused) are complex, to the point where the Constitution cannot plausibly be interpreted to rule out categorically all local efforts to use means that are "conscious" of the race of individuals.

In both Seattle and Louisville, the local school districts began with schools that were highly segregated in fact. In both cities plaintiffs filed lawsuits claiming unconstitutional segregation.

[Justice Breyer then described in detail the history of segregation in the Seattle and Louisville school systems.]

II

A longstanding and unbroken line of legal authority tells us that the Equal Protection Clause permits local school boards to use race-conscious criteria to achieve positive race-related goals, even when the Constitution does not compel it. Because of its importance, I shall repeat what this Court said about the matter in Swann. Chief Justice Burger, on behalf of a unanimous Court in a case of exceptional importance, wrote: "School authorities are traditionally charged with broad power to formulate and implement educational policy and might well conclude, for example, that in order to prepare students to live in a pluralistic society each school should have a prescribed ratio of Negro to white students reflecting the proportion for the district as a whole. To do this as an educational policy is within the broad discretionary powers of school authorities."

The statement was not a technical holding in the case. But the Court set forth in *Swann* a basic principle of constitutional law—a principle of law that has found "wide acceptance in the legal culture." If there were doubts before *Swann* was decided, they did not survive this Court's decision. Numerous state and federal courts explicitly relied upon *Swann*'s guidance for decades to follow.

Courts are not alone in accepting as constitutionally valid the legal principle that *Swann* enunciated—i.e., that the government may voluntarily adopt race-conscious measures to improve conditions of race even when it is not under a constitutional obligation to do so. That principle has been accepted by every branch of government and is rooted in the history of the Equal Protection Clause itself.

There is reason to believe that those who drafted an Amendment with this basic purpose in mind would have understood the legal and practical difference between the use of race-conscious criteria in defiance of that purpose, namely to keep the races apart, and the use of race-conscious criteria to further that purpose, namely to bring the races together.

Here, the context is one in which school districts seek to advance or to maintain racial integration in primary and secondary schools. It is a context, as *Swann* makes clear, where history has required special administrative remedies. And it is a context in which the school boards' plans simply set race-conscious limits at the outer boundaries of a broad range.

This context is not a context that involves the use of race to decide who will receive goods or services that are normally distributed on the basis of merit and which are in short supply. It is not one in which race-conscious limits stigmatize or exclude; the limits at issue do not pit the races against each other or otherwise significantly exacerbate racial tensions. They do not impose burdens unfairly upon members of one race alone but instead seek benefits for members of all races alike. The context here is one of racial limits that seek, not to keep the races apart, but to bring them together.

In my view, this contextual approach to scrutiny is altogether fitting. I believe that the law requires application here of a standard of review that is not "strict" in the traditional sense of that word, although it does require the careful review I have just described.

Nonetheless, in light of *Grutter* and other precedents, I shall adopt the first alternative. I shall apply the version of strict scrutiny that those cases embody. I shall consequently ask whether the school boards in Seattle and Louisville adopted these plans to serve a "compelling governmental interest" and, if so, whether the plans are "narrowly tailored" to achieve that interest. If the plans survive this strict review, they would survive less exacting review a fortiori. Hence, I conclude that the plans before us pass both parts of the strict scrutiny test. Consequently I must conclude that the plans here are permitted under the Constitution.

III

A

Compelling Interest

The principal interest advanced in these cases to justify the use of race-based criteria goes by various names. Sometimes a court refers to it as an interest in achieving racial "diversity." Other times a court, like the plurality here, refers to it as an interest in racial "balancing." I have used more general terms to signify that interest, describing it, for example, as an interest in promoting or preserving greater racial "integration" of public schools. By this term, I mean the school districts' interest in eliminating school-by-school racial isolation and increasing the degree to which racial mixture characterizes each of the district's schools and each individual student's public school experience.

Regardless of its name, however, the interest at stake possesses three essential elements. First, there is a historical and remedial element: an interest in setting right the consequences of prior conditions of segregation. This refers back to a time when public schools were highly segregated, often as a result of legal or administrative policies that facilitated racial segregation in public schools. It is an interest in continuing to combat the remnants of segregation caused in whole or in part by these school-related policies, which have often affected not only schools, but also housing patterns, employment practices, economic conditions, and social attitudes. It is an interest in maintaining hard-won gains. And it has its roots in preventing what gradually may become the de facto resegregation of America's public schools.

Second, there is an educational element: an interest in overcoming the adverse educational effects produced by and associated with highly segregated schools. Studies suggest that children taken from those schools and placed in integrated settings often show positive academic gains. Other studies reach different conclusions. See, e.g., D. Armor, Forced Justice (1995). But the evidence supporting an educational interest in racially integrated schools is well established and strong enough to permit a democratically elected school board reasonably to determine that this interest is a compelling one.

Third, there is a democratic element: an interest in producing an educational environment that reflects the "pluralistic society" in which our children will live.It is an interest in helping our children learn to work and play together with children of different racial backgrounds. It is an interest in teaching children to engage in the kind of cooperation among Americans of all races that is necessary to make a land of three hundred million people one Nation.

If we are to insist upon unanimity in the social science literature before finding a compelling interest, we might never find one. I believe only that the Constitution allows democratically elected school boards to make up their own minds as to how best to include people of all races in one America.

B

Narrow Tailoring

I next ask whether the plans before us are "narrowly tailored" to achieve these "compelling" objectives. I shall not accept the school board's assurances on faith, and I shall subject the "tailoring" of their plans to "rigorous judicial review." Several factors, taken together, nonetheless lead me to conclude that the boards' use of race-conscious criteria in these plans passes even the strictest "tailoring" test.

First, the race-conscious criteria at issue only help set the outer bounds of broad ranges. They constitute but one part of plans that depend primarily upon other, nonracial elements. To use race in this way is not to set a forbidden "quota." In fact, the defining feature of both plans is greater emphasis upon student choice. In Seattle, for example, in more than 80% of all cases, that choice alone determines which high schools Seattle's ninth graders will attend.

Second, broad-range limits on voluntary school choice plans are less burdensome, and hence more narrowly tailored, than other race-conscious restrictions this Court has previously approved. Indeed, the plans before us are more narrowly tailored than the race-conscious admission plans that this Court approved in *Grutter*. Here, race becomes a factor only in a fraction of students' non-merit-based assignments—not in large numbers of students' merit-based applications. Moreover, the effect of applying race-conscious criteria here affects potentially disadvantaged students less severely, not more severely, than the criteria at issue in *Grutter*. Disappointed students are not rejected from a State's flagship graduate program; they simply attend a different one of the district's many public schools, which in aspiration and in fact are substantially equal. And, in Seattle, the disadvantaged student loses at most one year at the high school of his choice. One will search *Grutter* in vain for similarly persuasive evidence of narrow tailoring as the school districts have presented here.

Third, the manner in which the school boards developed these plans itself reflects "narrow tailoring." Each plan was devised to overcome a history of segregated public schools. Each plan embodies the results of local experience and community consultation. Each plan is the product of a process that has sought to enhance student choice, while diminishing the need for mandatory busing. And each plan's use of race-conscious elements is diminished compared to the use of race in preceding integration plans.

The school boards' widespread consultation, their experimentation with numerous other plans, indeed, the 40-year history that Part I sets forth, make clear that plans that are less explicitly race-based are unlikely to achieve the board's "compelling" objectives. The history of each school system reveals highly segregated schools, followed by remedial plans that involved forced busing, followed by efforts to attract or retain students through the use of plans that abandoned busing and replaced it with greater student choice. Both cities once tried to achieve more integrated schools by relying solely upon measures such as redrawn district boundaries, new school building construction, and unrestricted voluntary transfers. In neither city did these prior attempts prove sufficient to achieve the city's integration goals.

Moreover, giving some degree of weight to a local school board's knowledge, expertise, and concerns in these particular matters is not inconsistent with rigorous judicial scrutiny. It simply recognizes that judges are not well suited to act as school administrators. Indeed, in the context of school desegregation, this Court has repeatedly stressed the importance of acknowledging that local school boards better understand their own communities and have a better knowledge of what in practice will best meet the educational needs of their pupils.

Nor could the school districts have accomplished their desired aims (e.g., avoiding forced busing, countering white flight, maintaining racial diversity) by other means. Nothing in the extensive history of desegregation efforts over the past 50 years gives the districts, or this Court, any reason to believe that another method is possible to accomplish these goals. Nevertheless, Justice Kennedy suggests that school boards: "may pursue the goal of bringing together students of diverse backgrounds and races through other means, including strategic site selection of new schools; drawing attendance zones with general recognition of the demographics of neighborhoods; allocating resources for special programs; recruiting students and faculty in a targeted fashion; and tracking enrollments, performance, and other statistics by race."

But, as to "strategic site selection," Seattle has built one new high school in the last 44 years (and that specialized school serves only 300 students). As to "allocating resources for special programs," Seattle and Louisville have both experimented with this; indeed, these programs are often referred to as "magnet schools," but the limited desegregation effect of these efforts extends at most to those few schools to which additional resources are granted. In addition, there is no evidence from the experience of these school districts that it will make any meaningful impact. As to "recruiting faculty" on the basis of race, both cities have tried, but only as one part of a broader program. As to "tracking enrollments, performance and other statistics by race," tracking reveals the problem; it does not cure it.

[IV]

Consequences

The Founders meant the Constitution as a practical document that would transmit its basic values to future generations through principles that remained workable over time. Hence it is important to consider the potential consequences of the plurality's approach, as measured against the Constitution's objectives. To do so provides further reason to believe that the plurality's approach is legally unsound.

At a minimum, the plurality's views would threaten a surge of race-based litigation. Hundreds of state and federal statutes and regulations use racial classifications for educational or other purposes. In many such instances, the contentious force of legal challenges to these classifications, meritorious or not, would displace earlier calm.

As I have pointed out, supra, de facto resegregation is on the rise. It is reasonable to conclude that such resegregation can create serious educational, social, and civic problems. Given the conditions in which school boards work to set policy, they may need all of the means presently at their disposal to combat those problems. Yet the plurality would deprive them of at least one tool that some districts now consider vital—the limited use of broad race-conscious student population ranges.

I use the words "may need" here deliberately. The plurality, or at least those who follow Justice Thomas' "'color-blind'" approach, may feel confident that, to end invidious discrimination, one must end all governmental use of race-conscious criteria including those with inclusive objectives. By way of contrast, I do not claim to know how best to stop harmful discrimination; how best to create a society that includes all Americans; how best to overcome our serious problems of increasing de facto segregation, troubled inner city schooling, and poverty correlated with race. But, as a judge, I do know that the Constitution does not authorize judges to dictate solutions to these problems. Rather, the Constitution creates a democratic political system through which the people themselves must together find answers. And it is for them to debate how best to educate the Nation's children and how best to administer America's schools to achieve that aim. The Court should leave them to their work. And it is for them to decide, to quote the plurality's slogan, whether the best "way to stop discrimination on the basis of race is to stop discriminating on the basis of race." That is why the Equal Protection Clause outlaws invidious discrimination, but does not similarly forbid all use of race-conscious criteria.

Until today, this Court understood the Constitution as affording the people, acting through their elected representatives, freedom to select the use of "race-conscious" criteria from among their available options. Today, however, the Court restricts (and some Members would eliminate) that leeway. I fear the consequences of doing so for the law, for the schools, for the democratic process, and for America's efforts to create, out of its diversity, one Nation.

The last half-century has witnessed great strides toward racial equality, but we have not yet realized the promise of *Brown*. To invalidate the plans under review is to threaten the promise of *Brown*. The plurality's position, I fear, would break that promise. This is a decision that the Court and the Nation will come to regret.

Chapter 8

Fundamental Rights Under Due Process and Equal Protection

D. Constitutional Protection for Reproductive Autonomy

3. The Right to Abortion

b. Government regulation of abortion (casebook p. 878)

In *Stenberg v. Carhart* [casebook p. 878], the Supreme Court invalidated a Nebraska law prohibited so-called "partial birth abortion." In April 2007, in *Gonzales v. Carhart*, the Court upheld a federal law prohibiting partial birth abortion. The Court did not overrule its earlier decision. In reading the case, it is important to consider whether there is a meaningful distinction between these decisions.

GONZALES v. CARHART
127 S.Ct. 1610 (2007)

Justice KENNEDY delivered the opinion of the Court.

These cases require us to consider the validity of the Partial-Birth Abortion Ban Act of 2003, a federal statute regulating abortion procedures. In recitations preceding its operative provisions the Act refers to the Court's opinion in *Stenberg v. Carhart* (2000), which also addressed the subject of abortion procedures used in the later stages of pregnancy. Compared to the state statute at issue in *Stenberg*, the Act is more specific concerning the instances to which it applies and in this respect more precise in its coverage. We conclude the Act should be sustained against the objections lodged by the broad, facial attack brought against it.

I

A

The Act proscribes a particular manner of ending fetal life, so it is necessary here, as it was in *Stenberg*, to discuss abortion procedures in some detail.

Abortion methods vary depending to some extent on the preferences of the physician and, of course, on the term of the pregnancy and the resulting stage of the unborn child's development. Between 85 and 90 percent of the approximately 1.3 million abortions performed each year in the United States take place in the first three months of pregnancy, which is to say in the first trimester. The most common first-trimester abortion method is vacuum aspiration (otherwise known as suction curettage) in which the physician vacuums out the embryonic tissue. Early in this trimester an alternative is to use medication, such as mifepristone (commonly known as RU-486), to terminate the pregnancy. The Act does not regulate these procedures.

Of the remaining abortions that take place each year, most occur in the second trimester. The surgical procedure referred to as "dilation and evacuation" or "D&E" is the usual abortion method in this trimester. Although individual techniques for performing D&E differ, the general steps are the same.

A doctor must first dilate the cervix at least to the extent needed to insert surgical instruments into the uterus and to maneuver them to evacuate the fetus. The steps taken to cause dilation differ by physician and gestational age of the fetus. After sufficient dilation the surgical operation can commence. The woman is placed under general anesthesia or conscious sedation. The doctor, often guided by ultrasound, inserts grasping forceps through the woman's cervix and into the uterus to grab the fetus. The doctor grips a fetal part with the forceps and pulls it back through the cervix and vagina, continuing to pull even after meeting resistance from the cervix. The friction causes the fetus to tear apart. For example, a leg might be ripped off the fetus as it is pulled through the cervix and out of the woman. The process of evacuating the fetus piece by piece continues until it has been completely removed. A doctor may make 10 to 15 passes with the forceps to evacuate the fetus in its entirety, though sometimes removal is completed with fewer passes. Once the fetus has been evacuated, the placenta and any remaining fetal material are suctioned or scraped out of the uterus. The doctor examines the different parts to ensure the entire fetal body has been removed.

Some doctors, especially later in the second trimester, may kill the fetus a day or two before performing the surgical evacuation. They inject digoxin or potassium chloride into the fetus, the umbilical cord, or the amniotic fluid. Fetal demise may cause contractions and make greater dilation possible. Once dead, moreover, the fetus' body will soften, and its removal will be easier. Other doctors refrain from injecting chemical agents, believing it adds risk with little or no medical benefit.

The abortion procedure that was the impetus for the numerous bans on "partial-birth abortion," including the Act, is a variation of this standard D&E. The medical community has not reached unanimity on the appropriate name for this D&E variation. It has been referred to as "intact D&E," "dilation and extraction" (D&X), and "intact D&X." For discussion purposes this D&E variation will be referred to as intact D&E. The main difference between the two procedures is that in intact D&E a doctor extracts the fetus intact or largely intact with only a few passes. There are no comprehensive statistics indicating what percentage of all D&Es are performed in this manner.

Intact D&E, like regular D&E, begins with dilation of the cervix. Sufficient dilation is essential for the procedure. In an intact D&E procedure the doctor extracts the fetus in a way conducive to pulling out its entire body, instead of ripping it apart. One doctor, for example, testified: " '[T]he surgeon then forces the scissors into the base of the skull or into the foramen magnum. Having safely entered the skull, he spreads the scissors to enlarge the opening. The surgeon removes the scissors and introduces a suction catheter into this hole and evacuates the skull contents. With the catheter still in place, he applies traction to the fetus, removing it completely from the patient.' "

This is an abortion doctor's clinical description. Dr. Haskell's approach is not the only method of killing the fetus once its head lodges in the cervix, and "the process has evolved" since his presentation. Another doctor, for example, squeezes the skull after it has been pierced "so that enough brain tissue exudes to allow the head to pass through." Still other physicians reach into the cervix with their forceps and crush the fetus' skull. Others continue to pull the fetus out of the woman until it disarticulates at the neck, in effect decapitating it. These doctors then grasp the head with forceps, crush it, and remove it.

D&E and intact D&E are not the only second-trimester abortion methods. Doctors also may abort a fetus through medical induction. The doctor medicates the woman to induce labor, and contractions occur to deliver the fetus. Induction, which unlike D&E should occur in a hospital, can last as little as 6 hours but can take longer than 48. It accounts for about five percent of second-trimester abortions before 20 weeks of gestation and 15 percent of those after 20 weeks. Doctors turn to two other methods of second-trimester abortion, hysterotomy and hysterectomy, only in emergency situations because they carry increased risk of complications. In a hysterotomy, as in a cesarean section, the doctor removes the fetus by making an incision through the abdomen and uterine wall to gain access to the uterine cavity. A hysterectomy requires the removal of the entire uterus. These two procedures represent about .07% of second-trimester abortions.

B

By the time of the Stenberg decision, about 30 States had enacted bans designed to prohibit the procedure. In 2003, after this Court's decision in Stenberg, Congress passed the Act at issue here.

The Act responded to Stenberg in two ways. First, Congress made factual findings. Congress found, among other things, that "[a] moral, medical, and ethical consensus exists that the practice of performing a partial-birth abortion . . . is a gruesome and inhumane procedure that is never medically necessary and should be prohibited."

Second, and more relevant here, the Act's language differs from that of the Nebraska statute struck down in *Stenberg*. The operative provisions of the Act provide in relevant part:

"(a) Any physician who, in or affecting interstate or foreign commerce, knowingly performs a partial-birth abortion and thereby kills a human fetus shall be fined under this title or imprisoned not more than 2 years, or both. This subsection does not apply to a partial-birth abortion that is necessary to save the life of a mother whose life is endangered by a physical disorder, physical illness, or physical injury, including a life-endangering physical condition caused by or arising from the pregnancy itself. This subsection takes effect 1 day after the enactment.

"(b) As used in this section-

"(1) the term 'partial-birth abortion' means an abortion in which the person performing the abortion-

"(A) deliberately and intentionally vaginally delivers a living fetus until, in the case of a head-first presentation, the entire fetal head is outside the body of the mother, or, in the case of breech presentation, any part of the fetal trunk past the navel is outside the body of the mother, for the purpose of performing an overt act that the person knows will kill the partially delivered living fetus; and

"(B) performs the overt act, other than completion of delivery, that kills the partially delivered living fetus."

"(d)(1) A defendant accused of an offense under this section may seek a hearing before the State Medical Board on whether the physician's conduct was necessary to save the life of the mother whose life was endangered by a physical disorder, physical illness, or physical injury, including a life-endangering physical condition caused by or arising from the pregnancy itself."

"(e) A woman upon whom a partial-birth abortion is performed may not be prosecuted under this section, for a conspiracy to violate this section, or for an offense under section 2, 3, or 4 of this title based on a violation of this section."

II

We assume the following principles for the purposes of this opinion. Before viability, a State "may not prohibit any woman from making the ultimate decision to terminate her pregnancy." It also may not impose upon this right an undue burden, which exists if a regulation's "purpose or effect is to place a substantial obstacle in the path of a woman seeking an abortion before the fetus attains viability." On the other hand, "[r]egulations which do no more than create a structural mechanism by which the State, or the parent or guardian of a minor, may express profound respect for the life of the unborn are permitted, if they are not a substantial obstacle to the woman's exercise of the right to choose." *Planned Parenthood v. Casey* (1992), in short, struck a balance. The balance was central to its holding. We now apply its standard to the cases at bar.

III

Respondents agree the Act encompasses intact D&E, but they contend its additional reach is both unclear and excessive. Respondents assert that, at the least, the Act is void for vagueness because its scope is indefinite. In the alternative, respondents argue the Act's text proscribes all D&Es. Because D&E is the most common second-trimester abortion method, respondents suggest the Act imposes an undue burden. In this litigation the Attorney General does not dispute that the Act would impose an undue burden if it covered standard D&E.

We conclude that the Act is not void for vagueness, does not impose an undue burden from any overbreadth, and is not invalid on its face.

A

The Act punishes "knowingly perform[ing]" a "partial-birth abortion." It defines the unlawful abortion in explicit terms. First, the person performing the abortion must "vaginally delive[r] a living fetus." The Act does not restrict an abortion procedure involving the delivery of an expired fetus. The Act, furthermore, is inapplicable to abortions that do not involve vaginal delivery (for instance, hysterotomy or hysterectomy). The Act does apply both previability and postviability because, by common understanding and scientific terminology, a fetus is a living organism while within the womb, whether or not it is viable outside the womb.

Second, the Act's definition of partial-birth abortion requires the fetus to be delivered "until, in the case of a head-first presentation, the entire fetal head is outside the body of the mother, or, in the case of breech presentation, any part of the fetal trunk past the navel is outside the body of the mother." The Attorney General concedes, and we agree, that if an abortion procedure does not involve the delivery of a living fetus to one of these "anatomical 'landmarks' "—where, depending on the presentation, either the fetal head or the fetal trunk past the navel is outside the body of the mother—the prohibitions of the Act do not apply.

Third, to fall within the Act, a doctor must perform an "overt act, other than completion of delivery, that kills the partially delivered living fetus." For purposes of criminal liability, the overt act causing the fetus' death must be separate from delivery. And the overt act must occur after the delivery to an anatomical landmark.

Fourth, the Act contains scienter requirements concerning all the actions involved in the prohibited abortion. To begin with, the physician must have "deliberately and intentionally" delivered the fetus to one of the Act's anatomical landmarks. If a living fetus is delivered past the critical point by accident or inadvertence, the Act is inapplicable. In addition, the fetus must have been delivered "for the purpose of performing an overt act that the [doctor] knows will kill [it]." If either intent is absent, no crime has occurred. This follows from the general principle that where scienter is required no crime is committed absent the requisite state of mind.

B

Respondents contend the language described above is indeterminate, and they thus argue the Act is unconstitutionally vague on its face. "As generally stated, the void-for-vagueness doctrine requires that a penal statute define the criminal offense with sufficient definiteness that ordinary people can understand what conduct is prohibited and in a manner that does not encourage arbitrary and discriminatory enforcement." The Act satisfies both requirements.

The Act provides doctors "of ordinary intelligence a reasonable opportunity to know what is prohibited." Indeed, it sets forth "relatively clear guidelines as to prohibited conduct" and provides "objective criteria" to evaluate whether a doctor has performed a prohibited procedure. Unlike the statutory language in *Stenberg* that prohibited the delivery of a " 'substantial portion' " of the fetus— where a doctor might question how much of the fetus is a substantial portion— the Act defines the line between potentially criminal conduct on the one hand and lawful abortion on the other. Doctors performing D&E will know that if they do not deliver a living fetus to an anatomical landmark they will not face criminal liability.

This conclusion is buttressed by the intent that must be proved to impose liability. The Court has made clear that scienter requirements alleviate vagueness concerns. The Act requires the doctor deliberately to have delivered the fetus to an anatomical landmark. Because a doctor performing a D&E will not face criminal liability if he or she delivers a fetus beyond the prohibited point by mistake, the Act cannot be described as "a trap for those who act in good faith."

Respondents likewise have failed to show that the Act should be invalidated on its face because it encourages arbitrary or discriminatory enforcement. Just as the Act's anatomical landmarks provide doctors with objective standards, they also "establish minimal guidelines to govern law enforcement." The scienter requirements narrow the scope of the Act's prohibition and limit prosecutorial discretion. It cannot be said that the Act "vests virtually complete discretion in the hands of [law enforcement] to determine whether the [doctor] has satisfied [its provisions]." Respondents' arguments concerning arbitrary enforcement, furthermore, are somewhat speculative. This is a preenforcement challenge, where "no evidence has been, or could be, introduced to indicate whether the [Act] has been enforced in a discriminatory manner or with the aim of inhibiting [constitutionally protected conduct]." The Act is not vague.

C

We next determine whether the Act imposes an undue burden, as a facial matter, because its restrictions on second-trimester abortions are too broad. A review of the statutory text discloses the limits of its reach. The Act prohibits intact D&E; and, notwithstanding respondents' arguments, it does not prohibit the D&E procedure in which the fetus is removed in parts.

The Act prohibits a doctor from intentionally performing an intact D&E. The Act excludes most D&Es in which the fetus is removed in pieces, not intact. If the doctor intends to remove the fetus in parts from the outset, the doctor will not have the requisite intent to incur criminal liability. Removing the fetus in this manner does not violate the Act because the doctor will not have delivered the living fetus to one of the anatomical landmarks or committed an additional overt act that kills the fetus after partial delivery.

A comparison of the Act with the Nebraska statute struck down in *Stenberg* confirms this point. The statute in *Stenberg* prohibited " 'deliberately and intentionally delivering into the vagina a living unborn child, or a substantial portion thereof, for the purpose of performing a procedure that the person performing such procedure knows will kill the unborn child and does kill the unborn child.' " The Court concluded that this statute encompassed D&E because "D&E will often involve a physician pulling a 'substantial portion' of a still living fetus, say, an arm or leg, into the vagina prior to the death of the fetus."

Congress, it is apparent, responded to these concerns because the Act departs in material ways from the statute in *Stenberg*. It adopts the phrase "delivers a living fetus," instead of " 'delivering . . . a living unborn child, or a substantial portion thereof.' "

The identification of specific anatomical landmarks to which the fetus must be partially delivered also differentiates the Act from the statute at issue in *Stenberg*. The Court in *Stenberg* interpreted " 'substantial portion' " of the fetus to include an arm or a leg. The Act's anatomical landmarks, by contrast, clarify that the removal of a small portion of the fetus is not prohibited. The landmarks also require the fetus to be delivered so that it is partially "outside the body of the mother." To come within the ambit of the Nebraska statute, on the other hand, a substantial portion of the fetus only had to be delivered into the vagina; no part of the fetus had to be outside the body of the mother before a doctor could face criminal sanctions.

By adding an overt-act requirement Congress sought further to meet the Court's objections to the state statute considered in *Stenberg*. The Act makes the distinction the Nebraska statute failed to draw (but the Nebraska Attorney General advanced) by differentiating between the overall partial-birth abortion and the distinct overt act that kills the fetus. The fatal overt act must occur after delivery to an anatomical landmark, and it must be something "other than [the] completion of delivery." This distinction matters because, unlike intact D&E, standard D&E does not involve a delivery followed by a fatal act.

IV

Under the principles accepted as controlling here, the Act, as we have interpreted it, would be unconstitutional "if its purpose or effect is to place a substantial obstacle in the path of a woman seeking an abortion before the fetus attains viability." The abortions affected by the Act's regulations take place both previability and postviability; so the quoted language and the undue burden analysis it relies upon are applicable. The question is whether the Act, measured by its text in this facial attack, imposes a substantial obstacle to late-term, but previability, abortions. The Act does not on its face impose a substantial obstacle, and we reject this further facial challenge to its validity.

A

The Act's purposes are set forth in recitals preceding its operative provisions. A description of the prohibited abortion procedure demonstrates the rationale for the congressional enactment. The Act proscribes a method of abortion in which a fetus is killed just inches before completion of the birth process. Congress stated as follows: "Implicitly approving such a brutal and inhumane procedure by choosing not to prohibit it will further coarsen society to the humanity of not only newborns, but all vulnerable and innocent human life, making it increasingly difficult to protect such life." The Act expresses respect for the dignity of human life.

Congress was concerned, furthermore, with the effects on the medical community and on its reputation caused by the practice of partial-birth abortion. There can be no doubt the government "has an interest in protecting the integrity and ethics of the medical profession." *Washington v. Glucksberg* (1997). Under our precedents it is clear the State has a significant role to play in regulating the medical profession.

The Act's ban on abortions that involve partial delivery of a living fetus furthers the Government's objectives. No one would dispute that, for many, D & E is a procedure itself laden with the power to devalue human life.

Respect for human life finds an ultimate expression in the bond of love the mother has for her child. The Act recognizes this reality as well. Whether to have an abortion requires a difficult and painful moral decision. While we find no reliable data to measure the phenomenon, it seems unexceptionable to conclude some women come to regret their choice to abort the infant life they once created and sustained. Severe depression and loss of esteem can follow.

The State has an interest in ensuring so grave a choice is well informed. It is self-evident that a mother who comes to regret her choice to abort must struggle with grief more anguished and sorrow more profound when she learns, only after the event, what she once did not know: that she allowed a doctor to pierce the skull and vacuum the fast-developing brain of her unborn child, a child assuming the human form.

It is a reasonable inference that a necessary effect of the regulation and the knowledge it conveys will be to encourage some women to carry the infant to full term, thus reducing the absolute number of late-term abortions. The medical profession, furthermore, may find different and less shocking methods to abort the fetus in the second trimester, thereby accommodating legislative demand.

The State's interest in respect for life is advanced by the dialogue that better informs the political and legal systems, the medical profession, expectant mothers, and society as a whole of the consequences that follow from a decision to elect a late-term abortion.

It is objected that the standard D&E is in some respects as brutal, if not more, than the intact D&E, so that the legislation accomplishes little. What we have already said, however, shows ample justification for the regulation. Partial-birth abortion, as defined by the Act, differs from a standard D&E because the former occurs when the fetus is partially outside the mother to the point of one of the Act's anatomical landmarks. It was reasonable for Congress to think that partial-birth abortion, more than standard D&E, "undermines the public's perception of the appropriate role of a physician during the delivery process, and perverts a process during which life is brought into the world."

B

The Act's furtherance of legitimate government interests bears upon, but does not resolve, the next question: whether the Act has the effect of imposing an unconstitutional burden on the abortion right because it does not allow use of the barred procedure where " 'necessary, in appropriate medical judgment, for [the] preservation of the . . . health of the mother.' " The prohibition in the Act would be unconstitutional, under precedents we here assume to be controlling, if it "subject[ed] [women] to significant health risks." [W]hether the Act creates significant health risks for women has been a contested factual question. The evidence presented in the trial courts and before Congress demonstrates both sides have medical support for their position.

Respondents presented evidence that intact D&E may be the safest method of abortion, for reasons similar to those adduced in *Stenberg*. Abortion doctors testified, for example, that intact D&E decreases the risk of cervical laceration or uterine perforation because it requires fewer passes into the uterus with surgical instruments and does not require the removal of bony fragments of the dismembered fetus, fragments that may be sharp. Respondents also presented evidence that intact D&E was safer both because it reduces the risks that fetal parts will remain in the uterus and because it takes less time to complete. Respondents, in addition, proffered evidence that intact D&E was safer for women with certain medical conditions or women with fetuses that had certain anomalies.

These contentions were contradicted by other doctors who testified in the District Courts and before Congress. They concluded that the alleged health advantages were based on speculation without scientific studies to support them. They considered D&E always to be a safe alternative.

There is documented medical disagreement whether the Act's prohibition would ever impose significant health risks on women.

The question becomes whether the Act can stand when this medical uncertainty persists. The Court's precedents instruct that the Act can survive this facial attack. The Court has given state and federal legislatures wide discretion to pass legislation in areas where there is medical and scientific uncertainty.

This traditional rule is consistent with *Casey*, which confirms the State's interest in promoting respect for human life at all stages in the pregnancy. Physicians are not entitled to ignore regulations that direct them to use reasonable alternative procedures. The law need not give abortion doctors unfettered choice in the course of their medical practice, nor should it elevate their status above other physicians in the medical community.

Medical uncertainty does not foreclose the exercise of legislative power in the abortion context any more than it does in other contexts. The medical uncertainty over whether the Act's prohibition creates significant health risks provides a sufficient basis to conclude in this facial attack that the Act does not impose an undue burden.

The conclusion that the Act does not impose an undue burden is supported by other considerations. Alternatives are available to the prohibited procedure. As we have noted, the Act does not proscribe D&E. If the intact D&E procedure is truly necessary in some circumstances, it appears likely an injection that kills the fetus is an alternative under the Act that allows the doctor to perform the procedure.

In reaching the conclusion the Act does not require a health exception we reject certain arguments made by the parties on both sides of these cases. On the one hand, the Attorney General urges us to uphold the Act on the basis of the congressional findings alone. Although we review congressional factfinding under a deferential standard, we do not in the circumstances here place dispositive weight on Congress' findings. The Court retains an independent constitutional duty to review factual findings where constitutional rights are at stake. As respondents have noted, and the District Courts recognized, some recitations in the Act are factually incorrect. Uncritical deference to Congress' factual findings in these cases is inappropriate.

On the other hand, relying on the Court's opinion in *Stenberg*, respondents contend that an abortion regulation must contain a health exception "if 'substantial medical authority supports the proposition that banning a particular procedure could endanger women's health.'" A zero tolerance policy would strike down legitimate abortion regulations, like the present one, if some part of the medical community were disinclined to follow the proscription. This is too exacting a standard to impose on the legislative power, exercised in this instance under the Commerce Clause, to regulate the medical profession. Considerations of marginal safety, including the balance of risks, are within the legislative competence when the regulation is rational and in pursuit of legitimate ends. When standard medical options are available, mere convenience does not suffice to displace them; and if some procedures have different risks than others, it does not follow that the State is altogether barred from imposing reasonable regulations. The Act is not invalid on its face where there is uncertainty over whether the barred procedure is ever necessary to preserve a woman's health, given the availability of other abortion procedures that are considered to be safe alternatives.

V

The considerations we have discussed support our further determination that these facial attacks should not have been entertained in the first instance. In these circumstances the proper means to consider exceptions is by as-applied challenge. This is the proper manner to protect the health of the woman if it can be shown that in discrete and well-defined instances a particular condition has or is likely to occur in which the procedure prohibited by the Act must be used. In an as-applied challenge the nature of the medical risk can be better quantified and balanced than in a facial attack.

The latitude given facial challenges in the First Amendment context is inapplicable here. Broad challenges of this type impose "a heavy burden" upon the parties maintaining the suit. As the previous sections of this opinion explain, respondents have not demonstrated that the Act would be unconstitutional in a large fraction of relevant cases.

The Act is open to a proper as-applied challenge in a discrete case. No as-applied challenge need be brought if the prohibition in the Act threatens a woman's life because the Act already contains a life exception.

Justice THOMAS, with whom Justice SCALIA joins, concurring.

I join the Court's opinion because it accurately applies current jurisprudence, including *Planned Parenthood of Southeastern Pa. v. Casey* (1992). I write separately to reiterate my view that the Court's abortion jurisprudence, including *Casey* and *Roe v. Wade* (1973), has no basis in the Constitution. I also note that whether the Act constitutes a permissible exercise of Congress' power under the Commerce Clause is not before the Court. The parties did not raise or brief that issue; it is outside the question presented; and the lower courts did not address it.

Justice GINSBURG, with whom Justice STEVENS, Justice SOUTER, and Justice BREYER join, dissenting.

Today's decision is alarming. It refuses to take *Casey* and *Stenberg* seriously. It tolerates, indeed applauds, federal intervention to ban nationwide a procedure found necessary and proper in certain cases by the American College of Obstetricians and Gynecologists (ACOG). It blurs the line, firmly drawn in *Casey*, between previability and postviability abortions. And, for the first time since *Roe*, the Court blesses a prohibition with no exception safeguarding a woman's health.

I

A

As *Casey* comprehended, at stake in cases challenging abortion restrictions is a woman's "control over her [own] destiny." Their ability to realize their full potential, the Court recognized, is intimately connected to "their ability to control their reproductive lives." Thus, legal challenges to undue restrictions on abortion procedures do not seek to vindicate some generalized notion of privacy; rather, they center on a woman's autonomy to determine her life's course, and thus to enjoy equal citizenship stature.

In keeping with this comprehension of the right to reproductive choice, the Court has consistently required that laws regulating abortion, at any stage of pregnancy and in all cases, safeguard a woman's health. We have thus ruled that a State must avoid subjecting women to health risks not only where the pregnancy itself creates danger, but also where state regulation forces women to resort to less safe methods of abortion.

Adolescents and indigent women, research suggests, are more likely than other women to have difficulty obtaining an abortion during the first trimester of pregnancy. Minors may be unaware they are pregnant until relatively late in pregnancy, while poor women's financial constraints are an obstacle to timely receipt of services. Severe fetal anomalies and health problems confronting the pregnant woman are also causes of second-trimester abortions; many such conditions cannot be diagnosed or do not develop until the second trimester.

In *Stenberg*, we expressly held that a statute banning intact D&E was unconstitutional in part because it lacked a health exception. We noted that there existed a "division of medical opinion" about the relative safety of intact D&E, but we made clear that as long as "substantial medical authority supports the proposition that banning a particular abortion procedure could endanger women's health," a health exception is required.

B

In 2003, a few years after our ruling in *Stenberg*, Congress passed the Partial-Birth Abortion Ban Act—without an exception for women's health. The congressional findings on which the Partial-Birth Abortion Ban Act rests do not withstand inspection, as the lower courts have determined and this Court is obliged to concede. Many of the Act's recitations are incorrect. For example, Congress determined that no medical schools provide instruction on intact D&E. But in fact, numerous leading medical schools teach the procedure. More important, Congress claimed there was a medical consensus that the banned procedure is never necessary. But the evidence "very clearly demonstrate[d] the opposite."

Similarly, Congress found that "[t]here is no credible medical evidence that partial-birth abortions are safe or are safer than other abortion procedures." But the congressional record includes letters from numerous individual physicians stating that pregnant women's health would be jeopardized under the Act, as well as statements from nine professional associations, including ACOG, the American Public Health Association, and the California Medical Association, attesting that intact D&E carries meaningful safety advantages over other methods.

C

In contrast to Congress, the District Courts made findings after full trials at which all parties had the opportunity to present their best evidence. The courts had the benefit of "much more extensive medical and scientific evidence . . . concerning the safety and necessity of intact D&Es." During the District Court trials, "numerous" "extraordinarily accomplished" and "very experienced" medical experts explained that, in certain circumstances and for certain women, intact D&E is safer than alternative procedures and necessary to protect women's health.

According to the expert testimony plaintiffs introduced, the safety advantages of intact D&E are marked for women with certain medical conditions, for example, uterine scarring, bleeding disorders, heart disease, or compromised immune systems. Further, plaintiffs' experts testified that intact D&E is significantly safer for women with certain pregnancy-related conditions, such as placenta previa and accreta, and for women carrying fetuses with certain abnormalities, such as severe hydrocephalus.

Intact D&E, plaintiffs' experts explained, provides safety benefits over D&E by dismemberment for several reasons: First, intact D&E minimizes the number of times a physician must insert instruments through the cervix and into the uterus, and thereby reduces the risk of trauma to, and perforation of, the cervix and uterus—the most serious complication associated with nonintact D&E. Second, removing the fetus intact, instead of dismembering it in utero, decreases the likelihood that fetal tissue will be retained in the uterus, a condition that can cause infection, hemorrhage, and infertility. Third, intact D&E diminishes the chances of exposing the patient's tissues to sharp bony fragments sometimes resulting from dismemberment of the fetus. Fourth, intact D&E takes less operating time than D&E by dismemberment, and thus may reduce bleeding, the risk of infection, and complications relating to anesthesia.

Based on thoroughgoing review of the trial evidence and the congressional record, each of the District Courts to consider the issue rejected Congress' findings as unreasonable and not supported by the evidence. The trial courts concluded, in contrast to Congress' findings, that "significant medical authority supports the proposition that in some circumstances, [intact D&E] is the safest procedure." The District Courts' findings merit this Court's respect.[1]

---

1. The majority contends that "[i]f the intact D&E procedure is truly necessary in some circumstances, it appears likely an injection that kills the fetus is an alternative under the Act that allows the doctor to perform the procedure." But a "significant body of medical opinion believes that inducing fetal death by injection is almost always inappropriate to the preservation of the health of women undergoing abortion because it poses tangible risk and provides no benefit to the woman." The Court also identifies medical induction of labor as an alternative. That procedure, however, requires a hospital stay, ibid., rendering it inaccessible to patients who lack financial resources, and it too is considered less safe for many women, and impermissible for others. [Footnote by Justice Ginsburg]

II

The Court offers flimsy and transparent justifications for upholding a nation-wide ban on intact D&E sans any exception to safeguard a women's health. Today's ruling, the Court declares, advances "a premise central to [*Casey*'s] conclusion"— i.e., the Government's "legitimate and substantial interest in preserving and promoting fetal life." But the Act scarcely furthers that interest: The law saves not a single fetus from destruction, for it targets only a method of performing abortion. And surely the statute was not designed to protect the lives or health of pregnant women. In short, the Court upholds a law that, while doing nothing to "preserv[e] . . . fetal life," bars a woman from choosing intact D&E although her doctor "reasonably believes [that procedure] will best protect [her]."

As another reason for upholding the ban, the Court emphasizes that the Act does not proscribe the nonintact D&E procedure. But why not, one might ask. Nonintact D&E could equally be characterized as "brutal," involving as it does "tear[ing] [a fetus] apart" and "ripp[ing] off" its limbs. "[T]he notion that either of these two equally gruesome procedures . . . is more akin to infanticide than the other, or that the State furthers any legitimate interest by banning one but not the other, is simply irrational."

Ultimately, the Court admits that "moral concerns" are at work, concerns that could yield prohibitions on any abortion. Notably, the concerns expressed are untethered to any ground genuinely serving the Government's interest in preserving life. By allowing such concerns to carry the day and case, overriding fundamental rights, the Court dishonors our precedent. Revealing in this regard, the Court invokes an antiabortion shibboleth for which it concededly has no reliable evidence: Women who have abortions come to regret their choices, and consequently suffer from "[s]evere depression and loss of esteem." Because of women's fragile emotional state and because of the "bond of love the mother has for her child," the Court worries, doctors may withhold information about the nature of the intact D&E procedure. The solution the Court approves, then, is not to require doctors to inform women, accurately and adequately, of the different procedures and their attendant risks. Instead, the Court deprives women of the right to make an autonomous choice, even at the expense of their safety.[2]

This way of thinking reflects ancient notions about women's place in the family and under the Constitution—ideas that have long since been discredited. Though today's majority may regard women's feelings on the matter as "self-evident,"

---

2. The Court is surely correct that, for most women, abortion is a painfully difficult decision. But "neither the weight of the scientific evidence to date nor the observable reality of 33 years of legal abortion in the United States comports with the idea that having an abortion is any more dangerous to a woman's long-term mental health than delivering and parenting a child that she did not intend to have. . . . " [Footnote by Justice Ginsburg]

this Court has repeatedly confirmed that "[t]he destiny of the woman must be shaped . . . on her own conception of her spiritual imperatives and her place in society."

B

In cases on a "woman's liberty to determine whether to [continue] her pregnancy," this Court has identified viability as a critical consideration. "[T]here is no line [more workable] than viability," the Court explained in *Casey*, for viability is "the time at which there is a realistic possibility of maintaining and nourishing a life outside the womb, so that the independent existence of the second life can in reason and all fairness be the object of state protection that now overrides the rights of the woman. . . . In some broad sense it might be said that a woman who fails to act before viability has consented to the State's intervention on behalf of the developing child."

Today, the Court blurs that line, maintaining that "[t]he Act [legitimately] appl[ies] both previability and postviability because . . . a fetus is a living organism while within the womb, whether or not it is viable outside the womb." Instead of drawing the line at viability, the Court refers to Congress' purpose to differentiate "abortion and infanticide" based not on whether a fetus can survive outside the womb, but on where a fetus is anatomically located when a particular medical procedure is performed.

One wonders how long a line that saves no fetus from destruction will hold in face of the Court's "moral concerns." The Court's hostility to the right *Roe* and *Casey* secured is not concealed. Throughout, the opinion refers to obstetrician-gynecologists and surgeons who perform abortions not by the titles of their medical specialties, but by the pejorative label "abortion doctor." A fetus is described as an "unborn child," and as a "baby," second-trimester, previability abortions are referred to as "late-term," and the reasoned medical judgments of highly trained doctors are dismissed as "preferences" motivated by "mere convenience." Instead of the heightened scrutiny we have previously applied, the Court determines that a "rational" ground is enough to uphold the Act. And, most troubling, *Casey*'s principles, confirming the continuing vitality of "the essential holding of *Roe*," are merely "assume[d]" for the moment, rather than "retained" or "reaffirmed."

III

The Court further confuses our jurisprudence when it declares that "facial attacks" are not permissible in "these circumstances," i.e., where medical uncertainty exists. This holding is perplexing given that, in materially identical circumstances we held that a statute lacking a health exception was unconstitutional on its face.

Without attempting to distinguish *Stenberg* and earlier decisions, the majority asserts that the Act survives review because respondents have not shown that the ban on intact D&E would be unconstitutional "in a large fraction of relevant cases." But *Casey* makes clear that, in determining whether any restriction poses an undue burden on a "large fraction" of women, the relevant class is not "all women," nor "all pregnant women," nor even all women "seeking abortions." Rather, a provision restricting access to abortion, "must be judged by reference to those [women] for whom it is an actual rather than an irrelevant restriction." ibid. Thus the absence of a health exception burdens all women for whom it is relevant—women who, in the judgment of their doctors, require an intact D&E because other procedures would place their health at risk. It makes no sense to conclude that this facial challenge fails because respondents have not shown that a health exception is necessary for a large fraction of second-trimester abortions, including those for which a health exception is unnecessary: The very purpose of a health exception is to protect women in exceptional cases.

If there is anything at all redemptive to be said of today's opinion, it is that the Court is not willing to foreclose entirely a constitutional challenge to the Act. "The Act is open," the Court states, "to a proper as-applied challenge in a discrete case." Surely the Court cannot mean that no suit may be brought until a woman's health is immediately jeopardized by the ban on intact D&E. A woman "suffer[ing] from medical complications," needs access to the medical procedure at once and cannot wait for the judicial process to unfold.

The Court appears, then, to contemplate another lawsuit by the initiators of the instant actions. In such a second round, the Court suggests, the challengers could succeed upon demonstrating that "in discrete and well-defined instances a particular condition has or is likely to occur in which the procedure prohibited by the Act must be used." One may anticipate that such a preenforcement challenge will be mounted swiftly, to ward off serious, sometimes irremediable harm, to women whose health would be endangered by the intact D&E prohibition.

The Court's allowance only of an "as-applied challenge in a discrete case," jeopardizes women's health and places doctors in an untenable position. Even if courts were able to carve-out exceptions through piecemeal litigation for "discrete and well-defined instances," women whose circumstances have not been anticipated by prior litigation could well be left unprotected. In treating those women, physicians would risk criminal prosecution, conviction, and imprisonment if they exercise their best judgment as to the safest medical procedure for their patients. The Court is thus gravely mistaken to conclude that narrow as-applied challenges are "the proper manner to protect the health of the woman."

In sum, the notion that the Partial-Birth Abortion Ban Act furthers any legitimate governmental interest is, quite simply, irrational. The Court's defense of the statute provides no saving explanation. In candor, the Act, and the Court's defense of it, cannot be understood as anything other than an effort to chip away at a right declared again and again by this Court—and with increasing comprehension of its centrality to women's lives. When "a statute burdens constitutional rights and all that can be said on its behalf is that it is the vehicle that legislators have chosen for expressing their hostility to those rights, the burden is undue."

e. Parental Notice and Consent Requirements (casebook, p. 901)

In *Ayotte v. Planned Parenthood of Northern New England*, the Court considered the constitutionality of a state law requiring parental notification for abortions for unemancipated minors. The United States Court of Appeals for the First Circuit invalidated the law because of a lack of an exception permitting doctors to perform abortions without parental notification or judicial approval where the health of the minor warranted it. The Supreme Court did not decide the constitutionality of the statute, but instead remanded the case to see if the lower courts could interpret it narrowly to avoid the constitutional issues.

AYOTTE v. PLANNED PARENTHOOD
OF NORTHERN NEW ENGLAND
546 U.S. 320 (2006)

Justice O'CONNOR delivered the opinion of the Court.

We do not revisit our abortion precedents today, but rather address a question of remedy: If enforcing a statute that regulates access to abortion would be unconstitutional in medical emergencies, what is the appropriate judicial response? We hold that invalidating the statute entirely is not always necessary or justified, for lower courts may be able to render narrower declaratory and injunctive relief.

I

In 2003, New Hampshire enacted the Parental Notification Prior to Abortion Act. The Act prohibits physicians from performing an abortion on a pregnant minor (or a woman for whom a guardian or conservator has been appointed) until 48 hours after written notice of the pending abortion is delivered to her parent or guardian. Notice may be delivered personally or by certified mail. Violations of the Act are subject to criminal and civil penalties.

The Act allows for three circumstances in which a physician may perform an abortion without notifying the minor's parent. First, notice is not required if "[t]he attending abortion provider certifies in the pregnant minor's record that the abortion is necessary to prevent the minor's death and there is insufficient time to provide the required notice." Second, a person entitled to receive notice may certify that he or she has already been notified. Finally, a minor may petition a judge to authorize her physician to perform an abortion without parental notification. The judge must so authorize if he or she finds that the minor is mature and capable of giving informed consent, or that an abortion without notification is in the minor's best interests. These judicial bypass proceedings "shall be confidential and shall be given precedence over other pending matters so that the court may reach a decision promptly and without delay," and access to the courts "shall be afforded [to the] pregnant minor 24 hours a day, 7 days a week." The trial and appellate courts must each rule on bypass petitions within seven days.

The Act does not explicitly permit a physician to perform an abortion in a medical emergency without parental notification.

II

As the case comes to us, three propositions—two legal and one factual—are established. First, States unquestionably have the right to require parental involvement when a minor considers terminating her pregnancy, because of their "strong and legitimate interest in the welfare of [their] young citizens, whose immaturity, inexperience, and lack of judgment may sometimes impair their ability to exercise their rights wisely." Accordingly, we have long upheld state parental involvement statutes like the Act before us, and we cast no doubt on those holdings today.

Second, New Hampshire does not dispute, and our precedents hold, that a State may not restrict access to abortions that are " 'necessary, in appropriate medical judgment, for preservation of the life or health of the mother.' "

Third, New Hampshire has not taken real issue with the factual basis of this litigation: In some very small percentage of cases, pregnant minors, like adult women, need immediate abortions to avert serious and often irreversible damage to their health.

New Hampshire has maintained that in most if not all cases, the Act's judicial bypass and the State's "competing harms" statutes should protect both physician and patient when a minor needs an immediate abortion. But the District Court and Court of Appeals found neither of these provisions to protect minors' health reliably in all emergencies. And New Hampshire has conceded that, under our cases, it would be unconstitutional to apply the Act in a manner that subjects minors to significant health risks.

III

We turn to the question of remedy: When a statute restricting access to abortion may be applied in a manner that harms women's health, what is the appropriate relief? Generally speaking, when confronting a constitutional flaw in a statute, we try to limit the solution to the problem. We prefer, for example, to enjoin only the unconstitutional applications of a statute while leaving other applications in force, or to sever its problematic portions while leaving the remainder intact.

Three interrelated principles inform our approach to remedies. First, we try not to nullify more of a legislature's work than is necessary, for we know that "[a] ruling of unconstitutionality frustrates the intent of the elected representatives of the people." It is axiomatic that a "statute may be invalid as applied to one state of facts and yet valid as applied to another." Accordingly, the "normal rule" is that "partial, rather than facial, invalidation is the required course," such that a "statute may . . . be declared invalid to the extent that it reaches too far, but otherwise left intact."

Second, mindful that our constitutional mandate and institutional competence are limited, we restrain ourselves from "rewrit[ing] state law to conform it to constitutional requirements" even as we strive to salvage it. Our ability to devise a judicial remedy that does not entail quintessentially legislative work often depends on how clearly we have already articulated the background constitutional rules at issue and how easily we can articulate the remedy. But making distinctions in a murky constitutional context, or where line-drawing is inherently complex, may call for a "far more serious invasion of the legislative domain" than we ought to undertake.

Third, the touchstone for any decision about remedy is legislative intent, for a court cannot "use its remedial powers to circumvent the intent of the legislature." After finding an application or portion of a statute unconstitutional, we must next ask: Would the legislature have preferred what is left of its statute to no statute at all? All the while, we are wary of legislatures who would rely on our intervention, for "[i]t would certainly be dangerous if the legislature could set a net large enough to catch all possible offenders, and leave it to the courts to step inside" to announce to whom the statute may be applied. "This would, to some extent, substitute the judicial for the legislative department of the government."

In this case, the courts below chose the most blunt remedy—permanently enjoining the enforcement of New Hampshire's parental notification law and thereby invalidating it entirely. That is understandable, for we, too, have previously invalidated an abortion statute in its entirety because of the same constitutional flaw. In *Stenberg*, we addressed a Nebraska law banning so-called "partial birth abortion" unless the procedure was necessary to save the pregnant woman's life. We held Nebraska's law unconstitutional because it lacked a health exception. But the parties in *Stenberg* did not ask for, and we did not contemplate, relief more finely drawn.

In the case that is before us, however, we agree with New Hampshire that the lower courts need not have invalidated the law wholesale. Respondents, too, recognize the possibility of a modest remedy: They pleaded for any relief "just and proper," and conceded at oral argument that carefully crafted injunctive relief may resolve this case. Only a few applications of New Hampshire's parental notification statute would present a constitutional problem. So long as they are faithful to legislative intent, then, in this case the lower courts can issue a declaratory judgment and an injunction prohibiting the statute's unconstitutional application.

There is some dispute as to whether New Hampshire's legislature intended the statute to be susceptible to such a remedy. New Hampshire notes that the

Act contains a severability clause providing that "[i]f any provision of this subdivision or the application thereof to any person or circumstance is held invalid, such invalidity shall not affect the provisions or applications of this subdivision which can be given effect without the invalid provisions or applications." Respondents, on the other hand, contend that New Hampshire legislators preferred no statute at all to a statute enjoined in the way we have described. Because this is an open question, we remand for the lower courts to determine legislative intent in the first instance.

Either an injunction prohibiting unconstitutional applications or a holding that consistency with legislative intent requires invalidating the statute in toto should obviate any concern about the Act's life exception. We therefore need not pass on the lower courts' alternative holding. Finally, if the Act does survive in part on remand, the Court of Appeals should address respondents' separate objection to the judicial bypass' confidentiality provision.

I. The Right to Vote

2. Restrictions on the Right to Vote (casebook, p. 944)

In *Crawford v. Marion County Election Board*, the Supreme Court considered the constitutionality of a requirement for photo identification for voting. There was no majority opinion for the Court as there was a 3-3-3 split among the Justices, with six voting to allow the regulation. In reading the case, it is important to focus on what test each group of Justices would use. Also, it is important to consider whether this case can be reconciled with other decisions concerning the right to vote, such as those striking down poll taxes and property ownership requirements for voting.

CRAWFORD v. MARION COUNTY ELECTION BOARD
128 S.Ct. 1610 (2008)

Justice STEVENS announced the judgment of the Court and delivered an opinion in which THE CHIEF JUSTICE and Justice Kennedy join.

At issue in these cases is the constitutionality of an Indiana statute requiring citizens voting in person on election day, or casting a ballot in person at the office of the circuit court clerk prior to election day, to present photo identification issued by the government.

Referred to as either the "Voter ID Law", or SEA 483, the statute applies to in-person voting at both primary and general elections. The requirement does not apply to absentee ballots submitted by mail, and the statute contains an exception for persons living and voting in a state-licensed facility such as a nursing home. A voter who is indigent or has a religious objection to being photographed may cast a provisional ballot that will be counted only if she executes an appropriate affidavit before the circuit court clerk within 10 days following the election. A voter who has photo identification but is unable to present that identification on election day may file a provisional ballot that will be counted if she brings her photo identification to the circuit county clerk's office within 10 days. No photo identification is required in order to register to vote, and the State offers free photo identification to qualified voters able to establish their residence and identity.

I

In Harper v. Virginia Bd. of Elections (1966), the Court held that Virginia could not condition the right to vote in a state election on the payment of a poll tax of $1.50. We rejected the dissenters' argument that the interest in promoting civic responsibility by weeding out those voters who did not care enough about public affairs to pay a small sum for the privilege of voting provided a rational basis for the tax. Applying a stricter standard, we concluded that a State "violates the Equal Protection Clause of the Fourteenth Amendment whenever it makes the affluence of the voter or payment of any fee an electoral standard." We used the term "invidiously discriminate" to describe conduct prohibited under that standard, noting that we had previously held that while a State may obviously impose "reasonable residence restrictions on the availability of the ballot," it "may not deny the opportunity to vote to a bona fide resident merely because he is a member of the armed services." Although the State's justification for the tax was rational, it was invidious because it was irrelevant to the voter's qualifications.

Thus, under the standard applied in Harper, even rational restrictions on the right to vote are invidious if they are unrelated to voter qualifications. In Anderson v. Celebrezze (1983), however, we confirmed the general rule that "evenhanded restrictions that protect the integrity and reliability of the electoral process itself" are not invidious and satisfy the standard set forth in Harper. Rather than applying any "litmus test" that would neatly separate valid from invalid restrictions, we concluded that a court must identify and evaluate the interests put forward by the State as justifications for the burden imposed by its rule, and then make the "hard judgment" that our adversary system demands.

In later election cases we have followed Anderson's balancing approach. Thus, in Norman v. Reed (1992), after identifying the burden Illinois imposed on a political party's access to the ballot, we "called for the demonstration of a corresponding interest sufficiently weighty to justify the limitation," and concluded that the "severe restriction" was not justified by a narrowly drawn state interest of compelling importance. Later, in Burdick v. Takushi, (1992), we applied Anderson's standard for "'reasonable, nondiscriminatory restrictions,'" and upheld Hawaii's prohibition on write-in voting despite the fact that it prevented a significant number of "voters from participating in Hawaii elections in a meaningful manner." We reaffirmed Anderson's requirement that a court evaluating a constitutional challenge to an election regulation weigh the asserted injury to the right to vote against the "'precise interests put forward by the State as justifications for the burden imposed by its rule."

In neither Norman nor Burdick did we identify any litmus test for measuring the severity of a burden that a state law imposes on a political party, an individual voter, or a discrete class of voters. However slight that burden may appear, as Harper demonstrates, it must be justified by relevant and legitimate state interests "sufficiently weighty to justify the limitation." We therefore begin our analysis of the constitutionality of Indiana's statute by focusing on those interests.

II

The State has identified several state interests that arguably justify the burdens that SEA 483 imposes on voters and potential voters. While petitioners argue that the statute was actually motivated by partisan concerns and dispute both the significance of the State's interests and the magnitude of any real threat to those interests, they do not question the legitimacy of the interests the State has identified. Each is unquestionably relevant to the State's interest in protecting the integrity and reliability of the electoral process.

The first is the interest in deterring and detecting voter fraud. The State has a valid interest in participating in a nationwide effort to improve and modernize election procedures that have been criticized as antiquated and inefficient. The State also argues that it has a particular interest in preventing voter fraud in response to a problem that is in part the product of its own maladministration-namely, that Indiana's voter registration rolls include a large number of names of persons who are either deceased or no longer live in Indiana. Finally, the State relies on its interest in safeguarding voter confidence. Each of these interests merits separate comment.

Election Modernization

Two recently enacted federal statutes have made it necessary for States to reexamine their election procedures. Both contain provisions consistent with a State's choice to use government-issued photo identification as a relevant source of information concerning a citizen's eligibility to vote.

In the National Voter Registration Act of 1993 (NVRA), Congress established procedures that would both increase the number of registered voters and protect the integrity of the electoral process. The statute requires state motor vehicle driver's license applications to serve as voter registration applications. While that requirement has increased the number of registered voters, the statute also contains a provision restricting States' ability to remove names from the lists of registered voters. These protections have been partly responsible for inflated lists of registered voters. For example, evidence credited by Judge Barker estimated that as of 2004 Indiana's voter rolls were inflated by as much as 41.4%, and data collected by the Election Assistance Committee in 2004 indicated that 19 of 92 Indiana counties had registration totals exceeding 100% of the 2004 voting-age population.

In HAVA, Congress required every State to create and maintain a computerized statewide list of all registered voters. HAVA also requires the States to verify voter information contained in a voter registration application and specifies either an "applicant's driver's license number" or "the last 4 digits of the applicant's social security number" as acceptable verifications.

HAVA also imposes new identification requirements for individuals registering to vote for the first time who submit their applications by mail. If the voter is casting his ballot in person, he must present local election officials with written identification, which may be either "a current and valid photo identification" or another form of documentation such as a bank statement or paycheck. If the voter is voting by mail, he must include a copy of the identification with his ballot. A voter may also include a copy of the documentation with his application or provide his driver's license number or Social Security number for verification. Finally, in a provision entitled "Fail-safe voting," HAVA authorizes the casting of provisional ballots by challenged voters. Of course, neither HAVA nor NVRA required Indiana to enact SEA 483, but they do indicate that Congress believes that photo identification is one effective method of establishing a voter's qualification to vote and that the integrity of elections is enhanced through improved technology. That conclusion is also supported by a report issued shortly after the enactment of SEA 483 by the Commission on Federal Election Reform chaired by former President Jimmy Carter and former Secretary of State James A. Baker III, which is a part of the record in these cases.

Voter Fraud

The only kind of voter fraud that SEA 483 addresses is in-person voter impersonation at polling places. The record contains no evidence of any such fraud actually occurring in Indiana at any time in its history. Moreover, petitioners argue that provisions of the Indiana Criminal Code punishing such conduct as a felony provide adequate protection against the risk that such conduct will occur in the future. It remains true, however, that flagrant examples of such fraud in other parts of the country have been documented throughout this Nation's history by respected historians and journalists, that occasional examples have surfaced in recent years, and that Indiana's own experience with fraudulent voting in the 2003 Democratic primary for East Chicago Mayor—though perpetrated using absentee ballots and not in-person fraud—demonstrate that not only is the risk of voter fraud real but that it could affect the outcome of a close election.

There is no question about the legitimacy or importance of the State's interest in counting only the votes of eligible voters. Moreover, the interest in orderly administration and accurate recordkeeping provides a sufficient justification for carefully identifying all voters participating in the election process. While the most effective method of preventing election fraud may well be debatable, the propriety of doing so is perfectly clear.

In its brief, the State argues that the inflation of its voter rolls provides further support for its enactment of SEA 483. The record contains a November 5, 2000, newspaper article asserting that as a result of NVRA and "sloppy record keeping," Indiana's lists of registered voters included the names of thousands of persons who had either moved, died, or were not eligible to vote because they had been convicted of felonies. Even though Indiana's own negligence may have contributed to the serious inflation of its registration lists when SEA 483 was enacted, the fact of inflated voter rolls does provide a neutral and nondiscriminatory reason supporting the State's decision to require photo identification.

Safeguarding Voter Confidence

Finally, the State contends that it has an interest in protecting public confidence "in the integrity and legitimacy of representative government." While that interest is closely related to the State's interest in preventing voter fraud, public confidence in the integrity of the electoral process has independent significance, because it encourages citizen participation in the democratic process. As the Carter-Baker Report observed, the "electoral system cannot inspire public confidence if no safeguards exist to deter or detect fraud or to confirm the identity of voters."

III

States employ different methods of identifying eligible voters at the polls. Some merely check off the names of registered voters who identify themselves; others require voters to present registration cards or other documentation before they can vote; some require voters to sign their names so their signatures can be compared with those on file; and in recent years an increasing number of States have relied primarily on photo identification. A photo identification requirement imposes some burdens on voters that other methods of identification do not share. For example, a voter may lose his photo identification, may have his wallet stolen on the way to the polls, or may not resemble the photo in the identification because he recently grew a beard. Burdens of that sort arising from life's vagaries, however, are neither so serious nor so frequent as to raise any question about the constitutionality of SEA 483; the availability of the right to cast a provisional ballot provides an adequate remedy for problems of that character.

The burdens that are relevant to the issue before us are those imposed on persons who are eligible to vote but do not possess a current photo identification that complies with the requirements of SEA The fact that most voters already possess a valid driver's license, or some other form of acceptable identification, would not save the statute under our reasoning in Harper, if the State required voters to pay a tax or a fee to obtain a new photo identification. But just as other States provide free voter registration cards, the photo identification cards issued by Indiana's BMV are also free. For most voters who need them, the inconvenience of making a trip to the BMV, gathering the required documents, and posing for a photograph surely does not qualify as a substantial burden on the right to vote, or even represent a significant increase over the usual burdens of voting.

Both evidence in the record and facts of which we may take judicial notice, however, indicate that a somewhat heavier burden may be placed on a limited number of persons. They include elderly persons born out-of-state, who may have difficulty obtaining a birth certificate; persons who because of economic or other personal limitations may find it difficult either to secure a copy of their birth certificate or to assemble the other required documentation to obtain a state-issued identification; homeless persons; and persons with a religious objection to being photographed. If we assume, as the evidence suggests, that some members of these classes were registered voters when SEA 483 was enacted, the new identification requirement may have imposed a special burden on their right to vote.

The severity of that burden is, of course, mitigated by the fact that, if eligible, voters without photo identification may cast provisional ballots that will ultimately be counted. To do so, however, they must travel to the circuit court clerk's office within 10 days to execute the required affidavit. It is unlikely that such a requirement would pose a constitutional problem unless it is wholly unjustified. And even assuming that the burden may not be justified as to a few voters, that conclusion is by no means sufficient to establish petitioners' right to the relief they seek in this litigation.

IV

Given the fact that petitioners have advanced a broad attack on the constitutionality of SEA 483, seeking relief that would invalidate the statute in all its applications, they bear a heavy burden of persuasion. Petitioners ask this Court, in effect, to perform a unique balancing analysis that looks specifically at a small number of voters who may experience a special burden under the statute and weighs their burdens against the State's broad interests in protecting election integrity. Petitioners urge us to ask whether the State's interests justify the burden imposed on voters who cannot afford or obtain a birth certificate and who must make a second trip to the circuit court clerk's office after voting. But on the basis of the evidence in the record it is not possible to quantify either the magnitude of the burden on this narrow class of voters or the portion of the burden imposed on them that is fully justified.

First, the evidence in the record does not provide us with the number of registered voters without photo identification; Judge Barker found petitioners' expert's report to be "utterly incredible and unreliable." Much of the argument about the numbers of such voters comes from extrarecord, postjudgment studies, the accuracy of which has not been tested in the trial court. The record says virtually nothing about the difficulties faced by either indigent voters or voters with religious objections to being photographed.

In sum, on the basis of the record that has been made in this litigation, we cannot conclude that the statute imposes "excessively burdensome requirements" on any class of voters. When we consider only the statute's broad application to all Indiana voters we conclude that it "imposes only a limited burden on voters' rights." The "'precise interests" advanced by the State are therefore sufficient to defeat petitioners' facial challenge to SEA 483.

Finally we note that petitioners have not demonstrated that the proper remedy—even assuming an unjustified burden on some voters—would be to invalidate the entire statute. When evaluating a neutral, nondiscriminatory regulation of voting procedure, "[w]e must keep in mind that '[a] ruling of unconstitutionality frustrates the intent of the elected representatives of the people.'"

V

In their briefs, petitioners stress the fact that all of the Republicans in the General Assembly voted in favor of SEA 483 and the Democrats were unanimous in opposing it. It is fair to infer that partisan considerations may have played a significant role in the decision to enact SEA 483. If such considerations had provided the only justification for a photo identification requirement, we may also assume that SEA 483 would suffer the same fate as the poll tax at issue in Harper.

But if a nondiscriminatory law is supported by valid neutral justifications, those justifications should not be disregarded simply because partisan interests may have provided one motivation for the votes of individual legislators. The state interests identified as justifications for SEA 483 are both neutral and sufficiently strong to require us to reject petitioners' facial attack on the statute. The application of the statute to the vast majority of Indiana voters is amply justified by the valid interest in protecting "the integrity and reliability of the electoral process."

Justice SCALIA, with whom Justice THOMAS and Justice ALITO join, concurring in the judgment.

The lead opinion assumes petitioners' premise that the voter-identification law "may have imposed a special burden on" some voters, but holds that petitioners have not assembled evidence to show that the special burden is severe enough to warrant strict scrutiny. That is true enough, but for the sake of clarity and finality (as well as adherence to precedent), I prefer to decide these cases on the grounds that petitioners' premise is irrelevant and that the burden at issue is minimal and justified.

To evaluate a law respecting the right to vote-whether it governs voter qualifications, candidate selection, or the voting process-we use the approach set out in Burdick v. Takushi (1992). This calls for application of a deferential "important regulatory interests" standard for nonsevere, nondiscriminatory restrictions, reserving strict scrutiny for laws that severely restrict the right to vote. The lead opinion resists the import of Burdick by characterizing it as simply adopting "the balancing approach" of Anderson v. Celebrezze (1983). Although Burdick liberally quoted Anderson, Burdick forged Anderson's amorphous "flexible standard" into something resembling an administrable rule. Since Burdick, we have repeatedly reaffirmed the primacy of its two-track approach. Thus, the first step is to decide whether a challenged law severely burdens the right to vote. Ordinary and widespread burdens, such as those requiring "nominal effort" of everyone, are not severe. Burdens are severe if they go beyond the merely inconvenient.

Of course, we have to identify a burden before we can weigh it. The Indiana law affects different voters differently, but what petitioners view as the law's several light and heavy burdens are no more than the different impacts of the single burden that the law uniformly imposes on all voters. To vote in person in Indiana, everyone must have and present a photo identification that can be obtained for free. The State draws no classifications, let alone discriminatory ones, except to establish optional absentee and provisional balloting for certain poor, elderly, and institutionalized voters and for religious objectors. Nor are voters who already have photo identifications exempted from the burden, since those voters must maintain the accuracy of the information displayed on the identifications, renew them before they expire, and replace them if they are lost.

The Indiana photo-identification law is a generally applicable, nondiscriminatory voting regulation, and our precedents refute the view that individual impacts are relevant to determining the severity of the burden it imposes. Insofar as our election-regulation cases rest upon the requirements of the Fourteenth Amendment, weighing the burden of a nondiscriminatory voting law upon each voter and concomitantly requiring exceptions for vulnerable voters would effectively turn back decades of equal-protection jurisprudence. A voter complaining about such a law's effect on him has no valid equal-protection claim because, without proof of discriminatory intent, a generally applicable law with disparate impact is not unconstitutional. See, e.g., Washington v. Davis (1976). The Fourteenth Amendment does not regard neutral laws as invidious ones, even when their burdens purportedly fall disproportionately on a protected class. A fortiori it does not do so when, as here, the classes complaining of disparate impact are not even protected.[1]

---

1. A number of our early right-to-vote decisions, purporting to rely upon the Equal Protection Clause, strictly scrutinized nondiscriminatory voting laws requiring the payment of fees. See, e.g., Harper v. Virginia Bd. of Elections (1966) (poll tax); Bullock v. Carter (1972) (ballot-access fee); Lubin v. Panish (1974) (ballot-access fee). To the extent those decisions continue to stand for a principle that Burdick v. Takushi (1992), does not already encompass, it suffices to note that we have never held that legislatures must calibrate all election laws, even those totally unrelated to money, for their impacts on poor voters or must otherwise accommodate wealth disparities. [Footnote by Justice Scalia]

Even if I thought that stare decisis did not foreclose adopting an individual-focused approach, I would reject it as an original matter. This is an area where the dos and don'ts need to be known in advance of the election, and voter-by-voter examination of the burdens of voting regulations would prove especially disruptive. A case-by-case approach naturally encourages constant litigation. Very few new election regulations improve everyone's lot, so the potential allegations of severe burden are endless. A State reducing the number of polling places would be open to the complaint it has violated the rights of disabled voters who live near the closed stations. Indeed, it may even be the case that some laws already on the books are especially burdensome for some voters, and one can predict lawsuits demanding that a State adopt voting over the Internet or expand absentee balloting.

That sort of detailed judicial supervision of the election process would flout the Constitution's express commitment of the task to the States. See Art. I, § 4. It is for state legislatures to weigh the costs and benefits of possible changes to their election codes, and their judgment must prevail unless it imposes a severe and unjustified overall burden upon the right to vote, or is intended to disadvantage a particular class. Judicial review of their handiwork must apply an objective, uniform standard that will enable them to determine, ex ante, whether the burden they impose is too severe.

The lead opinion's record-based resolution of these cases, which neither rejects nor embraces the rule of our precedents, provides no certainty, and will embolden litigants who surmise that our precedents have been abandoned. There is no good reason to prefer that course.

The universally applicable requirements of Indiana's voter-identification law are eminently reasonable. The burden of acquiring, possessing, and showing a free photo identification is simply not severe, because it does not "even represent a significant increase over the usual burdens of voting." And the State's interests, are sufficient to sustain that minimal burden. That should end the matter. That the State accommodates some voters by permitting (not requiring) the casting of absentee or provisional ballots, is an indulgence-not a constitutional imperative that falls short of what is required.

Justice SOUTER, with whom Justice GINSBURG joins, dissenting.

Indiana's "Voter ID Law" threatens to impose nontrivial burdens on the voting right of tens of thousands of the State's citizens, and a significant percentage of those individuals are likely to be deterred from voting. The statute is unconstitutional under the balancing standard of Burdick v. Takushi (1992): a State may not burden the right to vote merely by invoking abstract interests, be they legitimate, or even compelling, but must make a particular, factual showing that threats to its interests outweigh the particular impediments it has imposed. The State has made no such justification here, and as to some aspects of its law, it has hardly even tried. I therefore respectfully dissent from the Court's judgment sustaining the statute.

I

Voting-rights cases raise two competing interests, the one side being the fundamental right to vote. The Judiciary is obliged to train a skeptical eye on any qualification of that right.

As against the unfettered right, however, lies the "[c]ommon sense, as well as constitutional law . . . that government must play an active role in structuring elections; 'as a practical matter, there must be a substantial regulation of elections if they are to be fair and honest and if some sort of order, rather than chaos, is to accompany the democratic processes.'"

Given the legitimacy of interests on both sides, we have avoided pre-set levels of scrutiny in favor of a sliding-scale balancing analysis: the scrutiny varies with the effect of the regulation at issue. And whatever the claim, the Court has long made a careful, ground-level appraisal both of the practical burdens on the right to vote and of the State's reasons for imposing those precise burdens.

The lead opinion does not disavow these basic principles. But I think it does not insist enough on the hard facts that our standard of review demands.

II

Under Burdick, "the rigorousness of our inquiry into the propriety of a state election law depends upon the extent to which a challenged regulation burdens First and Fourteenth Amendment rights," upon an assessment of the "character and magnitude of the asserted [threatened] injury," and an estimate of the number of voters likely to be affected.

A

The first set of burdens shown in these cases is the travel costs and fees necessary to get one of the limited variety of federal or state photo identifications needed to cast a regular ballot under the Voter ID Law. The travel is required for the personal visit to a license branch of the Indiana Bureau of Motor Vehicles (BMV), which is demanded of anyone applying for a driver's license or nondriver photo identification. The need to travel to a BMV branch will affect voters according to their circumstances, with the average person probably viewing it as nothing more than an inconvenience. Poor, old, and disabled voters who do not drive a car, however, may find the trip prohibitive, witness the fact that the BMV has far fewer license branches in each county than there are voting precincts.

The burden of traveling to a more distant BMV office rather than a conveniently located polling place is probably serious for many of the individuals who lack photo identification, and public transportation in Indiana is fairly limited. According to a report published by Indiana's Department of Transportation in August 2007, 21 of Indiana's 92 counties have no public transportation system at all, and as of 2000, nearly 1 in every 10 voters lived within 1 of these 21 counties. State officials recognize the effect that travel costs can have on voter turnout, as in Marion County, for example, where efforts have been made to "establis[h] most polling places in locations even more convenient than the statutory minimum," in order to "provid[e] for neighborhood voting." Although making voters travel farther than what is convenient for most and possible for some does not amount to a "severe" burden under Burdick, that is no reason to ignore the burden altogether. It translates into an obvious economic cost (whether in work time lost, or getting and paying for transportation) that an Indiana voter must bear to obtain an ID.

For those voters who can afford the roundtrip, a second financial hurdle appears: in order to get photo identification for the first time, they need to present "'a birth certificate, a certificate of naturalization, U.S. veterans photo identification, U.S. military photo identification, or a U.S. passport.'" As the lead opinion says, the two most common of these documents come at a price: Indiana counties charge anywhere from $3 to $12 for a birth certificate (and in some other States the fee is significantly higher), and that same price must usually be paid for a first-time passport, since a birth certificate is required to prove U.S. citizenship by birth. The total fees for a passport, moreover, are up to about $100. So most voters must pay at least one fee to get the ID necessary to cast a regular ballot. As with the travel costs, these fees are far from shocking on their face, but in the Burdick analysis it matters that both the travel costs and the fees are disproportionately heavy for, and thus disproportionately likely to deter, the poor, the old, and the immobile.

B

To be sure, Indiana has a provisional-ballot exception to the ID requirement for individuals the State considers "indigent" as well as those with religious objections to being photographed, and this sort of exception could in theory provide a way around the costs of procuring an ID. But Indiana's chosen exception does not amount to much relief.

The law allows these voters who lack the necessary ID to sign the poll book and cast a provisional ballot. As the lead opinion recognizes, though, that is only the first step; to have the provisional ballot counted, a voter must then appear in person before the circuit court clerk or county election board within 10 days of the election, to sign an affidavit attesting to indigency or religious objection to being photographed (or to present an ID at that point). Unlike the trip to the BMV (which, assuming things go smoothly, needs to be made only once every four years for renewal of nondriver photo identification, see id.), this one must be taken every time a poor person or religious objector wishes to vote, because the State does not allow an affidavit to count in successive elections. And unlike the trip to the BMV (which at least has a handful of license branches in the more populous counties), a county has only one county seat. Forcing these people to travel to the county seat every time they try to vote is particularly onerous for the reason noted already, that most counties in Indiana either lack public transportation or offer only limited coverage.

That the need to travel to the county seat each election amounts to a high hurdle is shown in the results of the 2007 municipal elections in Marion County, to which Indiana's Voter ID Law applied. Thirty-four provisional ballots were cast, but only two provisional voters made it to the County Clerk's Office within the 10 days.

All of this suggests that provisional ballots do not obviate the burdens of getting photo identification. And even if that were not so, the provisional-ballot option would be inadequate for a further reason: the indigency exception by definition offers no relief to those voters who do not consider themselves (or would not be considered) indigent but as a practical matter would find it hard, for nonfinancial reasons, to get the required ID (most obviously the disabled).

c

Indiana's Voter ID Law thus threatens to impose serious burdens on the voting right, even if not "severe" ones, and the next question under Burdick is whether the number of individuals likely to be affected is significant as well. Record evidence and facts open to judicial notice answer yes.

Although the District Court found that petitioners failed to offer any reliable empirical study of numbers of voters affected, we may accept that court's rough calculation that 43,000 voting-age residents lack the kind of identification card required by Indiana's law. The District Court made that estimate by comparing BMV records reproduced in petitioners' statistician's report with U.S. Census Bureau figures for Indiana's voting-age population in 2004, and the State does not argue that these raw data are unreliable.

So a fair reading of the data supports the District Court's finding that around 43,000 Indiana residents lack the needed identification, and will bear the burdens the law imposes. To be sure, the 43,000 figure has to be discounted to some extent, residents of certain nursing homes being exempted from the photo identification requirement. But the State does not suggest that this narrow exception could possibly reduce 43,000 to an insubstantial number.

The upshot is this. Tens of thousands of voting-age residents lack the necessary photo identification. A large proportion of them are likely to be in bad shape economically. The Voter ID Law places hurdles in the way of either getting an ID or of voting provisionally, and they translate into nontrivial economic costs. There is accordingly no reason to doubt that a significant number of state residents will be discouraged or disabled from voting.[2]

---

2. Studies in other States suggest that the burdens of an ID requirement may also fall disproportionately upon racial minorities. See Overton, Voter Identification, 105 Mich. L.Rev. 631, 659 (2007) ("In 1994, the U.S. Department of Justice found that African-Americans in Louisiana were four to five

Petitioners, to be sure, failed to nail down precisely how great the cohort of discouraged and totally deterred voters will be, but empirical precision beyond the foregoing numbers has never been demanded for raising a voting-rights claim. Cf. Washington State Grange v. Washington State Republican Party, 552 U.S. ____, ____, 128 S.Ct. 1184, 1197, 170 L.Ed.2d 151 (2008) (ROBERTS, C. J., concurring) ("Nothing in my analysis requires the parties to produce studies regarding voter perceptions on this score"); Dunn v. Blumstein, 405 U. S. 330, 335, n. 5, 92 S.Ct. 995, 31 L.Ed.2d 274 (1972) ("[I]t would be difficult to determine precisely how many would-be voters throughout the country cannot vote because of durational residence requirements"); Bullock, supra, at 144, 92 S.Ct. 849 (taking account of "the obvious likelihood" that candidate filing fees would "fall more heavily on the less affluent segment of the community, whose favorites may be unable to pay the large costs"). While of course it would greatly aid a plaintiff to establish his claims beyond mathematical doubt, he does enough to show that serious burdens are likely.

III

Because the lead opinion finds only "limited" burdens on the right to vote, it avoids a hard look at the State's claimed interests. But having found the Voter ID Law burdens far from trivial, I have to make a rigorous assessment of "'the precise interests put forward by the State as justifications for the burden imposed by its rule,' [and] 'the extent to which those interests make it necessary to burden the plaintiff's rights.'"

As the lead opinion sees it, the State has offered four related concerns that suffice to justify the Voter ID Law: modernizing election procedures, combating voter fraud, addressing the consequences of the State's bloated voter rolls, and protecting public confidence in the integrity of the electoral process. On closer look, however, it appears that the first two (which are really just one) can claim modest weight at best, and the latter two if anything weaken the State's case.

A

The lead opinion's discussion of the State's reasons begins with the State's asserted interests in "election modernization," and in combating voter fraud. Although these are given separate headings, any line drawn between them is unconvincing; as I understand it, the "effort to modernize elections," is not for modernity's sake, but to reach certain practical (or political) objectives. The

---

times less likely than white residents to have government sanctioned photo identification"); (describing June 2005 study by the Employment and Training Institute at the University of Wisconsin Milwaukee, which found that while 17% of voting age whites lacked a valid driver's license, 55% of black males and 49% of black females were unlicensed, and 46% of Latino males and 59% of Latino females were similarly unlicensed). [Footnote by Justice Souter]

State says that it adopted the ID law principally to combat voter fraud, and it is this claim, not the slogan of "election modernization," that warrants attention.

There is no denying the abstract importance, the compelling nature, of combating voter fraud. But it takes several steps to get beyond the level of abstraction here.

To begin with, requiring a voter to show photo identification before casting a regular ballot addresses only one form of voter fraud: in-person voter impersonation. The photo ID requirement leaves untouched the problems of absentee-ballot fraud, which (unlike in-person voter impersonation) is a documented problem in Indiana); of registered voters voting more than once (but maintaining their own identities) in different counties or in different States; of felons and other disqualified individuals voting in their own names; of vote buying; or, for that matter, of ballot-stuffing, ballot miscounting, voter intimidation, or any other type of corruption on the part of officials administering elections.

And even the State's interest in deterring a voter from showing up at the polls and claiming to be someone he is not must, in turn, be discounted for the fact that the State has not come across a single instance of in-person voter impersonation fraud in all of Indiana's history. Neither the District Court nor the Indiana General Assembly that passed the Voter ID Law was given any evidence whatsoever of in-person voter impersonation fraud in the State.

The State responds to the want of evidence with the assertion that in-person voter impersonation fraud is hard to detect. But this is like saying the "man who wasn't there" is hard to spot, and to know whether difficulty in detection accounts for the lack of evidence one at least has to ask whether in-person voter impersonation is (or would be) relatively harder to ferret out than other kinds of fraud (e.g., by absentee ballot) which the State has had no trouble documenting. The answer seems to be no; there is reason to think that "impersonation of voters is . . . the most likely type of fraud to be discovered." This is in part because an individual who impersonates another at the polls commits his fraud in the open, under the scrutiny of local poll workers who may well recognize a fraudulent voter when they hear who he claims to be.

The relative ease of discovering in-person voter impersonation is also owing to the odds that any such fraud will be committed by "organized groups such as campaigns or political parties" rather than by individuals acting alone. It simply is not worth it for individuals acting alone to commit in-person voter impersonation, which is relatively ineffectual for the foolish few who may commit it. If an imposter gets caught, he is subject to severe criminal penalties.

In sum, fraud by individuals acting alone, however difficult to detect, is unlikely. And while there may be greater incentives for organized groups to engage in broad-gauged in-person voter impersonation fraud, it is also far more difficult to conceal larger enterprises of this sort. The State's argument about the difficulty of detecting the fraud lacks real force.

What is left of the State's claim must be downgraded further for one final reason: regardless of the interest the State may have in adopting a photo identification requirement as a general matter, that interest in no way necessitates the particular burdens the Voter ID Law imposes on poor people and religious objectors. Individuals unable to get photo identification are forced to travel to the county seat every time they wish to exercise the franchise, and they have to get there within 10 days of the election. Nothing about the State's interest in fighting voter fraud justifies this requirement of a post-election trip to the county seat instead of some verification process at the polling places.

In briefing this Court, the State responds by pointing to an interest in keeping lines at polling places short. But this argument fails on its own terms, for whatever might be the number of individuals casting a provisional ballot, the State could simply allow voters to sign the indigency affidavit at the polls subject *1641 to review there after the election. After all, the Voter ID Law already requires voters lacking photo identification to sign, at the polling site, an affidavit attesting to proper registration.

Indeed, the State's argument more than fails; it backfires, in implicitly conceding that a not-insignificant number of individuals will need to rely on the burdensome provisional-ballot mechanism. What is more, as the District Court found, the Voter ID Law itself actually increases the likelihood of delay at the polls. Since any minor discrepancy between a voter's photo identification card and the registration information may lead to a challenge, "the opportunities for presenting challenges ha[ve] increased as a result of the photo identification requirements."

B

The State's asserted interests in modernizing elections and combating fraud are decidedly modest; at best, they fail to offset the clear inference that thousands of Indiana citizens will be discouraged from voting. The two remaining justifications, meanwhile, actually weaken the State's case.

The lead opinion agrees with the State that "the inflation of its voter rolls is further support for its enactment of" the Voter ID Law. How any of this can justify restrictions on the right to vote is difficult to say. The State is simply trying to take advantage of its own wrong: if it is true that the State's fear of in-person voter impersonation fraud arises from its bloated voter checklist, the answer to the problem is in the State's own hands. The claim that the State has an interest in addressing a symptom of the problem (alleged impersonation) rather than the problem itself (the negligently maintained bloated rolls) is thus self-defeating; it shows that the State has no justifiable need to burden the right to vote as it does, and it suggests that the State is not as serious about combating fraud as it claims to be.

The State's final justification, its interest in safeguarding voter confidence, similarly collapses. The problem with claiming this interest lies in its connection to the bloated voter rolls; the State has come up with nothing to suggest that its citizens doubt the integrity of the State's electoral process, except its own failure to maintain its rolls. The answer to this problem is not to burden the right to vote, but to end the official negligence.

It should go without saying that none of this is to deny States' legitimate interest in safeguarding public confidence. But the force of the interest depends on the facts (or plausibility of the assumptions) said to justify invoking it.

c

Without a shred of evidence that in-person voter impersonation is a problem in the State, much less a crisis, Indiana has adopted one of the most restrictive photo identification requirements in the country. The State recognizes that tens of thousands of qualified voters lack the necessary federally issued or state-issued identification, but it insists on implementing the requirement immediately, without allowing a transition period for targeted efforts to distribute the required identification to individuals who need it. The State hardly even tries to explain its decision to force indigents or religious objectors to travel all the way to their county seats every time they wish to vote, and if there is any waning of confidence in the administration of elections it probably owes more to the State's violation of federal election law than to any imposters at the polling places. It is impossible to say, on this record, that the State's interest in adopting its signally inhibiting photo identification requirement has been shown to outweigh the serious burdens it imposes on the right to vote.

The Indiana Voter ID Law is thus unconstitutional: the state interests fail to justify the practical limitations placed on the right to vote, and the law imposes an unreasonable and irrelevant burden on voters who are poor and old. I would vacate the judgment of the Seventh Circuit, and remand for further proceedings.

L. Procedural Due Process (casebook, p. 1006)

1. What Is a Deprivation?

There were two important procedural due process cases in October Term 2004. They were in different contexts and raised different issues. In DeShaney v. Winnebago County Department of Social Services (1989) (casebook, p. 1011), the Court held that generally the government has no duty to protect people from privately inflicted harms. In Town of Castle Rock v. Gonzales, excerpted below, the Court considered whether state law, and a restraining order pursuant to it, might be used to create a duty to provide protection as a property right.

In Wilkinson v. Austin, which appears after *Castle Rock*, the Court considered whether placing a prisoner in a "Supermax" facility, with 23 hours a day of solitary confinement, is a deprivation of liberty, and if so, what due process requires.

TOWN OF CASTLE ROCK v. GONZALES
545 U.S. 748 (2005)

Justice SCALIA delivered the opinion of the Court.

We decide in this case whether an individual who has obtained a state-law restraining order has a constitutionally protected property interest in having the police enforce the restraining order when they have probable cause to believe it has been violated.

I

The horrible facts of this case are contained in the complaint that respondent Jessica Gonzales filed in Federal District Court. (Because the case comes to us on appeal from a dismissal of the complaint, we assume its allegations are true.) Respondent alleges that petitioner, the town of Castle Rock, Colorado, violated the Due Process Clause of the Fourteenth Amendment to the United States Constitution when its police officers, acting pursuant to official policy or custom, failed to respond properly to her repeated reports that her estranged husband was violating the terms of a restraining order.

The restraining order had been issued by a state trial court several weeks earlier in conjunction with respondent's divorce proceedings. The original form order, issued on May 21, 1999, and served on respondent's husband on June 4, 1999, commanded him not to "molest or disturb the peace of [respondent] or of any child," and to remain at least 100 yards from the family home at all times. The bottom of the pre-printed form noted that the reverse side contained "IMPOR-TANT NOTICES FOR RESTRAINED PARTIES AND LAW ENFORCEMENT OFFICIALS." the preprinted text on the back of the form included the following "WARNING":

> A KNOWING VIOLATION OF A RESTRAINING ORDER IS A CRIME. . . . A VIOLATION WILL ALSO CONSTITUTE CONTEMPT OF COURT. YOU MAY BE ARRESTED WITHOUT NOTICE IF A LAW ENFORCEMENT OFFICER HAS PROBABLE CAUSE TO BELIEVE THAT YOU HAVE KNOWINGLY VI-OLATED THIS ORDER.

The preprinted text on the back of the form also included a "NOTICE TO LAW ENFORCEMENT OFFICIALS," which read in part:

> YOU SHALL USE EVERY REASONABLE MEANS TO ENFORCE THIS RESTRAINING ORDER. YOU SHALL ARREST, OR, IF AN ARREST WOULD BE IMPRACTICAL UNDER THE CIRCUMSTANCES, SEEK A WARRANT FOR THE ARREST OF THE RESTRAINED PERSON WHEN YOU HAVE INFORMA-TION AMOUNTING TO PROBABLE CAUSE THAT THE RESTRAINED PER-SON HAS VIOLATED OR ATTEMPTED TO VIOLATE ANY PROVISION OF THIS ORDER AND THE RESTRAINED PERSON HAS BEEN PROPERLY SERVED WITH A COPY OF THIS ORDER OR HAS RECEIVED ACTUAL NOTICE OF THE EXISTENCE OF THIS ORDER.

On June 4, 1999, the state trial court modified the terms of the restraining order and made it permanent. The modified order gave respondent's husband the right to spend time with his three daughters (ages 10, 9, and 7) on alternate weekends, for two weeks during the summer, and, " 'upon reasonable notice,' " for a midweek dinner visit " 'arranged by the parties' "; the modified order also allowed him to visit the home to collect the children for such "parenting time."

According to the complaint, at about 5 or 5:30 p.m. on Tuesday, June 22, 1999, respondent's husband took the three daughters while they were playing outside the family home. No advance arrangements had been made for him to see the daughters that evening. When respondent noticed the children were missing, she suspected her husband had taken them. At about 7:30 p.m., she called the Castle Rock Police Department, which dispatched two officers. The complaint continues: "When [the officers] arrived ..., she showed them a copy of the TRO and requested that it be enforced and the three children be returned to her immediately. [The officers] stated that there was nothing they could do about the TRO and suggested that [respondent] call the Police Department again if the three children did not return home by 10:00 p.m."

At approximately 8:30 p.m., respondent talked to her husband on his cellular telephone. He told her "he had the three children [at an] amusement park in Denver." She called the police again and asked them to "have someone check for" her husband or his vehicle at the amusement park and "put out an [all points bulletin]" for her husband, but the officer with whom she spoke "refused to do so," again telling her to "wait until 10:00 p.m. and see if" her husband returned the girls.

At approximately 10:10 p.m., respondent called the police and said her children were still missing, but she was now told to wait until midnight. She called at midnight and told the dispatcher her children were still missing. She went to her husband's apartment and, finding nobody there, called the police at 12:10 a.m.; she was told to wait for an officer to arrive. When none came, she went to the police station at 12:50 a.m. and submitted an incident report. The officer who took the report "made no reasonable effort to enforce the TRO or locate the three children. Instead, he went to dinner."

At approximately 3:20 a.m., respondent's husband arrived at the police station and opened fire with a semiautomatic handgun he had purchased earlier that evening. Police shot back, killing him. Inside the cab of his pickup truck, they found the bodies of all three daughters, whom he had already murdered.

On the basis of the foregoing factual allegations, respondent brought an action claiming that the town violated the Due Process Clause because its police department had "an official policy or custom of failing to respond properly to complaints of restraining order violations" and "tolerate[d] the non-enforcement of restraining orders by its police officers." The complaint also alleged that the town's actions "were taken either willfully, recklessly or with such gross negligence as to indicate wanton disregard and deliberate indifference to" respondent's civil rights.

II

The Fourteenth Amendment to the United States Constitution provides that a State shall not "deprive any person of life, liberty, or property, without due process of law." Amdt. 14, § 1. In 42 U.S.C. § 1983, Congress has created a federal cause of action for "the deprivation of any rights, privileges, or immunities secured by the Constitution and laws." Respondent claims the benefit of this provision on the ground that she had a property interest in police enforcement of the restraining order against her husband; and that the town deprived her of this property without due process by having a policy that tolerated nonenforcement of restraining orders.

As the Court of Appeals recognized, we left a similar question unanswered in DeShaney v. Winnebago County Dept. of Social Servs. (1989), another case with "undeniably tragic" facts: Local child-protection officials had failed to protect a young boy from beatings by his father that left him severely brain damaged. We held that the so-called "substantive" component of the Due Process Clause does not "requir[e] the State to protect the life, liberty, and property of its citizens against invasion by private actors."

The procedural component of the Due Process Clause does not protect everything that might be described as a "benefit": "To have a property interest in a benefit, a person clearly must have more than an abstract need or desire" and "more than a unilateral expectation of it. He must, instead, have a legitimate claim of entitlement to it." Board of Regents of State Colleges v. Roth (1972). Such entitlements are " 'of course, . . . not created by the Constitution. Rather, they are created and their dimensions are defined by existing rules or understandings that stem from an independent source such as state law.' " Paul v. Davis (1976).

A

Our cases recognize that a benefit is not a protected entitlement if government officials may grant or deny it in their discretion. The Court of Appeals in this case determined that Colorado law created an entitlement to enforcement of the restraining order because the "court-issued restraining order . . . specifically dictated that its terms must be enforced" and a "state statute command[ed]" enforcement of the order when certain objective conditions were met (probable cause to believe that the order had been violated and that the object of the order had received notice of its existence).

B

The critical language in the restraining order came not from any part of the order itself (which was signed by the state-court trial judge and directed to the restrained party, respondent's husband), but from the preprinted notice to law-enforcement personnel that appeared on the back of the order. That notice effectively restated the statutory provision describing "peace officers' duties" related to the crime of violation of a restraining order. We do not believe that these provisions of Colorado law truly made enforcement of restraining orders mandatory. A well established tradition of police discretion has long coexisted with apparently mandatory arrest statutes.

"In each and every state there are long-standing statutes that, by their terms, seem to preclude nonenforcement by the police. . . . However, for a number of reasons, including their legislative history, insufficient resources, and sheer physical impossibility, it has been recognized that such statutes cannot be interpreted literally. . . . [T]hey clearly do not mean that a police officer may not lawfully decline to make an arrest. As to third parties in these states, the full-enforcement statutes simply have no effect, and their significance is further diminished." 1 ABA Standards for Criminal Justice (2d ed.1980).

The deep-rooted nature of law-enforcement discretion, even in the presence of seemingly mandatory legislative commands, is illustrated by Chicago v. Morales (1999), which involved an ordinance that said a police officer " 'shall order' " persons to disperse in certain circumstances. This Court rejected out of hand the possibility that "the mandatory language of the ordinance . . . afford[ed] the police no discretion." It is, the Court proclaimed, simply "common sense that all police officers must use some discretion in deciding when and where to enforce city ordinances."

Against that backdrop, a true mandate of police action would require some stronger indication from the Colorado Legislature than "shall use every reasonable means to enforce a restraining order" (or even "shall arrest . . . or . . . seek a warrant"). That language is not perceptibly more mandatory than the Colorado statute which has long told municipal chiefs of police that they "shall pursue and arrest any person fleeing from justice in any part of the state" and that they "shall apprehend any person in the act of committing any offense . . . and, forthwith and without any warrant, bring such person before a . . . competent authority for examination and trial." It is hard to imagine that a Colorado peace officer would not have some discretion to determine that—despite probable cause to believe a restraining order has been violated—the circumstances of the violation or the competing duties of that officer or his agency counsel decisively against enforcement in a particular instance. The practical necessity for discretion is particularly apparent in a case such as this one, where the suspected violator is not actually present and his whereabouts are unknown.

The dissent correctly points out that, in the specific context of domestic violence, mandatory-arrest statutes have been found in some States to be more mandatory than traditional mandatory-arrest statutes. Even in the domestic-violence context, however, it is unclear how the mandatory-arrest paradigm applies to cases in which the offender is not present to be arrested.

Respondent does not specify the precise means of enforcement that the Colorado restraining-order statute assertedly mandated—whether her interest lay in having police arrest her husband, having them seek a warrant for his arrest, or having them "use every reasonable means, up to and including arrest, to enforce the order's terms." Such indeterminacy is not the hallmark of a duty that is mandatory. Nor can someone be safely deemed "entitled" to something when the identity of the alleged entitlement is vague.

Even if the statute could be said to have made enforcement of restraining orders "mandatory" because of the domestic-violence context of the underlying statute, that would not necessarily mean that state law gave respondent an entitlement to enforcement of the mandate. Making the actions of government employees obligatory can serve various legitimate ends other than the conferral of a benefit on a specific class of people. The serving of public rather than private ends is the normal course of the criminal law because criminal acts, "besides the injury [they do] to individuals, . . . strike at the very being of society; which cannot possibly subsist, where actions of this sort are suffered to escape with impunity." This principle underlies, for example, a Colorado district attorney's discretion to prosecute a domestic assault, even though the victim withdraws her charge.

C

Even if we were to think otherwise concerning the creation of an entitlement by Colorado, it is by no means clear that an individual entitlement to enforcement of a restraining order could constitute a "property" interest for purposes of the Due Process Clause. Such a right would not, of course, resemble any traditional conception of property. Although that alone does not disqualify it from due process protection, as *Roth* and its progeny show, the right to have a restraining order enforced does not "have some ascertainable monetary value," as even our "*Roth*-type property-as-entitlement" cases have implicitly required.

Perhaps most radically, the alleged property interest here arises incidentally, not out of some new species of government benefit or service, but out of a function that government actors have always performed—to wit, arresting people who they have probable cause to believe have committed a criminal offense.

III

We conclude, therefore, that respondent did not, for purposes of the Due Process Clause, have a property interest in police enforcement of the restraining order against her husband. In light of today's decision and that in *DeShaney*, the benefit that a third party may receive from having someone else arrested for a crime generally does not trigger protections under the Due Process Clause, neither in its procedural nor in its "substantive" manifestations. This result reflects our continuing reluctance to treat the Fourteenth Amendment as " 'a font of tort law,' " *Parratt v. Taylor* (1981), but it does not mean States are powerless to provide victims with personally enforceable remedies. Although the framers of the Fourteenth Amendment and the Civil Rights Act of 1871 did not create a system by which police departments are generally held financially accountable for crimes that better policing might have prevented, the people of Colorado are free to craft such a system under state law.

Justice SOUTER, with whom Justice BREYER joins, concurring.

The Due Process Clause extends procedural protection to guard against unfair deprivation by state officials of substantive state-law property rights or entitlements; the federal process protects the property created by state law. But Gonzales claims a property interest in a state-mandated process in and of itself. This argument is at odds with the rule that "[p]rocess is not an end in itself. Its constitutional purpose is to protect a substantive interest to which the individual has a legitimate claim of entitlement."

Just as a State cannot diminish a property right, once conferred, by attaching less than generous procedure to its deprivation, neither does a State create a property right merely by ordaining beneficial procedure unconnected to some articulable substantive guarantee. This is not to say that state rules of executive procedure may not provide significant reasons to infer an articulable property right meant to be protected; but it is to say that we have not identified property with procedure as such. State rules of executive procedure, however important, may be nothing more than rules of executive procedure.

Thus, in every instance of property recognized by this Court as calling for federal procedural protection, the property has been distinguishable from the procedural obligations imposed on state officials to protect it. [T]he property interest recognized in our cases has always existed apart from state procedural protection before the Court has recognized a constitutional claim to protection by federal process. To accede to Gonzales's argument would therefore work a sea change in the scope of federal due process, for she seeks federal process as a substitute simply for state process. There is no articulable distinction between the object of Gonzales's asserted entitlement and the process she desires in order to protect her entitlement; both amount to certain steps to be taken by the police to protect her family and herself. Gonzales's claim would thus take us beyond *Roth* or any other recognized theory of Fourteenth Amendment due process, by collapsing the distinction between property protected and the process that protects it, and would federalize every mandatory state-law direction to executive officers whose performance on the job can be vitally significant to individuals affected.

Justice STEVENS, with whom Justice GINSBURG joins, dissenting.

The issue presented to us is much narrower than is suggested by the far-ranging arguments of the parties and their amici. Neither the tragic facts of the case, nor the importance of according proper deference to law enforcement professionals, should divert our attention from that issue. That issue is whether the restraining order entered by the Colorado trial court on June 4, 1999, created a "property" interest that is protected from arbitrary deprivation by the Due Process Clause of the Fourteenth Amendment.

It is perfectly clear, on the one hand, that neither the Federal Constitution itself, nor any federal statute, granted respondent or her children any individual entitlement to police protection. See DeShaney v. Winnebago County Dept. of Social Servs. (1989). Nor, I assume, does any Colorado statute create any such entitlement for the ordinary citizen. On the other hand, it is equally clear that federal law imposes no impediment to the creation of such an entitlement by Colorado law. Respondent certainly could have entered into a contract with a private security firm, obligating the firm to provide protection to respondent's family; respondent's interest in such a contract would unquestionably constitute "property" within the meaning of the Due Process Clause. If a Colorado statute enacted for her benefit, or a valid order entered by a Colorado judge, created the functional equivalent of such a private contract by granting respondent an entitlement to mandatory individual protection by the local police force, that state-created right would also qualify as "property" entitled to constitutional protection.

I do not understand the majority to rule out the foregoing propositions, although it does express doubts. Moreover, the majority does not contest that if respondent did have a cognizable property interest in this case, the deprivation of that interest violated due process. As the Court notes, respondent has alleged that she presented the police with a copy of the restraining order issued by the Colorado court and requested that it be enforced. In response, she contends, the officers effectively ignored her. If these allegations are true, a federal statute, 42 U.S.C. § 1983, provides her with a remedy against the petitioner, even if Colorado law does not.

The central question in this case is therefore whether, as a matter of Colorado law, respondent had a right to police assistance comparable to the right she would have possessed to any other service the government or a private firm might have undertaken to provide.

Even if the Court had good reason to doubt the Court of Appeals' determination of state law, it would, in my judgment, be a far wiser course to certify the question to the Colorado Supreme Court. Powerful considerations support certification in this case. First, principles of federalism and comity favor giving a State's high court the opportunity to answer important questions of state law, particularly when those questions implicate uniquely local matters such as law enforcement and might well require the weighing of policy considerations for their correct resolution. Second, by certifying a potentially dispositive state-law issue, the Court would adhere to its wise policy of avoiding the unnecessary adjudication of difficult questions of constitutional law. Third, certification would promote both judicial economy and fairness to the parties. After all, the Colorado Supreme Court is the ultimate authority on the meaning of Colorado law, and if in later litigation it should disagree with this Court's provisional state-law holding, our efforts will have been wasted and respondent will have been deprived of the opportunity to have her claims heard under the authoritative view of Colorado law. The unique facts of this case only serve to emphasize the importance of employing a procedure that will provide the correct answer to the central question of state law.

Three flaws in the Court's rather superficial analysis of the merits highlight the unwisdom of its decision to answer the state-law question de novo. First, the Court places undue weight on the various statutes throughout the country that seemingly mandate police enforcement but are generally understood to preserve police discretion. As a result, the Court gives short shrift to the unique case of "mandatory arrest" statutes in the domestic violence context; States passed a wave of these statutes in the 1980's and 1990's with the unmistakable goal of eliminating police discretion in this area. Second, the Court's formalistic analysis fails to take seriously the fact that the Colorado statute at issue in this case was enacted for the benefit of the narrow class of persons who are beneficiaries of domestic restraining orders, and that the order at issue in this case was specifically intended to provide protection to respondent and her children. Finally, the Court is simply wrong to assert that a citizen's interest in the government's commitment to provide police enforcement in certain defined circumstances does not resemble any "traditional conception of property"; in fact, a citizen's property interest in such a commitment is just as concrete and worthy of protection as her interest in any other important service the government or a private firm has undertaken to provide.

Given that Colorado law has quite clearly eliminated the police's discretion to deny enforcement, respondent is correct that she had much more than a "unilateral expectation" that the restraining order would be enforced; rather, she had a "legitimate claim of entitlement" to enforcement. Recognizing respondent's property interest in the enforcement of her restraining order is fully consistent with our precedent. This Court has "made clear that the property interests protected by procedural due process extend well beyond actual ownership of real estate, chattels, or money." The "types of interests protected as 'property' are varied and, as often as not, intangible, 'relating to the whole domain of social and economic fact.'" Police enforcement of a restraining order is a government service that is no less concrete and no less valuable than other government services, such as education.

The relative novelty of recognizing this type of property interest is explained by the relative novelty of the domestic violence statutes creating a mandatory arrest duty; before this innovation, the unfettered discretion that characterized police enforcement defeated any citizen's "legitimate claim of entitlement" to this service. Novel or not, respondent's claim finds strong support in the principles that underlie our due process jurisprudence. In this case, Colorado law guaranteed the provision of a certain service, in certain defined circumstances, to a certain class of beneficiaries, and respondent reasonably relied on that guarantee. As we observed in *Roth*, "[i]t is a purpose of the ancient institution of property to protect those claims upon which people rely in their daily lives, reliance that must not be arbitrarily undermined." Surely, if respondent had contracted with a private security firm to provide her and her daughters with protection from her husband, it would be apparent that she possessed a property interest in such a contract. Here, Colorado undertook a comparable obligation, and respondent—with restraining order in hand—justifiably relied on that undertaking. Respondent's claim of entitlement to this promised service is no less legitimate than the other claims our cases have upheld, and no less concrete than a hypothetical agreement with a private firm. The fact that it is based on a statutory enactment and a judicial order entered for her special protection, rather than on a formal contract, does not provide a principled basis for refusing to consider it "property" worthy of constitutional protection.

Because respondent had a property interest in the enforcement of the restraining order, state officials could not deprive her of that interest without observing fair procedures. Her description of the police behavior in this case and the department's callous policy of failing to respond properly to reports of restraining order violations clearly alleges a due process violation. At the very least, due process requires that the relevant state decisionmaker listen to the claimant and then apply the relevant criteria in reaching his decision.

2. Is It a Deprivation of "Life, Liberty, or Property"?

Liberty Interests for Prisoners (casebook, p. 1032)

In *Wilkinson v. Austin*, below, the Court considered whether prisoners placed in "super-max" facilities are deprived of liberty and, if so, whether the state's procedures are sufficient to meet due process.

WILKINSON v. AUSTIN
545 U.S. 209 (2005)

Justice KENNEDY delivered the opinion of the Court

This case involves the process by which Ohio classifies prisoners for placement at its highest security prison, known as a "Supermax" facility. Supermax facilities are maximum-security prisons with highly restrictive conditions, designed to segregate the most dangerous prisoners from the general prison population. We must consider what process the Fourteenth Amendment to the United States Constitution requires Ohio to afford to inmates before assigning them to Supermax. We hold that the procedures Ohio has adopted provide sufficient procedural protection to comply with due process requirements.

I

The use of Supermax prisons has increased over the last 20 years, in part as a response to the rise in prison gangs and prison violence. About 30 States now operate Supermax prisons, in addition to the two operated by the Federal Government. In 1998, Ohio opened its only Supermax facility, the Ohio State Penitentiary (OSP), after a riot in one of its maximum-security prisons. OSP has the capacity to house up to 504 inmates in single-inmate cells and is designed to "separate the most predatory and dangerous prisoners from the rest of the . . . general [prison] population."

Conditions at OSP are more restrictive than any other form of incarceration in Ohio, including conditions on its death row or in its administrative control units. In the OSP almost every aspect of an inmate's life is controlled and monitored. Inmates must remain in their cells, which measure 7 by 14 feet, for 23 hours per day. A light remains on in the cell at all times, though it is sometimes dimmed, and an inmate who attempts to shield the light to sleep is subject to further discipline. During the one hour per day that an inmate may leave his cell, access is limited to one of two indoor recreation cells.

Incarceration at OSP is synonymous with extreme isolation. In contrast to any other Ohio prison, including any segregation unit, OSP cells have solid metal doors with metal strips along their sides and bottoms which prevent conversation or communication with other inmates. All meals are taken alone in the inmate's cell instead of in a common eating area. Opportunities for visitation are rare and in all events are conducted through glass walls. It is fair to say OSP inmates are deprived of almost any environmental or sensory stimuli and of almost all human contact.

Aside from the severity of the conditions, placement at OSP is for an indefinite period of time, limited only by an inmate's sentence. For an inmate serving a life sentence, there is no indication how long he may be incarcerated at OSP once assigned there. Inmates otherwise eligible for parole lose their eligibility while incarcerated at OSP.

Placement at OSP is determined in the following manner: Upon entering the prison system, all Ohio inmates are assigned a numerical security classification from level 1 through level 5, with 1 the lowest security risk and 5 the highest. The initial security classification is based on numerous factors (e.g., the nature of the underlying offense, criminal history, or gang affiliation) but is subject to modification at any time during the inmate's prison term if, for instance, he engages in misconduct or is deemed a security risk. Level 5 inmates are placed in OSP, and levels 1 through 4 inmates are placed at lower security facilities throughout the State.

Ohio concedes that when OSP first became operational, the procedures used to assign inmates to the facility were inconsistent and undefined. For a time, no official policy governing placement was in effect. Haphazard placements were not uncommon, and some individuals who did not pose high-security risks were designated, nonetheless, for OSP. In an effort to establish guidelines for the selection and classification of inmates suitable for OSP, Ohio issued Department of Rehabilitation and Correction Policy 111-07 (Aug. 31, 1998). This policy has been revised at various points but relevant here are two versions: the "Old Policy" and the "New Policy." The New Policy provided more guidance regarding the factors to be considered in placement decisions and afforded inmates more procedural protection against erroneous placement at OSP.

Although the record is not altogether clear regarding the precise manner in which the New Policy operates, we construe it based on the policy's text, the accompanying forms, and the parties' representations at oral argument and in their briefs. The New Policy appears to operate as follows: A classification review for OSP placement can occur either (1) upon entry into the prison system if the inmate was convicted of certain offenses, e.g., organized crime, or (2) during the term of incarceration if an inmate engages in specified conduct, e.g., leads a prison gang. The review process begins when a prison official prepares a "Security Designation Long Form." This three-page form details matters such as the inmate's recent violence, escape attempts, gang affiliation, underlying offense, and other pertinent details. A three-member Classification Committee (Committee) convenes to review the proposed classification and to hold a hearing. At least 48 hours before the hearing, the inmate is provided with written notice summarizing the conduct or offense triggering the review. At the time of notice, the inmate also has access to the Long Form, which details why the review was initiated. The inmate may attend the hearing, may "offer any pertinent information, explanation and/or objections to [OSP] placement," and may submit a written statement. He may not call witnesses.

If the Committee does not recommend OSP placement, the process terminates. If the Committee does recommend OSP placement, it documents the decision on a "Classification Committee Report" (CCR), setting forth "the nature of the threat the inmate presents and the committee's reasons for the recommendation," as well as a summary of any information presented at the hearing. The Committee sends the completed CCR to the warden of the prison where the inmate is housed or, in the case of an inmate just entering the prison system, to another designated official.

If, after reviewing the CCR, the warden (or the designated official) disagrees and concludes that OSP is inappropriate, the process terminates and the inmate is not placed in OSP. If the warden agrees, he indicates his approval on the CCR, provides his reasons, and forwards the annotated CCR to the Bureau of Classification (Bureau) for a final decision. The annotated CCR is served upon the inmate, notifying him of the Classification Committee's and warden's recommendations and reasons. The inmate has 15 days to file any objections with the Bureau of Classification.

After the 15-day period, the Bureau of Classification reviews the CCR and makes a final determination. If it concludes OSP placement is inappropriate, the process terminates. If the Bureau approves the warden's recommendation, the inmate is transferred to OSP. The Bureau's chief notes the reasons for the decision on the CCR, and the CCR is again provided to the inmate.

Inmates assigned to OSP receive another review within 30 days of their arrival. That review is conducted by a designated OSP staff member, who examines the inmate's file. If the OSP staff member deems the inmate inappropriately placed, he prepares a written recommendation to the OSP warden that the inmate be transferred to a lower security institution. If the OSP warden concurs, he forwards that transfer recommendation to the Bureau of Classification for appropriate action. If the inmate is deemed properly placed, he remains in OSP and his placement is reviewed on at least an annual basis according to the initial three-tier classification review process outlined above.

[II]

Withdrawing from the position taken in the Court of Appeals, Ohio in its briefs to this Court conceded that the inmates have a liberty interest in avoiding assignment at OSP. The United States, supporting Ohio as amicus curiae, disagrees with Ohio's concession and argues that the inmates have no liberty interest in avoiding assignment to a prison facility with more restrictive conditions of confinement. At oral argument Ohio initially adhered to its earlier concession, but when pressed, the State backtracked. We need reach the question of what process is due only if the inmates establish a constitutionally protected liberty interest, so it is appropriate to address this threshold question at the outset.

The Fourteenth Amendment's Due Process Clause protects persons against deprivations of life, liberty, or property; and those who seek to invoke its procedural protection must establish that one of these interests is at stake. A liberty interest may arise from the Constitution itself, by reason of guarantees implicit in the word "liberty," or it may arise from an expectation or interest created by state laws or policies. We have held that the Constitution itself does not give rise to a liberty interest in avoiding transfer to more adverse conditions of confinement. Meachum v. Fano (1976) (no liberty interest arising from Due Process Clause itself in transfer from low-to maximum-security prison because "[c]onfinement in any of the State's institutions is within the normal limits or range of custody which the conviction has authorized the State to impose"). We have also held, however, that a liberty interest in avoiding particular conditions of confinement may arise from state policies or regulations, subject to the important limitations set forth in Sandin v. Conner (1995).

After *Sandin*, it is clear that the touchstone of the inquiry into the existence of a protected, state-created liberty interest in avoiding restrictive conditions of confinement is not the language of regulations regarding those conditions but the nature of those conditions themselves "in relation to the ordinary incidents of prison life." The *Sandin* standard requires us to determine if assignment to OSP "imposes atypical and significant hardship on the inmate in relation to the ordinary incidents of prison life." In *Sandin*'s wake the Courts of Appeals have not reached consistent conclusions for identifying the baseline from which to measure what is atypical and significant in any particular prison system. We need not resolve the issue here, however, for we are satisfied that assignment to OSP imposes an atypical and significant hardship under any plausible baseline.

For an inmate placed in OSP, almost all human contact is prohibited, even to the point that conversation is not permitted from cell to cell; the light, though it may be dimmed, is on for 24 hours; exercise is for 1 hour per day, but only in a small indoor room. Save perhaps for the especially severe limitations on all human contact, these conditions likely would apply to most solitary confinement facilities, but here there are two added components. First is the duration.

Unlike the 30-day placement in *Sandin*, placement at OSP is indefinite and, after an initial 30-day review, is reviewed just annually. Second is that placement disqualifies an otherwise eligible inmate for parole consideration. While any of these conditions standing alone might not be sufficient to create a liberty interest, taken together they impose an atypical and significant hardship within the correctional context. It follows that respondents have a liberty interest in avoiding assignment to OSP.

OSP's harsh conditions may well be necessary and appropriate in light of the danger that high-risk inmates pose both to prison officials and to other prisoners. That necessity, however, does not diminish our conclusion that the conditions give rise to a liberty interest in their avoidance.

[III]

A liberty interest having been established, we turn to the question of what process is due an inmate whom Ohio seeks to place in OSP. Because the requirements of due process are "flexible and cal[l] for such procedural protections as the particular situation demands," Morrissey v. Brewer (1972), we generally have declined to establish rigid rules and instead have embraced a framework to evaluate the sufficiency of particular procedures. The framework, established in Mathews v. Eldridge (1976), requires consideration of three distinct factors:

"First, the private interest that will be affected by the official action; second, the risk of an erroneous deprivation of such interest through the procedures used, and the probable value, if any, of additional or substitute procedural safeguards; and finally, the Government's interest, including the function involved and the fiscal and administrative burdens that the additional or substitute procedural requirement would entail."

Applying the three factors set forth in *Mathews*, we find Ohio's New Policy provides a sufficient level of process. We first consider the significance of the inmate's interest in avoiding erroneous placement at OSP. Prisoners held in lawful confinement have their liberty curtailed by definition, so the procedural protections to which they are entitled are more limited than in cases where the right at stake is the right to be free from confinement at all. The private interest at stake here, while more than minimal, must be evaluated, nonetheless, within the context of the prison system and its attendant curtailment of liberties.

The second factor addresses the risk of an erroneous placement under the procedures in place, and the probable value, if any, of additional or alternative procedural safeguards. The New Policy provides that an inmate must receive notice of the factual basis leading to consideration for OSP placement and a fair opportunity for rebuttal. Our procedural due process cases have consistently observed that these are among the most important procedural mechanisms for purposes of avoiding erroneous deprivations. Requiring officials to provide a brief summary of the factual basis for the classification review and allowing the inmate a rebuttal opportunity safeguards against the inmate's being mistaken for another or singled out for insufficient reason. In addition to having the opportunity to be heard at the Classification Committee stage, Ohio also invites the inmate to submit objections prior to the final level of review. This second opportunity further reduces the possibility of an erroneous deprivation.

Although a subsequent reviewer may overturn an affirmative recommendation for OSP placement, the reverse is not true; if one reviewer declines to recommend OSP placement, the process terminates. This avoids one of problems apparently present under the Old Policy, where, even if two levels of reviewers recommended against placement, a later reviewer could overturn their recommendation without explanation.

If the recommendation is OSP placement, Ohio requires that the decision-maker provide a short statement of reasons. This requirement guards against arbitrary decisionmaking while also providing the inmate a basis for objection before the next decisionmaker or in a subsequent classification review. The statement also serves as a guide for future behavior.

As we have noted, Ohio provides multiple levels of review for any decision recommending OSP placement, with power to overturn the recommendation at each level. In addition to these safeguards, Ohio further reduces the risk of erroneous placement by providing for a placement review within 30 days of an inmate's initial assignment to OSP.

The third *Mathews* factor addresses the State's interest. In the context of prison management, and in the specific circumstances of this case, this interest is a dominant consideration. Ohio has responsibility for imprisoning nearly 44,000 inmates. The State's first obligation must be to ensure the safety of guards and prison personnel, the public, and the prisoners themselves.

Prison security, imperiled by the brutal reality of prison gangs, provides the backdrop of the State's interest. Clandestine, organized, fueled by race-based hostility, and committed to fear and violence as a means of disciplining their own members and their rivals, gangs seek nothing less than to control prison life and to extend their power outside prison walls. Murder of an inmate, a guard, or one of their family members on the outside is a common form of gang discipline and control, as well as a condition for membership in some gangs.

The problem of scarce resources is another component of the State's interest. The cost of keeping a single prisoner in one of Ohio's ordinary maximum-security prisons is $34,167 per year, and the cost to maintain each inmate at OSP is $49,007 per year. We can assume that Ohio, or any other penal system, faced with costs like these will find it difficult to fund more effective education and vocational assistance programs to improve the lives of the prisoners. It follows that courts must give substantial deference to prison management decisions before mandating additional expenditures for elaborate procedural safeguards when correctional officials conclude that a prisoner has engaged in disruptive behavior.

The State's interest must be understood against this background. Were Ohio to allow an inmate to call witnesses or provide other attributes of an adversary hearing before ordering transfer to OSP, both the State's immediate objective of controlling the prisoner and its greater objective of controlling the prison could be defeated. This problem, moreover, is not alleviated by providing an exemption for witnesses who pose a hazard, for nothing in the record indicates simple mechanisms exist to determine when witnesses may be called without fear of reprisal. The danger to witnesses, and the difficulty in obtaining their cooperation, make the probable value of an adversary-type hearing doubtful in comparison to its obvious costs.

A balance of the *Mathews* factors yields the conclusion that Ohio's New Policy is adequate to safeguard an inmate's liberty interest in not being assigned to OSP. Prolonged confinement in Supermax may be the State's only option for the control of some inmates, and claims alleging violation of the Eighth Amendment's prohibition of cruel and unusual punishments were resolved, or withdrawn, by settlement in an early phase of this case. Here, any claim of excessive punishment in individual circumstances is not before us.

3.   What Procedures Are Required? (casebook, p. 1037)

In *Jones v. Flowers*, below, the Court considered what type of notice is required before the government sells a person's property. In a 5-4 decision with Chief Justice Roberts writing the majority opinion, joined by Justices Stevens, Souter, Ginsburg, and Breyer, the Court held that notice requires more than sending a letter by certified mail and publishing a notice in a newspaper.

JONES v. FLOWERS

126 S. Ct. 1708 (2006)

Chief Justice ROBERTS delivered the opinion of the Court.

Before a State may take property and sell it for unpaid taxes, the Due Process Clause of the Fourteenth Amendment requires the government to provide the owner "notice and opportunity for hearing appropriate to the nature of the case." We granted certiorari to determine whether, when notice of a tax sale is mailed to the owner and returned undelivered, the government must take additional reasonable steps to provide notice before taking the owner's property.

I

In 1967, petitioner Gary Jones purchased a house at 717 North Bryan Street in Little Rock, Arkansas. He lived in the house with his wife until they separated in 1993. Jones then moved into an apartment in Little Rock, and his wife continued to live in the North Bryan Street house. Jones paid his mortgage each month for 30 years, and the mortgage company paid Jones' property taxes. After Jones paid off his mortgage in 1997, the property taxes went unpaid, and the property was certified as delinquent.

In April 2000, respondent Mark Wilcox, the Commissioner of State Lands (Commissioner), attempted to notify Jones of his tax delinquency, and his right to redeem the property, by mailing a certified letter to Jones at the North Bryan Street address. The packet of information stated that unless Jones redeemed the property, it would be subject to public sale two years later on April 17, 2002. Nobody was home to sign for the letter, and nobody appeared at the post office to retrieve the letter within the next 15 days. The post office returned the unopened packet to the Commissioner marked "unclaimed."

Two years later, and just a few weeks before the public sale, the Commissioner published a notice of public sale in the Arkansas Democrat Gazette. No bids were submitted, which permitted the State to negotiate a private sale of the property. Several months later, respondent Linda Flowers submitted a purchase offer. The Commissioner mailed another certified letter to Jones at the North Bryan Street address, attempting to notify him that his house would be sold to Flowers if he did not pay his taxes. Like the first letter, the second was also returned to the Commissioner marked "unclaimed". Flowers purchased the house, which the parties stipulated in the trial court had a fair market value of $80,000, for $21,042.15. Immediately after the 30-day period for postsale redemption passed, Flowers had an unlawful detainer notice delivered to the property. The notice was served on Jones' daughter, who contacted Jones and notified him of the tax sale.

Jones filed a lawsuit in Arkansas state court against the Commissioner and Flowers, alleging that the Commissioner's failure to provide notice of the tax sale and of Jones' right to redeem resulted in the taking of his property without due process.

We granted certiorari, to resolve a conflict among the Circuits and State Supreme Courts concerning whether the Due Process Clause requires the government to take additional reasonable steps to notify a property owner when notice of a tax sale is returned undelivered. We hold that when mailed notice of a tax sale is returned unclaimed, the State must take additional reasonable steps to attempt to provide notice to the property owner before selling his property, if it is practicable to do so. Under the circumstances presented here, additional reasonable steps were available to the State.

II

A

Due process does not require that a property owner receive actual notice before the government may take his property. Rather, we have stated that due process requires the government to provide "notice reasonably calculated, under all the circumstances, to apprise interested parties of the pendency of the action and afford them an opportunity to present their objections." The Commissioner argues that once the State provided notice reasonably calculated to apprise Jones of the impending tax sale by mailing him a certified letter, due process was satisfied. The Arkansas statutory scheme is reasonably calculated to provide notice, the Commissioner continues, because it provides for notice by certified mail to an address that the property owner is responsible for keeping up to date. The Commissioner notes this Court's ample precedent condoning notice by mail, and adds that the Arkansas scheme exceeds constitutional requirements by requiring the Commissioner to use certified mail.

It is true that this Court has deemed notice constitutionally sufficient if it was reasonably calculated to reach the intended recipient when sent. In each of these cases, the government attempted to provide notice and heard nothing back indicating that anything had gone awry, and we stated that "[t]he reasonableness and hence the constitutional validity of [the] chosen method may be defended on the ground that it is in itself reasonably certain to inform those affected." But we have never addressed whether due process entails further responsibility when the government becomes aware prior to the taking that its attempt at notice has failed.

We do not think that a person who actually desired to inform a real property owner of an impending tax sale of a house he owns would do nothing when a certified letter sent to the owner is returned unclaimed. If the Commissioner prepared a stack of letters to mail to delinquent taxpayers, handed them to the postman, and then watched as the departing postman accidentally dropped the letters down a storm drain, one would certainly expect the Commissioner's office to prepare a new stack of letters and send them again. No one "desirous of actually informing" the owners would simply shrug his shoulders as the letters disappeared and say "I tried." Failure to follow up would be unreasonable, despite the fact that the letters were reasonably calculated to reach their intended recipients when delivered to the postman.

By the same token, when a letter is returned by the post office, the sender will ordinarily attempt to resend it, if it is practicable to do so. This is especially true when, as here, the subject matter of the letter concerns such an important and irreversible prospect as the loss of a house. Although the State may have made a reasonable calculation of how to reach Jones, it had good reason to suspect when the notice was returned that Jones was "no better off than if the notice had never been sent." Deciding to take no further action is not what someone "desirous of actually informing" Jones would do; such a person would take further reasonable steps if any were available.

The Commissioner has three further arguments for why reasonable followup measures were not required in this case. First, notice was sent to an address that Jones provided and had a legal obligation to keep updated. Second, "after failing to receive a property tax bill and pay property taxes, a property holder is on inquiry—notice that his property is subject to governmental taking." Third, Jones was obliged to ensure that those in whose hands he left his property would alert him if it was in jeopardy. None of these contentions relieves the State of its constitutional obligation to provide adequate notice.

The Commissioner does not argue that Jones' failure to comply with a statutory obligation to keep his address updated forfeits his right to constitutionally sufficient notice, and we agree. Although Ark.Code Ann. § 26-35-705 provides strong support for the Commissioner's argument that mailing a certified letter to Jones at 717 North Bryan Street was reasonably calculated to reach him, it does not alter the reasonableness of the Commissioner's position that he must do nothing more when the notice is promptly returned "unclaimed."

As for the Commissioner's inquiry notice argument, the common knowledge that property may become subject to government taking when taxes are not paid does not excuse the government from complying with its constitutional obligation of notice before taking private property. We have previously stated the opposite: An interested party's "knowledge of delinquency in the payment of taxes is not equivalent to notice that a tax sale is pending."

Finally, the Commissioner reminds us that the State can assume an owner leaves his property in the hands of one who will inform him if his interest is in jeopardy. An occupant, however, is not charged with acting as the owner's agent in all respects, and it is quite a leap from Justice Jackson's examples to conclude that it is an obligation of tenancy to follow up with certified mail of unknown content addressed to the owner. In fact, the State makes it impossible for the occupant to learn why the Commissioner is writing the owner, because an occupant cannot call for a certified letter without first obtaining the owner's signature. For all the occupant knows, the Commissioner of State Lands might write to certain residents about a variety of matters he finds important, such as state parks or highway construction; it would by no means be obvious to an occupant observing a certified mail slip from the Commissioner that the owner is in danger of losing his property. In any event, there is no record evidence that notices of attempted delivery were left at 717 North Bryan Street.

Mr. Jones should have been more diligent with respect to his property, no question. People must pay their taxes, and the government may hold citizens accountable for tax delinquency by taking their property. But before forcing a citizen to satisfy his debt by forfeiting his property, due process requires the government to provide adequate notice of the impending taking.

We think there were several reasonable steps the State could have taken. What steps are reasonable in response to new information depends upon what the new information reveals. The return of the certified letter marked "unclaimed" meant either that Jones still lived at 717 North Bryan Street, but was not home when the postman called and did not retrieve the letter at the post office, or that Jones no longer resided at that address. One reasonable step primarily addressed to the former possibility would be for the State to resend the notice by regular mail, so that a signature was not required. The Commissioner says that use of certified mail makes actual notice more likely, because requiring the recipient's signature protects against misdelivery. But that is only true, of course, when someone is home to sign for the letter, or to inform the mail carrier that he has arrived at the wrong address. Otherwise, "[c]ertified mail is dispatched and handled in transit as ordinary mail," and the use of certified mail might make actual notice less likely in some cases—the letter cannot be left like regular mail to be examined at the end of the day, and it can only be retrieved from the post office for a specified period of time. Following up with regular mail might also increase the chances of actual notice to Jones if—as it turned out—he had moved. Even occupants who ignored certified mail notice slips addressed to the owner (if any had been left) might scrawl the owner's new address on the notice packet and leave it for the postman to retrieve, or notify Jones directly.

Other reasonable followup measures, directed at the possibility that Jones had moved as well as that he had simply not retrieved the certified letter, would have been to post notice on the front door, or to address otherwise undeliverable mail to "occupant." Most States that explicitly outline additional procedures in their tax sale statutes require just such steps. Either approach would increase the likelihood that the owner would be notified that he was about to lose his property, given the failure of a letter deliverable only to the owner in person. That is clear in the case of an owner who still resided at the premises. It is also true in the case of an owner who has moved: Occupants who might disregard a certified mail slip not addressed to them are less likely to ignore posted notice, and a letter addressed to them (even as "occupant") might be opened and read. In either case, there is a significant chance the occupants will alert the owner, if only because a change in ownership could well affect their own occupancy. In fact, Jones first learned of the State's effort to sell his house when he was alerted by one of the occupants—his daughter—after she was served with an unlawful detainer notice.

There is no reason to suppose that the State will ever be less than fully zealous in its efforts to secure the tax revenue it needs. The same cannot be said for the State's efforts to ensure that its citizens receive proper notice before the State takes action against them. In this case, the State is exerting extraordinary power against a property owner—taking and selling a house he owns. It is not too much to insist that the State do a bit more to attempt to let him know about it when the notice letter addressed to him is returned unclaimed. The Commissioner's effort to provide notice to Jones of an impending tax sale of his house was insufficient to satisfy due process given the circumstances of this case.

Justice ALITO took no part in the consideration or decision of this case.

Justice THOMAS, with whom Justice SCALIA and Justice KENNEDY join, dissenting.

Adopting petitioner's arguments, the Court holds today that "when mailed notice of a tax sale is returned unclaimed, the State must take additional reasonable steps to attempt to provide notice to the property owner before selling his property, if it is practicable to do so." Because, under this Court's precedents, the State's notice methods clearly satisfy the requirements of the Due Process Clause, I respectfully dissent.

I

The methods of notice employed by Arkansas were reasonably calculated to inform petitioner of proceedings affecting his property interest and thus satisfy the requirements of the Due Process Clause. The State mailed a notice by certified letter to the address provided by petitioner. The certified letter was returned to the State marked "unclaimed" after three attempts to deliver it. The State then published a notice of public sale containing redemption information in the Arkansas Democrat Gazette newspaper. After Flowers submitted a purchase offer, the State sent yet another certified letter to petitioner at his record address. That letter, too, was returned to the State marked "unclaimed" after three delivery attempts.

Arkansas' attempts to contact petitioner by certified mail at his "record address," without more, satisfy due process. Because the notices were sent to the address provided by petitioner himself, the State had an especially sound basis for determining that notice would reach him. Moreover, Arkansas exceeded the constitutional minimum by additionally publishing notice in a local newspaper. Due process requires nothing more—and certainly not here, where petitioner had a statutory duty to pay his taxes and to report any change of address to the state taxing authority.

My conclusion that Arkansas' notice methods satisfy due process is reinforced by the well-established presumption that individuals, especially those owning property, act in their own interest. Recognizing that "[i]t is the part of common prudence for all those who have any interest in [a thing], to guard that interest by persons who are in a situation to protect it," this Court has concluded that "[t]he ways of an owner with tangible property are such that he usually arranges means to learn of any direct attack upon his possessory or proprietary rights." Consistent with this observation, Arkansas was free to "indulge the assumption" that petitioner had either provided the State taxing authority with a correct and up-to-date mailing address—as required by state law—"or that he left some caretaker under a duty to let him know that [his property was] being jeopardized."

II

The Court's proposed methods, aside from being constitutionally unnecessary, are also burdensome, impractical, and no more likely to effect notice than the methods actually employed by the State.

In Arkansas, approximately 18,000 parcels of delinquent real estate are certified annually. Under the Court's rule, the State will bear the burden of locating thousands of delinquent property owners. These administrative burdens are not compelled by the Due Process Clause. Here, Arkansas has determined that its law requiring property owners to maintain a current address with the state taxing authority, in conjunction with its authorization to send property notices to the record address, is an efficient and fair way to administer its tax collection system. The Court's decision today forecloses such a reasonable system and burdens the State with inefficiencies caused by delinquent taxpayers.

Moreover, the Court's proposed methods are no more reasonably calculated to achieve notice than the methods employed by the State here. Regular mail is hardly foolproof; indeed, it is arguably less effective than certified mail. Certified mail is tracked, delivery attempts are recorded, actual delivery is logged, and notices are posted to alert someone at the residence that certified mail is being held at a local post office. By creating a record, these features give parties grounds for defending or challenging notice. By contrast, regular mail is untraceable; there is no record of either delivery or receipt. Had the State used regular mail, petitioner would presumably argue that it should have sent notice by certified mail because it creates a paper trail.

The meaning of the Constitution should not turn on the antics of tax evaders and scofflaws. Nor is the self-created conundrum in which petitioner finds himself a legitimate ground for imposing additional constitutional obligations on the State. The State's attempts to notify petitioner by certified mail at the address that he provided and, additionally, by publishing notice in a local newspaper satisfy due process.

Chapter 9

First Amendment: Freedom of Expression

B. Free Speech Methodology

4. What Is an Infringement of Freedom of Speech?

Compelled Speech (casebook, p. 1129)

In the last three years, the Supreme Court has decided two cases concerning compelled speech. In *Johanns v. Livestock Marketing Association*, below, the Court considered whether forcing beef producers to fund generic advertising is a violation of the First Amendment. In concluding that there was not a violation of the First Amendment, Justice Scalia emphasized that this is government speech and the government may tax, even selectively, to fund this. After this case, it is worth considering whether there are any limits on the government's ability to tax some to advertise or advance messages—even messages that those taxed disagree with.

In *Rumsfeld v. Forum for Academic and Institutional Rights*, also below, the Court rejected a challenge to a federal law that requires universities receiving federal funds to allow military recruiters equal access to campus facilities. The law was adopted because many law schools refused to allow military recruiters access to career services facilities because of policies preventing employers from recruiting on campus if they discriminate based on race, gender, religion, or sexual orientation. A federal statute bars gays and lesbians from the military. The Court rejected challenges based on compelled speech and association.

JOHANNS v. LIVESTOCK MARKETING ASSOCIATION
544 U.S. 550 (2005)

Justice SCALIA delivered the opinion of the Court

We consider whether a federal program that finances generic advertising to promote an agricultural product violates the First Amendment. [T]he dispositive question is whether the generic advertising at issue is the Government's own speech and therefore is exempt from First Amendment scrutiny.

I.

The Beef Promotion and Research Act of 1985 (Beef Act or Act), announces a federal policy of promoting the marketing and consumption of "beef and beef products," using funds raised by an assessment on cattle sales and importation. The Secretary is to impose a $1-per-head assessment (or "checkoff") on all sales or importation of cattle and a comparable assessment on imported beef products. And the assessment is to be used to fund beef-related projects, including promotional campaigns, designed by the Operating Committee and approved by the Secretary.

Respondents are two associations whose members collect and pay the check-off, and several individuals who raise and sell cattle subject to the checkoff. Respondents noted that the advertising promotes beef as a generic commodity, which, they contended, impedes their efforts to promote the superiority of American beef, grain-fed beef, or certified Angus or Hereford beef.

II

We have sustained First Amendment challenges to allegedly compelled expression in two categories of cases: true "compelled speech" cases, in which an individual is obliged personally to express a message he disagrees with, imposed by the government; and "compelled subsidy" cases, in which an individual is required by the government to subsidize a message he disagrees with, expressed by a private entity. We have not heretofore considered the First Amendment consequences of government-compelled subsidy of the government's own speech.

In all of the cases invalidating exactions to subsidize speech, the speech was, or was presumed to be, that of an entity other than the government itself. Our compelled-subsidy cases have consistently respected the principle that "[c]ompelled support of a private association is fundamentally different from compelled support of government." "Compelled support of government"— even those programs of government one does not approve—is of course perfectly constitutional, as every taxpayer must attest. And some government programs involve, or entirely consist of, advocating a position. "The government, as a general rule, may support valid programs and policies by taxes or other exactions binding on protesting parties. Within this broader principle it seems inevitable that funds raised by the government will be spent for speech and other expression to advocate and defend its own policies." We have generally assumed, though not yet squarely held, that compelled funding of government speech does not alone raise First Amendment concerns.

III

Respondents do not seriously dispute these principles, nor do they contend that, as a general matter, their First Amendment challenge requires them to show only that their checkoff dollars pay for speech with which they disagree. Rather, they assert that the challenged promotional campaigns differ dispositively from the type of government speech that, our cases suggest, is not susceptible to First Amendment challenge. They point to the role of the Beef Board and its Operating Committee in designing the promotional campaigns, and to the use of a mandatory assessment on beef producers to fund the advertising. We consider each in turn.

A

The Secretary of Agriculture does not write ad copy himself. Rather, the Beef Board's promotional campaigns are designed by the Beef Board's Operating Committee, only half of whose members are Beef Board members appointed by the Secretary. (All members of the Operating Committee are subject to *removal* by the Secretary.) Respondents contend that speech whose content is effectively controlled by a nongovernmental entity—the Operating Committee—cannot be considered "government speech." We need not address this contention, because we reject its premise: The message of the promotional campaigns is effectively controlled by the Federal Government itself.

The message set out in the beef promotions is from beginning to end the message established by the Federal Government. Congress has directed the implementation of a "coordinated program" of promotion, "including paid advertising, to advance the image and desirability of beef and beef products." Congress and the Secretary have also specified, in general terms, what the promotional campaigns shall contain (campaigns "shall . . . take into account" different types of beef products), and what they shall not (campaigns shall not, without prior approval, refer "to a brand or trade name of any beef product"). Thus, Congress and the Secretary have set out the overarching message and some of its elements, and they have left the development of the remaining details to an entity whose members are answerable to the Secretary (and in some cases appointed by him as well).

Moreover, the record demonstrates that the Secretary exercises final approval authority over every word used in every promotional campaign. All proposed promotional messages are reviewed by Department officials both for substance and for wording, and some proposals are rejected or rewritten by the Department. Nor is the Secretary's role limited to final approval or rejection: officials of the Department also attend and participate in the open meetings at which proposals are developed. When, as here, the government sets the overall message to be communicated and approves every word that is disseminated, it is not precluded from relying on the government-speech doctrine merely because it solicits assistance from nongovernmental sources in developing specific messages.

B

Respondents also contend that the beef program does not qualify as "government speech" because it is funded by a targeted assessment on beef producers, rather than by general revenues. This funding mechanism, they argue, has two relevant effects: it gives control over the beef program not to politically accountable legislators, but to a narrow interest group that will pay no heed to respondents' dissenting views, and it creates the perception that the advertisements speak for beef producers such as respondents.

We reject the first point. The compelled-*subsidy* analysis is altogether un-affected by whether the funds for the promotions are raised by general taxes or through a targeted assessment. Citizens may challenge compelled support of private speech, but have no First Amendment right not to fund government speech. And that is no less true when the funding is achieved through targeted assessments devoted exclusively to the program to which the assessed citizens object.

Some of our cases have justified compelled funding of government speech by pointing out that government speech is subject to democratic accountability. But our references to "traditional political controls" do not signify that the First Amendment duplicates the Appropriations Clause, or that every instance of government speech must be funded by a line item in an appropriations bill. Here, the beef advertisements are subject to political safeguards more than adequate to set them apart from private messages. The program is authorized and the basic message prescribed by federal statute, and specific requirements for the promotions' content are imposed by federal regulations promulgated after notice and comment. The Secretary of Agriculture, a politically accountable official, oversees the program, appoints and dismisses the key personnel, and retains absolute veto power over the advertisements' content, right down to the wording. And Congress, of course, retains oversight authority, not to mention the ability to reform the program at any time. No more is required.

As to the second point, respondents' argument proceeds as follows: They contend that crediting the advertising to "America's Beef Producers" impermissibly uses not only their money but also their seeming endorsement to promote a message with which they do not agree. Communications cannot be "government speech," they argue, if they are attributed to someone other than the government; and the person to whom they are attributed, when he is, by compulsory funding, made the unwilling instrument of communication, may raise a First Amendment objection.

We need not determine the validity of this argument—which relates to compelled *speech* rather than compelled *subsidy*—with regard to respondents' facial challenge. Since neither the Beef Act nor the Beef Order requires attribution, neither can be the cause of any possible First Amendment harm.

On some set of facts, this second theory might (again, we express no view on the point) form the basis for an as-applied challenge—if it were established, that is, that individual beef advertisements were attributed to respondents. The record, however, includes only a stipulated sampling of these promotional materials, and none of the exemplars provides any support for this attribution theory except for the tagline identifying the funding. Respondents apparently presented no other evidence of attribution at trial, and the District Court made no factual findings on the point.

Justice THOMAS, concurring.

I join the Court's opinion. I continue to believe that "[a]ny regulation that compels the funding of advertising must be subjected to the most stringent First Amendment scrutiny." At the same time, I recognize that this principle must be qualified where the regulation compels the funding of speech that is the government's own. It cannot be that all taxpayers have a First Amendment objection to taxpayer-funded government speech, even if the funded speech is not "germane" to some broader regulatory program. Like the Court, I see no analytical distinction between "pure" government speech funded from general tax revenues and from speech funded from targeted exactions; the practice of using targeted taxes to fund government operations, such as excise taxes, dates from the founding.

Still, if the advertisements associated their generic pro-beef message with either the individual or organization respondents, then respondents would have a valid as-applied First Amendment challenge. The government may not, consistent with the First Amendment, associate individuals or organizations involuntarily with speech by attributing an unwanted message to them, whether or not those individuals fund the speech, and whether or not the message is under the government's control. This principle follows not only from our cases establishing that the government may not compel individuals to convey messages with which they disagree, but also from our expressive-association cases, which prohibit the government from coercively associating individuals or groups with unwanted messages. The present record, however, does not show that the advertisements objectively associate their message with any individual respondent.

Justice SOUTER, with whom Justice STEVENS and Justice KENNEDY join, dissenting.

The Beef Promotion and Research Act of 1985, known as the Beef Act, taxes cattle sold in or imported into the United States at one dollar a head. Much of the revenue is spent urging people to eat beef, as in advertisements with the slogan, "Beef. It's What's for Dinner." Respondent taxpayers object to the tax because they disagree with the advertisements' content, which they see as a generic message that "beef is good." This message, the ranchers say, ignores the fact that not all beef is the same; the ads fail to distinguish, for example, the American ranchers' grain-fed beef from the grass-fed beef predominant in the imports, which the Americans consider inferior.

[T]he Government argues here that the beef advertising is its own speech, exempting it from the First Amendment bar against extracting special subsidies from those unwilling to underwrite an objectionable message.

The Court accepts the defense unwisely. The error is not that government speech can never justify compelling a subsidy, but that a compelled subsidy should not be justifiable by speech unless the government must put that speech forward as its own. Otherwise there is no check whatever on government's power to compel special speech subsidies. I take the view that if government relies on the government-speech doctrine to compel specific groups to fund speech with targeted taxes, it must make itself politically accountable by indicating that the content actually is a government message, not just the statement of one self-interested group the government is currently willing to invest with power. Sometimes, as in these very cases, government can make an effective disclosure only by explicitly labeling the speech as its own. Because the Beef Act fails to require the Government to show its hand, I would affirm the judgment of the Court of Appeals holding the Act unconstitutional, and I respectfully dissent from the Court's decision to condone this compelled subsidy.

RUMSFELD v. FORUM FOR ACADEMIC AND INSTITUTIONAL RIGHTS, INC.
126 S. Ct. 1297 (2006)

Chief Justice ROBERTS delivered the opinion of the Court.

When law schools began restricting the access of military recruiters to their students because of disagreement with the Government's policy on homosexuals in the military, Congress responded by enacting the Solomon Amendment. See 10 U.S.C.A. § 983. That provision specifies that if any part of an institution of higher education denies military recruiters access equal to that provided other recruiters, the entire institution would lose certain federal funds. The law schools responded by suing, alleging that the Solomon Amendment infringed their First Amendment freedoms of speech and association. The District Court disagreed but was reversed by a divided panel of the Court of Appeals for the Third Circuit, which ordered the District Court to enter a preliminary injunction against enforcement of the Solomon Amendment.

I

Respondent Forum for Academic and Institutional Rights, Inc. (FAIR), is an association of law schools and law faculties. They would like to restrict military recruiting on their campuses because they object to the policy Congress has adopted with respect to homosexuals in the military. See 10 U.S.C. § 654.[2] The Solomon Amendment, however, forces institutions to choose between enforcing their nondiscrimination policy against military recruiters in this way and continuing to receive specified federal funding.

---

2. Under this policy, a person generally may not serve in the Armed Forces if he has engaged in homosexual acts, stated that he is a homosexual, or married a person of the same sex. Respondents do not challenge that policy in this litigation. [Footnote by Court]

II

The Solomon Amendment denies federal funding to an institution of higher education that "has a policy or practice . . . that either prohibits, or in effect prevents" the
military "from gaining access to campuses, or access to students . . . on campuses,
for purposes of military recruiting in a manner that is at least equal in quality and
scope to the access to campuses and to students that is provided to any other
employer." 10 U.S.C.A. § 983(b). The statute provides an exception for an institution with "a longstanding policy of pacifism based on historical religious
affiliation." The Government and FAIR agree on what this statute requires: In
order for a law school and its university to receive federal funding, the law school
must offer military recruiters the same access to its campus and students that it
provides to the nonmilitary recruiter receiving the most favorable access.

III

The Constitution grants Congress the power to "provide for the common Defence,"
"[t]o raise and support Armies," and "[t]o provide and maintain a Navy." Art. I,
§ 8, cls. 1, 12-13. Congress' power in this area "is broad and sweeping," and there is
no dispute in this case that it includes the authority to require campus access for
military recruiters. That is, of course, unless Congress exceeds constitutional
limitations on its power in enacting such legislation. But the fact that legislation
that raises armies is subject to First Amendment constraints does not mean that we
ignore the purpose of this legislation when determining its constitutionality; as we
[have] recognized "judicial deference . . . is at its apogee" when Congress legis-
lates under its authority to raise and support armies. Id., at 70.

  Although Congress has broad authority to legislate on matters of military recruiting, it nonetheless chose to secure campus access for military recruiters indirectly,
through its Spending Clause power. The Solomon Amendment gives universities a
choice: Either allow military recruiters the same access to students afforded any
other recruiter or forgo certain federal funds. Congress' decision to proceed indirectly does not reduce the deference given to Congress in the area of military affairs.
Congress' choice to promote its goal by creating a funding condition deserves at
least as deferential treatment as if Congress had imposed a mandate on universities.

  This case does not require us to determine when a condition placed on
university funding goes beyond the "reasonable" choice and becomes an
unconstitutional condition. It is clear that a funding condition cannot be unconstitutional if it could be constitutionally imposed directly. Because the First
Amendment would not prevent Congress from directly imposing the Solomon
Amendment's access requirement, the statute does not place an unconstitutional
condition on the receipt of federal funds.

A

The Solomon Amendment neither limits what law schools may say nor
requires them to say anything. Law schools remain free under the statute to

express whatever views they may have on the military's congressionally mandated employment policy, all the while retaining eligibility for federal funds. As a general matter, the Solomon Amendment regulates conduct, not speech. It affects what law schools must do—afford equal access to military recruiters—not what they may or may not say.

Nevertheless, the Third Circuit concluded that the Solomon Amendment violates law schools' freedom of speech in a number of ways. First, in assisting military recruiters, law schools provide some services, such as sending e-mails and distributing flyers, that clearly involve speech. The Court of Appeals held that in supplying these services law schools are unconstitutionally compelled to speak the Government's message. Second, military recruiters are, to some extent, speaking while they are on campus. The Court of Appeals held that, by forcing law schools to permit the military on campus to express its message, the Solomon Amendment unconstitutionally requires law schools to host or accommodate the military's speech. Third, although the Court of Appeals thought that the Solomon Amendment regulated speech, it held in the alternative that, if the statute regulates conduct, this conduct is expressive and regulating it unconstitutionally infringes law schools' right to engage in expressive conduct. We consider each issue in turn.

1

Some of this Court's leading First Amendment precedents have established the principle that freedom of speech prohibits the government from telling people what they must say. In *West Virginia Bd. of Ed. v. Barnette* (1943), we held unconstitutional a state law requiring schoolchildren to recite the Pledge of Allegiance and to salute the flag. And in *Wooley v. Maynard* (1977), we held unconstitutional another that required New Hampshire motorists to display the state motto—"Live Free or Die"—on their license plates.

The Solomon Amendment does not require any similar expression by law schools. Nonetheless, recruiting assistance provided by the schools often includes elements of speech. For example, schools may send e-mails or post notices on bulletin boards on an employer's behalf. Law schools offering such services to other recruiters must also send e-mails and post notices on behalf of the military to comply with the Solomon Amendment. As FAIR points out, these compelled statements of fact ("The U.S. Army recruiter will meet interested students in Room 123 at 11 a.m."), like compelled statements of opinion, are subject to First Amendment scrutiny.

This sort of recruiting assistance, however, is a far cry from the compelled speech in *Barnette* and *Wooley*. The Solomon Amendment, unlike the laws at issue in those cases, does not dictate the content of the speech at all, which is only "compelled" if, and to the extent, the school provides such speech for other recruiters. There is nothing in this case approaching a government-mandated pledge or motto that the school must endorse.

The compelled speech to which the law schools point is plainly incidental to the Solomon Amendment's regulation of conduct, and "it has never been deemed an abridgment of freedom of speech or press to make a course of conduct illegal merely because the conduct was in part initiated, evidenced, or carried out by means of language, either spoken, written, or printed." Congress, for example, can prohibit employers from discriminating in hiring on the basis of race. The fact that this will require an employer to take down a sign reading "White Applicants Only" hardly means that the law should be analyzed as one regulating the employer's speech rather than conduct. Compelling a law school that sends scheduling e-mails for other recruiters to send one for a military recruiter is simply not the same as forcing a student to pledge allegiance, or forcing a Jehovah's Witness to display the motto "Live Free or Die," and it trivializes the freedom protected in *Barnette* and *Wooley* to suggest that it is.

2

Our compelled-speech cases are not limited to the situation in which an individual must personally speak the government's message. We have also in a number of instances limited the government's ability to force one speaker to host or accommodate another speaker's message. See *Hurley v. Irish-American Gay, Lesbian and Bisexual Group of Boston, Inc.* (1995) (state law cannot require a parade to include a group whose message the parade's organizer does not wish to send); *Pacific Gas & Elec. Co. v. Public Util. Comm'n of Cal.* (1986) (state agency cannot require a utility company to include a third-party newsletter in its billing envelope); *Miami Herald Publishing Co. v. Tornillo* (right-of-reply statute violates editors' right to determine the content of their newspapers). Relying on these precedents, the Third Circuit concluded that the Solomon Amendment unconstitutionally compels law schools to accommodate the military's message "[b]y requiring schools to include military recruiters in the interviews and recruiting receptions the schools arrange."

The compelled-speech violation in each of our prior cases, however, resulted from the fact that the complaining speaker's own message was affected by the speech it was forced to accommodate. The expressive nature of a parade was central to our holding in *Hurley*. We concluded that because "every participating unit affects the message conveyed by the [parade's] private organizers," a law dictating that a particular group must be included in the parade "alter[s] the expressive content of th[e] parade." As a result, we held that the State's public accommodation law, as applied to a private parade, "violates the fundamental rule of protection under the First Amendment, that a speaker has the autonomy to choose the content of his own message."

In this case, accommodating the military's message does not affect the law schools' speech, because the schools are not speaking when they host interviews and recruiting receptions. Unlike a parade organizer's choice of parade contingents, a law school's decision to allow recruiters on campus is not inherently expressive. Law schools facilitate recruiting to assist their students in obtaining jobs. A law school's recruiting services lack the expressive quality of a parade, a newsletter, or the editorial page of a newspaper; its accommodation of a military recruiter's message is not compelled speech because the accommodation does not sufficiently interfere with any message of the school.

The schools respond that if they treat military and nonmilitary recruiters alike in order to comply with the Solomon Amendment, they could be viewed as sending the message that they see nothing wrong with the military's policies, when they do. We rejected a similar argument in *PruneYard Shopping Center v. Robins* (1980). In that case, we upheld a state law requiring a shopping center owner to allow certain expressive activities by others on its property. We explained that there was little likelihood that the views of those engaging in the expressive activities would be identified with the owner, who remained free to disassociate himself from those views and who was "not . . . being compelled to affirm [a] belief in any governmentally prescribed position or view."

The same is true here. Nothing about recruiting suggests that law schools agree with any speech by recruiters, and nothing in the Solomon Amendment restricts what the law schools may say about the military's policies.

3

Having rejected the view that the Solomon Amendment impermissibly regulates speech, we must still consider whether the expressive nature of the conduct regulated by the statute brings that conduct within the First Amendment's protection. [W]e have extended First Amendment protection only to conduct that is inherently expressive. In *Texas v. Johnson* (1989), for example, we held that burning the American flag was sufficiently expressive to warrant First Amendment protection.

Unlike flag burning, the conduct regulated by the Solomon Amendment is not inherently expressive. Prior to the adoption of the Solomon Amendment's equal-access requirement, law schools "expressed" their disagreement with the military by treating military recruiters differently from other recruiters. But these actions were expressive only because the law schools accompanied their conduct with speech explaining it. For example, the point of requiring military interviews to be conducted on the undergraduate campus is not "overwhelmingly apparent." An observer who sees military recruiters interviewing away from the law school has no way of knowing whether the law school is expressing its disapproval of the military, all the law school's interview rooms are full, or the military recruiters decided for reasons of their own that they would rather interview someplace else. The expressive component of a law school's actions is not created by the conduct itself but by the speech that accompanies it. The fact that such explanatory speech is necessary is strong evidence that the conduct at issue here is not so inherently expressive that it warrants protection. If combining speech and conduct were enough to create expressive conduct, a regulated party could always transform conduct into "speech" simply by talking about it.

B

The Solomon Amendment does not violate law schools' freedom of speech, but the First Amendment's protection extends beyond the right to speak. We have recognized a First Amendment right to associate for the purpose of speaking, which we have termed a "right of expressive association." See, e.g., *Boy Scouts of America v. Dale* (2000). The reason we have extended First Amendment protection in this way is clear: The right to speak is often exercised most effectively by combining one's voice with the voices of others. If the government were free to restrict individuals' ability to join together and speak, it could essentially silence views that the First Amendment is intended to protect.

FAIR argues that the Solomon Amendment violates law schools' freedom of expressive association. According to FAIR, law schools' ability to express their message that discrimination on the basis of sexual orientation is wrong is significantly affected by the presence of military recruiters on campus and the schools' obligation to assist them.

The Solomon Amendment, however, does not similarly affect a law school's associational rights. To comply with the statute, law schools must allow military recruiters on campus and assist them in whatever way the school chooses to assist other employers. Law schools therefore "associate" with military recruiters in the sense that they interact with them. But recruiters are not part of the law school. Recruiters are, by definition, outsiders who come onto campus for the limited purpose of trying to hire students—not to become members of the school's expressive association. This distinction is critical. Unlike the public accommodations law in *Dale*, the Solomon Amendment does not force a law school "to accept members it does not desire." The law schools say that allowing military recruiters equal access impairs their own expression by requiring them to associate with the recruiters, but just as saying conduct is undertaken for expressive purposes cannot make it symbolic speech, so too a speaker cannot "erect a shield" against laws requiring access "simply by asserting" that mere association "would impair its message."

The Solomon Amendment has no similar effect on a law school's associational rights. Students and faculty are free to associate to voice their disapproval of the military's message; nothing about the statute affects the composition of the group by making group membership less desirable. The Solomon Amendment therefore does not violate a law school's First Amendment rights. A military recruiter's mere presence on campus does not violate a law school's right to associate, regardless of how repugnant the law school considers the recruiter's message.

In this case, FAIR has attempted to stretch a number of First Amendment doctrines well beyond the sort of activities these doctrines protect. The law schools object to having to treat military recruiters like other recruiters, but that regulation of conduct does not violate the First Amendment. To the extent that the Solomon Amendment incidentally affects expression, the law schools' effort to cast themselves as just like the schoolchildren in *Barnette*, the parade organizers in *Hurley*, and the Boy Scouts in *Dale* plainly overstates the expressive nature of their activity and the impact of the Solomon Amendment on it, while exaggerating the reach of our First Amendment precedents.

C. Types of Unprotected and Less Protected Speech

3. Sexually Explicit Speech

b. Child pornography (casebook p. 1213)

After the Supreme Court's decision in *Ashcroft v. Free Speech Coalition* (casebook p. 1216), Congress adopted a new law regulating child pornography. It attempted to cure the problem identified in *Ashcroft* by requiring proof that children were used in producing the material. However, the new law makes it a crime to solicit or offer what is believed to be child pornography, even if it turns out that the material is not actually child pornography. The issue in *United States v. Williams* is whether this violates the First Amendment.

UNITED STATES v. WILLIAMS
128 S.Ct. 1830 (2008)

Justice SCALIA delivered the opinion of the Court.

Section 2252A(a)(3)(B) of Title 18, United States Code, criminalizes, in certain specified circumstances, the pandering or solicitation of child pornography. This case presents the question whether that statute is overbroad under the First Amendment or impermissibly vague under the Due Process Clause of the Fifth Amendment.

I

A

We have long held that obscene speech—sexually explicit material that violates fundamental notions of decency—is not protected by the First Amendment. See Roth v. United States (1957). But to protect explicit material that has social value, we have limited the scope of the obscenity exception, and have overturned convictions for the distribution of sexually graphic but nonobscene material. See Miller v. California (1973).

Over the last 25 years, we have confronted a related and overlapping category of proscribable speech: child pornography. This consists of sexually explicit visual portrayals that feature children. We have held that a statute which proscribes the distribution of all child pornography, even material that does not qualify as obscenity, does not on its face violate the First Amendment. Moreover, we have held that the government may criminalize the possession of child pornography, even though it may not criminalize the mere possession of obscene material involving adults.

The broad authority to proscribe child pornography is not, however, unlimited. Four Terms ago [in Free Speech Coalition v. Ashcroft (2004)], we held facially overbroad two provisions of the federal Child Pornography Protection Act of 1996 (CPPA). The first of these banned the possession and distribution of "'any visual depiction'" that "'is, or appears to be, of a minor engaging in sexually explicit conduct,'" even if it contained only youthful-looking adult actors or virtual images of children generated by a computer. This was invalid, we explained, because the child-protection rationale for speech restriction does not apply to materials produced without children. The second provision at issue criminalized the possession and distribution of material that had been pandered as child pornography, regardless of whether it actually was that. A person could thus face prosecution for possessing unobjectionable material that someone else had pandered. We held that this prohibition, which did "more than prohibit pandering," was also facially overbroad.

After our decision in Free Speech Coalition, Congress went back to the drawing board and produced legislation with the unlikely title of the Prosecutorial Remedies and Other Tools to end the Exploitation of Children Today Act of 2003. Section 503 of the Act amended 18 U.S.C. § 2252A to add a new pandering and solicitation provision, relevant portions of which now read as follows:

"(a) Any person who–
(3) knowingly–
(B) advertises, promotes, presents, distributes, or solicits through the mails, or in interstate or foreign commerce by any means, including by computer, any material or purported material in a manner that reflects the belief, or that is intended to cause another to believe, that the material or purported material is, or contains–

(i) an obscene visual depiction of a minor engaging in sexually explicit conduct; or
(ii) a visual depiction of an actual minor engaging in sexually explicit conduct, shall be punished as provided in subsection (b)."

Section 2256(2)(A) defines "sexually explicit conduct" as

"actual or simulated–

>   (i) sexual intercourse, including genital-genital, oral-genital, anal-genital, or
>   oral-anal, whether between persons of the same or opposite sex;
>   (ii) bestiality;
> (iii) masturbation;
>   (iv) sadistic or masochistic abuse; or
>   (v) lascivious exhibition of the genitals or pubic area of any person."

Violation of § 2252A(a)(3)(B) incurs a minimum sentence of 5 years imprisonment and a maximum of 20 years.

The Act's express findings indicate that Congress was concerned that limiting the child-pornography prohibition to material that could be proved to feature actual children, as our decision in Free Speech Coalition required, would enable many child pornographers to evade conviction. The emergence of new technology and the repeated retransmission of picture files over the Internet could make it nearly impossible to prove that a particular image was produced using real children-even though "[t]here is no substantial evidence that any of the child pornography images being trafficked today were made other than by the abuse of real children," virtual imaging being prohibitively expensive.

B

On April 26, 2004, respondent Michael Williams, using a sexually explicit screen name, signed in to a public Internet chat room. A Secret Service agent had also signed in to the chat room under the moniker "Lisa n Miami." The agent noticed that Williams had posted a message that read: "Dad of toddler has 'good' pics of her an [sic] me for swap of your toddler pics, or live cam." The agent struck up a conversation with Williams, leading to an electronic exchange of nonpornographic pictures of children. (The agent's picture was in fact a doctored photograph of an adult.) Soon thereafter, Williams messaged that he had photographs of men molesting his 4-year-old daughter. Suspicious that "Lisa n Miami" was a law-enforcement agent, before proceeding further Williams demanded that the agent produce additional pictures. When he did not, Williams posted the following public message in the chat room: "HERE ROOM; I CAN PUT UPLINK CUZ IM FOR REAL—SHE CANT." Appended to this declaration was a hyperlink that, when clicked, led to seven pictures of actual children, aged approximately 5 to 15, engaging in sexually explicit conduct and displaying their genitals. The Secret Service then obtained a search warrant for Williams's home, where agents seized two hard drives containing at least 22 images of real children engaged in sexually explicit conduct, some of it sadomasochistic.

Williams was charged with one count of pandering child pornography under § 2252A(a)(3)(B) and one count of possessing child pornography under § 2252A (a)(5)(B). He pleaded guilty to both counts but reserved the right to challenge the constitutionality of the pandering conviction. The District Court rejected his challenge, and sentenced him to concurrent 60-month sentences on the two counts. The United States Court of Appeals for the Eleventh Circuit reversed the pandering conviction, holding that the statute was both overbroad and impermissibly vague.

II

According to our First Amendment overbreadth doctrine, a statute is facially invalid if it prohibits a substantial amount of protected speech. The doctrine seeks to strike a balance between competing social costs. On the one hand, the threat of enforcement of an overbroad law deters people from engaging in constitutionally protected speech, inhibiting the free exchange of ideas. On the other hand, invalidating a law that in some of its applications is perfectly constitutional—particularly a law directed at conduct so antisocial that it has been made criminal—has obvious harmful effects. In order to maintain an appropriate balance, we have vigorously enforced the requirement that a statute's overbreadth be substantial, not only in an absolute sense, but also relative to the statute's plainly legitimate sweep.

The first step in overbreadth analysis is to construe the challenged statute; it is impossible to determine whether a statute reaches too far without first knowing what the statute covers. Generally speaking, § 2252A(a)(3)(B) prohibits offers to provide and requests to obtain child pornography. The statute does not require the actual existence of child pornography. Rather than targeting the underlying material, this statute bans the collateral speech that introduces such material into the child-pornography distribution network. Thus, an Internet user who solicits child pornography from an undercover agent violates the statute, even if the officer possesses no child pornography. Likewise, a person who advertises virtual child pornography as depicting actual children also falls within the reach of the statute.

A number of features of the statute are important to our analysis: First, the statute includes a scienter requirement. The first word of § 2252A(a)(3)—"knowingly" applies to every element of the two provisions. This is not a case where grammar or structure enables the challenged provision or some of its parts to be read apart from the "knowingly" requirement. Here "knowingly" introduces the challenged provision itself, making clear that it applies to that provision in its entirety; and there is no grammatical barrier to reading it that way.

Second, the statute's string of operative verbs—"advertises, promotes, presents, distributes, or solicits"—is reasonably read to have a transactional connotation. That is to say, the statute penalizes speech that accompanies or seeks to induce a transfer of child pornography—via reproduction or physical delivery—from one person to another.

To be clear, our conclusion that all the words in this list relate to transactions is not to say that they relate to commercial transactions. One could certainly "distribute" child pornography without expecting payment in return. Indeed, in much Internet file sharing of child pornography each participant makes his files available for free to other participants—as Williams did in this case. "Distribution may involve sophisticated pedophile rings or organized crime groups that operate for profit, but in many cases, is carried out by individual amateurs who seek no financial reward." To run afoul of the statute, the speech need only accompany or seek to induce the transfer of child pornography from one person to another.

Third, the phrase "in a manner that reflects the belief" includes both subjective and objective components. "[A] manner that reflects the belief" is quite different from "a manner that would give one cause to believe." The first formulation suggests that the defendant must actually have held the subjective "belief" that the material or purported material was child pornography. Thus, a misdescription that leads the listener to believe the defendant is offering child pornography, when the defendant in fact does not believe the material is child pornography, does not violate this prong of the statute. (It may, however, violate the "manner . . . that is intended to cause another to believe" prong if the misdescription is intentional.) There is also an objective component to the phrase "manner that reflects the belief." The statement or action must objectively manifest a belief that the material is child pornography; a mere belief, without an accompanying statement or action that would lead a reasonable person to understand that the defendant holds that belief, is insufficient.

Fourth, the other key phrase, "in a manner . . . that is intended to cause another to believe," contains only a subjective element: The defendant must "intend" that the listener believe the material to be child pornography, and must select a manner of "advertising, promoting, presenting, distributing, or soliciting" the material that he thinks will engender that belief—whether or not a reasonable person would think the same. (Of course in the ordinary case the proof of the defendant's intent will be the fact that, as an objective matter, the manner of "advertising, promoting, presenting, distributing, or soliciting" plainly sought to convey that the material was child pornography.)

Fifth, the definition of "sexually explicit conduct" (the visual depiction of which, engaged in by an actual minor, is covered by the Act's pandering and soliciting prohibition even when it is not obscene) is very similar to the definition of "sexual conduct" in the New York statute we upheld against an overbreadth challenge in New York v. Ferber. That defined "sexual conduct" as "'actual or simulated sexual intercourse, deviate sexual intercourse, sexual bestiality, masturbation, sado-masochistic abuse, or lewd exhibition of the genitals." Congress used essentially the same constitutionally approved definition in the present Act. If anything, the fact that the defined term here is "sexually explicit conduct," rather than (as in Ferber) merely "sexual conduct," renders the definition more immune from facial constitutional attack.

Critically, unlike in Free Speech Coalition, § 2252A(a)(3)(B)(ii)'s requirement of a "visual depiction of an actual minor" makes clear that, although the sexual intercourse may be simulated, it must involve actual children (unless it is obscene). This change eliminates any possibility that virtual child pornography or sex between youthful-looking adult actors might be covered by the term "simulated sexual intercourse."

B

We now turn to whether the statute, as we have construed it, criminalizes a substantial amount of protected expressive activity.

Offers to engage in illegal transactions are categorically excluded from First Amendment protection. One would think that this principle resolves the present case, since the statute criminalizes only offers to provide or requests to obtain contraband-child obscenity and child pornography involving actual children, both of which are proscribed, and the proscription of which is constitutional.

The Eleventh Circuit, however, believed that the exclusion of First Amendment protection extended only to commercial offers to provide or receive contraband: "Because [the statute] is not limited to commercial speech but extends also to non-commercial promotion, presentation, distribution, and solicitation, we must subject the content-based restriction of the PROTECT Act pandering provision to strict scrutiny. . . . "

This mistakes the rationale for the categorical exclusion. It is based not on the less privileged First Amendment status of commercial speech, but on the principle that offers to give or receive what it is unlawful to possess have no social value and thus, like obscenity, enjoy no First Amendment protection. Many long established criminal proscriptions—such as laws against conspiracy, incitement, and solicitation—criminalize speech (commercial or not) that is intended to induce or commence illegal activities. Offers to provide or requests to obtain unlawful material, whether as part of a commercial exchange or not, are similarly undeserving of First Amendment protection. It would be an odd constitutional principle that permitted the government to prohibit offers to sell illegal drugs, but not offers to give them away for free.

To be sure, there remains an important distinction between a proposal to engage in illegal activity and the abstract advocacy of illegality. See Brandenburg v. Ohio (1969) (per curiam). The Act before us does not prohibit advocacy of child pornography, but only offers to provide or requests to obtain it. There is no doubt that this prohibition falls well within constitutional bounds.

In sum, we hold that offers to provide or requests to obtain child pornography are categorically excluded from the First Amendment. The Eleventh Circuit believed it a constitutional difficulty that no child pornography need exist to trigger the statute. In its view, the fact that the statute could punish a "braggart, exaggerator, or outright liar" rendered it unconstitutional. That seems to us a strange constitutional calculus. Although we have held that the government can ban both fraudulent offers, and offers to provide illegal products, the Eleventh Circuit would forbid the government from punishing fraudulent offers to provide illegal products. We see no logic in that position; if anything, such statements are doubly excluded from the First Amendment.

The Eleventh Circuit found "particularly objectionable" the fact that the "reflects the belief" prong of the statute could ensnare a person who mistakenly believes that material is child pornography. This objection has two conceptually distinct parts. First, the Eleventh Circuit thought that it would be unconstitutional to punish someone for mistakenly distributing virtual child pornography as real child pornography. We disagree. Offers to deal in illegal products or otherwise engage in illegal activity do not acquire First Amendment protection when the offeror is mistaken about the factual predicate of his offer. The pandering and solicitation made unlawful by the Act are sorts of inchoate crimes—acts looking toward the commission of another crime, the delivery of child pornography. As with other inchoate crimes—attempt and conspiracy, for example—impossibility of completing the crime because the facts were not as the defendant believed is not a defense. "All courts are in agreement that what is usually referred to as 'factual impossibility' is no defense to a charge of attempt."

Finally, the dissent accuses us of silently overruling our prior decisions in Ferber and Free Speech Coalition. According to the dissent, Congress has made an end-run around the First Amendment's protection of virtual child pornography by prohibiting proposals to transact in such images rather than prohibiting the images themselves. But an offer to provide or request to receive virtual child pornography is not prohibited by the statute. A crime is committed only when the speaker believes or intends the listener to believe that the subject of the proposed transaction depicts real children. It is simply not true that this means "a protected category of expression [will] inevitably be suppressed." Simulated child pornography will be as available as ever, so long as it is offered and sought as such, and not as real child pornography. The dissent would require an exception from the statute's prohibition when, unbeknownst to one or both of the parties to the proposal, the completed transaction would not have been unlawful because it is (we have said) protected by the First Amendment. We fail to see what First Amendment interest would be served by drawing a distinction between two defendants who attempt to acquire contraband, one of whom happens to be mistaken about the contraband nature of what he would acquire. Is Congress forbidden from punishing those who attempt to acquire what they believe to be national-security documents, but which are actually fakes? To ask is to answer. There is no First Amendment exception from the general principle of criminal law that a person attempting to commit a crime need not be exonerated because he has a mistaken view of the facts.

III

As an alternative ground for facial invalidation, the Eleventh Circuit held that § 2252A(a)(3)(B) is void for vagueness. Vagueness doctrine is an outgrowth not of the First Amendment, but of the Due Process Clause of the Fifth Amendment. A conviction fails to comport with due process if the statute under which it is obtained fails to provide a person of ordinary intelligence fair notice of what is prohibited, or is so standardless that it authorizes or encourages seriously discriminatory enforcement.

The Eleventh Circuit believed that the phrases "'in a manner that reflects the belief'" and "'in a manner . . . that is intended to cause another to believe'" are "so vague and standardless as to what may not be said that the public is left with no objective measure to which behavior can be conformed."

What renders a statute vague is not the possibility that it will sometimes be difficult to determine whether the incriminating fact it establishes has been proved; but rather the indeterminacy of precisely what that fact is. Thus, we have struck down statutes that tied criminal culpability to whether the defendant's conduct was "annoying" or "indecent"—wholly subjective judgments without statutory definitions, narrowing context, or settled legal meanings.

There is no such indeterminacy here. The statute requires that the defendant hold, and make a statement that reflects, the belief that the material is child pornography; or that he communicate in a manner intended to cause another so to believe. Those are clear questions of fact. Whether someone held a belief or had an intent is a true-or-false determination, not a subjective judgment such as whether conduct is "annoying" or "indecent." Similarly true or false is the determination whether a particular formulation reflects a belief that material or purported material is child pornography. To be sure, it may be difficult in some cases to determine whether these clear requirements have been met. "But courts and juries every day pass upon knowledge, belief and intent-the state of men's minds-having before them no more than evidence of their words and conduct, from which, in ordinary human experience, mental condition may be inferred."

* * *

Child pornography harms and debases the most defenseless of our citizens. Both the State and Federal Governments have sought to suppress it for many years, only to find it proliferating through the new medium of the Internet. This Court held unconstitutional Congress's previous attempt to meet this new threat, and Congress responded with a carefully crafted attempt to eliminate the First Amendment problems we identified. As far as the provision at issue in this case is concerned, that effort was successful.

Justice SOUTER, with whom Justice GINSBURG joins, dissenting.

I accept the Court's explanation that Congress may criminalize proposals unrelated to any extant image. I part ways from the Court, however, on the regulation of proposals made with regard to specific, existing representations. Under the new law, the elements of the pandering offense are the same, whether or not the images are of real children. As to those that do not show real children, of course, a transaction in the material could not be prosecuted consistently with the First Amendment, and I believe that maintaining the First Amendment protection of expression we have previously held to cover fake child pornography requires a limit to the law's criminalization of pandering proposals. In failing to confront the tension between ostensibly protecting the material pandered while approving prosecution of the pandering of that same material, and in allowing the new pandering prohibition to suppress otherwise protected speech, the Court undermines Ferber and Free Speech Coalition in both reasoning and result. This is the significant element of today's holding, and I respectfully dissent from it.

The easy case for applying the Act would be a proposal to obtain or supply child pornography supposedly showing a real child, when the solicitation or offer is unrelated to any image (that is, when the existence of pornographic "material" was merely "purported"). On the other side of that sort of proposed transaction, someone with nothing to supply or having only non-expressive matter who purports to present, distribute, advertise, or promote child pornography also proposes an illegal transaction. In both cases, the activity would amount to an offer to traffic in child pornography that may be suppressed, and the First Amendment does not categorically protect offers to engage in illegal transactions. To the extent the speaker intended to mislead others, a conviction would also square with the unprotected status of fraud; and even a non-fraudulent speaker who mistakenly believed he could obtain the forbidden contraband to transfer to anyone who accepted an offer could be validly convicted consistent with the general rule of criminal law, that attempting to commit a crime is punishable even though the completed crime might (or would) turn out to be impossible in fact.

The easy cases for constitutional application of the Act are over, however, when one gets to proposals for transactions related to extant pornographic objects, like photos in a dealer's inventory, for example. These will in fact be the common cases, as the legislative findings attest. Congress did not pass the Act to catch unsuccessful solicitors or fraudulent offerors with no photos to sell.

But even when actual pictures thus occasion proposals, the Act requires no finding that an actual child be shown in the pornographic setting in order to prove a violation. And the fair assumption (apparently made by Congress) is that in some instances, the child pornography in question will be fake, with the picture showing only a simulation of a child, for example, or a very young-looking adult convincingly passed off as a child; in those cases the proposal is for a transaction that could not itself be made criminal, because the absence of a child model means that the image is constitutionally protected. But under the Act, that is irrelevant. What matters is not the inclusion of an actual child in the image, or the validity of forbidding the transaction proposed; what counts is simply the manifest belief or intent to cause a belief that a true minor is shown in the pornographic depiction referred to.

The tension with existing constitutional law is obvious. Free Speech Coalition reaffirmed that non-obscene virtual pornographic images are protected, because they fail to trigger the concern for child safety that disentitles child pornography to First Amendment protection. The Act, however, punishes proposals regarding images when the inclusion of actual children is not established by the prosecution, as well as images that show no real children at all; and this, despite the fact that, under Free Speech Coalition, the first proposed transfer could not be punished without the very proof the Act is meant to dispense with, and the second could not be made criminal at all.

What justification can there be for making independent crimes of proposals to engage in transactions that may include protected materials? The Court gives three answers, none of which comes to grips with the difficulty raised by the question. The first says it is simply wrong to say that the Act makes it criminal to propose a lawful transaction, since an element of the forbidden proposal must express a belief or inducement to believe that the subject of the proposed transaction shows actual children. But this does not go to the point. The objection is not that the Act criminalizes a proposal for a transaction described as being in virtual (that is, protected) child pornography. The point is that some proposals made criminal, because they express a belief that they refer to real child pornography, will relate to extant material that does not, or cannot be, demonstrated to show real children and so may not be prohibited. When a proposal covers existing photographs, the Act does not require that the requisite belief (manifested or encouraged) in the reality of the subjects be a correct belief. Prohibited proposals may relate to transactions in lawful, as well as unlawful, pornography.

Much the same may be said about the Court's second answer, that a proposal to commit a crime enjoys no speech protection. For the reason just given, that answer does not face up to the source of the difficulty: the action actually contemplated in the proposal, the transfer of the particular image, is not criminal if it turns out that an actual child is not shown in the photograph. If Ferber and Free Speech Coalition are good law, the facts sufficient for conviction under the Act do not suffice to show that the image (perhaps merely simulated), and thus a transfer of that image, are outside the bounds of constitutional protection. For this reason, it is not enough just to say that the First Amendment does not protect proposals to commit crimes. For that rule rests on the assumption that the proposal is actually to commit a crime, not to do an act that may turn out to be no crime at all. Why should the general rule of unprotected criminal proposals cover a case like the proposal to transfer what may turn out to be fake child pornography?

The Court's third answer analogizes the proposal to an attempt to commit a crime, and relies on the rule of criminal law that an attempt is criminal even when some impediment makes it impossible to complete the criminal act (the possible impediment here being the advanced age, say, or simulated character of the child-figure). Although the actual transfer the speaker has in mind may not turn out to be criminal, the argument goes, the transfer intended by the speaker is criminal, because the speaker believes that the contemplated transfer will be of real child pornography, and transfer of real child pornography is criminal. The fact that the circumstances are not as he believes them to be, because the material does not depict actual minors, is no defense to his attempt to engage in an unlawful transaction.

The more serious failure of the attempt analogy, however, is its unjustifiable extension of the classic factual frustration rule, under which the action specifically intended would be a criminal act if completed. The intending killer who mistakenly grabs the pistol loaded with blanks would have committed homicide if bullets had been in the gun; it was only the impossibility of completing the very intended act of shooting bullets that prevented the completion of the crime. This is not so, however, in the proposed transaction in an identified pornographic image without the showing of a real child; no matter what the parties believe, and no matter how exactly a defendant's actions conform to his intended course of conduct in completing the transaction he has in mind, if there turns out to be reasonable doubt that a real child was used to make the photos, or none was, there could be, respectively, no conviction and no crime. Thus, in the classic impossibility example, there is attempt liability when the course of conduct intended cannot be completed owing to some fact which the defendant was mistaken about, and which precludes completing the intended physical acts. But on the Court's reasoning there would be attempt liability even when the contemplated acts had been completed exactly as intended, but no crime had been committed. Why should attempt liability be recognized here (thus making way for "proposal" liability, under the Court's analogy)?

The Court's first response is to demur, with its example of the drug dealer who sells something else. (A package of baking powder, not powder cocaine, would be an example.) No one doubts the dealer may validly be convicted of an attempted drug sale even if he didn't know it was baking powder he was selling. Yet selling baking powder is no more criminal than selling virtual child pornography.

This response does not suffice, however, because it overlooks a difference between the lawfulness of selling baking powder and the lawful character of virtual child pornography. Powder sales are lawful but not constitutionally privileged. Any justification within the bounds of rationality would suffice for limiting baking powder transactions, just as it would for regulating the discharge of blanks from a pistol. Virtual pornography, however, has been held to fall within the First Amendment speech privilege, and thus is affirmatively protected, not merely allowed as a matter of course. The question stands: why should a proposal that may turn out to cover privileged expression be subject to standard attempt liability?

The Court's next response deals with the privileged character of the underlying material. It gives another example of attempt that presumably could be made criminal, in the case of the mistaken spy, who passes national security documents thinking they are classified and secret, when in fact they have been declassified and made subject to public inspection. Publishing unclassified documents is subject to the First Amendment privilege and can claim a value that fake child pornography cannot. The Court assumes that the document publication may be punished as an attempt to violate state-secret restrictions (and I assume so too); then why not attempt-proposals based on a mistaken belief that the underlying material is real child pornography? As the Court looks at it, the deterrent value that justifies prosecuting the mistaken spy (like the mistaken drug dealer and the intending killer) would presumably validate prosecuting those who make proposals about fake child pornography. But it would not, for there are significant differences between the cases of security documents and pornography without real children.

Eliminating the line between protected and unprotected speech, guaranteeing the suppression of a category of expression previously protected, and reducing recent and carefully considered First Amendment precedents to empty shells are heavy prices, not to be paid without a substantial offset, which is missing from this case. Hence, my answer that there is no justification for saving the Act's attempt to get around our holdings. We should hold that a transaction in what turns out to be fake pornography is better understood, not as an incomplete attempt to commit a crime, but as a completed series of intended acts that simply do not add up to a crime, owing to the privileged character of the material the parties were in fact about to deal in.

Perhaps I am wrong, but without some demonstration that juries have been rendering exploitation of children unpunishable, there is no excuse for cutting back on the First Amendment and no alternative to finding overbreadth in this Act. I would hold it unconstitutional on the authority of Ferber and Free Speech Coalition.

6. Conduct that Communicates

v. The Continuing Distinction Between Contributions and Expenditures (casebook, p. 1332)

There have been two important cases in the last two years concerning campaign finance. In *Randall v. Sorrell*, the Court considered the constitutionality of a Vermont law regulating campaign expenditures and contributions. Although the Court was very fragmented, the following clearly emerged: A majority of the Justices accept the *Buckley* framework (restrictions on contributions in election campaigns are allowed, but restrictions on expenditures are unconstitutional); and restrictions on contributions violate the First Amendment if they are too low. Justice Breyer's plurality opinion articulated reasons for finding the limit in this case to be too low. Because this is the first case ever to invalidate contributions as being too low, it undoubtedly will lead to challenges to many campaign finance laws around the country. The other case *Federal Election Commission v. Wisconsin Right to Life, Inc.*, involved an "as applied" challenge to the Bipartisan Campaign Finance Reform Act of 2002. In *McConnell v. Federal Election Commission* [casebook, p. 1336], the Court upheld the facial constitutionality of the Act. In *Wisconsin Right to Life*, the Court held that one of the provisions which it had upheld is unconstitutional as applied.

RANDALL v. SORRELL
548 U.S. 230 (2006)

Justice BREYER announced the judgment of the Court, and delivered an opinion in which THE CHIEF JUSTICE joins, and in which Justice ALITO joins except as to Parts II-B-1 and II-B-2.

We here consider the constitutionality of a Vermont campaign finance statute that limits both (1) the amounts that candidates for state office may spend on their campaigns (expenditure limitations) and (2) the amounts that individuals, organizations, and political parties may contribute to those campaigns (contribution limitations). We hold that both sets of limitations are inconsistent with the First Amendment. Well-established precedent makes clear that the expenditure limits violate the First Amendment. *Buckley v. Valeo* (1976) (per curiam). The contribution limits are unconstitutional because in their specific details (involving low maximum levels and other restrictions) they fail to satisfy the First Amendment's requirement of careful tailoring. That is to say, they impose burdens upon First Amendment interests that (when viewed in light of the statute's legitimate objectives) are disproportionately severe.

I

Prior to 1997, Vermont's campaign finance law imposed no limit upon the amount a candidate for state office could spend. It did, however, impose limits upon the amounts that individuals, corporations, and political committees could contribute to the campaign of such a candidate.

In 1997, Vermont enacted a more stringent campaign finance law, Pub. Act No. 64, the statute at issue here. Act 64, which took effect immediately after the 1998 elections, imposes mandatory expenditure limits on the total amount a candidate for state office can spend during a "two-year general election cycle," i.e., the primary plus the general election, in approximately the following amounts: governor, $300,000; lieutenant governor, $100,000; other statewide offices, $45,000; state senator, $4,000 (plus an additional $2,500 for each additional seat in the district); state representative (two-member district), $3,000; and state representative (single member district), $2,000. These limits are adjusted for inflation in odd-numbered years based on the Consumer Price Index. Incumbents seeking reelection to statewide office may spend no more than 85% of the above amounts, and incumbents seeking reelection to the State Senate or House may spend no more than 90% of the above amounts. The Act defines "[e]xpenditure" broadly to mean the "payment, disbursement, distribution, advance, deposit, loan or gift of money or anything of value, paid or promised to be paid, for the purpose of influencing an election, advocating a position on a public question, or supporting or opposing one or more candidates."

Act 64 also imposes strict contribution limits. The amount any single individual can contribute to the campaign of a candidate for state office during a "two-year general election cycle" is limited as follows: governor, lieutenant governor, and other statewide offices, $400; state senator, $300; and state representative, $200. § 2805(a). Unlike its expenditure limits, Act 64's contribution limits are not indexed for inflation.

A political committee is subject to these same limits. So is a political party, defined broadly to include "any subsidiary, branch or local unit" of a party, as well as any "national or regional affiliates" of a party (taken separately or together). Thus, for example, the statute treats the local, state, and national affiliates of the Democratic Party as if they were a single entity and limits their total contribution to a single candidate's campaign for governor (during the primary and the general election together) to $400.

The Act also imposes a limit of $2,000 upon the amount any individual can give to a political party during a 2-year general election cycle. The Act defines "contribution" broadly in approximately the same way it defines "expenditure."

II

We turn first to the Act's expenditure limits. Do those limits violate the First Amendment's free speech guarantees? In *Buckley v. Valeo*, the Court considered the constitutionality of the Federal Election Campaign Act of 1971 (FECA), a statute that, much like the Act before us, imposed both expenditure and contribution limitations on campaigns for public office. The Court, while upholding FECA's contribution limitations as constitutional, held that the statute's expenditure limitations violated the First Amendment. Over the last 30 years, in considering the constitutionality of a host of different campaign finance statutes, this Court has repeatedly adhered to *Buckley's* constraints, including those on expenditure limits.

The respondents recognize that, in respect to expenditure limits, *Buckley* appears to be a controlling—and unfavorable—precedent. They seek to overcome that precedent in two ways. First, they ask us in effect to overrule *Buckley*. Post-*Buckley* experience, they believe, has shown that contribution limits (and disclosure requirements) alone cannot effectively deter corruption or its appearance; hence experience has undermined an assumption underlying that case. Indeed, the respondents have devoted several pages of their briefs to attacking *Buckley's* holding on expenditure limits.

Second, in the alternative, they ask us to limit the scope of *Buckley* significantly by distinguishing *Buckley* from the present case. They advance as a ground for distinction a justification for expenditure limitations that, they say, *Buckley* did not consider, namely that such limits help to protect candidates from spending too much time raising money rather than devoting that time to campaigning among ordinary voters. We find neither argument persuasive.

The Court has often recognized the "fundamental importance" of stare decisis, the basic legal principle that commands judicial respect for a court's earlier decisions and the rules of law they embody. The Court has pointed out that stare decisis "promotes the evenhanded, predictable, and consistent development of legal principles, fosters reliance on judicial decisions, and contributes to the actual and perceived integrity of the judicial process." Stare decisis thereby avoids the instability and unfairness that accompany disruption of settled legal expectations. For this reason, the rule of law demands that adhering to our prior case law be the norm. Departure from precedent is exceptional, and requires "special justification." This is especially true where, as here, the principle has become settled through iteration and reiteration over a long period of time.

We can find here no such special justification that would require us to overrule *Buckley*. Subsequent case law has not made *Buckley* a legal anomaly or otherwise undermined its basic legal principles. We cannot find in the respondents' claims any demonstration that circumstances have changed so radically as to undermine *Buckley's* critical factual assumptions. The respondents have not shown, for example, any dramatic increase in corruption or its appearance in Vermont; nor have they shown that expenditure limits are the only way to attack that problem. At the same time, *Buckley* has promoted considerable reliance. Congress and state legislatures have used *Buckley* when drafting campaign finance laws. And, as we have said, this Court has followed *Buckley*, upholding and applying its reasoning in later cases. Overruling *Buckley* now would dramatically undermine this reliance on our settled precedent.

For all these reasons, we find this a case that fits the stare decisis norm. And we do not perceive the strong justification that would be necessary to warrant overruling so well established a precedent. We consequently decline the respondents' invitation to reconsider *Buckley*.

The respondents also ask us to distinguish these cases from *Buckley*. But we can find no significant basis for that distinction. Act 64's expenditure limits are not substantially different from those at issue in *Buckley*. In both instances the limits consist of a dollar cap imposed upon a candidate's expenditures. Nor is Vermont's primary justification for imposing its expenditure limits significantly different from Congress' rationale for the *Buckley* limits: preventing corruption and its appearance.

The sole basis on which the respondents seek to distinguish *Buckley* concerns a further supporting justification. They argue that expenditure limits are necessary in order to reduce the amount of time candidates must spend raising money. Increased campaign costs, together with the fear of a better-funded opponent, mean that, without expenditure limits, a candidate must spend too much time raising money instead of meeting the voters and engaging in public debate.

In our view, it is highly unlikely that fuller consideration of this time protection rationale would have changed *Buckley's* result. The *Buckley* Court was aware of the connection between expenditure limits and a reduction in fundraising time. In a section of the opinion dealing with FECA's public financing provisions, it wrote that Congress was trying to "free candidates from the rigors of fundraising." And, in any event, the connection between high campaign expenditures and increased fundraising demands seems perfectly obvious. Under these circumstances, the respondents' argument amounts to no more than an invitation so to limit Buckley's holding as effectively to overrule it. For the reasons set forth above, we decline that invitation as well. And, given Buckley's continued authority, we must conclude that Act 64's expenditure limits violate the First Amendment.

III

We turn now to a more complex question, namely the constitutionality of Act 64's contribution limits. The parties, while accepting *Buckley's* approach, dispute whether, despite *Buckley's* general approval of statutes that limit campaign contributions, Act 64's contribution limits are so severe that in the circumstances its particular limits violate the First Amendment.

Following *Buckley*, we must determine whether Act 64's contribution limits prevent candidates from "amassing the resources necessary for effective [campaign] advocacy," whether they magnify the advantages of incumbency to the point where they put challengers to a significant disadvantage; in a word, whether they are too low and too strict to survive First Amendment scrutiny. In answering these questions, we recognize, as *Buckley* stated, that we have "no scalpel to probe" each possible contribution level. We cannot determine with any degree of exactitude the precise restriction necessary to carry out the statute's legitimate objectives. In practice, the legislature is better equipped to make such empirical judgments, as legislators have "particular expertise" in matters related to the costs and nature of running for office. Thus ordinarily we have deferred to the legislature's determination of such matters.

Nonetheless, as *Buckley* acknowledged, we must recognize the existence of some lower bound. At some point the constitutional risks to the democratic electoral process become too great. After all, the interests underlying contribution limits, preventing corruption and the appearance of corruption, "directly implicate the integrity of our electoral process." Yet that rationale does not simply mean "the lower the limit, the better." That is because contribution limits that are too low can also harm the electoral process by preventing challengers from mounting effective campaigns against incumbent officeholders, thereby reducing democratic accountability. Thus, we see no alternative to the exercise of independent judicial judgment as a statute reaches those outer limits. And, where there is strong indication in a particular case, i.e., danger signs, that such risks exist (both present in kind and likely serious in degree), courts, including appellate courts, must review the record independently and carefully with an eye toward assessing the statute's "tailoring," that is, toward assessing the proportionality of the restrictions.

We find those danger signs present here. As compared with the contribution limits upheld by the Court in the past, and with those in force in other States, Act 64's limits are sufficiently low as to generate suspicion that they are not closely drawn. The Act sets its limits per election cycle, which includes both a primary and a general election. Thus, in a gubernatorial race with both primary and final election contests, the Act's contribution limit amounts to $200 per election per candidate (with significantly lower limits for contributions to candidates for State Senate and House of Representatives.) These limits apply both to contributions from individuals and to contributions from political parties, whether made in cash or in expenditures coordinated (or presumed to be coordinated) with the candidate.

In sum, Act 64's contribution limits are substantially lower than both the limits we have previously upheld and comparable limits in other States. These are danger signs that Act 64's contribution limits may fall outside tolerable First Amendment limits. We consequently must examine the record independently and carefully to determine whether Act 64's contribution limits are "closely drawn" to match the State's interests.

C

Our examination of the record convinces us that, from a constitutional perspective, Act 64's contribution limits are too restrictive. We reach this conclusion based not merely on the low dollar amounts of the limits themselves, but also on the statute's effect on political parties and on volunteer activity in Vermont elections. Taken together, Act 64's substantial restrictions on the ability of candidates to raise the funds necessary to run a competitive election, on the ability of political parties to help their candidates get elected, and on the ability of individual citizens to volunteer their time to campaigns show that the Act is not closely drawn to meet its objectives. In particular, five factors together lead us to this decision.

First, the record suggests, though it does not conclusively prove, that Act 64's contribution limits will significantly restrict the amount of funding available for challengers to run competitive campaigns.

Second, Act 64's insistence that political parties abide by exactly the same low contribution limits that apply to other contributors threatens harm to a particularly important political right, the right to associate in a political party.

Third, the Act's treatment of volunteer services aggravates the problem. Like its federal statutory counterpart, the Act excludes from its definition of "contribution" all "services provided without compensation by individuals volunteering their time on behalf of a candidate." But the Act does not exclude the expenses those volunteers incur, such as travel expenses, in the course of campaign activities. The Act's broad definitions would seem to count those expenses against the volunteer's contribution limit, at least where the spending was facilitated or approved by campaign officials. The absence of some such exception may matter in the present context, where contribution limits are very low.

Fourth, unlike the contribution limits we upheld in *Shrink*, Act 64's contribution limits are not adjusted for inflation. Its limits decline in real value each year.

Fifth, we have found nowhere in the record any special justification that might warrant a contribution limit so low or so restrictive as to bring about the serious associational and expressive problems that we have described. Rather, the basic justifications the State has advanced in support of such limits are those present in *Buckley*. The record contains no indication that, for example, corruption (or its appearance) in Vermont is significantly more serious a matter than elsewhere.

Justice ALITO, concurring in part and concurring in the judgment.

Whether or not a case can be made for reexamining *Buckley* in whole or in part, what matters is that respondents do not do so here, and so I think it unnecessary to reach the issue.

Justice KENNEDY, concurring in the judgment.

The Court decides the constitutionality of the limitations Vermont places on campaign expenditures and contributions. I agree that both limitations violate the First Amendment. As the plurality notes, our cases hold that expenditure limitations "place substantial and direct restrictions on the ability of candidates, citizens, and associations to engage in protected political expression, restrictions that the First Amendment cannot tolerate."

The universe of campaign finance regulation is one this Court has in part created and in part permitted by its course of decisions. That new order may cause more problems than it solves. On a routine, operational level the present system requires us to explain why $200 is too restrictive a limit while $1,500 is not. Our own experience gives us little basis to make these judgments, and certainly no traditional or well-established body of law exists to offer guidance. On a broader, systemic level political parties have been denied basic First Amendment rights. Entering to fill the void have been new entities such as political action committees, which are as much the creatures of law as of traditional forces of speech and association. Those entities can manipulate the system and attract their own elite power brokers, who operate in ways obscure to the ordinary citizen. Viewed within the legal universe we have ratified and helped create, the result the plurality reaches is correct; given my own skepticism regarding that system and its operation, however, it seems to me appropriate to concur only in the judgment.

Justice THOMAS, with whom Justice SCALIA joins, concurring in the judgment.

Although I agree with the plurality that Act 64, is unconstitutional, I disagree with its rationale for striking down that statute. I continue to believe that *Buckley* provides insufficient protection to political speech, the core of the First Amendment. The illegitimacy of *Buckley* is further underscored by the continuing inability of the Court (and the plurality here) to apply *Buckley* in a coherent and principled fashion. As a result, stare decisis should pose no bar to overruling *Buckley* and replacing it with a standard faithful to the First Amendment. Accordingly, I concur only in the judgment.

I adhere to my view that this Court erred in *Buckley* when it distinguished between contribution and expenditure limits, finding the former to be a less severe infringement on First Amendment rights. Likewise, *Buckley's* suggestion that contribution caps only marginally restrict speech, because "[a] contribution serves as a general expression of support for the candidate and his views, but does not communicate the underlying basis for the support," even if descriptively accurate, does not support restrictions on contributions.

The plurality opinion, far from making the case for Buckley as a rule of law, itself demonstrates that Buckley's limited scrutiny of contribution limits is "insusceptible of principled application," and accordingly is not entitled to stare decisis effect. Today's newly minted, multifactor test, particularly when read in combination with the Court's decision in *Shrink*, places this Court in the position of addressing the propriety of regulations of political speech based upon little more than its impression of the appropriate limits.

Given that these contribution limits severely impinge on the ability of candidates to run campaigns and on the ability of citizens to contribute to campaigns, and do so without any demonstrable need to avoid corruption, they cannot possibly satisfy even *Buckley's* ambiguous level of scrutiny.

Justice STEVENS, dissenting.

I am convinced that *Buckley's* holding on expenditure limits is wrong, and that the time has come to overrule it. I have not reached this conclusion lightly. As Justice Breyer correctly observes, stare decisis is a principle of "fundamental importance." But it is not an inexorable command, and several factors, taken together, provide special justification for revisiting the constitutionality of statutory limits on candidate expenditures.

To begin with, *Buckley's* holding on expenditure limits itself upset a long-established practice. For the preceding 65 years, congressional races had been subject to statutory limits on both expenditures and contributions. There are further reasons for reexamining *Buckley's* holding on candidate expenditure limits that do not apply to its holding on candidate contribution limits.

The interest in freeing candidates from the fundraising straitjacket is even more compelling. Without expenditure limits, fundraising devours the time and attention of political leaders, leaving them too busy to handle their public responsibilities effectively.

Additionally, there is no convincing evidence that these important interests favoring expenditure limits are fronts for incumbency protection. And only by "permit[ting] States nationwide to experiment with these critically needed reforms,"—as 18 States urge us to do—will we enable further research on how expenditure limits relate to our incumbent reelection rates. In the meantime, a legislative judgment that "enough is enough" should command the greatest possible deference from judges interpreting a constitutional provision that, at best, has an indirect relationship to activity that affects the quantity—rather than the quality or the content—of repetitive speech in the marketplace of ideas.

Justice SOUTER, with whom Justice GINSBURG joins, and with whom Justice STEVENS joins dissenting.

In 1997, the Legislature of Vermont passed Act 64 after a series of public hearings persuaded legislators that rehabilitating the State's political process required campaign finance reform. A majority of the Court today decides that the expenditure and contribution limits enacted are irreconcilable with the Constitution's guarantee of free speech. I would adhere to the Court of Appeals's decision to remand for further enquiry bearing on the limitations on candidates' expenditures, and I think the contribution limits satisfy controlling precedent. I respectfully dissent.

We said in *Buckley* that "expenditure limitations impose far greater restraints on the freedom of speech and association than do . . . contribution limitations," but the *Buckley* Court did not categorically foreclose the possibility that some spending limit might comport with the First Amendment. Instead, *Buckley* held that the constitutionality of an expenditure limitation "turns on whether the governmental interests advanced in its support satisfy the [applicable] exacting scrutiny." In applying that standard in *Buckley* itself, the Court gave no indication that it had given serious consideration to an aim that Vermont's statute now pursues: to alleviate the drain on candidates' and officials' time caused by the endless fundraising necessary to aggregate many small contributions to meet the opportunities for ever more expensive campaigning.

Vermont's argument therefore does not ask us to overrule *Buckley*; it asks us to apply *Buckley's* framework to determine whether its evidence here on a need to slow the fundraising treadmill suffices to support the enacted limitations. Vermont's claim is serious. Three decades of experience since *Buckley* have taught us much, and the findings made by the Vermont Legislature on the pernicious effect of the nonstop pursuit of money are significant. Thus, the constitutionality of the expenditure limits was not conclusively decided by the Second Circuit, and I believe the evidentiary work that remained to be done would have raised the prospect for a sound answer to that question, whatever the answer might have been. Instead, we are left with an unresolved question of narrow tailoring and with consequent doubt about the justifiability of the spending limits as necessary and appropriate correctives. This is not the record on which to foreclose the ability of a State to remedy the impact of the money chase on the democratic process. I would not, therefore, disturb the Court of Appeals's stated intention to remand.

II

Although I would defer judgment on the merits of the expenditure limitations, I believe the Court of Appeals correctly rejected the challenge to the contribution limits. Low though they are, one cannot say that "the contribution limitation[s are] so radical in effect as to render political association ineffective, drive the sound of a candidate's voice below the level of notice, and render contributions pointless."

The limits set by Vermont are not remarkable departures either from those previously upheld by this Court or from those lately adopted by other States.

Still, our cases do not say deference should be absolute. We can all imagine dollar limits that would be laughable, and per capita comparisons that would be meaningless because aggregated donations simply could not sustain effective campaigns. The plurality thinks that point has been reached in Vermont, and in particular that the low contribution limits threaten the ability of challengers to run effective races against incumbents. Thus, the plurality's limit of deference is substantially a function of suspicion that political incumbents in the legislature set low contribution limits because their public recognition and easy access to free publicity will effectively augment their own spending power beyond anything a challenger can muster. The suspicion is, in other words, that incumbents cannot be trusted to set fair limits, because facially neutral limits do not in fact give challengers an even break. But this received suspicion is itself a proper subject of suspicion. The petitioners offered, and the plurality invokes, no evidence that the risk of a pro-incumbent advantage has been realized; in fact, the record evidence runs the other way, as the plurality concedes.

Because I would not pass upon the constitutionality of Vermont's expenditure limits prior to further enquiry into their fit with the problem of fundraising demands on candidates, and because I do not see the contribution limits as depressed to the level of political inaudibility, I respectfully dissent.

FEDERAL ELECTION COMMISSION v. WISCONSIN RIGHT TO LIFE, INC.
127 S.Ct. 2652 (2007)

Chief Justice ROBERTS announced the judgment of the Court and delivered the opinion of the Court with respect to Parts I and II, and an opinion with respect to Parts III and IV, in which Justice ALITO joins.

Section 203 of the Bipartisan Campaign Reform Act of 2002 (BCRA) makes it a federal crime for any corporation to broadcast, shortly before an election, any communication that names a federal candidate for elected office and is targeted to the electorate. In *McConnell v. Federal Election Comm'n* (2003), this Court considered whether § 203 was facially overbroad under the First Amendment because it captured within its reach not only campaign speech, or "express advocacy," but also speech about public issues more generally, or "issue advocacy," that mentions a candidate for federal office. The Court concluded that there was no overbreadth concern to the extent the speech in question was the "functional equivalent" of express campaign speech. On the other hand, the Court "assume[d]" that the interests it had found to "justify the regulation of campaign speech might not apply to the regulation of genuine issue ads." The Court nonetheless determined that § 203 was not facially overbroad. Even assuming § 203 "inhibit[ed] some constitutionally protected corporate and union speech," the Court concluded that those challenging the law on its face had failed to carry their "heavy burden" of establishing that all enforcement of the law should therefore be prohibited.

We now confront such an as-applied challenge. Resolving it requires us first to determine whether the speech at issue is the "functional equivalent" of speech expressly advocating the election or defeat of a candidate for federal office, or instead a "genuine issue a[d]." We have long recognized that the distinction between campaign advocacy and issue advocacy "may often dissolve in practical application. Candidates, especially incumbents, are intimately tied to public issues involving legislative proposals and governmental actions." Our development of the law in this area requires us, however, to draw such a line, because we have recognized that the interests held to justify the regulation of campaign speech and its "functional equivalent" "might not apply" to the regulation of issue advocacy.

In drawing that line, the First Amendment requires us to err on the side of protecting political speech rather than suppressing it. We conclude that the speech at issue in this as-applied challenge is not the "functional equivalent" of express campaign speech. We further conclude that the interests held to justify restricting corporate campaign speech or its functional equivalent do not justify restricting issue advocacy, and accordingly we hold that BCRA § 203 is unconstitutional as applied to the advertisements at issue in these cases.

I

Prior to BCRA, corporations were free under federal law to use independent expenditures to engage in political speech so long as that speech did not expressly advocate the election or defeat of a clearly identified federal candidate. BCRA significantly cut back on corporations' ability to engage in political speech. BCRA § 203, at issue in these cases, makes it a crime for any labor union or incorporated entity—whether the United Steelworkers, the American Civil Liberties Union, or General Motors—to use its general treasury funds to pay for any "electioneering communication." BCRA's definition of "electioneering communication" is clear and expansive. It encompasses any broadcast, cable, or satellite communication that refers to a candidate for federal office and that is aired within 30 days of a federal primary election or 60 days of a federal general election in the jurisdiction in which that candidate is running for office.

Appellee Wisconsin Right to Life, Inc. (WRTL), is a nonprofit, nonstock, ideological advocacy corporation recognized by the Internal Revenue Service as tax exempt under § 501(c)(4) of the Internal Revenue Code. On July 26, 2004, as part of what it calls a "grassroots lobbying campaign," began broadcasting a radio advertisement [criticizing Wisconsin's Senators, Russell Feingold and Herbert Kohl from participating in filibusters of President Bush's judicial nominees.]

Believing that it nonetheless possessed a First Amendment right to broadcast these ads, WRTL filed suit against the Federal Election Commission (FEC) on July 28, 2004, seeking declaratory and injunctive relief before a three-judge District Court.

II

[The Court found that the case was not moot even though the election was over because it was a "wrong capable of repetition but evading review." This aspect of the decision is presented in Chapter 1.]

III

WRTL rightly concedes that its ads are prohibited by BCRA § 203. Each ad clearly identifies Senator Feingold, who was running (unopposed) in the Wisconsin Democratic primary on September 14, 2004, and each ad would have been "targeted to the relevant electorate," during the BCRA blackout period. WRTL further concedes that its ads do not fit under any of BCRA's exceptions to the term "electioneering communication." The only question, then, is whether it is consistent with the First Amendment for BCRA § 203 to prohibit WRTL from running these three ads.

A

Because BCRA § 203 burdens political speech, it is subject to strict scrutiny. The strict scrutiny analysis is, of course, informed by our precedents. This Court has already ruled that BCRA survives strict scrutiny to the extent it regulates express advocacy or its functional equivalent. So to the extent the ads in these cases fit this description, the FEC's burden is not onerous; all it need do is point to *McConnell* and explain why it applies here. If, on the other hand, WRTL's ads are not express advocacy or its equivalent, the Government's task is more formidable. It must then demonstrate that banning such ads during the blackout periods is narrowly tailored to serve a compelling interest. No precedent of this Court has yet reached that conclusion.

B

The FEC, intervenors, and the dissent below contend that *McConnell* already established the constitutional test for determining if an ad is the functional equivalent of express advocacy: whether the ad is intended to influence elections and has that effect. WRTL and the District Court majority, on the other hand, claim that *McConnell* did not adopt any test as the standard for future as-applied challenges. We agree. *McConnell*'s analysis was grounded in the evidentiary record before the Court. When the *McConnell* Court considered the possible facial overbreadth of § 203, it looked to the studies in the record analyzing ads broadcast during the blackout periods, and those studies had classified the ads in terms of intent and effect. The Court's assessment was accordingly phrased in the same terms, which the Court regarded as sufficient to conclude, on the record before it, that the plaintiffs had not "carried their heavy burden of proving" that § 203 was facially overbroad and could not be enforced in any circumstances. The Court did not explain that it was adopting a particular test for determining what constituted the "functional equivalent" of express advocacy.

For the reasons regarded as sufficient in *Buckley* [*v. Valeo* (1976)], we decline to adopt a test for as-applied challenges turning on the speaker's intent to affect an election. The test to distinguish constitutionally protected political speech from speech that BCRA may proscribe should provide a safe harbor for those who wish to exercise First Amendment rights. The test should also "reflec[t] our 'profound national commitment to the principle that debate on public issues should be uninhibited, robust, and wide-open.' " A test turning on the intent of the speaker does not remotely fit the bill.

Far from serving the values the First Amendment is meant to protect, an intent-based test would chill core political speech by opening the door to a trial on every ad within the terms of § 203, on the theory that the speaker actually intended to affect an election, no matter how compelling the indications that the ad concerned a pending legislative or policy issue. No reasonable speaker would choose to run an ad covered by BCRA if its only defense to a criminal prosecution would be that its motives were pure. An intent-based standard "blankets with uncertainty whatever may be said," and "offers no security for free discussion." A test focused on the speaker's intent could lead to the bizarre result that identical ads aired at the same time could be protected speech for one speaker, while leading to criminal penalties for another.

Buckley also explains the flaws of a test based on the actual effect speech will have on an election or on a particular segment of the target audience. Such a test "'puts the speaker . . . wholly at the mercy of the varied understanding of his hearers.'" It would also typically lead to a burdensome, expert-driven inquiry, with an indeterminate result. Litigation on such a standard may or may not accurately predict electoral effects, but it will unquestionably chill a substantial amount of political speech.

C

"The freedom of speech . . . guaranteed by the Constitution embraces at the least the liberty to discuss publicly and truthfully all matters of public concern without previous restraint or fear of subsequent punishment." To safeguard this liberty, the proper standard for an as-applied challenge to BCRA § 203 must be objective, focusing on the substance of the communication rather than amorphous considerations of intent and effect. It must entail minimal if any discovery, to allow parties to resolve disputes quickly without chilling speech through the threat of burdensome litigation. And it must eschew "the open-ended rough-and-tumble of factors," which "invit[es] complex argument in a trial court and a virtually inevitable appeal." In short, it must give the benefit of any doubt to protecting rather than stifling speech.

In light of these considerations, a court should find that an ad is the functional equivalent of express advocacy only if the ad is susceptible of no reasonable interpretation other than as an appeal to vote for or against a specific candidate. Under this test, WRTL's three ads are plainly not the functional equivalent of express advocacy. First, their content is consistent with that of a genuine issue ad: The ads focus on a legislative issue, take a position on the issue, exhort the public to adopt that position, and urge the public to contact public officials with respect to the matter. Second, their content lacks indicia of express advocacy:

The ads do not mention an election, candidacy, political party, or challenger; and they do not take a position on a candidate's character, qualifications, or fitness for office.

At best, appellants have shown what we have acknowledged at least since *Buckley*: that "the distinction between discussion of issues and candidates and advocacy of election or defeat of candidates may often dissolve in practical application." Under the test set forth above, that is not enough to establish that the ads can only reasonably be viewed as advocating or opposing a candidate in a federal election. "Freedom of discussion, if it would fulfill its historic function in this nation, must embrace all issues about which information is needed or appropriate to enable the members of society to cope with the exigencies of their period." Discussion of issues cannot be suppressed simply because the issues may also be pertinent in an election. Where the First Amendment is implicated, the tie goes to the speaker, not the censor.

Because WRTL's ads may reasonably be interpreted as something other than as an appeal to vote for or against a specific candidate, we hold they are not the functional equivalent of express advocacy, and therefore fall outside the scope of *McConnell*'s holding.

IV

BCRA § 203 can be constitutionally applied to WRTL's ads only if it is narrowly tailored to further a compelling interest. This Court has never recognized a compelling interest in regulating ads, like WRTL's, that are neither express advocacy nor its functional equivalent.

Appellants argue that an expansive definition of "functional equivalent" is needed to ensure that issue advocacy does not circumvent the rule against express advocacy, which in turn helps protect against circumvention of the rule against contributions. But such a prophylaxis-upon-prophylaxis approach to regulating expression is not consistent with strict scrutiny. "[T]he desire for a bright-line rule . . . hardly constitutes the compelling state interest necessary to justify any infringement on First Amendment freedom."

A second possible compelling interest recognized by this Court lies in addressing a "different type of corruption in the political arena: the corrosive and distorting effects of immense aggregations of wealth that are accumulated with the help of the corporate form and that have little or no correlation to the public's support for the corporation's political ideas." These cases did not suggest, however, that the interest in combating "a different type of corruption" extended beyond campaign speech.

These cases are about political speech. The importance of the cases to speech and debate on public policy issues is reflected in the number of diverse organizations that have joined in supporting WRTL before this Court: the American Civil Liberties Union, the National Rifle Association, the American Federation of Labor and Congress of Industrial Organizations, the Chamber of

Commerce of the United States of America, Focus on the Family, the Coalition of Public Charities, the Cato Institute, and many others.

Yet, as is often the case in this Court's First Amendment opinions, we have gotten this far in the analysis without quoting the Amendment itself: "Congress shall make no law . . . abridging the freedom of speech." The Framers' actual words put these cases in proper perspective. Our jurisprudence over the past 216 years has rejected an absolutist interpretation of those words, but when it comes to drawing difficult lines in the area of pure political speech—between what is protected and what the Government may ban—it is worth recalling the language we are applying. *McConnell* held that express advocacy of a candidate or his opponent by a corporation shortly before an election may be prohibited, along with the functional equivalent of such express advocacy. We have no occasion to revisit that determination today. But when it comes to defining what speech qualifies as the functional equivalent of express advocacy subject to such a ban—the issue we do have to decide—we give the benefit of the doubt to speech, not censorship. The First Amendment's command that "Congress shall make no law . . . abridging the freedom of speech" demands at least that.

Justice SCALIA, with whom Justice KENNEDY and Justice THOMAS join, concurring in part and concurring in the judgment.

A Moroccan cartoonist once defended his criticism of the Moroccan monarch (lèse majesté being a serious crime in Morocco) as follows: " 'I'm not a revolutionary, I'm just defending freedom of speech. . . . I never said we had to change the king—no, no, no, no! But I said that some things the king is doing, I do not like. Is that a crime?' " Well, in the United States (making due allowance for the fact that we have elected representatives instead of a king) it is a crime, at least if the speaker is a union or a corporation (including not-for-profit public-interest corporations) and if the representative is identified by name within a certain period before a primary or congressional election in which he is running. That is the import of § 203 of the Bipartisan Campaign Reform Act of 2002 (BCRA), the constitutionality of which we upheld three Terms ago in *McConnell v. Federal Election Comm'n* (2003).

As an element essential to that determination of constitutionality, our opinion left open the possibility that a corporation or union could establish that, in the particular circumstances of its case, the ban was unconstitutional because it was (to pursue the analogy) only the king's policies and not his tenure in office that was criticized. Today's cases present the question of what sort of showing is necessary for that purpose. For the reasons I set forth below, it is my view that no test for such a showing can both (1) comport with the requirement of clarity that unchilled freedom of political speech demands, and (2) be compatible with the facial validity of § 203 (as pronounced in *McConnell*). I would therefore reconsider the decision that sets us the unsavory task of separating issue-speech from election-speech with no clear criterion.

McConnell was mistaken in its belief that as-applied challenges could eliminate the unconstitutional applications of § 203. They can do so only if a test is adopted which contradicts the holding of McConnell—that § 203 is facially valid because the vast majority of pre-election issue ads can constitutionally be proscribed. Today's cases make it apparent that the adventure is a flop, and that *McConnell*'s holding concerning § 203 was wrong.

Which brings me to the question of stare decisis. "Stare decisis is not an inexorable command" or " 'a mechanical formula of adherence to the latest decision.' " It is instead " 'a principle of policy,' " and this Court has a "considered practice" not to apply that principle of policy "as rigidly in constitutional as in nonconstitutional cases." This Court has not hesitated to overrule decisions offensive to the First Amendment and to do so promptly where fundamental error was apparent. Overruling a constitutional case decided just a few years earlier is far from unprecedented.

Of particular relevance to the stare decisis question in these cases is the impracticability of the regime created by *McConnell*. Stare decisis considerations carry little weight when an erroneous "governing decisio[n]" has created an "unworkable" legal regime. As described above, the *McConnell* regime is unworkable because of the inability of any acceptable as-applied test to validate the facial constitutionality of § 203—that is, its inability to sustain proscription of the vast majority of issue ads. We could render the regime workable only by effectively overruling *McConnell* without saying so—adopting a clear as-applied rule protective of speech in the "heartland" of what Congress prohibited. The promise of an administrable as-applied rule that is both effective in the vindication of First Amendment rights and consistent with *McConnell*'s holding is illusory. It is not as though *McConnell* produced a settled body of law. Indeed, it is far more accurate to say that *McConnell* unsettled a body of law.

Neither do any of the other considerations relevant to stare decisis suggest adherence to *McConnell*. These cases do not involve property or contract rights, where reliance interests are involved. And *McConnell*'s § 203 holding has assuredly not become "embedded" in our "national culture." If § 203 has had any cultural impact, it has been to undermine the traditional and important role of grassroots advocacy in American politics by burdening the "budget-strapped nonprofit entities upon which many of our citizens rely for political commentary and advocacy."

There is wondrous irony to be found in both the genesis and the consequences of BCRA. In the fact that the institutions it was designed to muzzle-unions and nearly all manner of corporations—for all the "corrosive and distorting effects" of their "immense aggregations of wealth," were utterly impotent to prevent the passage of this legislation that forbids them to criticize candidates (including incumbents). In the fact that the effect of BCRA has been to concentrate more political power in the hands of the country's wealthiest individuals and their so-called 527 organizations, unregulated by § 203. (In the 2004 election cycle, a mere 24 individuals contributed an astounding total of $142 million to 527s. And in the fact that while these wealthy individuals dominate political discourse, it is this small, grass-roots organization of Wisconsin Right to Life that is muzzled.

I would overrule that part of the Court's decision in *McConnell* upholding
§ 203(a) of BCRA.

Justice SOUTER, with whom Justice STEVENS, Justice GINSBURG, and Justice
BREYER join, dissenting.

The significance and effect of today's judgment, from which I respectfully
dissent, turn on three things: the demand for campaign money in huge amounts
from large contributors, whose power has produced a cynical electorate; the
congressional recognition of the ensuing threat to democratic integrity as
reflected in a century of legislation restricting the electoral leverage of concentrations of money in corporate and union treasuries; and declaring the facial
validity of the most recent Act of Congress in that tradition, a decision that is
effectively, and unjustifiably, overruled today.

I

The indispensable ingredient of a political candidacy is money for advertising.
In the 2004 campaign, more than half of the combined expenditures by the two
principal presidential candidates (excluding fundraising) went for media time
and space. And in the 2005-2006 election cycle, the expenditure of more than
$2 billion on television shattered the previous record, even without a presiden-
tial contest. The portent is for still greater spending. By the end of March 2007,
almost a year before the first primary and more than 18 months before the
general election, presidential candidates had already raised over $150 million.

The indispensability of these huge sums has two significant consequences for
American Government that are particularly on point here. The enormous
demands, first, assign power to deep pockets. Candidates occasionally boast
about the number of contributors they have, but the headlines speaking in
dollars reflect political reality. Some major contributors get satisfaction from
pitching in for their candidates, but political preference fails to account for the
frequency of giving "substantial sums to both major national parties," a practice driven "by stark political pragmatism, not by ideological support for either
party or their candidates." What the high-dollar pragmatists of either variety get
is special access to the officials they help elect, and with it a disproportionate
influence on those in power. At a critical level, contributions that underwrite
elections are leverage for enormous political influence.

Voters know this. Hence, the second important consequence of the demand
for big money to finance publicity: pervasive public cynicism. A 2002 poll
found that 71 percent of Americans think Members of Congress cast votes based
on the views of their big contributors, even when those views differ from the
Member's own beliefs about what is best for the country. The same percentage
believes that the will of contributors tempts Members to vote against the
majority view of their constituents. Almost half of Americans believe that
Members often decide how to vote based on what big contributors to their

party want, while only a quarter think Members often base their votes on perceptions of what is best for the country or their constituents.

Devoting concentrations of money in self-interested hands to the support of political campaigning therefore threatens the capacity of this democracy to represent its constituents and the confidence of its citizens in their capacity to govern themselves. These are the elements summed up in the notion of political integrity, giving it a value second to none in a free society.

II

If the threat to this value flowing from concentrations of money in politics has reached an unprecedented enormity, it has been gathering force for generations. Before the turn of the last century, as now, it was obvious that the purchase of influence and the cynicism of voters threaten the integrity and stability of democratic government, each derived from the responsiveness of its law to the interests of citizens and their confidence in that focus. The danger has traditionally seemed at its apex when no reasonable limits constrain the campaign activities of organizations whose "unique legal and economic characteristics" are tailored to "facilitat[e] the amassing of large treasuries." Corporations were the earliest subjects of concern; the same characteristics that have made them engines of the Nation's extraordinary prosperity have given them the financial muscle to gain "advantage in the political marketplace" when they turn from core corporate activity to electioneering, and in "Congress' judgment" the same concern extends to labor unions as to corporations.

As was expectable, narrowing the corporate-union electioneering limitation to magic words soon reduced it to futility. "[P]olitical money . . . is a moving target," and the "ingenuity and resourcefulness" of political financiers revealed the massive regulatory gap left by the "magic words" test. It proved to be the door through which so-called "issue ads" of current practice entered American politics.

An issue ad is an advertisement on a political subject urging the reader or listener to let a politician know what he thinks, but containing no magic words telling the recipient to vote for or against anyone. By the 1996 election cycle, between $135 and $150 million was being devoted to these ads, and because they had no magic words, they failed to trigger the limitation on union or corporate expenditures for electioneering. Experience showed, however, that the line between "issue" broadcasts and outright electioneering was a patent fiction. Nor was it surprising that the Senate Committee heard testimony that " '[w]ithout taming' " the vast sums flowing into issue ads, " 'campaign finance reform—no matter how thoroughly it addresses . . . perceived problems-will come to naught.' " The Committee predicted that "if the course of non-action is followed, . . . Congress would be encouraging further growth of union, corporate nonprofit and individual independent expenditures." The next two elections validated the prediction: during the 1998 cycle, spending on issue ads doubled to between $270 and $340 million, and the figure climbed to $500 million in the 2000 cycle.

The congressional response was § 203 of the Bipartisan Campaign Reform Act of 2002 (BCRA), 116 Stat. 91, which redefined prohibited "expenditure" so as to restrict corporations and unions from funding "electioneering communication[s]" out of their general treasuries.

III

In *McConnell*, we found this definition to be "easily understood and objectiv[e]," and we held that the resulting line separating regulated election speech from general political discourse does not, on its face, violate the First Amendment. We rejected any suggestion "that *Buckley* drew a constitutionally mandated line between express advocacy [with magic words] and so-called issue advocacy [without them], and that speakers possess an inviolable First Amendment right to engage in the latter category of speech." We thus found "[l]ittle difference . . . between an ad that urged viewers to 'vote against Jane Doe' and one that condemned Jane Doe's record on a particular issue before exhorting viewers to 'call Jane Doe and tell her what you think.' "

We understood that Congress had a compelling interest in limiting this sort of electioneering by corporations and unions, for § 203 exemplified a tradition of "repeatedly sustained legislation aimed at 'the corrosive and distorting effects of immense aggregations of wealth that are accumulated with the help of the corporate form and that have little or no correlation to the public's support for the corporation's political ideas.' " Nor did we see any plausible claim of substantial overbreadth from incidentally prohibiting ads genuinely focused on issues rather than elections, given the limitation of "electioneering communication" by time, geographical coverage, and clear reference to candidate.

We may add that a nonprofit corporation, no matter what its source of funding, is free to pelt a federal candidate like Jane Doe with criticism or shower her with praise, by name and within days of an election, if it speaks through a newspaper ad or on a website, rather than a "broadcast, cable, or satellite communication."

In sum, Congress in 1907 prohibited corporate contributions to candidates and in 1943 applied the same ban to unions. In 1947, Congress extended the complete ban from contributions to expenditures "in connection with" an election, a phrase so vague that in 1986 we held it must be confined to instances of express advocacy using magic words. Congress determined, in 2002, that corporate and union expenditures for fake issue ads devoid of magic words should be regulated using a narrow definition of "electioneering communication" to reach only broadcast ads that were the practical equivalents of express advocacy. In 2003, this Court found the provision free from vagueness and justified by the concern that drove its enactment.

This century-long tradition of legislation and judicial precedent rests on facing undeniable facts and testifies to an equally undeniable value. Campaign finance reform has been a series of reactions to documented threats to electoral integrity obvious to any voter, posed by large sums of money from corporate or union treasuries, with no redolence of "grassroots" about them. Neither Congress's decisions nor our own have understood the corrupting influence of money in politics as being limited to outright bribery or discrete quid pro quo; campaign finance reform has instead consistently focused on the more pervasive distortion of electoral institutions by concentrated wealth, on the special access and guaranteed favor that sap the representative integrity of American government and defy public confidence in its institutions. From early in the 20th century through the decision in *McConnell*, we have acknowledged that the value of democratic integrity justifies a realistic response when corporations and labor organizations commit the concentrated moneys in their treasuries to electioneering.

IV

The corporate appellee in these cases, Wisconsin Right to Life (WRTL), is a nonprofit corporation funded to a significant extent by contributions from other corporations. Throughout the 2004 senatorial campaign, WRTL made no secret of its views about who should win the election and explicitly tied its position to the filibuster issue. In sum, any Wisconsin voter who paid attention would have known that Democratic Senator Feingold supported filibusters against Republican presidential judicial nominees, that the propriety of the filibusters was a major issue in the senatorial campaign, and that WRTL along with the Senator's Republican challengers opposed his reelection because of his position on filibusters. Any alert voters who heard or saw WRTL's ads would have understood that WRTL was telling them that the Senator's position on the filibusters should be grounds to vote against him.

Given these facts, it is beyond all reasonable debate that the ads are constitutionally subject to regulation under *McConnell*. There, we noted that BCRA was meant to remedy the problem of "[s]o-called issue ads" being used "to advocate the election or defeat of clearly identified federal candidates." *McConnell*'s holding that § 203 is facially constitutional is overruled.

The price of *McConnell*'s demise as authority on § 203 seems to me to be a high one. The Court (and, I think, the country) loses when important precedent is overruled without good reason, and there is no justification for departing from our usual rule of stare decisis here. The same combination of alternatives that was available to corporations affected by *McConnell* in 2003 is available today: WRTL could have run a newspaper ad, could have paid for the broadcast ads through its PAC, could have established itself as an MCFL organization free of corporate money, and could have said "call your Senators" instead of naming Senator Feingold in its ads broadcasted just before the election. Nothing in the related law surrounding § 203 has changed in any way, let alone in any way that undermines *McConnell*'s rationale.

Nor can any serious argument be made that *McConnell*'s holding has been "unworkable in practice." *McConnell* validated a clear rule resting on mostly bright-line conditions, and there is no indication that the statute has been difficult to apply. Finally, it goes without saying that nothing has changed about the facts.

After today, the ban on contributions by corporations and unions and the limitation on their corrosive spending when they enter the political arena are open to easy circumvention, and the possibilities for regulating corporate and union campaign money are unclear. The ban on contributions will mean nothing much, now that companies and unions can save candidates the expense of advertising directly, simply by running "issue ads" without express advocacy, or by funneling the money through an independent corporation like WRTL.

But the understanding of the voters and the Congress that this kind of corporate and union spending seriously jeopardizes the integrity of democratic government will remain. The facts are too powerful to be ignored, and further efforts at campaign finance reform will come. It is only the legal landscape that now is altered, and it may be that today's departure from precedent will drive further reexamination of the constitutional analysis: of the distinction between contributions and expenditures, or the relation between spending and speech, which have given structure to our thinking since Buckley itself was decided.

I cannot tell what the future will force upon us, but I respectfully dissent from this judgment today.

****

In 2008, the Supreme Court dealt with the constitutionality of another provision of the Bipartisan Campaign Finance Reform Act: the so-called millionaires provision which raises contribution limits for candidates if their opponents spend a significant amount of their own money. In a 5-4 decision, the Court invalidated the provision. The key disagreement between the majority and the dissent is whether creating more equal election opportunities is a compelling government interest.

DAVIS v. FEDERAL ELECTION COMMISSION
128 S.Ct. 2759 (2008)

Justice ALITO delivered the opinion of the Court.

In this appeal, we consider the constitutionality of federal election law provisions that, under certain circumstances, impose different campaign contribution limits on candidates competing for the same congressional seat.

I

A

Federal law limits the amount of money that a candidate for the House of Representatives and the candidate's authorized committee may receive from an individual, as well as the amount that the candidate's party may devote to coordinated campaign expenditures. Under the usual circumstances, the same restrictions apply to all the competitors for a seat and their authorized committees. Contributions from individual donors during a 2-year election cycle are subject to a cap, which is currently set at $2,300. In addition, no funds may be accepted from an individual whose aggregate contributions to candidates and their committees during the election cycle have reached the legal limit, currently $42,700. A candidate also may not accept general election coordinated expenditures by national or state political party committees that exceed an imposed limit.

Section 319(a) of the Bipartisan Campaign Reform Act of 2002 (BCRA), part of the so-called "Millionaire's Amendment," fundamentally alters this scheme when, as a result of a candidate's expenditure of personal funds, the "opposition personal funds amount" (OPFA) exceeds $350,000. When a candidate's expenditure of personal funds causes the OPFA to pass the $350,000 mark (for convenience, such candidates will be referred to as "self-financing"), a new, asymmetrical regulatory scheme comes into play. The self-financing candidate remains subject to the limitations noted above, but the candidate's opponent (the "non-self-financing" candidate) may receive individual contributions at treble the normal limit (e.g., $6,900 rather than the current $2,300), even from individuals who have reached the normal aggregate contributions cap, and may accept coordinated party expenditures without limit. Once the non-self-financing candidate's receipts exceed the OPFA, the prior limits are revived. A candidate who does not spend the contributions received under the asymmetrical limits must return them.

In order to calculate the OPFA, certain information is needed about the self-financing candidate's campaign assets and personal expenditures. A non-self-financing candidate and the candidate's committee face less extensive disclosure requirements.

B

Appellant Jack Davis was the Democratic candidate for the House of Representatives from New York's 26th Congressional District in 2004 and 2006. In both elections, he lost to the incumbent. In his brief, Davis discloses having spent $1.2 million, principally his own funds, on his 2004 campaign. He reports spending $2.3 million in 2006, all but $126,000 of which came from personal funds. His opponent in 2006 spent no personal funds. Indeed, although the OPFA calculation provided the opportunity for Davis' opponent to raise nearly $1.5 million under §319(a)'s asymmetrical limits, Davis' opponent adhered to the normal contribution limits.

Davis' 2006 candidacy began in March 2006, when he filed with the FEC a "Statement of Candidacy" and, in compliance with §319(b), declared that he intended to spend $1 million in personal funds during the general election. After Davis declared his candidacy but before he filed suit, the FEC's general counsel notified him that it had reason to believe that he had violated § 319 by failing to report personal expenditures during the 2004 campaign.

Davis filed this action in the United States District Court for the District of Columbia.

[II]

We turn to the merits of Davis' claim that the First Amendment is violated by the contribution limits that apply when § 319(a) comes into play. Under this scheme, as previously noted, when a candidate spends more than $350,000 in personal funds and creates what the statute apparently regards as a financial imbalance, that candidate's opponent may qualify to receive both larger individual contributions than would otherwise be allowed and unlimited coordinated party expenditures. Davis contends that § 319(a) unconstitutionally burdens his exercise of his First Amendment right to make unlimited expenditures of his personal funds because making expenditures that create the imbalance has the effect of enabling his opponent to raise more money and to use that money to finance speech that counteracts and thus diminishes the effectiveness of Davis' own speech.

A

If § 319(a) simply raised the contribution limits for all candidates, Davis' argument would plainly fail. This Court has previously sustained the facial constitutionality of limits on discrete and aggregate individual contributions and on coordinated party expenditures. At the same time, the Court has recognized that such limits implicate First Amendment interests and that they cannot stand unless they are "closely drawn" to serve a "sufficiently important interest," such as preventing corruption and the appearance of corruption. See, e.g., McConnell v. Federal Election Comm'n (2003).

There is, however, no constitutional basis for attacking contribution limits on the ground that they are too high. Congress has no constitutional obligation to limit contributions at all; and if Congress concludes that allowing contributions of a certain amount does not create an undue risk of corruption or the appearance of corruption, a candidate who wishes to restrict an opponent's fundraising cannot argue that the Constitution demands that contributions be regulated more strictly. Consequently, if § 319(a)'s elevated contribution limits applied across the board, Davis would not have any basis for challenging those limits.

B

Section 319(a), however, does not raise the contribution limits across the board. Rather, it raises the limits only for the non-self-financing candidate and does so only when the self-financing candidate's expenditure of personal funds causes the OPFA threshold to be exceeded. We have never upheld the constitutionality of a law that imposes different contribution limits for candidates who are competing against each other, and we agree with Davis that this scheme impermissibly burdens his First Amendment right to spend his own money for campaign speech.

In Buckley, we soundly rejected a cap on a candidate's expenditure of personal funds to finance campaign speech. We held that a "candidate . . . has a First Amendment right to engage in the discussion of public issues and vigorously and tirelessly to advocate his own election" and that a cap on personal expenditures imposes "a substantial," "clea[r]" and "direc[t]" restraint on that right. We found that the cap at issue was not justified by "[t]he primary governmental interest" proffered in its defense, i.e., "the prevention of actual and apparent corruption of the political process." Far from preventing these evils, "the use of personal funds," we observed, "reduces the candidate's dependence on outside contributions and thereby counteracts the coercive pressures and attendant risks of abuse to which . . . contribution limitations are directed." We also rejected the argument that the expenditure cap could be justified on the ground that it served "[t]he ancillary interest in equalizing the relative financial resources of candidates competing for elective office." This putative interest, we noted, was "clearly not sufficient to justify the . . . infringement of fundamental First Amendment rights."

Buckley's emphasis on the fundamental nature of the right to spend personal funds for campaign speech is instructive. While BCRA does not impose a cap on a candidate's expenditure of personal funds, it imposes an unprecedented penalty on any candidate who robustly exercises that First Amendment right. Section 319(a) requires a candidate to choose between the First Amendment right to engage in unfettered political speech and subjection to discriminatory fundraising limitations. Many candidates who can afford to make large personal expenditures to support their campaigns may choose to do so despite § 319(a), but they must shoulder a special and potentially significant burden if they make that choice.

Because § 319(a) imposes a substantial burden on the exercise of the First Amendment right to use personal funds for campaign speech, that provision cannot stand unless it is "justified by a compelling state interest." No such justification is present here.

The burden imposed by § 319(a) on the expenditure of personal funds is not justified by any governmental interest in eliminating corruption or the perception of corruption.

The Government maintains that § 319(a)'s asymmetrical limits are justified because they "level electoral opportunities for candidates of different personal wealth." [I]n Buckley, we held that "[t]he interest in equalizing the financial resources of candidates" did not provide a "justification for restricting" candidates' overall campaign expenditures, particularly where equalization "might serve . . . to handicap a candidate who lacked substantial name recognition or exposure of his views before the start of the campaign." We have similarly held that the interest "in equalizing the relative ability of individuals and groups to influence the outcome of elections" cannot support a cap on expenditures for "express advocacy of the election or defeat of candidates," as "the concept that government may restrict the speech of some elements of our society in order to enhance the relative voice of others is wholly foreign to the First Amendment."

The argument that a candidate's speech may be restricted in order to "level electoral opportunities" has ominous implications because it would permit Congress to arrogate the voters' authority to evaluate the strengths of candidates competing for office. Different candidates have different strengths. Some are wealthy; others have wealthy supporters who are willing to make large contributions. Some are celebrities; some have the benefit of a well-known family name. Leveling electoral opportunities means making and implementing judgments about which strengths should be permitted to contribute to the outcome of an election. The Constitution, however, confers upon voters, not Congress, the power to choose the Members of the House of Representatives, Art. I, § 2, and it is a dangerous business for Congress to use the election laws to influence the voters' choices.

[III]

The remaining issue that we must consider is the constitutionality of § 319(b)'s disclosure requirements. "[W]e have repeatedly found that compelled disclosure, in itself, can seriously infringe on privacy of association and belief guaranteed by the First Amendment." As a result, we have closely scrutinized disclosure requirements, including requirements governing independent expenditures made to further individuals' political speech. To survive this scrutiny, significant encroachments "cannot be justified by a mere showing of some legitimate governmental interest." Instead, there must be "a 'relevant correlation' or 'substantial relation' between the governmental interest and the information required to be disclosed," and the governmental interest "must survive exacting scrutiny." That is, the strength of the governmental interest must reflect the seriousness of the actual burden on First Amendment rights.

The § 319(b) disclosure requirements were designed to implement the asymmetrical contribution limits provided for in § 319(a), and as discussed above, § 319(a) violates the First Amendment. In light of that holding, the burden imposed by the § 319(b) requirements cannot be justified, and it follows that they too are unconstitutional.

Justice STEVENS, with whom Justice SOUTER, Justice GINSBURG, and Justice BREYER join as to Part II, concurring in part and dissenting in part.

The "Millionaire's Amendment" of the Bipartisan Campaign Reform Act of 2002 (BCRA), is the product of a congressional judgment that candidates who are willing and able to spend over $350,000 of their own money in seeking election to Congress enjoy an advantage over opponents who must rely on contributions to finance their campaigns. To reduce that advantage, and to combat the perception that congressional seats are for sale to the highest bidder, Congress has relaxed the restrictions that would otherwise limit the amount of contributions that the opponents of self-funding candidates may accept from their supporters. In a thorough and well—reasoned opinion, the District Court held that because the Millionaire's Amendment does not impose any burden whatsoever on the self-funding candidate's freedom to speak, it does not violate the First Amendment, and because it does no more than diminish the unequal strength of the self-funding candidate, it does not violate the equal protection component of the Fifth Amendment. I agree completely with the District Court's opinion.

While I would affirm for the reasons given by the District Court, I believe it appropriate to add these additional comments on the premise that underlies the constitutional prohibition on expenditure limitations, and on my reasons for concluding that the Millionaire's Amendment represents a modest, sensible, and plainly constitutional attempt by Congress to minimize the advantages enjoyed by wealthy candidates vis-á-vis those who must rely on the support of others to fund their pursuit of public office.

I

In my view, a number of purposes, both legitimate and substantial, may justify the imposition of reasonable limitations on the expenditures permitted during the course of any single campaign. For one, such limitations would "free candidates and their staffs from the interminable burden of fundraising." Moreover, the imposition of reasonable limitations would likely have the salutary effect of improving the quality of the exposition of ideas. After all, orderly debate is always more enlightening than a shouting match that awards points on the basis of decibels rather than reasons. Quantity limitations are commonplace in any number of other contexts in which high-value speech occurs. Litigants in this Court pressing issues of the utmost importance to the Nation are allowed only a fixed time for oral debate and a maximum number of pages for written argument. As listeners and as readers, judges need time to reflect on the merits of an issue. It seems to me that Congress is entitled to make the judgment that voters deserve the same courtesy and the same opportunity to reflect as judges; flooding the airwaves with slogans and sound-bites may well do more to obscure the issues than to enlighten listeners.

If, as I have come to believe, Congress could attempt to reduce the millionaire candidate's advantage by imposing reasonable limits on all candidates' expenditures, it follows a fortiori that the eminently reasonable scheme before us today survives constitutional scrutiny.

II

Even accepting the Buckley Court's holding that expenditure limits as such are uniquely incompatible with the First Amendment, it remains my firm conviction that the Millionaire's Amendment represents a good-faith attempt by Congress to regulate, within the bounds of the Constitution, one particularly pernicious feature of many contemporary political campaigns.

It cannot be gainsaid that the twin rationales at the heart of the Millionaire's Amendment—reducing the importance of wealth as a criterion for public office and countering the perception that seats in the United States Congress are available for purchase by the wealthiest bidder—are important Government interests. It is also evident that Congress, in enacting the provision, crafted a solution that was carefully tailored to those concerns. Davis insists, however, that the Government's interests are insufficiently weighty to justify what he believes are intrusions upon his rights under the First Amendment and the equal protection component of the Fifth Amendment, and that, regardless of the strength of the justifications offered, Congress' solution is not sufficiently tailored to addressing the twin concerns it has identified. His arguments are unpersuasive on all counts.

The thrust of Davis' First Amendment challenge is that by relaxing the contribution limits applicable to the opponent of a self-funding candidate, the Millionaire's Amendment punishes the candidate who chooses to self-fund. Extrapolating from the zero-sum nature of a political race, Davis insists that any benefit conferred upon a self-funder's opponent thereby works a detriment to the self-funding candidate. Accordingly, he argues, the scheme burdens the self-funding candidate's First Amendment right to speak freely and to participate fully in the political process.

But Davis cannot show that the Millionaire's Amendment causes him—or any other self-funding candidate—any First Amendment injury whatsoever. The Millionaire's Amendment quiets no speech at all. On the contrary, it does no more than assist the opponent of a self-funding candidate in his attempts to make his voice heard; this amplification in no way mutes the voice of the millionaire, who remains able to speak as loud and as long as he likes in support of his campaign. Enhancing the speech of the millionaire's opponent, far from contravening the First Amendment, actually advances its core principles. If only one candidate can make himself heard, the voter's ability to make an informed choice is impaired. And the self-funding candidate's ability to engage meaningfully in the political process is in no way undermined by this provision.

Even were we to credit Davis' view that the benefit conferred on the self-funding candidate's opponent burdens the self-funder's First Amendment rights, the purposes of the Amendment surely justify its effects. The Court is simply wrong when it suggests that the "governmental interest in eliminating corruption or the perception of corruption," is the sole governmental interest sufficient to support campaign finance regulations.

Indeed, we have long recognized the strength of an independent governmental interest in reducing both the influence of wealth on the outcomes of elections, and the appearance that wealth alone dictates those results. In case after case, we have held that statutes designed to protect against the undue influence of aggregations of wealth on the political process—where such statutes are responsive to the identified evil—do not contravene the First Amendment. See, e.g., Austin v. Michigan Chamber of Commerce (1990).

Although the focus of our cases has been on aggregations of corporate rather than individual wealth, there is no reason that their logic—specifically, their concerns about the corrosive and distorting effects of wealth on our political process—is not equally applicable in the context of individual wealth. For, as we explained in McConnell, "Congress' historical concern with the 'political potentialities of wealth' and their 'untoward consequences for the democratic process' . . . has long reached beyond corporate money."

Minimizing the effect of concentrated wealth on our political process, and the concomitant interest in addressing the dangers that attend the perception that political power can be purchased, are, therefore, sufficiently weighty objectives to justify significant congressional action. And, not only was Congress motivated by proper and weighty goals in crafting the Millionaire's Amendment, the details of the scheme it devised are genuinely responsive to the problems it identified. The statute's "Opposition Personal Funds Amount" formula permits a self-funding candidate to spend as much money as he wishes, while taking into account fundraising by the relevant campaigns; it thereby ensures that a candidate who happens to enjoy a significant fundraising advantage against a self-funding opponent does not reap a windfall as a result of the enhanced contribution limits. Rather, the self-funder's opponent may avail himself of the enhanced contribution limits only until parity is achieved, at which point he becomes again ineligible for contributions above the normal maximum.

It seems uncontroversial that "there is no good reason to allow disparities in wealth to be translated into disparities in political power. A well-functioning democracy distinguishes between market processes of purchase and sale on the one hand and political processes of voting and reason-giving on the other." In light of that clear truth, Congress' carefully crafted attempt to reduce the distinct advantages enjoyed by wealthy candidates for congressional office does not offend the First Amendment.

Justice GINSBURG, with whom Justice BREYER joins, concurring in part and dissenting in part.

Agreeing with the Court that appellant Jack Davis has standing and that this case is not moot, on the merits, however, I part ways with the Court. I resist joining other portions of Justice Stevens' opinion, however, to the extent that they address Buckley's distinction between expenditure and contribution limits and, correspondingly, Buckley's holding that expenditure limits impose "direct quantity restrictions on political communication." Appellee Federal Election Commission has not asked us to overrule Buckley ; consequently, the issue has not been briefed. Convinced that the challenged statute encounters no constitutional shoal under our precedents, I would leave reconsideration of Buckley for a later day and case.

3. Compelled Association (casebook p. 1400)

In *Davenport v. Washington Education Association*, 127 S.Ct. 2372 (2007), the Supreme Court applied *Abood* to hold that a state could require that public sector unions could spend non-members' dues on political election activities only with their affirmative authorization. The Court ruled that it does not violate the First Amendment for a State to require its public-sector unions to receive affirmative authorization from a nonmember before spending that nonmember's agency fees for election-related purposes.

D. What Places Are Available for Speech?

3. Speech in Authoritarian Environments: Military, Prisons, and Schools

b. Prisons (casebook, p. 1380)

In *Beard v. Banks*, below, the Court upheld a Pennsylvania prison regulation that prevented some inmates from having any access to newspapers or magazines. The 6-3 decision, without a majority opinion, reflected great judicial deference to prison authorities.

BEARD v. BANKS

548 U.S. 521 (2006)

Justice BREYER announced the judgment of the Court, and delivered an opinion, in which THE CHIEF JUSTICE, Justice KENNEDY, and Justice SOUTER join.

We here consider whether a Pennsylvania prison policy that "denies newspapers, magazines, and photographs" to a group of specially dangerous and recalcitrant inmates "violate[s] the First Amendment." While we do not deny the constitutional importance of the interests in question, we find, on the basis of the record now before us, that prison officials have set forth adequate legal support for the policy. And the plaintiff, a prisoner who attacks the policy, has failed to set forth "specific facts" that, in light of the deference that courts must show to the prison officials, could warrant a determination in his favor.

I

The prison regulation at issue applies to certain prisoners housed in Pennsylvania's Long Term Segregation Unit. The LTSU is the most restrictive of the three special units that Pennsylvania maintains for difficult prisoners.

[T]hey (unlike all other prisoners in the Commonwealth) are restricted in the manner at issue here: They have no access to newspapers, magazines, or personal photographs. They are nonetheless permitted legal and personal correspondence, religious and legal materials, two library books, and writing paper.

II

Turner v. Safley (1987), and *Overton v. Bazzetta* (2003), contain the basic substantive legal standards governing this case. This Court recognized in *Turner* that imprisonment does not automatically deprive a prisoner of certain important constitutional protections, including those of the First Amendment. But at the same time the Constitution sometimes permits greater restriction of such rights in a prison than it would allow elsewhere. *Turner* [held] that restrictive prison regulations are permissible if they are " 'reasonably related' to legitimate penological interests," and are not an "exaggerated response" to such objectives.

Turner also sets forth four factors "relevant in determining the reasonableness of the regulation at issue." First, is there a " 'valid, rational connection' between the prison regulation and the legitimate governmental interest put forward to justify it"? Second, are there "alternative means of exercising the right that remain open to prison inmates"? Third, what "impact" will "accommodation of the asserted constitutional right . . . have on guards and other inmates, and on the allocation of prison resources generally"? And, fourth, are "ready alternatives" for furthering the governmental interest available?

III

The Secretary in his motion set forth several justifications for the prison's policy, including the need to motivate better behavior on the part of particularly difficult prisoners, the need to minimize the amount of property they control in their cells, and the need to assure prison safety, by, for example, diminishing the amount of material a prisoner might use to start a cell fire. We need go no further than the first justification, that of providing increased incentives for better prison behavior. Applying the well-established substantive and procedural standards set forth in Part II, we find, on the basis of the record before us, that the Secretary's justification is adequate. And that finding here warrants summary judgment in the Secretary's favor.

The Secretary rested his motion for summary judgment primarily upon the statement of undisputed facts along with Deputy Prison Superintendent Dickson's affidavit. The statement of undisputed facts says that the LTSU's 40 inmates, about 0.01 percent of the total prison population, constitute the " 'worst of the worst,' " those who "have proven by the history of their behavior in prison, the necessity of holding them in the rigorous regime of confinement" of the LTSU. It then sets forth three "penological rationales" for the Policy, summarized from the Dickson deposition:

(1) to "motivat[e]" better "behavior" on the part of these "particularly difficult prisoners," by providing them with an incentive to move to level 1, or out of the LTSU altogether, and to "discourage backsliding" on the part of level 1 inmates;

(2) to minimize the amount of property controlled by the prisoners, on the theory that the "less property these high maintenance, high supervision, obdurate troublemakers have, the easier it is for . . . correctional officer [s] to detect concealed contraband [and] to provide security"; and

(3) to diminish the amount of material (in particular newspapers and magazines) that prisoners might use as weapons of attack in the form of "spears" or "blow guns," or that they could employ "as tools to catapult feces at the guards without the necessity of soiling one's own hands," or use "as tinder for cell fires."

As we have said we believe that the first rationale itself satisfies Turner's requirements. First, the statement and deposition set forth a "valid, rational connection" between the Policy and "legitimate penological objectives." The articulated connections between newspapers and magazines, the deprivation of virtually the last privilege left to an inmate, and a significant incentive to improve behavior, are logical ones. Thus, the first factor supports the Policy's "reasonableness."

As to the second factor, the statement and deposition make clear that, as long as the inmate remains at level 2, no "alternative means of exercising the right" remain open to him. The absence of any alternative thus provides "some evidence that the regulations [a]re unreasonable," but is not "conclusive" of the reasonableness of the Policy.

As to the third factor, the statement and deposition indicate that, were prison authorities to seek to "accommodat[e] . . . the asserted constitutional right," the resulting "impact" would be negative. That circumstance is also inherent in the nature of the Policy: If the Policy (in the authorities' view) helps to produce better behavior, then its absence (in the authorities' view) will help to produce worse behavior, e.g., "backsliding" (and thus the expenditure of more "resources" at level 2). Similarly, as to the fourth factor, neither the statement nor the deposition describes, points to, or calls to mind any "alternative method of accommodating the claimant's constitutional complaint . . . that fully accommodates the prisoner's rights at de minimis cost to valid penological interests."

Here prison authorities responded adequately through their statement and deposition to the allegations in the complaint. And the plaintiff failed to point to "specific facts" in the record that could "lead a rational trier of fact to find" in his favor.

Justice THOMAS, with whom Justice SCALIA joins, concurring in the judgment.

Judicial scrutiny of prison regulations is an endeavor fraught with peril. Just last Term, this Court invalidated California's policy of racially segregating prisoners in its reception centers, notwithstanding that State's warning that its policy was necessary to prevent prison violence. See *Johnson v. California* (2005). California subsequently experienced several instances of severe race-based prison violence, including a riot that resulted in 2 fatalities and more than 100 injuries, and significant fighting along racial lines between newly arrived inmates, the very inmates that were subject to the policy invalidated by the Court in *Johnson*. This powerful reminder of the grave dangers inherent in prison administration confirms my view that the framework I set forth in *Overton v. Bazzetta* (2003) is the least perilous approach for resolving challenges to prison regulations, as well as the approach that is most faithful to the Constitution. Accordingly, I concur only in the judgment of the Court.

Both the plurality and the dissent evaluate the regulations challenged in this case pursuant to the approach set forth in *Turner v. Safley*, which permits prison regulations that "imping[e] on inmates' constitutional rights" if the regulations are "reasonably related to legitimate penological interests." But as I explained in *Overton*, *Turner* and its progeny "rest on the unstated (and erroneous) presumption that the Constitution contains an implicit definition of incarceration." Because the Constitution contains no such definition, "States are free to define and redefine all types of punishment, including imprisonment, to encompass various types of deprivations— provided only that those deprivations are consistent with the Eighth Amendment." Respondent has not challenged Pennsylvania's prison policy as a violation of the Eighth Amendment.

Although Pennsylvania "is free to alter its definition of incarceration to include the retention" of unfettered access to magazines, newspapers, and photographs, it appears that the Commonwealth instead sentenced respondent against the backdrop of its traditional conception of imprisonment, which affords no such privileges. Accordingly, respondent's challenge to Pennsylvania's prison regulations must fail.

Justice STEVENS, with whom Justice GINSBURG joins, dissenting.

By ratifying the Fourteenth Amendment, our society has made an unmistakable commitment to apply the rule of law in an evenhanded manner to all persons, even those who flagrantly violate their social and legal obligations. Thus, it is well settled that even the "'worst of the worst'" prisoners retain constitutional protection, specifically including their First Amendment rights. When a prison regulation impinges upon First Amendment freedoms, it is invalid unless "it is reasonably related to legitimate penological interests." *Turner v. Safley* (1987). Under this standard, a prison regulation cannot withstand constitutional scrutiny if "the logical connection between the regulation and the asserted goal is so remote as to render the policy arbitrary or irrational," or if the regulation represents an "exaggerated response" to legitimate penological objectives.

In this case, Pennsylvania prison officials have promulgated a rule that prohibits inmates in Long Term Segregation Unit, level 2 (LTSU-2), which is the most restrictive condition of confinement statewide, from possessing any secular, nonlegal newspaper, newsletter, or magazine during the indefinite duration of their solitary confinement. A prisoner in LTSU-2 may not even receive an individual article clipped from such a news publication unless the article relates to him or his family. In addition, under the challenged rule, any personal photograph, including those of spouses, children, deceased parents, or inspirational mentors, will be treated as contraband and confiscated.

It is indisputable that this prohibition on the possession of newspapers and photographs infringes upon respondent's First Amendment rights. Plainly, the rule at issue in this case strikes at the core of the First Amendment rights to receive, to read, and to think.

Petitioner does not dispute that the prohibition at issue infringes upon rights protected by the First Amendment. Instead, petitioner posits two penological interests, which, in his view, are sufficient to justify the challenged rule notwithstanding these constitutional infringements: prison security and inmate rehabilitation. Although these interests are certainly valid, petitioner has failed to establish, as a matter of law, that the challenged rule is reasonably related to these interests.

Turning first to the security rationale, which the plurality does not discuss, the Court of Appeals persuasively explained why, in light of the amount of materials LTSU-2 inmates may possess in their cells, petitioner has failed to demonstrate that the prohibition on newspapers, magazines, and photographs is likely to have any marginal effect on security.

The second rationale posited by petitioner in support of the prohibitions on newspapers, newsletters, magazines, and photographs is rehabilitation. According to petitioner, the ban "provides the [l]evel 2 inmates with the prospect of earning a privilege through compliance with orders and remission of various negative behaviors and serves to encourage the progress and discourage backsliding by the level 1 inmates." In the plurality's view, in light of the present record, this rationale is sufficient to warrant a reversal of the judgment below.

Rehabilitation is undoubtedly a legitimate penological interest. However, the particular theory of rehabilitation at issue in this case presents a special set of concerns for courts considering whether a prison regulation is consistent with the First Amendment. Specifically, petitioner advances a deprivation theory of rehabilitation: Any deprivation of something a prisoner desires gives him an added incentive to improve his behavior. This justification has no limiting principle; if sufficient, it would provide a "rational basis" for any regulation that deprives a prisoner of a constitutional right so long as there is at least a theoretical possibility that the prisoner can regain the right at some future time by modifying his behavior. Indeed, the more important the constitutional right at stake (at least from the prisoners' perspective), the stronger the justification for depriving prisoners of that right.

Indeed, the strong form of the deprivation theory of rehabilitation would mean that the prison rule we invalidated in *Turner* would have survived constitutional scrutiny if the State had simply posited an interest in rehabilitating prisoners through deprivation. In *Turner*, we held that a Missouri regulation that forbade inmates from marrying except with the permission of the prison superintendent was facially unconstitutional. We rejected the State's proffered security and rehabilitation concerns as not reasonably related to the marriage ban. Taken to its logical conclusion, however, the deprivation theory of rehabilitation would mean that the marriage ban in *Turner* could be justified because the prohibition furnished prisoners with an incentive to behave well and thus earn early release.

In sum, rehabilitation is a valid penological interest, and deprivation is undoubtedly one valid tool in promoting rehabilitation. Nonetheless, to ensure that Turner continues to impose meaningful limits on the promulgation of rules that infringe upon inmates' constitutional rights, courts must be especially cautious in evaluating the constitutionality of prison regulations that are supposedly justified primarily on that basis. When, as here, a reasonable factfinder could conclude that challenged deprivations have a tenuous logical connection to rehabilitation, or are exaggerated responses to a prison's legitimate interest in rehabilitation, prison officials are not entitled to judgment as a matter of law.

In any event, if we consider the severity of the other conditions of confinement in LTSU-2, it becomes obvious that inmates have a powerful motivation to escape those conditions irrespective of the ban on newspapers, magazines, and personal photographs. Inmates in LTSU-2 face 23 hours a day in solitary confinement, are allowed only one visitor per month, may not make phone calls except in cases of emergency, lack any access to radio or television, may not use the prison commissary, are not permitted General Educational Development (GED) or special education study, and may not receive compensation under the inmate compensation system if they work as a unit janitor. The logical conclusion from this is that, even if LTSU-2 prisoners were not deprived of access to newspapers and personal photographs, they would still have a strong incentive to gain promotion to LTSU-1.

In sum, the logical connection between the ban on newspapers and (especially) the ban on personal photographs, on one hand, and the rehabilitation interests posited by petitioner, on the other, is at best highly questionable. Moreover, petitioner did not introduce evidence that his proposed theory of behavior modification has any basis in human psychology, or that the challenged rule has in fact had any rehabilitative effect on LTSU-2 inmates.

What is perhaps most troubling about the prison regulation at issue in this case is that the rule comes perilously close to a state-sponsored effort at mind control. In this case, the complete prohibition on secular, nonlegal newspapers, newsletters, and magazines prevents prisoners from "receiv[ing] suitable access to social, political, esthetic, moral, and other ideas," which are central to the development and preservation of individual identity, and are clearly protected by the First Amendment. Similarly, the ban on personal photographs, for at least some inmates, interferes with the capacity to remember loved ones, which is undoubtedly a core part of a person's "sphere of intellect and spirit." Moreover, it is difficult to imagine a context in which these First Amendment infringements could be more severe; LTSU-2 inmates are in solitary confinement for 23 hours a day with no access to radio or television, are not permitted to make phone calls except in cases of emergency, and may only have one visitor per month. They are essentially isolated from any meaningful contact with the outside world. The severity of the constitutional deprivations at issue in this case should give us serious pause before concluding, as a matter of law, that the challenged regulation is consistent with the sovereign's duty to treat prisoners in accordance with "the ethical tradition that accords respect to the dignity and worth of every individual."

c. Schools (casebook, p. 1385)

For the first time in 20 years, the Supreme Court in *Morse v. Frederick* considered the free speech rights of students and the ability of schools to punish student speech.

MORSE v. FREDERICK
127 S.Ct. 2618 (2007)

Chief Justice ROBERTS delivered the opinion of the Court.

At a school-sanctioned and school-supervised event, a high school principal saw some of her students unfurl a large banner conveying a message she reasonably regarded as promoting illegal drug use. Consistent with established school policy prohibiting such messages at school events, the principal directed the students to take down the banner. One student—among those who had brought the banner to the event—refused to do so. The principal confiscated the banner and later suspended the student.

Our cases make clear that students do not "shed their constitutional rights to freedom of speech or expression at the schoolhouse gate." *Tinker v. Des Moines Independent Community School Dist.* (1969). At the same time, we have held that "the constitutional rights of students in public school are not automatically coextensive with the rights of adults in other settings," *Bethel School Dist. No. 403 v. Fraser* (1986), and that the rights of students "must be 'applied in light of the special characteristics of the school environment.'" *Hazelwood School Dist. v. Kuhlmeier* (1988). Consistent with these principles, we hold that schools may take steps to safeguard those entrusted to their care from speech that can reasonably be regarded as encouraging illegal drug use. We conclude that the school officials in this case did not violate the First Amendment by confiscating the pro-drug banner and suspending the student responsible for it.

I

On January 24, 2002, the Olympic Torch Relay passed through Juneau, Alaska, on its way to the winter games in Salt Lake City, Utah. The torchbearers were to proceed along a street in front of Juneau-Douglas High School (JDHS) while school was in session. Petitioner Deborah Morse, the school principal, decided to permit staff and students to participate in the Torch Relay as an approved social event or class trip. Students were allowed to leave class to observe the relay from either side of the street. Teachers and administrative officials monitored the students' actions.

Respondent Joseph Frederick, a JDHS senior, was late to school that day. When he arrived, he joined his friends (all but one of whom were JDHS students) across the street from the school to watch the event. Not all the students waited patiently. Some became rambunctious, throwing plastic cola bottles and snowballs and scuffling with their classmates. As the torchbearers and camera crews passed by, Frederick and his friends unfurled a 14-foot banner bearing the phrase: "BONG HiTS 4 JESUS." The large banner was easily readable by the students on the other side of the street.

Principal Morse immediately crossed the street and demanded that the banner be taken down. Everyone but Frederick complied. Morse confiscated the banner and told Frederick to report to her office, where she suspended him for 10 days. Morse later explained that she told Frederick to take the banner down because she thought it encouraged illegal drug use, in violation of established school policy. Juneau School Board Policy No. 5520 states: "The Board specifically prohibits any assembly or public expression that . . . advocates the use of substances that are illegal to minors. . . . " In addition, Juneau School Board Policy No. 5850 subjects "[p]upils who participate in approved social events and class trips" to the same student conduct rules that apply during the regular school program.

Frederick administratively appealed his suspension, but the Juneau School District Superintendent upheld it, limiting it to time served (8 days). In a memorandum setting forth his reasons, the superintendent determined that Frederick had displayed his banner "in the midst of his fellow students, during school hours, at a school-sanctioned activity." He further explained that Frederick "was not disciplined because the principal of the school 'disagreed' with his message, but because his speech appeared to advocate the use of illegal drugs." Id., at 61a.

The superintendent continued:

"The common-sense understanding of the phrase 'bong hits' is that it is a reference to a means of smoking marijuana. Given [Frederick's] inability or unwillingness to express any other credible meaning for the phrase, I can only agree with the principal and countless others who saw the banner as advocating the use of illegal drugs. [Frederick's] speech was not political. He was not advocating the legalization of marijuana or promoting a religious belief. He was displaying a fairly silly message promoting illegal drug usage in the midst of a school activity, for the benefit of television cameras covering the Torch Relay. [Frederick's] speech was potentially disruptive to the event and clearly disruptive of and inconsistent with the school's educational mission to educate students about the dangers of illegal drugs and to discourage their use."

Frederick then filed suit under 42 U.S.C. § 1983, alleging that the school board and Morse had violated his First Amendment rights. He sought declaratory and injunctive relief, unspecified compensatory damages, punitive damages, and attorney's fees.

II

At the outset, we reject Frederick's argument that this is not a school speech case. The event occurred during normal school hours. It was sanctioned by Principal Morse "as an approved social event or class trip," and the school district's rules expressly provide that pupils in "approved social events and class trips are subject to district rules for student conduct." Teachers and administrators were interspersed among the students and charged with supervising them. The high school band and cheerleaders performed. Frederick, standing among other JDHS students across the street from the school, directed his banner toward the school, making it plainly visible to most students. Under these circumstances, we agree with the superintendent that Frederick cannot "stand in the midst of his fellow students, during school hours, at a school-sanctioned activity and claim he is not at school."

III

The message on Frederick's banner is cryptic. It is no doubt offensive to some, perhaps amusing to others. To still others, it probably means nothing at all. Frederick himself claimed "that the words were just nonsense meant to attract television cameras." But Principal Morse thought the banner would be interpreted by those viewing it as promoting illegal drug use, and that interpretation is plainly a reasonable one.

As Morse later explained in a declaration, when she saw the sign, she thought that "the reference to a 'bong hit' would be widely understood by high school students and others as referring to smoking marijuana." She further believed that "display of the banner would be construed by students, District personnel, parents and others witnessing the display of the banner, as advocating or promoting illegal drug use"—in violation of school policy.

We agree with Morse. At least two interpretations of the words on the banner demonstrate that the sign advocated the use of illegal drugs. First, the phrase could be interpreted as an imperative: "[Take] bong hits . . ."—a message equivalent, as Morse explained in her declaration, to "smoke marijuana" or "use an illegal drug." Alternatively, the phrase could be viewed as celebrating drug use—"bong hits [are a good thing]," or "[we take] bong hits"—and we discern no meaningful distinction between celebrating illegal drug use in the midst of fellow students and outright advocacy or promotion.

Elsewhere in its opinion, the dissent emphasizes the importance of political speech and the need to foster "national debate about a serious issue," as if to suggest that the banner is political speech. But not even Frederick argues that the banner conveys any sort of political or religious message. Contrary to the dissent's suggestion, this is plainly not a case about political debate over the criminalization of drug use or possession.

IV

The question thus becomes whether a principal may, consistent with the First Amendment, restrict student speech at a school event, when that speech is reasonably viewed as promoting illegal drug use. We hold that she may.

In *Tinker*, this Court made clear that "First Amendment rights, applied in light of the special characteristics of the school environment, are available to teachers and students." *Tinker* involved a group of high school students who decided to wear black armbands to protest the Vietnam War. School officials learned of the plan and then adopted a policy prohibiting students from wearing armbands. When several students nonetheless wore armbands to school, they were suspended. The students sued, claiming that their First Amendment rights had been violated, and this Court agreed.

Tinker held that student expression may not be suppressed unless school officials reasonably conclude that it will "materially and substantially disrupt the work and discipline of the school."

This Court's next student speech case was *Fraser*. Matthew Fraser was suspended for delivering a speech before a high school assembly in which he employed what this Court called "an elaborate, graphic, and explicit sexual metaphor." Analyzing the case under *Tinker*, the District Court and Court of Appeals found no disruption, and therefore no basis for disciplining Fraser. This Court reversed, holding that the "School District acted entirely within its permissible authority in imposing sanctions upon Fraser in response to his offensively lewd and indecent speech."

The mode of analysis employed in *Fraser* is not entirely clear. The Court was plainly attuned to the content of Fraser's speech, citing the "marked distinction between the political 'message' of the armbands in *Tinker* and the sexual content of [Fraser's] speech." But the Court also reasoned that school boards have the authority to determine "what manner of speech in the classroom or in school assembly is inappropriate."

We need not resolve this debate to decide this case. For present purposes, it is enough to distill from *Fraser* two basic principles. First, *Fraser*'s holding demonstrates that "the constitutional rights of students in public school are not automatically coextensive with the rights of adults in other settings." Had Fraser delivered the same speech in a public forum outside the school context, it would have been protected. In school, however, Fraser's First Amendment rights were circumscribed "in light of the special characteristics of the school environment." Second, *Fraser* established that the mode of analysis set forth in *Tinker* is not absolute. Whatever approach *Fraser* employed, it certainly did not conduct the "substantial disruption" analysis prescribed by *Tinker*.

Our most recent student speech case, *Kuhlmeier*, concerned "expressive activities that students, parents, and members of the public might reasonably perceive to bear the imprimatur of the school." Staff members of a high school newspaper sued their school when it chose not to publish two of their articles. The Court of Appeals analyzed the case under *Tinker*, ruling in favor of the students because it found no evidence of material disruption to classwork or school discipline. This Court reversed, holding that "educators do not offend the First Amendment by exercising editorial control over the style and content of student speech in school-sponsored expressive activities so long as their actions are reasonably related to legitimate pedagogical concerns."

Kuhlmeier does not control this case because no one would reasonably believe that Frederick's banner bore the school's imprimatur. The case is nevertheless instructive because it confirms both principles cited above. *Kuhlmeier* acknowledged that schools may regulate some speech "even though the government could not censor similar speech outside the school." And, like *Fraser*, it confirms that the rule of *Tinker* is not the only basis for restricting student speech.

Drawing on the principles applied in our student speech cases, we have held in the Fourth Amendment context that "while children assuredly do not 'shed their constitutional rights . . . at the schoolhouse gate,' . . . the nature of those rights is what is appropriate for children in school."

Even more to the point, these cases also recognize that deterring drug use by schoolchildren is an "important—indeed, perhaps compelling" interest. Drug abuse can cause severe and permanent damage to the health and well-being of young people. The problem remains serious today. See generally 1 National Institute on Drug Abuse, National Institutes of Health, Monitoring the Future: National Survey Results on Drug Use, 1975-2005, Secondary School Students (2006). About half of American 12th graders have used an illicit drug, as have more than a third of 10th graders and about one-fifth of 8th graders. Nearly one in four 12th graders has used an illicit drug in the past month. Some 25% of high schoolers say that they have been offered, sold, or given an illegal drug on school property within the past year.

The "special characteristics of the school environment," and the governmental interest in stopping student drug abuse—reflected in the policies of Congress and myriad school boards, allow schools to restrict student expression that they reasonably regard as promoting illegal drug use. Tinker warned that schools may not prohibit student speech because of "undifferentiated fear or apprehension of disturbance" or "a mere desire to avoid the discomfort and unpleasantness that always accompany an unpopular viewpoint." The danger here is far more serious and palpable. The particular concern to prevent student drug abuse at issue here, embodied in established school policy, App. 92-95;

App. to Pet. for Cert. 53a, extends well beyond an abstract desire to avoid controversy.

School principals have a difficult job, and a vitally important one. When Frederick suddenly and unexpectedly unfurled his banner, Morse had to decide to act—or not act—on the spot. It was reasonable for her to conclude that the banner promoted illegal drug use—in violation of established school policy—and that failing to act would send a powerful message to the students in her charge, including Frederick, about how serious the school was about the dangers of illegal drug use. The First Amendment does not require schools to tolerate at school events student expression that contributes to those dangers.

Justice THOMAS, concurring.

The Court today decides that a public school may prohibit speech advocating illegal drug use. I agree and therefore join its opinion in full. I write separately to state my view that the standard set forth in *Tinker v. Des Moines Independent Community School Dist.* (1969), is without basis in the Constitution.

In my view, the history of public education suggests that the First Amendment, as originally understood, does not protect student speech in public schools. Although colonial schools were exclusively private, public education proliferated in the early 1800's. By the time the States ratified the Fourteenth Amendment, public schools had become relatively common. If students in public schools were originally understood as having free-speech rights, one would have expected 19th-century public schools to have respected those rights and courts to have enforced them. They did not.

Teachers instilled these values not only by presenting ideas but also through strict discipline. Schools punished students for behavior the school considered disrespectful or wrong. Rules of etiquette were enforced, and courteous behavior was demanded. To meet their educational objectives, schools required absolute obedience. In short, in the earliest public schools, teachers taught, and students listened. Teachers commanded, and students obeyed. Teachers did not rely solely on the power of ideas to persuade; they relied on discipline to maintain order.

Through the legal doctrine of in loco parentis, courts upheld the right of schools to discipline students, to enforce rules, and to maintain order. Applying in loco parentis, the judiciary was reluctant to interfere in the routine business of school administration, allowing schools and teachers to set and enforce rules and to maintain order.Thus, in the early years of public schooling, schools and teachers had considerable discretion in disciplinary matters.

Tinker effected a sea change in students' speech rights, extending them well beyond traditional bounds. *Tinker*'s reasoning conflicted with the traditional understanding of the judiciary's role in relation to public schooling, a role limited by in loco parentis.

Today, the Court creates another exception. In doing so, we continue to distance ourselves from *Tinker*, but we neither overrule it nor offer an explanation of when it operates and when it does not. I am afraid that our jurisprudence now says that students have a right to speak in schools except when they don't—a standard continuously developed through litigation against local schools and their administrators. In my view, petitioners could prevail for a much simpler reason: As originally understood, the Constitution does not afford students a right to free speech in public schools.

I join the Court's opinion because it erodes *Tinker*'s hold in the realm of student speech, even though it does so by adding to the patchwork of exceptions to the *Tinker* standard. I think the better approach is to dispense with *Tinker* altogether, and given the opportunity, I would do so.

Justice ALITO, with whom Justice KENNEDY joins, concurring.

I join the opinion of the Court on the understanding that (a) it goes no further than to hold that a public school may restrict speech that a reasonable observer would interpret as advocating illegal drug use and (b) it provides no support for any restriction of speech that can plausibly be interpreted as commenting on any political or social issue, including speech on issues such as "the wisdom of the war on drugs or of legalizing marijuana for medicinal use."

The opinion of the Court correctly reaffirms the recognition in *Tinker v. Des Moines Independent Community School Dist.* (1969), of the fundamental principle that students do not "shed their constitutional rights to freedom of speech or expression at the schoolhouse gate." The Court is also correct in noting that *Tinker*, which permits the regulation of student speech that threatens a concrete and "substantial disruption," does not set out the only ground on which in-school student speech may be regulated by state actors in a way that would not be constitutional in other settings.

But I do not read the opinion to mean that there are necessarily any grounds for such regulation that are not already recognized in the holdings of this Court. In addition to *Tinker*, the decision in the present case allows the restriction of speech advocating illegal drug use; *Bethel School Dist. No. 403 v. Fraser* (1986), permits the regulation of speech that is delivered in a lewd or vulgar manner as part of a middle school program; and *Hazelwood School Dist. v. Kuhlmeier*, (1988), allows a school to regulate what is in essence the school's own speech, that is, articles that appear in a publication that is an official school organ. I join the opinion of the Court on the understanding that the opinion does not hold that the special characteristics of the public schools necessarily justify any other speech restrictions.

In most settings, the First Amendment strongly limits the government's ability to suppress speech on the ground that it presents a threat of violence. But due to the special features of the school environment, school officials must have greater authority to intervene before speech leads to violence. And, in most cases, *Tinker*'s "substantial disruption" standard permits school officials to step in before actual violence erupts.

Speech advocating illegal drug use poses a threat to student safety that is just as serious, if not always as immediately obvious. As we have recognized in the past and as the opinion of the Court today details, illegal drug use presents a grave and in many ways unique threat to the physical safety of students. I therefore conclude that the public schools may ban speech advocating illegal drug use. But I regard such regulation as standing at the far reaches of what the First Amendment permits. I join the opinion of the Court with the understanding that the opinion does not endorse any further extension.

Justice BREYER, concurring in the judgment in part and dissenting in part. [Justice Breyer would have found that the principal was protected by qualified immunity; that is, that the principal could not be held liable for money damages because she did not violate clearly established law that the reasonable officer should know.]

Justice STEVENS, with whom Justice SOUTER and Justice GINSBURG join, dissenting.

A significant fact barely mentioned by the Court sheds a revelatory light on the motives of both the students and the principal of Juneau-Douglas High School (JDHS). On January 24, 2002, the Olympic Torch Relay gave those Alaska residents a rare chance to appear on national television. As Joseph Frederick repeatedly explained, he did not address the curious message— "BONG HiTS 4 JESUS"—to his fellow students. He just wanted to get the camera crews' attention. Moreover, concern about a nationwide evaluation of the conduct of the JDHS student body would have justified the principal's decision to remove an attention-grabbing 14-foot banner, even if it had merely proclaimed "Glaciers Melt!"

I agree with the Court that the principal should not be held liable for pulling down Frederick's banner [because of qualified immunity]. I would hold, however, that the school's interest in protecting its students from exposure to speech "reasonably regarded as promoting illegal drug use," cannot justify disciplining Frederick for his attempt to make an ambiguous statement to a television audience simply because it contained an oblique reference to drugs. The First Amendment demands more, indeed, much more.

The Court holds otherwise only after laboring to establish two uncontroversial propositions: first, that the constitutional rights of students in school settings are not coextensive with the rights of adults; and second, that deterring drug use by schoolchildren is a valid and terribly important interest. As to the first, I take the Court's point that the message on Frederick's banner is not necessarily protected speech, even though it unquestionably would have been had the banner been unfurled elsewhere. As to the second, I am willing to assume that the Court is correct that the pressing need to deter drug use supports JDHS's rule prohibiting willful conduct that expressly "advocates the use of substances that are illegal to minors." But it is a gross non sequitur to draw from these two unremarkable propositions the remarkable conclusion that the school may suppress student speech that was never meant to persuade anyone to do anything.

In my judgment, the First Amendment protects student speech if the message itself neither violates a permissible rule nor expressly advocates conduct that is illegal and harmful to students. This nonsense banner does neither, and the Court does serious violence to the First Amendment in upholding—indeed, lauding—a school's decision to punish Frederick for expressing a view with which it disagreed.

I

In December 1965, we were engaged in a controversial war, a war that "divided this country as few other issues ever have." *Tinker v. Des Moines Independent Community School Dist.* (1969) (Black, J., dissenting). Two cardinal First Amendment principles animate both the Court's opinion in *Tinker* and Justice Harlan's dissent. First, censorship based on the content of speech, particularly censorship that depends on the viewpoint of the speaker, is subject to the most rigorous burden of justification. Second, punishing someone for advocating illegal conduct is constitutional only when the advocacy is likely to provoke the harm that the government seeks to avoid. See *Brandenburg v. Ohio* (1969) (per curiam).

Yet today the Court fashions a test that trivializes the two cardinal principles upon which *Tinker* rests. The Court's test invites stark viewpoint discrimination. In this case, for example, the principal has unabashedly acknowledged that she disciplined Frederick because she disagreed with the pro-drug viewpoint she ascribed to the message on the banner. It is also perfectly clear that "promoting illegal drug use," comes nowhere close to proscribable "incitement to imminent lawless action." Encouraging drug use might well increase the likelihood that a listener will try an illegal drug, but that hardly justifies censorship:

No one seriously maintains that drug advocacy (much less Frederick's ridiculous sign) comes within the vanishingly small category of speech that can be prohibited because of its feared consequences. Such advocacy, to borrow from Justice Holmes, "ha[s] no chance of starting a present conflagration."

II

The Court rejects outright these twin foundations of *Tinker* because, in its view, the unusual importance of protecting children from the scourge of drugs supports a ban on all speech in the school environment that promotes drug use. Whether or not such a rule is sensible as a matter of policy, carving out pro-drug speech for uniquely harsh treatment finds no support in our case law and is inimical to the values protected by the First Amendment.

I will nevertheless assume for the sake of argument that the school's concededly powerful interest in protecting its students adequately supports its restriction on "any assembly or public expression that . . . advocates the use of substances that are illegal to minors. . . . " But it is one thing to restrict speech that advocates drug use. It is another thing entirely to prohibit an obscure message with a drug theme that a third party subjectively—and not very reasonably—thinks is tantamount to express advocacy.

There is absolutely no evidence that Frederick's banner's reference to drug paraphernalia "willful[ly]" infringed on anyone's rights or interfered with any of the school's educational programs. Therefore, just as we insisted in Tinker that the school establish some likely connection between the armbands and their feared consequences, so too JDHS must show that Frederick's supposed advocacy stands a meaningful chance of making otherwise-abstemious students try marijuana.

But instead of demanding that the school make such a showing, the Court punts. To the extent the Court independently finds that "BONG HiTS 4 JESUS" objectively amounts to the advocacy of illegal drug use—in other words, that it can most reasonably be interpreted as such—that conclusion practically refutes itself. This is a nonsense message, not advocacy. The Court's feeble effort to divine its hidden meaning is strong evidence of that (positing that the banner might mean, alternatively, " '[Take] bong hits,' " " 'bong hits [are a good thing],' " or " '[we take] bong hits' "). Admittedly, some high school students (including those who use drugs) are dumb. Most students, however, do not shed their brains at the schoolhouse gate, and most students know dumb advocacy when they see it. The notion that the message on this banner would actually persuade either the average student or even the dumbest one to change his or her behavior is most implausible. That the Court believes such a silly message can be proscribed as advocacy underscores the novelty of its position, and suggests that the principle it articulates has no stopping point.

Among other things, the Court's ham-handed, categorical approach is deaf to the constitutional imperative to permit unfettered debate, even among high-school students, about the wisdom of the war on drugs or of legalizing marijuana for medicinal use. If Frederick's stupid reference to marijuana can in the Court's view justify censorship, then high school students everywhere could be forgiven for zipping their mouths about drugs at school lest some "reasonable" observer censor and then punish them for promoting drugs.

Although this case began with a silly, nonsensical banner, it ends with the Court inventing out of whole cloth a special First Amendment rule permitting the censorship of any student speech that mentions drugs, at least so long as someone could perceive that speech to contain a latent pro-drug message.

Even in high school, a rule that permits only one point of view to be expressed is less likely to produce correct answers than the open discussion of countervailing views. In the national debate about a serious issue, it is the expression of the minority's viewpoint that most demands the protection of the First Amendment. Whatever the better policy may be, a full and frank discussion of the costs and benefits of the attempt to prohibit the use of marijuana is far wiser than suppression of speech because it is unpopular.

d. The Speech Rights of Government Employees (new)

The Supreme Court has held that the government may not punish the speech of public employees if it involves matters of public concern unless the state can prove that the needs of the government outweigh the speech rights of the employee. In other words, speech by public employees is clearly less protected than other speech; First Amendment protection does not exist unless the expression is about public concern, and even then, the employee can be disciplined or fired if the government can show, on balance, that the efficient operation of the office justified the action. *See, e.g., Pickering v. Board of Education*, 391 U.S. 563 (1968).

In *Garcetti v. Ceballos*, below, the Court imposed a significant new limit on constitutional protection for the speech of government employees. The Court held that such speech is not protected if it is by a government employee while on the job and as part of his or her duties.

GARCETTI v. CEBALLOS
126 S. Ct. 1951 (2006)

Justice KENNEDY delivered the opinion of the Court.

It is well settled that "a State cannot condition public employment on a basis that infringes the employee's constitutionally protected interest in freedom of expression." *Connick v. Myers* (1983). The question presented by the instant case is whether the First Amendment protects a government employee from discipline based on speech made pursuant to the employee's official duties.

I

Respondent Richard Ceballos has been employed since 1989 as a deputy district attorney for the Los Angeles County District Attorney's Office. During the period relevant to this case, Ceballos was a calendar deputy in the office's Pomona branch, and in this capacity he exercised certain supervisory responsibilities over other lawyers. In February 2000, a defense attorney contacted Ceballos about a pending criminal case. The defense attorney said there were inaccuracies in an affidavit used to obtain a critical search warrant. The attorney informed Ceballos that he had filed a motion to traverse, or challenge, the warrant, but he also wanted Ceballos to review the case. According to Ceballos, it was not unusual for defense attorneys to ask calendar deputies to investigate aspects of pending cases. After examining the affidavit and visiting the location it described, Ceballos determined the affidavit contained serious misrepresentations. The affidavit called a long driveway what Ceballos thought should have been referred to as a separate roadway. Ceballos also questioned the affidavit's statement that tire tracks led from a stripped-down truck to the premises covered by the warrant. His doubts arose from his conclusion that the roadway's composition in some places made it difficult or impossible to leave visible tire tracks.

Ceballos spoke on the telephone to the warrant affiant, a deputy sheriff from the Los Angeles County Sheriff's Department, but he did not receive a satisfactory explanation for the perceived inaccuracies. He relayed his findings to his supervisors, petitioners Carol Najera and Frank Sundstedt, and followed up by preparing a disposition memorandum. The memo explained Ceballos' concerns and recommended dismissal of the case.

Despite Ceballos' concerns, Sundstedt decided to proceed with the prosecution, pending disposition of the defense motion to traverse. The trial court held a hearing on the motion. Ceballos was called by the defense and recounted his observations about the affidavit, but the trial court rejected the challenge to the warrant.

Ceballos claims that in the aftermath of these events he was subjected to a series of retaliatory employment actions. The actions included reassignment from his calendar deputy position to a trial deputy position, transfer to another courthouse, and denial of a promotion. 25 S.Ct. 1395, 161 L.Ed.2d 188 (2005), and we now reverse.

II

As the Court's decisions have noted, for many years "the unchallenged dogma was that a public employee had no right to object to conditions placed upon the terms of employment—including those which restricted the exercise of constitutional rights." That dogma has been qualified in important respects. The Court has made clear that public employees do not surrender all their First Amendment rights by reason of their employment. Rather, the First Amendment protects a public employee's right, in certain circumstances, to speak as a citizen addressing matters of public concern.

Pickering and the cases decided in its wake identify two inquiries to guide interpretation of the constitutional protections accorded to public employee speech. The first requires determining whether the employee spoke as a citizen on a matter of public concern. If the answer is no, the employee has no First Amendment cause of action based on his or her employer's reaction to the speech. If the answer is yes, then the possibility of a First Amendment claim arises. The question becomes whether the relevant government entity had an adequate justification for treating the employee differently from any other member of the general public. This consideration reflects the importance of the relationship between the speaker's expressions and employment. A government entity has broader discretion to restrict speech when it acts in its role as employer, but the restrictions it imposes must be directed at speech that has some potential to affect the entity's operations.

When a citizen enters government service, the citizen by necessity must accept certain limitations on his or her freedom. Government employers, like private employers, need a significant degree of control over their employees' words and actions; without it, there would be little chance for the efficient provision of public services. Public employees, moreover, often occupy trusted positions in society. When they speak out, they can express views that contravene governmental policies or impair the proper performance of governmental functions.

At the same time, the Court has recognized that a citizen who works for the government is nonetheless a citizen. The First Amendment limits the ability of a public employer to leverage the employment relationship to restrict, incidentally or intentionally, the liberties employees enjoy in their capacities as private citizens. So long as employees are speaking as citizens about matters of public concern, they must face only those speech restrictions that are necessary for their employers to operate efficiently and effectively.

III

With these principles in mind we turn to the instant case. Respondent Ceballos believed the affidavit used to obtain a search warrant contained serious misrepresentations. He conveyed his opinion and recommendation in a memo to his supervisor. That Ceballos expressed his views inside his office, rather than publicly, is not dispositive. Employees in some cases may receive First Amendment protection for expressions made at work. Many citizens do much of their talking inside their respective workplaces, and it would not serve the goal of treating public employees like "any member of the general public," to hold that all speech within the office is automatically exposed to restriction.

The memo concerned the subject matter of Ceballos' employment, but this, too, is nondispositive. The First Amendment protects some expressions related to the speaker's job.

The controlling factor in Ceballos' case is that his expressions were made pursuant to his duties as a calendar deputy. That consideration – the fact that Ceballos spoke as a prosecutor fulfilling a responsibility to advise his supervisor about how best to proceed with a pending case – distinguishes Ceballos' case from those in which the First Amendment provides protection against discipline. We hold that when public employees make statements pursuant to their official duties, the employees are not speaking as citizens for First Amendment purposes, and the Constitution does not insulate their communications from employer discipline. Ceballos wrote his disposition memo because that is part of what he, as a calendar deputy, was employed to do. It is immaterial whether he experienced some personal gratification from writing the memo; his First Amendment rights do not depend on his job satisfaction. The significant point is that the memo was written pursuant to Ceballos' official duties. Restricting speech that owes its existence to a public employee's professional responsibilities does not infringe any liberties the employee might have enjoyed as a private citizen. It simply reflects the exercise of employer control over what the employer itself has commissioned or created.

Ceballos did not act as a citizen when he went about conducting his daily professional activities, such as supervising attorneys, investigating charges, and preparing filings. In the same way he did not speak as a citizen by writing a memo that addressed the proper disposition of a pending criminal case. When he went to work and performed the tasks he was paid to perform, Ceballos acted as a government employee. The fact that his duties sometimes required him to speak or write does not mean his supervisors were prohibited from evaluating his performance.

This result is consistent with our precedents' attention to the potential societal value of employee speech. Our holding likewise is supported by the emphasis of our precedents on affording government employers sufficient discretion to manage their operations. Employers have heightened interests in controlling speech made by an employee in his or her professional capacity. Official communications have official consequences, creating a need for substantive consistency and clarity. Supervisors must ensure that their employees' official communications are accurate, demonstrate sound judgment, and promote the employer's mission. Ceballos' memo is illustrative. It demanded the attention of his supervisors and led to a heated meeting with employees from the sheriff's department. If Ceballos' superiors thought his memo was inflammatory or misguided, they had the authority to take proper corrective action.

Ceballos' proposed contrary rule, adopted by the Court of Appeals, would commit state and federal courts to a new, permanent, and intrusive role, mandating judicial oversight of communications between and among government employees and their superiors in the course of official business. This displacement of managerial discretion by judicial supervision finds no support in our precedents. When an employee speaks as a citizen addressing a matter of public concern, the First Amendment requires a delicate balancing of the competing interests surrounding the speech and its consequences. When, however, the employee is simply performing his or her job duties, there is no warrant for a similar degree of scrutiny. To hold otherwise would be to demand permanent judicial intervention in the conduct of governmental operations to a degree inconsistent with sound principles of federalism and the separation of powers.

Exposing governmental inefficiency and misconduct is a matter of considerable significance. As the Court noted in Connick, public employers should, "as a matter of good judgment," be "receptive to constructive criticism offered by their employees." The dictates of sound judgment are reinforced by the powerful network of legislative enactments—such as whistle-blower protection laws and labor codes—available to those who seek to expose wrongdoing. Cases involving government attorneys implicate additional safeguards in the form of, for example, rules of conduct and constitutional obligations apart from the First Amendment. These imperatives, as well as obligations arising from any other applicable constitutional provisions and mandates of the criminal and civil laws, protect employees and provide checks on supervisors who would order unlawful or otherwise inappropriate actions.

We reject, however, the notion that the First Amendment shields from discipline the expressions employees make pursuant to their professional duties. Our precedents do not support the existence of a constitutional cause of action behind every statement a public employee makes in the course of doing his or her job.

Justice STEVENS, dissenting.

The proper answer to the question "whether the First Amendment protects a government employee from discipline based on speech made pursuant to the employee's official duties," is "Sometimes," not "Never." Of course a supervisor may take corrective action when such speech is "inflammatory or misguided." But what if it is just unwelcome speech because it reveals facts that the supervisor would rather not have anyone else discover?

As Justice Souter explains, public employees are still citizens while they are in the office. The notion that there is a categorical difference between speaking as a citizen and speaking in the course of one's employment is quite wrong. Over a quarter of a century has passed since then-Justice Rehnquist, writing for a unanimous Court, rejected "the conclusion that a public employee forfeits his protection against governmental abridgment of freedom of speech if he decides to express his views privately rather than publicly." *Givhan v. Western Line Consol. School Dist.* (1979). We had no difficulty recognizing that the First Amendment applied when Bessie Givhan, an English teacher, raised concerns about the school's racist employment practices to the principal. Our silence as to whether or not her speech was made pursuant to her job duties demonstrates that the point was immaterial. That is equally true today, for it is senseless to let constitutional protection for exactly the same words hinge on whether they fall within a job description. Moreover, it seems perverse to fashion a new rule that provides employees with an incentive to voice their concerns publicly before talking frankly to their superiors.

Justice SOUTER, with whom Justice STEVENS and Justice GINSBURG join, dissenting.

The Court holds that "when public employees make statements pursuant to their official duties, the employees are not speaking as citizens for First Amendment purposes, and the Constitution does not insulate their communications from employer discipline." I respectfully dissent. I agree with the majority that a government employer has substantial interests in effectuating its chosen policy and objectives, and in demanding competence, honesty, and judgment from employees who speak for it in doing their work. But I would hold that private and public interests in addressing official wrongdoing and threats to health and safety can outweigh the government's stake in the efficient implementation of policy, and when they do public employees who speak on these matters in the course of their duties should be eligible to claim First Amendment protection.

Open speech by a private citizen on a matter of public importance lies at the heart of expression subject to protection by the First Amendment. At the other extreme, a statement by a government employee complaining about nothing beyond treatment under personnel rules raises no greater claim to constitutional protection against retaliatory response than the remarks of a private employee. In between these points lies a public employee's speech unwelcome to the government but on a significant public issue. Such an employee speaking as a citizen, that is, with a citizen's interest, is protected from reprisal unless the statements are too damaging to the government's capacity to conduct public business to be justified by any individual or public benefit thought to flow from the statements. *Pickering v. Board of Ed. of Township High School Dist.* 205, Will Cty. (1968). Entitlement to protection is thus not absolute.

This significant, albeit qualified, protection of public employees who irritate the government is understood to flow from the First Amendment, in part, because a government paycheck does nothing to eliminate the value to an individual of speaking on public matters, and there is no good reason for categorically discounting a speaker's interest in commenting on a matter of public concern just because the government employs him. Still, the First Amendment safeguard rests on something more, being the value to the public of receiving the opinions and information that a public employee may disclose. "Government employees are often in the best position to know what ails the agencies for which they work." The reason that protection of employee speech is qualified is that it can distract co-workers and supervisors from their tasks at hand and thwart the implementation of legitimate policy, the risks of which grow greater the closer the employee's speech gets to commenting on his own workplace and responsibilities. It is one thing for an office clerk to say there is waste in government and quite another to charge that his own department pays full-time salaries to part-time workers. Even so, we have regarded eligibility for protection by *Pickering* balancing as the proper approach when an employee speaks critically about the administration of his own government employer.

Nothing, then, accountable on the individual and public side of the *Pickering* balance changes when an employee speaks "pursuant" to public duties. On the side of the government employer, however, something is different, and to this extent, I agree with the majority of the Court. The majority is rightly concerned that the employee who speaks out on matters subject to comment in doing his own work has the greater leverage to create office uproars and fracture the government's authority to set policy to be carried out coherently through the ranks. "Official communications have official consequences, creating a need for substantive consistency and clarity. Supervisors must ensure that their employees' official communications are accurate, demonstrate sound judgment, and promote the employer's mission." Up to a point, then, the majority makes good points: government needs civility in the workplace, consistency in policy, and honesty and competence in public service.

But why do the majority's concerns, which we all share, require categorical exclusion of First Amendment protection against any official retaliation for things said on the job? Is it not possible to respect the unchallenged individual and public interests in the speech through a *Pickering* balance without drawing the strange line I mentioned before? This is, to be sure, a matter of judgment, but the judgment has to account for the undoubted value of speech to those, and by those, whose specific public job responsibilities bring them face to face with wrongdoing and incompetence in government, who refuse to avert their eyes and shut their mouths. And it has to account for the need actually to disrupt government if its officials are corrupt or dangerously incompetent. It is thus no adequate justification for the suppression of potentially valuable information simply to recognize that the government has a huge interest in managing its employees and preventing the occasionally irresponsible one from turning his job into a bully pulpit. Even there, the lesson of *Pickering* (and the object of most constitutional adjudication) is still to the point: when constitutionally significant interests clash, resist the demand for winner-take-all; try to make adjustments that serve all of the values at stake.

Justice BREYER, dissenting.

This case asks whether the First Amendment protects public employees when they engage in speech that both (1) involves matters of public concern and (2) takes place in the ordinary course of performing the duties of a government job. The majority answers the question by holding that "when public employees make statements pursuant to their official duties, the employees are not speaking as citizens for First Amendment purposes, and the Constitution does not insulate their communications from employer discipline." Ante, at 1960. In a word, the majority says, "never." That word, in my view, is too absolute.

Like the majority, I understand the need to "affor[d] government employers sufficient discretion to manage their operations." And I agree that the Constitution does not seek to "displac[e] . . . managerial discretion by judicial supervision." Nonetheless, there may well be circumstances with special demand for constitutional protection of the speech at issue, where governmental justifications may be limited, and where administrable standards seem readily available—to the point where the majority's fears of department management by lawsuit are misplaced. In such an instance, I believe that courts should apply the *Pickering* standard, even though the government employee speaks upon matters of public concern in the course of his ordinary duties.

This is such a case. The respondent, a government lawyer, complained of retaliation, in part, on the basis of speech contained in his disposition memorandum that he says fell within the scope of his obligations under *Brady v. Maryland* (1963). The facts present two special circumstances that together justify First Amendment review.

First, the speech at issue is professional speech—the speech of a lawyer. Such speech is subject to independent regulation by canons of the profession. Those canons provide an obligation to speak in certain instances. And where that is so, the government's own interest in forbidding that speech is diminished.

Second, the Constitution itself here imposes speech obligations upon the government's professional employee. A prosecutor has a constitutional obligation to learn of, to preserve, and to communicate with the defense about exculpatory and impeachment evidence in the government's possession. Hence, I would find that the Constitution mandates special protection of employee speech in such circumstances. Thus I would apply the *Pickering* balancing test here.

I conclude that the First Amendment sometimes does authorize judicial actions based upon a government employee's speech that both (1) involves a matter of public concern and also (2) takes place in the course of ordinary job-related duties. But it does so only in the presence of augmented need for constitutional protection and diminished risk of undue judicial interference with governmental management of the public's affairs. In my view, these conditions are met in this case and *Pickering* balancing is consequently appropriate.

Chapter 10

First Amendment: Religion

B. The Free Exercise Clause (casebook, p. 1463)

Is a law to protect free exercise of religion a violation of the Establishment Clause? As described in Employment Division v. Smith (casebook, p. 1464), the Court narrowly interpreted the protections of the Free Exercise Clause of the First Amendment. The Religious Freedom Restoration Act was adopted in 1993 to restore religious freedom by statute to what it previously had been under the Constitution (casebook, p. 1477). But in City of Boerne v. Flores (casebook, p. 216), this law was declared unconstitutional as applied to state and local governments. Congress then adopted the Religious Land Use and Institutionalized Persons Act. It requires strict scrutiny for state and local government actions that significantly burden religion concerning land use or institutionalized persons. In *Cutter v. Wilkinson*, the Court considered whether this law violates the Establishment Clause.

CUTTER v. WILKINSON
544 U.S. 709 (2005)

Justice GINSBURG delivered the opinion of the Court.

Section 3 of the Religious Land Use and Institutionalized Persons Act of 2000 (RLUIPA), provides in part: "No government shall impose a substantial burden on the religious exercise of a person residing in or confined to an institution," unless the burden furthers "a compelling governmental interest," and does so by "the least restrictive means." Plaintiffs below, petitioners here, are current and former inmates of institutions operated by the Ohio Department of Rehabilitation and Correction and assert that they are adherents of "nonmainstream" religions: the Satanist, Wicca, and Asatru religions, and the Church of Jesus Christ Christian. They complain that Ohio prison officials (respondents here), in violation of RLUIPA, have failed to accommodate their religious exercise "in a variety of different ways, including retaliating and discriminating against them for exercising their nontraditional faiths, denying them access to religious literature, denying them the same opportunities for group worship that are granted to adherents of mainstream religions, forbidding them to adhere to the dress and appearance mandates of their religions, withholding religious ceremonial items that are substantially identical to those that the adherents of mainstream religions are permitted, and failing to provide a chaplain trained in their faith."

In response to petitioners' complaints, respondent prison officials have mounted a facial challenge to the institutionalized-persons provision of RLUIPA; respondents contend that the Act improperly advances religion in violation of the First Amendment's Establishment Clause. The District Court denied respondents' motion to dismiss petitioners' complaints, but the Court of Appeals reversed that determination. The appeals court held, as the prison officials urged, that the portion of RLUIPA applicable to institutionalized persons violates the Establishment Clause. We reverse the Court of Appeals' judgment.

"This Court has long recognized that the government may . . . accommodate religious practices . . . without violating the Establishment Clause." Just last Term, in Locke v. Davey (2004), the Court reaffirmed that "there is room for play in the joints between" the Free Exercise and Establishment Clauses, allowing the government to accommodate religion beyond free exercise requirements, without offense to the Establishment Clause. "At some point, accommodation may devolve into an unlawful fostering of religion." But § 3 of RLUIPA, we hold, does not, on its face, exceed the limits of permissible government accommodation of religious practices.[1]

The Religion Clauses of the First Amendment provide: "Congress shall make no law respecting an establishment of religion, or prohibiting the free exercise thereof." The first of the two Clauses, commonly called the Establishment Clause, commands a separation of church and state. The second, the Free Exercise Clause, requires government respect for, and noninterference with, the religious beliefs and practices of our Nation's people. While the two Clauses express complementary values, they often exert conflicting pressures.

Our decisions recognize that "there is room for play in the joints" between the Clauses, some space for legislative action neither compelled by the Free Exercise Clause nor prohibited by the Establishment Clause. In accord with the majority of Courts of Appeals that have ruled on the question, we hold that § 3 of RLUIPA fits within the corridor between the Religion Clauses: On its face, the Act qualifies as a permissible legislative accommodation of religion that is not barred by the Establishment Clause.

Foremost, we find RLUIPA's institutionalized-persons provision compatible with the Establishment Clause because it alleviates exceptional government-created

---

1. Respondents argued below that RLUIPA exceeds Congress' legislative powers under the Spending and Commerce Clauses and violates the Tenth Amendment. The Sixth Circuit, having determined that RLUIPA violates the Establishment Clause, did not rule on respondents' further arguments. Respondents renew those arguments in this Court. Because these defensive pleas were not addressed by the Court of Appeals, and mindful that we are a court of review, not of first view, we do not consider them here. [Footnote by Justice Ginsburg.]

burdens on private religious exercise. Furthermore, the Act on its face does not founder on shoals our prior decisions have identified: Properly applying RLUIPA, courts must take adequate account of the burdens a requested accommodation may impose on nonbeneficiaries, and they must be satisfied that the Act's prescriptions are and will be administered neutrally among different faiths.

"[T]he 'exercise of religion' often involves not only belief and profession but the performance of . . . physical acts [such as] assembling with others for a worship service [or] participating in sacramental use of bread and wine. . . ." Section 3 covers state-run institutions—mental hospitals, prisons, and the like— in which the government exerts a degree of control unparalleled in civilian society and severely disabling to private religious exercise. RLUIPA thus protects institutionalized persons who are unable freely to attend to their religious needs and are therefore dependent on the government's permission and accommodation for exercise of their religion.

We note in this regard the Federal Government's accommodation of religious practice by members of the military. In Goldman v. Weinberger (1986), we held that the Free Exercise Clause did not require the Air Force to exempt an Orthodox Jewish officer from uniform dress regulations so that he could wear a yarmulke indoors. Congress responded to Goldman by prescribing that "a member of the armed forces may wear an item of religious apparel while wearing the uniform," unless "the wearing of the item would interfere with the performance [of] military duties [or] the item of apparel is not neat and conservative."

We do not read RLUIPA to elevate accommodation of religious observances over an institution's need to maintain order and safety. Our decisions indicate that an accommodation must be measured so that it does not override other significant interests. We have no cause to believe that RLUIPA would not be applied in an appropriately balanced way, with particular sensitivity to security concerns. While the Act adopts a "compelling governmental interest" standard, "[c]ontext matters" in the application of that standard. Lawmakers supporting RLUIPA were mindful of the urgency of discipline, order, safety, and security in penal institutions. They anticipated that courts would apply the Act's standard with "due deference to the experience and expertise of prison and jail administrators in establishing necessary regulations and procedures to maintain good order, security and discipline, consistent with consideration of costs and limited resources."

Finally, RLUIPA does not differentiate among bona fide faiths. RLUIPA presents no such defect. It confers no privileged status on any particular religious sect, and singles out no bona fide faith for disadvantageous treatment.

The Sixth Circuit misread our precedents to require invalidation of RLUIPA as "impermissibly advancing religion by giving greater protection to religious rights than to other constitutionally protected rights." Were the Court of Appeals' view the correct reading of our decisions, all manner of religious accommodations would fall. Congressional permission for members of the military to wear religious apparel while in uniform would fail, as would accommodations Ohio itself makes. Ohio could not, as it now does, accommodate "traditionally recognized" religions. The State provides inmates with chaplains "but not with publicists or political consultants," and allows "prisoners to assemble for worship, but not for political rallies."

In upholding RLUIPA's institutionalized-persons provision, we emphasize that respondents "have raised a facial challenge to [the Act's] constitutionality, and have not contended that under the facts of any of [petitioners'] specific cases . . . [that] applying RLUIPA would produce unconstitutional results." Should inmate requests for religious accommodations become excessive, impose unjustified burdens on other institutionalized persons, or jeopardize the effective functioning of an institution, the facility would be free to resist the imposition. In that event, adjudication in as-applied challenges would be in order.

In *Gonzales v. O Centro Espirita Beneficente Uniao Do*, 546 U.S. 418 (2006), the Supreme Court applied the Religious Freedom Restoration Act to the federal government. Although the Court did not expressly address the issue of whether the statute is constitutional as applied to the federal government, the Court did use the Act to rule in favor of a religion and against the federal government. The case involved a small religion, with relatively few adherents in the United States, whose members receive communion by drinking hoasca, a tea brewed from plants unique to the Amazon rainforest that contains a hallucinogen regulated under Schedule I of the Controlled Substances Act. Members of the religion brought a suit seeking a declaratory judgment that their use of the tea was protected by the Religious Freedom Restoration Act.

Chief Justice Roberts wrote for a unanimous Court and ruled in favor of the religion. In response to the government's claim of a need to stop the availability of hallucinogenic drugs, the Court stated: "RFRA requires the Government to demonstrate that the compelling interest test is satisfied through application of the challenged law 'to the person'—the particular claimant whose sincere exercise of religion is being substantially burdened. RFRA expressly adopted the compelling interest test 'as set forth in *Sherbert v. Verner* (1963) and *Wisconsin v. Yoder* (1972).' In each of those cases, this Court looked beyond broadly formulated interests justifying the general applicability of government mandates and scrutinized the asserted harm of granting specific exemptions to particular religious claimants."

Applying this test, the Court concluded: "Under the more focused inquiry required by RFRA and the compelling interest test, the Government's mere invocation of the general characteristics of Schedule I substances, as set forth in the Controlled Substances Act, cannot carry the day. It is true, of course, that Schedule I substances are exceptionally dangerous. Nevertheless, there is no indication that Congress considered the harms posed by the particular use at issue here — the circumscribed, sacramental use of hoasca by [this religion]."

The case indicates that RFRA is applicable to the federal government and that the Court approves a rigorous application of strict scrutiny under the statute.

C. The Establishment Clause

1. Competing Theories of the Establishment Clause (casebook, p. 1486)

The competing theories of the Establishment Clause were very much in evidence in two Supreme Court decisions concerning Ten Commandments displays: McCreary County,. v. ACLU of Kentucky and Van Orden v. Perry. In reading these cases, it is important to identify the different approaches that the Justices take with regard to the Establishment Clause. The Court declared the display in *McCreary County* unconstitutional, but upheld the display in *Van Orden*. In reading the decisions, consider whether there is a meaningful distinction between these cases. Also, it is important to consider what lower courts should do, in light of these decisions, if they are confronted with cases involving Ten Commandments monuments or other religious symbols.

MCCREARY COUNTY v. AMERICAN CIVIL LIBERTIES UNION OF KENTUCKY
545 U.S. 844 (2005)

Justice SOUTER delivered the opinion of the Court.

Executives of two counties posted a version of the Ten Commandments on the walls of their courthouses. After suits were filed charging violations of the Establishment Clause, the legislative body of each county adopted a resolution calling for a more extensive exhibit meant to show that the Commandments are Kentucky's "precedent legal code." The result in each instance was a modified display of the Commandments surrounded by texts containing religious references as their sole common element. After changing counsel, the counties revised the exhibits again by eliminating some documents, expanding the text set out in another, and adding some new ones.

The issues are whether a determination of the counties' purpose is a sound basis for ruling on the Establishment Clause complaints, and whether evaluation of the counties' claim of secular purpose for the ultimate displays may take their evolution into account. We hold that the counties' manifest objective may be dispositive of the constitutional enquiry, and that the development of the presentation should be considered when determining its purpose.

I

In the summer of 1999, petitioners McCreary County and Pulaski County, Kentucky (hereinafter Counties), put up in their respective courthouses large, gold-framed copies of an abridged text of the King James version of the Ten Commandments, including a citation to the Book of Exodus. In McCreary

County, the placement of the Commandments responded to an order of the county legislative body requiring "the display [to] be posted in 'a very high traffic area' of the courthouse." In Pulaski County, amidst reported controversy over the propriety of the display, the Commandments were hung in a ceremony presided over by the county Judge-Executive, who called them "good rules to live by" and who recounted the story of an astronaut who became convinced "there must be a divine God" after viewing the Earth from the moon.

In November 1999, respondents American Civil Liberties Union of Kentucky et al. sued the Counties in Federal District Court and sought a preliminary injunction against maintaining the displays, which the ACLU charged were violations of the prohibition of religious establishment included in the First Amendment of the Constitution. Within a month, and before the District Court had responded to the request for injunction, the legislative body of each County authorized a second, expanded display, by nearly identical resolutions reciting that the Ten Commandments are "the precedent legal code upon which the civil and criminal codes of . . . Kentucky are founded," and stating several grounds for taking that position: that "the Ten Commandments are codified in Kentucky's civil and criminal laws"; that the Kentucky House of Representatives had in 1993 "voted unanimously . . . to adjourn . . . 'in remembrance and honor of Jesus Christ, the Prince of Ethics'"; that the "County Judge and . . . magistrates agree with the arguments set out by Judge [Roy] Moore" in defense of his "display [of] the Ten Commandments in his courtroom"; and that the "Founding Father[s] [had an] explicit understanding of the duty of elected officials to publicly acknowledge God as the source of America's strength and direction."

As directed by the resolutions, the Counties expanded the displays of the Ten Commandments in their locations, presumably along with copies of the resolution, which instructed that it, too, be posted. In addition to the first display's large framed copy of the edited King James version of the Commandments, the second included eight other documents in smaller frames, each either having a religious theme or excerpted to highlight a religious element. The documents were the "endowed by their Creator" passage from the Declaration of Independence; the Preamble to the Constitution of Kentucky; the national motto, "In God We Trust"; a page from the Congressional Record of February 2, 1983, proclaiming the Year of the Bible and including a statement of the Ten Commandments; a proclamation by President Abraham Lincoln designating April 30, 1863, a National Day of Prayer and Humiliation; an excerpt from President Lincoln's "Reply to Loyal Colored People of Baltimore upon Presentation of a Bible," reading that "[t]he Bible is the best gift God has ever given to man"; a proclamation by President Reagan marking 1983 the Year of the Bible; and the Mayflower Compact.

After argument, the District Court entered a preliminary injunction on May 5, 2000, ordering that the "display . . . be removed from [each] County Courthouse IMMEDIATELY" and that no county official "erect or cause to be erected similar displays."

The Counties filed a notice of appeal from the preliminary injunction but voluntarily dismissed it after hiring new lawyers. They then installed another display in each courthouse, the third within a year. No new resolution authorized this one, nor did the Counties repeal the resolutions that preceded the second. The posting consists of nine framed documents of equal size, one of them setting out the Ten Commandments explicitly identified as the "King James Version" at Exodus 20:3-17 and quoted at greater length than before:

Thou shalt have no other gods before me.

Thou shalt not make unto thee any graven image, or any likeness of any thing that is in heaven above, or that is in the earth beneath, or that is in the water underneath the earth: Thou shalt not bow down thyself to them, nor serve them: for I the LORD thy God am a jealous God, visiting the iniquity of the fathers upon the children unto the third and fourth generation of them that hate me.

Thou shalt not take the name of the LORD thy God in vain: for the LORD will not hold him guiltless that taketh his name in vain.

Remember the sabbath day, to keep it holy.

Honour thy father and thy mother: that thy days may be long upon the land which the LORD thy God giveth thee.

Thou shalt not kill.

Thou shalt not commit adultery.

Thou shalt not steal.

Thou shalt not bear false witness against thy neighbour.

Thou shalt not covet thy neighbour's house, thou shalt not covet th[y] neighbor's wife, nor his manservant, nor his maidservant, nor his ox, nor his ass, nor anything that is th[y] neighbour's.

Assembled with the Commandments are framed copies of the Magna Carta, the Declaration of Independence, the Bill of Rights, the lyrics of the Star Spangled Banner, the Mayflower Compact, the National Motto, the Preamble to the Kentucky Constitution, and a picture of Lady Justice. The collection is entitled "The Foundations of American Law and Government Display" and each document comes with a statement about its historical and legal significance. The comment on the Ten Commandments reads:

The Ten Commandments have profoundly influenced the formation of Western legal thought and the formation of our country. That influence is clearly seen in the Declaration of Independence, which declared that "We hold these truths to be self-evident, that all men are created equal, that they are endowed by their Creator with certain unalienable Rights, that among these are Life, Liberty, and the pursuit of Happiness." The Ten Commandments provide the moral background of the Declaration of Independence and the foundation of our legal tradition.

II

Twenty-five years ago in a case prompted by posting the Ten Commandments in Kentucky's public schools, this Court recognized that the Commandments "are undeniably a sacred text in the Jewish and Christian faiths" and held that their display in public classrooms violated the First Amendment's bar against establishment of religion. Stone v. Graham (1980). *Stone* found a predominantly religious purpose in the government's posting of the Commandments, given their prominence as " 'an instrument of religion.' " The Counties ask for a different approach here by arguing that official purpose is unknowable and the search for it inherently vain. In the alternative, the Counties would avoid the District Court's conclusion by having us limit the scope of the purpose enquiry so severely that any trivial rationalization would suffice, under a standard oblivious to the history of religious government action like the progression of exhibits in this case.

A

Ever since Lemon v. Kurtzman (1971) summarized the three familiar considerations for evaluating Establishment Clause claims, looking to whether government action has "a secular legislative purpose" has been a common, albeit seldom dispositive, element of our cases. Though we have found government action motivated by an illegitimate purpose only four times since *Lemon*, and "the secular purpose requirement alone may rarely be determinative . . . , it nevertheless serves an important function."

The touchstone for our analysis is the principle that the "First Amendment mandates governmental neutrality between religion and religion, and between religion and nonreligion." When the government acts with the ostensible and predominant purpose of advancing religion, it violates that central Establishment Clause value of official religious neutrality, there being no neutrality when the government's ostensible object is to take sides. Manifesting a purpose to favor one faith over another, or adherence to religion generally, clashes with the "understanding, reached . . . after decades of religious war, that liberty and social stability demand a religious tolerance that respects the religious views of all citizens. . . ." By showing a purpose to favor religion, the government "sends the . . . message to . . . nonadherents 'that they are outsiders, not full members of the political community, and an accompanying message to adherents that they are insiders, favored members. . . .' "

Indeed, the purpose apparent from government action can have an impact more significant than the result expressly decreed: when the government maintains Sunday closing laws, it advances religion only minimally because many working people would take the day as one of rest regardless, but if the government justified its decision with a stated desire for all Americans to honor Christ, the divisive thrust of the official action would be inescapable. This is the teaching of McGowan v. Maryland (1961), which upheld Sunday closing statutes on practical, secular grounds after finding that the government had forsaken the religious purposes behind centuries-old predecessor laws.

B

Despite the intuitive importance of official purpose to the realization of Establishment Clause values, the Counties ask us to abandon *Lemon*'s purpose test, or at least to truncate any enquiry into purpose here. Their first argument is that the very consideration of purpose is deceptive: according to them, true "purpose" is unknowable, and its search merely an excuse for courts to act selectively and unpredictably in picking out evidence of subjective intent. The assertions are as seismic as they are unconvincing.

Examination of purpose is a staple of statutory interpretation that makes up the daily fare of every appellate court in the country, and governmental purpose is a key element of a good deal of constitutional doctrine, e.g., Washington v. Davis (1976) (discriminatory purpose required for Equal Protection violation); Hunt v. Washington State Apple Advertising Comm'n (1977) (discriminatory purpose relevant to dormant Commerce Clause claim); Church of Lukumi Babalu Aye, Inc. v. Hialeah (1993) (discriminatory purpose raises level of scrutiny required by free exercise claim). With enquiries into purpose this common, if they were nothing but hunts for mares' nests deflecting attention from bare judicial will, the whole notion of purpose in law would have dropped into disrepute long ago.

But scrutinizing purpose does make practical sense, as in Establishment Clause analysis, where an understanding of official objective emerges from readily discoverable fact, without any judicial psychoanalysis of a drafter's heart of hearts. The eyes that look to purpose belong to an " 'objective observer,' " one who takes account of the traditional external signs that show up in the " 'text, legislative history, and implementation of the statute,' " or comparable official act. There is, then, nothing hinting at an unpredictable or disingenuous exercise when a court enquires into purpose after a claim is raised under the Establishment Clause.

Nor is there any indication that the enquiry is rigged in practice to finding a religious purpose dominant every time a case is filed. In the past, the test has not been fatal very often, presumably because government does not generally act unconstitutionally, with the predominant purpose of advancing religion. That said, one consequence of the corollary that Establishment Clause analysis does not look to the veiled psyche of government officers could be that in some of the cases in which establishment complaints failed, savvy officials had disguised their religious intent so cleverly that the objective observer just missed it.

But that is no reason for great constitutional concern. If someone in the government hides religious motive so well that the "'objective observer, acquainted with the text, legislative history, and implementation of the statute,'" cannot see it, then without something more the government does not make a divisive announcement that in itself amounts to taking religious sides. A secret motive stirs up no strife and does nothing to make outsiders of nonadherents, and it suffices to wait and see whether such government action turns out to have (as it may even be likely to have) the illegitimate effect of advancing religion.

C

After declining the invitation to abandon concern with purpose wholesale, we also have to avoid the Counties' alternative tack of trivializing the enquiry into it. The Counties would read the cases as if the purpose enquiry were so naive that any transparent claim to secularity would satisfy it, and they would cut context out of the enquiry, to the point of ignoring history, no matter what bearing it actually had on the significance of current circumstances. There is no precedent for the Counties' arguments, or reason supporting them.

Lemon said that government action must have "a secular . . . purpose," and after a host of cases it is fair to add that although a legislature's stated reasons will generally get deference, the secular purpose required has to be genuine, not a sham, and not merely secondary to a religious objective.

The Counties' second proffered limitation can be dispatched quickly. They argue that purpose in a case like this one should be inferred, if at all, only from the latest news about the last in a series of governmental actions, however close they may all be in time and subject. But the world is not made brand new every morning, and the Counties are simply asking us to ignore perfectly probative evidence; they want an absentminded objective observer, not one presumed to be familiar with the history of the government's actions and competent to learn what history has to show. The Counties' position just bucks common sense: reasonable observers have reasonable memories, and our precedents sensibly forbid an observer "to turn a blind eye to the context in which [the] policy arose."

III

This case comes to us on appeal from a preliminary injunction. We accordingly review the District Court's legal rulings de novo, and its ultimate conclusion for abuse of discretion.

We take *Stone* as the initial legal benchmark, our only case dealing with the constitutionality of displaying the Commandments. *Stone* recognized that the Commandments are an "instrument of religion" and that, at least on the facts before it, the display of their text could presumptively be understood as meant to advance religion: although state law specifically required their posting in public school classrooms, their isolated exhibition did not leave room even for an argument that secular education explained their being there. But *Stone* did not purport to decide the constitutionality of every possible way the Commandments might be set out by the government, and under the Establishment Clause detail is key. Hence, we look to the record of evidence showing the progression leading up to the third display of the Commandments.

The display rejected in *Stone* had two obvious similarities to the first one in the sequence here: both set out a text of the Commandments as distinct from any traditionally symbolic representation, and each stood alone, not part of an arguably secular display. *Stone* stressed the significance of integrating the Commandments into a secular scheme to forestall the broadcast of an otherwise clearly religious message, and for good reason, the Commandments being a central point of reference in the religious and moral history of Jews and Christians. They proclaim the existence of a monotheistic god (no other gods). They regulate details of religious obligation (no graven images, no sabbath breaking, no vain oath swearing). And they unmistakably rest even the universally accepted prohibitions (as against murder, theft, and the like) on the sanction of the divinity proclaimed at the beginning of the text. Displaying that text is thus different from a symbolic depiction, like tablets with 10 roman numerals, which could be seen as alluding to a general notion of law, not a sectarian conception of faith. Where the text is set out, the insistence of the religious message is hard to avoid in the absence of a context plausibly suggesting a message going beyond an excuse to promote the religious point of view. The display in *Stone* had no context that might have indicated an object beyond the religious character of the text, and the Counties' solo exhibit here did nothing more to counter the sectarian implication than the postings at issue in *Stone*. Actually, the posting by the Counties lacked even the *Stone* display's implausible disclaimer that the Commandments were set out to show their effect on the civil law. What is more, at the ceremony for posting the framed Commandments in Pulaski County, the county executive was accompanied by his pastor, who testified to the certainty of the existence of God. The reasonable observer could only think that the Counties meant to emphasize and celebrate the Commandments' religious message.

This is not to deny that the Commandments have had influence on civil or secular law; a major text of a majority religion is bound to be felt. The point is simply that the original text viewed in its entirety is an unmistakably religious statement dealing with religious obligations and with morality subject to religious sanction. When the government initiates an effort to place this statement alone in public view, a religious object is unmistakable.

Once the Counties were sued, they modified the exhibits and invited additional insight into their purpose in a display that hung for about six months. This new one was the product of forthright and nearly identical Pulaski and McCreary County resolutions listing a series of American historical documents with theistic and Christian references, which were to be posted in order to furnish a setting for displaying the Ten Commandments and any "other

Kentucky and American historical documen[t]" without raising concern about "any Christian or religious references" in them. As mentioned, the resolutions expressed support for an Alabama judge who posted the Commandments in his courtroom, and cited the fact the Kentucky Legislature once adjourned a session in honor of "Jesus Christ, Prince of Ethics."

In this second display, unlike the first, the Commandments were not hung in isolation, merely leaving the Counties' purpose to emerge from the pervasively religious text of the Commandments themselves. Instead, the second version was required to include the statement of the government's purpose expressly set out in the county resolutions, and underscored it by juxtaposing the Commandments to other documents with highlighted references to God as their sole common element. The display's unstinting focus was on religious passages, showing that the Counties were posting the Commandments precisely because of their sectarian content. That demonstration of the government's objective was enhanced by serial religious references and the accompanying resolution's claim about the embodiment of ethics in Christ. Together, the display and resolution presented an indisputable, and undisputed, showing of an impermissible purpose.

Today, the Counties make no attempt to defend their undeniable objective, but instead hopefully describe version two as "dead and buried." Their refusal to defend the second display is understandable, but the reasonable observer could not forget it.

After the Counties changed lawyers, they mounted a third display, without a new resolution or repeal of the old one. The result was the "Foundations of American Law and Government" exhibit, which placed the Commandments in the company of other documents the Counties thought especially significant in the historical foundation of American government.

These new statements of purpose were presented only as a litigating position, there being no further authorizing action by the Counties' governing boards. And although repeal of the earlier county authorizations would not have erased them from the record of evidence bearing on current purpose, the extraordinary resolutions for the second display passed just months earlier were not repealed or otherwise repudiated. Indeed, the sectarian spirit of the common resolution found enhanced expression in the third display, which quoted more of the purely religious language of the Commandments than the first two displays had done. No reasonable observer could swallow the claim that the Counties had cast off the objective so unmistakable in the earlier displays.

In holding the preliminary injunction adequately supported by evidence that the Counties' purpose had not changed at the third stage, we do not decide that the Counties' past actions forever taint any effort on their part to deal with the subject matter. We hold only that purpose needs to be taken seriously under the Establishment Clause and needs to be understood in light of context; an implausible claim that governmental purpose has changed should not carry the day in a court of law any more than in a head with common sense. It is enough to say here that district courts are fully capable of adjusting preliminary relief to take account of genuine changes in constitutionally significant conditions.

Nor do we have occasion here to hold that a sacred text can never be integrated constitutionally into a governmental display on the subject of law, or American history. We do not forget, and in this litigation have frequently been reminded, that our own courtroom frieze was deliberately designed in the exercise of governmental authority so as to include the figure of Moses holding tablets exhibiting a portion of the Hebrew text of the later, secularly phrased Commandments; in the company of 17 other lawgivers, most of them secular figures, there is no risk that Moses would strike an observer as evidence that the National Government was violating neutrality in religion.

IV

The importance of neutrality as an interpretive guide is no less true now than it was when the Court broached the principle in Everson v. Board of Ed. of Ewing (1947), and a word needs to be said about the different view taken in today's dissent. We all agree, of course, on the need for some interpretative help. The First Amendment contains no textual definition of "establishment," and the term is certainly not self-defining. No one contends that the prohibition of establishment stops at a designation of a national (or with Fourteenth Amendment incorporation, a state) church, but nothing in the text says just how much more it covers. There is no simple answer, for more than one reason.

The prohibition on establishment covers a variety of issues from prayer in widely varying government settings, to financial aid for religious individuals and institutions, to comment on religious questions. In these varied settings, issues of about interpreting inexact Establishment Clause language, like difficult interpretative issues generally, arise from the tension of competing values, each constitutionally respectable, but none open to realization to the logical limit.

The dissent, however, puts forward a limitation on the application of the neutrality principle, with citations to historical evidence said to show that the Framers understood the ban on establishment of religion as sufficiently narrow to allow the government to espouse submission to the divine will. The dissent identifies God as the God of monotheism, all of whose three principal strains (Jewish, Christian, and Muslim) acknowledge the religious importance of the Ten Commandments. On the dissent's view, it apparently follows that even rigorous espousal of a common element of this common monotheism is consistent with the establishment ban.

But the dissent's argument for the original understanding is flawed from the outset by its failure to consider the full range of evidence showing what the Framers believed. The dissent is certainly correct in putting forward evidence that some of the Framers thought some endorsement of religion was compatible with the establishment ban.

But the fact is that we do have more to go on, for there is also evidence supporting the proposition that the Framers intended the Establishment Clause to require governmental neutrality in matters of religion, including neutrality in statements acknowledging religion. The very language of the Establishment

Clause represented a significant departure from early drafts that merely prohibited a single national religion, and, the final language instead "extended [the] prohibition to state support for 'religion' in general."

The historical record, moreover, is complicated beyond the dissent's account by the writings and practices of figures no less influential than Thomas Jefferson and James Madison. Jefferson, for example, refused to issue Thanksgiving Proclamations because he believed that they violated the Constitution. And Madison, whom the dissent claims as supporting its thesis, criticized Virginia's general assessment tax not just because it required people to donate "three pence" to religion, but because "it is itself a signal of persecution. It degrades from the equal rank of Citizens all those whose opinions in Religion do not bend to those of the Legislative authority."

The fair inference is that there was no common understanding about the limits of the establishment prohibition, and the dissent's conclusion that its narrower view was the original understanding stretches the evidence beyond tensile capacity. What the evidence does show is a group of statesmen, like others before and after them, who proposed a guarantee with contours not wholly worked out, leaving the Establishment Clause with edges still to be determined. And none the worse for that. Indeterminate edges are the kind to have in a constitution meant to endure, and to meet "exigencies which, if foreseen at all, must have been seen dimly, and which can be best provided for as they occur."

While the dissent fails to show a consistent original understanding from which to argue that the neutrality principle should be rejected, it does manage to deliver a surprise. As mentioned, the dissent says that the deity the Framers had in mind was the God of monotheism, with the consequence that government may espouse a tenet of traditional monotheism. This is truly a remarkable view. Today's dissent, however, apparently means that government should be free to approve the core beliefs of a favored religion over the tenets of others, a view that should trouble anyone who prizes religious liberty. Certainly history cannot justify it; on the contrary, history shows that the religion of concern to the Framers was not that of the monotheistic faiths generally, but Christianity in particular, a fact that no member of this Court takes as a premise for construing the Religion Clauses.

Historical evidence thus supports no solid argument for changing course (whatever force the argument might have when directed at the existing precedent), whereas public discourse at the present time certainly raises no doubt about the value of the interpretative approach invoked for 60 years now. We are centuries away from the St. Bartholomew's Day massacre and the treatment of heretics in early Massachusetts, but the divisiveness of religion in current public life is inescapable. This is no time to deny the prudence of understanding the Establishment Clause to require the Government to stay neutral on religious belief, which is reserved for the conscience of the individual.

Justice O'CONNOR, concurring.

I join in the Court's opinion. The First Amendment expresses our Nation's fundamental commitment to religious liberty by means of two provisions—one protecting the free exercise of religion, the other barring establishment of religion. They were written by the descendents of people who had come to this land precisely so that they could practice their religion freely. Together with the other First Amendment guarantees—of free speech, a free press, and the rights to assemble and petition— the Religion Clauses were designed to safeguard the freedom of conscience and belief that those immigrants had sought. They embody an idea that was once considered radical: Free people are entitled to free and diverse thoughts, which government ought neither to constrain nor to direct.

Reasonable minds can disagree about how to apply the Religion Clauses in a given case. But the goal of the Clauses is clear: to carry out the Founders' plan of preserving religious liberty to the fullest extent possible in a pluralistic society.

By enforcing the Clauses, we have kept religion a matter for the individual conscience, not for the prosecutor or bureaucrat. At a time when we see around the world the violent consequences of the assumption of religious authority by government, Americans may count themselves fortunate: Our regard for constitutional boundaries has protected us from similar travails, while allowing private religious exercise to flourish. The well-known statement that "[w]e are a religious people" has proved true. Americans attend their places of worship more often than do citizens of other developed nations, and describe religion as playing an especially important role in their lives. Those who would renegotiate the boundaries between church and state must therefore answer a difficult question: Why would we trade a system that has served us so well for one that has served others so poorly?

When we enforce these restrictions, we do so for the same reason that guided the Framers—respect for religion's special role in society. Our Founders conceived of a Republic receptive to voluntary religious expression, and provided for the possibility of judicial intervention when government action threatens or impedes such expression. Voluntary religious belief and expression may be as threatened when government takes the mantle of religion upon itself as when government directly interferes with private religious practices. When the government associates one set of religious beliefs with the state and identifies nonadherents as outsiders, it encroaches upon the individual's decision about whether and how to worship. In the marketplace of ideas, the government has vast resources and special status. Government religious expression therefore risks crowding out private observance and distorting the natural interplay between competing beliefs. Allowing government to be a potential mouthpiece for competing religious ideas risks the sort of division that might easily spill over into suppression of rival beliefs. Tying secular and religious authority together poses risks to both.

Given the history of this particular display of the Ten Commandments, the Court correctly finds an Establishment Clause violation. The purpose behind the counties' display is relevant because it conveys an unmistakable message of endorsement to the reasonable observer. It is true that many Americans find the Commandments in accord with their personal beliefs. But we do not count heads before enforcing the First Amendment. Nor can we accept the theory that

Americans who do not accept the Commandments' validity are outside the First Amendment's protections. There is no list of approved and disapproved beliefs appended to the First Amendment—and the Amendment's broad terms do not admit of such a cramped reading.

It is true that the Framers lived at a time when our national religious diversity was neither as robust nor as well recognized as it is now. They may not have foreseen the variety of religions for which this Nation would eventually provide a home. They surely could not have predicted new religions, some of them born in this country. But they did know that line-drawing between religions is an enterprise that, once begun, has no logical stopping point. They worried that "the same authority which can establish Christianity, in exclusion of all other Religions, may establish with the same ease any particular sect of Christians, in exclusion of all other Sects." The Religion Clauses, as a result, protect adherents of all religions, as well as those who believe in no religion at all.

We owe our First Amendment to a generation with a profound commitment to religion and a profound commitment to religious liberty—visionaries who held their faith "with enough confidence to believe that what should be rendered to God does not need to be decided and collected by Caesar." In my opinion, the display at issue was an establishment of religion in violation of our Constitution. For the reasons given above, I join in the Court's opinion.

Justice SCALIA, with whom THE CHIEF JUSTICE and Justice THOMAS join, and with whom Justice KENNEDY joins as to Parts II and III, dissenting.

I would uphold McCreary County and Pulaski County, Kentucky's (hereinafter Counties) displays of the Ten Commandments. I shall discuss first, why the Court's oft repeated assertion that the government cannot favor religious practice is false; second, why today's opinion extends the scope of that falsehood even beyond prior cases; and third, why even on the basis of the Court's false assumptions the judgment here is wrong.

I

A

On September 11, 2001 I was attending in Rome, Italy an international conference of judges and lawyers, principally from Europe and the United States. That night and the next morning virtually all of the participants watched, in their hotel rooms, the address to the Nation by the President of the United States concerning the murderous attacks upon the Twin Towers and the Pentagon, in which thousands of Americans had been killed. The address ended, as Presidential addresses often do, with the prayer "God bless America." The next afternoon I was approached by one of the judges from a European country, who, after extending his profound condolences for my country's loss, sadly observed "How I wish that the Head of State of my country, at a similar time of national tragedy and distress, could conclude his address 'God bless _____.' It is of course absolutely forbidden."

That is one model of the relationship between church and state—a model spread across Europe by the armies of Napoleon, and reflected in the Constitution of France, which begins "France is [a] . . . secular . . . Republic." France Const., Art. 1. Religion is to be strictly excluded from the public forum. This is not, and never was, the model adopted by America. George Washington added to the form of Presidential oath prescribed by Art. II, § 1, cl. 8, of the Constitution, the concluding words "so help me God." The Supreme Court under John Marshall opened its sessions with the prayer, "God save the United States and this Honorable Court." The First Congress instituted the practice of beginning its legislative sessions with a prayer. The same week that Congress submitted the Establishment Clause as part of the Bill of Rights for ratification by the States, it enacted legislation providing for paid chaplains in the House and Senate. The day after the First Amendment was proposed, the same Congress that had proposed it requested the President to proclaim "a day of public thanksgiving and prayer, to be observed, by acknowledging, with grateful hearts, the many and signal favours of Almighty God." President Washington offered the first Thanksgiving Proclamation shortly thereafter, devoting November 26, 1789 on behalf of the American people " 'to the service of that great and glorious Being who is the beneficent author of all the good that is, that was, or that will be,' " thus beginning a tradition of offering gratitude to God that continues today. The same Congress also reenacted the Northwest Territory Ordinance of 1787, Article III of which provided: "Religion, morality, and knowledge, being necessary to good government and the happiness of mankind, schools and the means of education shall forever be encouraged." And of course the First Amendment itself accords religion (and no other manner of belief) special constitutional protection.

These actions of our First President and Congress and the Marshall Court were not idiosyncratic; they reflected the beliefs of the period. Those who wrote the Constitution believed that morality was essential to the well-being of society and that encouragement of religion was the best way to foster morality. The "fact that the Founding Fathers believed devotedly that there was a God and that the unalienable rights of man were rooted in Him is clearly evidenced in their writings, from the Mayflower Compact to the Constitution itself."

Nor have the views of our people on this matter significantly changed. Presidents continue to conclude the Presidential oath with the words "so help me God." Our legislatures, state and national, continue to open their sessions with prayer led by official chaplains. The sessions of this Court continue to open with the prayer "God save the United States and this Honorable Court." Invocation of the Almighty by our public figures, at all levels of government, remains commonplace. Our coinage bears the motto "IN GOD WE TRUST." And our Pledge of Allegiance contains the acknowledgment that we are a Nation "under God." As one of our Supreme Court opinions rightly observed, "We are a religious people whose institutions presuppose a Supreme Being." Zorach v. Clauson (1952).

With all of this reality (and much more) staring it in the face, how can the Court possibly assert that " 'the First Amendment mandates governmental neutrality between . . . religion and nonreligion,' " and that "[m]anifesting a purpose to favor . . . adherence to religion generally," is unconstitutional? Who says so? Surely not the words of the Constitution. Surely not the history and traditions that reflect our society's constant understanding of those words. Surely not even the current sense of our society, recently reflected in an Act of Congress adopted unanimously by the Senate and with only 5 nays in the House of Representatives, criticizing a Court of Appeals opinion that had held "under God" in the Pledge of Allegiance unconstitutional. Nothing stands behind the Court's assertion that governmental affirmation of the society's belief in God is unconstitutional except the Court's own say-so, citing as support only the unsubstantiated say-so of earlier Courts going back no farther than the mid-20th century. And it is, moreover, a thoroughly discredited say-so. It is discredited, to begin with, because a majority of the Justices on the current Court (including at least one Member of today's majority) have, in separate opinions, repudiated the brainspun *Lemon test* that embodies the supposed principle of neutrality between religion and irreligion. And it is discredited because the Court has not had the courage (or the foolhardiness) to apply the neutrality principle consistently.

What distinguishes the rule of law from the dictatorship of a shifting Supreme Court majority is the absolutely indispensable requirement that judicial opinions be grounded in consistently applied principle. That is what prevents judges from ruling now this way, now that—thumbs up or thumbs down—as their personal preferences dictate.

Besides appealing to the demonstrably false principle that the government cannot favor religion over irreligion, today's opinion suggests that the posting of the Ten Commandments violates the principle that the government cannot favor one religion over another. That is indeed a valid principle where public aid or assistance to religion is concerned, or where the free exercise of religion is at issue, but it necessarily applies in a more limited sense to public acknowledgment of the Creator. If religion in the public forum had to be entirely nondenominational, there could be no religion in the public forum at all. One cannot say the word "God," or "the Almighty," one cannot offer public supplication or thanksgiving, without contradicting the beliefs of some people that there are many gods, or that God or the gods pay no attention to human affairs. With respect to public acknowledgment of religious belief, it is entirely clear from our Nation's historical practices that the Establishment Clause permits this disregard of polytheists and believers in unconcerned deities, just as it permits the disregard of devout atheists. The Thanksgiving Proclamation issued by George Washington at the instance of the First Congress was scrupulously nondenominational—but it was monotheistic. In Marsh v. Chambers (1983), we said that the fact the particular prayers offered in the Nebraska Legislature were "in the Judeo-Christian tradition" posed no additional problem, because "there is no indication that the prayer opportunity has been exploited to proselytize or advance any one, or to disparage any other, faith or belief."

Historical practices thus demonstrate that there is a distance between the acknowledgment of a single Creator and the establishment of a religion. The former is, as Marsh v. Chambers put it, "a tolerable acknowledgment of beliefs widely held among the people of this country." The three most popular religions in the United States, Christianity, Judaism, and Islam—which combined account for 97.7% of all believers—are monotheistic. All of them, moreover (Islam included), believe that the Ten Commandments were given by God to Moses, and are divine prescriptions for a virtuous life. Publicly honoring the Ten Commandments is thus indistinguishable, insofar as discriminating against other religions is concerned, from publicly honoring God. Both practices are recognized across such a broad and diverse range of the population—from Christians to Muslims—that they cannot be reasonably understood as a government endorsement of a particular religious viewpoint.

B

A few remarks are necessary in response to the criticism of this dissent by the Court. What is more probative of the meaning of the Establishment Clause than the actions of the very Congress that proposed it, and of the first President charged with observing it?

I must respond to Justice Stevens' assertion that I would "marginaliz[e] the belief systems of more than 7 million Americans" who adhere to religions that are not monotheistic. Surely that is a gross exaggeration. The beliefs of those citizens are entirely protected by the Free Exercise Clause, and by those aspects of the Establishment Clause that do not relate to government acknowledgment of the Creator. Invocation of God despite their beliefs is permitted not because nonmonotheistic religions cease to be religions recognized by the religion clauses of the First Amendment, but because governmental invocation of God is not an establishment. Justice Stevens fails to recognize that in the context of public acknowledgments of God there are legitimate competing interests: On the one hand, the interest of that minority in not feeling "excluded"; but on the other, the interest of the overwhelming majority of religious believers in being able to give God thanks and supplication as a people, and with respect to our national endeavors. Our national tradition has resolved that conflict in favor of the majority. It is not for this Court to change a disposition that accounts, many Americans think, for the phenomenon remarked upon in a quotation attributed to various authors, including Bismarck, but which I prefer to associate with Charles de Gaulle: "God watches over little children, drunkards, and the United States of America."

II

As bad as the *Lemon* test is, it is worse for the fact that, since its inception, its seemingly simple mandates have been manipulated to fit whatever result the Court aimed to achieve. Today's opinion is no different. In two respects it modifies *Lemon* to ratchet up the Court's hostility to religion. First, the Court justifies inquiry into legislative purpose, not as an end itself, but as a means to ascertain the appearance of the government action to an " 'objective observer.' " Because in the Court's view the true danger to be guarded against is that the objective observer would feel like an "outside[r]" or "not [a] full membe[r] of the political community," its inquiry focuses not on the actual purpose of government action, but the "purpose apparent from government action." Under this approach, even if a government could show that its actual purpose was not to advance religion, it would presumably violate the Constitution as long as the Court's objective observer would think otherwise.

I have remarked before that it is an odd jurisprudence that bases the unconstitutionality of a government practice that does not actually advance religion on the hopes of the government that it would do so. But that oddity pales in comparison to the one invited by today's analysis: the legitimacy of a government action with a wholly secular effect would turn on the misperception of an imaginary observer that the government officials behind the action had the intent to advance religion.

Second, the Court replaces *Lemon*'s requirement that the government have "a secular . . . purpose" with the heightened requirement that the secular purpose "predominate" over any purpose to advance religion. The Court treats this extension as a natural outgrowth of the longstanding requirement that the government's secular purpose not be a sham, but simple logic shows the two to be unrelated. If the government's proffered secular purpose is not genuine, then the government has no secular purpose at all. The new demand that secular purpose predominate contradicts *Lemon*'s more limited requirement, and finds no support in our cases.

I have urged that *Lemon*'s purpose prong be abandoned, because (as I have discussed in Part I) even an exclusive purpose to foster or assist religious practice is not necessarily invalidating. But today's extension makes things even worse. By shifting the focus of *Lemon*'s purpose prong from the search for a genuine, secular motivation to the hunt for a predominantly religious purpose, the Court converts what has in the past been a fairly limited inquiry into a rigorous review of the full record. Those responsible for the adoption of the Religion Clauses would surely regard it as a bitter irony that the religious values they designed those Clauses to protect have now become so distasteful to this Court that if they constitute anything more than a subordinate motive for government action they will invalidate it.

III

Even accepting the Court's *Lemon*-based premises, the displays at issue here were constitutional. To any person who happened to walk down the hallway of the McCreary or Pulaski County Courthouse during the roughly nine months when the Foundations Displays were exhibited, the displays must have seemed unremarkable—if indeed they were noticed at all. The walls of both courthouses were already lined with historical documents and other assorted portraits; each Foundations Display was exhibited in the same format as these other displays and nothing in the record suggests that either County took steps to give it greater prominence. On its face, the Foundations Displays manifested the purely secular purpose that the Counties asserted before the District Court: "to display documents that played a significant role in the foundation of our system of law and government." That the Displays included the Ten Commandments did not transform their apparent secular purpose into one of impermissible advocacy for Judeo-Christian beliefs.

Acknowledgment of the contribution that religion has made to our Nation's legal and governmental heritage partakes of a centuries-old tradition. Display of the Ten Commandments is well within the mainstream of this practice of acknowledgment. Federal, State, and local governments across the Nation have engaged in such display. The Supreme Court Building itself includes depictions of Moses with the Ten Commandments in the Courtroom and on the east pediment of the building, and symbols of the Ten Commandments "adorn the metal gates lining the north and south sides of the Courtroom as well as the doors leading into the Courtroom." Similar depictions of the Decalogue appear on public buildings and monuments throughout our Nation's Capital. The frequency of these displays testifies to the popular understanding that the Ten Commandments are a foundation of the rule of law, and a symbol of the role that religion played, and continues to play, in our system of government.

VAN ORDEN v. PERRY
545 U.S. 677 (2005)

Chief Justice REHNQUIST announced the judgment of the Court and delivered an opinion, in which Justice SCALIA, Justice KENNEDY, and Justice THOMAS join.

The question here is whether the Establishment Clause of the First Amendment allows the display of a monument inscribed with the Ten Commandments on the Texas State Capitol grounds. We hold that it does.

The 22 acres surrounding the Texas State Capitol contain 17 monuments and 21 historical markers commemorating the "people, ideals, and events that compose Texan identity." The monolith challenged here stands 6-feet high and 3½ feet wide. It is located to the north of the Capitol building, between the Capitol and the Supreme Court building. Its primary content is the text of the Ten Commandments. An eagle grasping the American flag, an eye inside of a pyramid, and two small tablets with what appears to be an ancient script are carved above the text of the Ten Commandments. Below the text are two Stars of David and the superimposed Greek letters Chi and Rho, which represent Christ. The bottom of the monument bears the inscription "PRESENTED TO THE PEOPLE AND YOUTH OF TEXAS BY THE FRATERNAL ORDER OF EAGLES OF TEXAS 1961."

The legislative record surrounding the State's acceptance of the monument from the Eagles—a national social, civic, and patriotic organization—is limited to legislative journal entries. After the monument was accepted, the State selected a site for the monument based on the recommendation of the state organization responsible for maintaining the Capitol grounds. The Eagles paid the cost of erecting the monument, the dedication of which was presided over by two state legislators.

Petitioner Thomas Van Orden is a native Texan and a resident of Austin. At one time he was a licensed lawyer, having graduated from Southern Methodist Law School. Van Orden testified that, since 1995, he has encountered the Ten Commandments monument during his frequent visits to the Capitol grounds. Forty years after the monument's erection and six years after Van Orden began to encounter the monument frequently, he sued numerous state officials in their official capacities seeking both a declaration that the monument's placement violates the Establishment Clause and an injunction requiring its removal.

Our cases, Januslike, point in two directions in applying the Establishment Clause. One face looks toward the strong role played by religion and religious traditions throughout our Nation's history. The other face looks toward the principle that governmental intervention in religious matters can itself endanger religious freedom.

This case, like all Establishment Clause challenges, presents us with the difficulty of respecting both faces. Our institutions presuppose a Supreme Being, yet these institutions must not press religious observances upon their citizens. One face looks to the past in acknowledgment of our Nation's heritage, while the other looks to the present in demanding a separation between church and state. Reconciling these two faces requires that we neither abdicate our responsibility to maintain a division between church and state nor evince a hostility to religion by disabling the government from in some ways recognizing our religious heritage.

These two faces are evident in representative cases both upholding and invalidating laws under the Establishment Clause. Over the last 25 years, we have sometimes pointed to Lemon v. Kurtzman (1971) as providing the governing test in Establishment Clause challenges. Yet, just two years after *Lemon* was decided, we noted that the factors identified in *Lemon* serve as "no more than helpful signposts." Many of our recent cases simply have not applied the *Lemon* test. Others have applied it only after concluding that the challenged practice was invalid under a different Establishment Clause test.

Whatever may be the fate of the *Lemon* test in the larger scheme of Establishment Clause jurisprudence, we think it not useful in dealing with the sort of passive monument that Texas has erected on its Capitol grounds. Instead, our analysis is driven both by the nature of the monument and by our Nation's history.

As we explained in Lynch v. Donnelly (1984): "There is an unbroken history of official acknowledgment by all three branches of government of the role of religion in American life from at least 1789." For example, both Houses passed resolutions in 1789 asking President George Washington to issue a Thanksgiving Day Proclamation to "recommend to the people of the United States a day of public thanksgiving and prayer, to be observed by acknowledging, with grateful hearts, the many and signal favors of Almighty God." President Washington's proclamation directly attributed to the Supreme Being the foundations and successes of our young Nation.

Recognition of the role of God in our Nation's heritage has also been reflected in our decisions. We have acknowledged, for example, that "religion has been closely identified with our history and government," and that "[t]he history of man is inseparable from the history of religion." This recognition has led us to hold that the Establishment Clause permits a state legislature to open its daily sessions with a prayer by a chaplain paid by the State. Marsh v. Chambers (1982). With similar reasoning, we have upheld laws, which originated from one of the Ten Commandments, that prohibited the sale of merchandise on Sunday. McGowan v. Maryland (1961).

In this case we are faced with a display of the Ten Commandments on government property outside the Texas State Capitol. Such acknowledgments of the role played by the Ten Commandments in our Nation's heritage are common throughout America. We need only look within our own Courtroom. Since 1935, Moses has stood, holding two tablets that reveal portions of the Ten Commandments written in Hebrew, among other lawgivers in the south frieze. Representations of the Ten Commandments adorn the metal gates lining the north and south sides of the Courtroom as well as the doors leading into the Courtroom. Moses also sits on the exterior east facade of the building holding the Ten Commandments tablets.

Similar acknowledgments can be seen throughout a visitor's tour of our Nation's Capital. For example, a large statue of Moses holding the Ten Commandments, alongside a statue of the Apostle Paul, has overlooked the rotunda of the Library of Congress' Jefferson Building since 1897. And the Jefferson Building's Great Reading Room contains a sculpture of a woman beside the Ten Commandments with a quote above her from the Old Testament (Micah 6:8). A medallion with two tablets depicting the Ten Commandments decorates the floor of the National Archives. Inside the Department of Justice, a statue entitled "The Spirit of Law" has two tablets representing the Ten Commandments lying at its feet. In front of the Ronald Reagan Building is another sculpture that includes a depiction of the Ten Commandments. So too a 24-foot-tall sculpture, depicting, among other things, the Ten Commandments and a cross, stands outside the federal courthouse that houses both the Court of Appeals and the District Court for the District of Columbia. Moses is also prominently featured in the Chamber of the United States House of Representatives.

Of course, the Ten Commandments are religious—they were so viewed at their inception and so remain. The monument, therefore, has religious significance. According to Judeo-Christian belief, the Ten Commandments were given to Moses by God on Mt. Sinai. But Moses was a lawgiver as well as a religious leader. And the Ten Commandments have an undeniable historical meaning, as the foregoing examples demonstrate. Simply having religious content or promoting a message consistent with a religious doctrine does not run afoul of the Establishment Clause.

There are, of course, limits to the display of religious messages or symbols. For example, we held unconstitutional a Kentucky statute requiring the posting of the Ten Commandments in every public schoolroom. Stone v. Graham (1980) (per curiam). In the classroom context, we found that the Kentucky statute had an improper and plainly religious purpose.

The placement of the Ten Commandments monument on the Texas State Capitol grounds is a far more passive use of those texts than was the case in *Stone*, where the text confronted elementary school students every day. Indeed, Van Orden, the petitioner here, apparently walked by the monument for a number of years before bringing this lawsuit. Texas has treated her Capitol grounds monuments as representing the several strands in the State's political and legal history. The inclusion of the Ten Commandments monument in this group has a dual significance, partaking of both religion and government. We cannot say that Texas' display of this monument violates the Establishment Clause of the First Amendment.

Justice SCALIA, concurring.

I join the opinion of The Chief Justice because I think it accurately reflects our current Establishment Clause jurisprudence—or at least the Establishment Clause jurisprudence we currently apply some of the time. I would prefer to reach the same result by adopting an Establishment Clause jurisprudence that is in accord with our Nation's past and present practices, and that can be consistently applied—the central relevant feature of which is that there is nothing unconstitutional in a State's favoring religion generally, honoring God through public prayer and acknowledgment, or, in a nonproselytizing manner, venerating the Ten Commandments.

Justice THOMAS, concurring.

The Court holds that the Ten Commandments monument found on the Texas State Capitol grounds does not violate the Establishment Clause. Rather than trying to suggest meaninglessness where there is meaning, The Chief Justice rightly recognizes that the monument has "religious significance." He properly recognizes the role of religion in this Nation's history and the permissibility of government displays acknowledging that history. For those reasons, I join The Chief Justice's opinion in full.

This case would be easy if the Court were willing to abandon the inconsistent guideposts it has adopted for addressing Establishment Clause challenges, and return to the original meaning of the Clause. I have previously suggested that the Clause's text and history "resis[t] incorporation" against the States. If the Establishment Clause does not restrain the States, then it has no application here, where only state action is at issue.

Even if the Clause is incorporated, or if the Free Exercise Clause limits the power of States to establish religions, our task would be far simpler if we returned to the original meaning of the word "establishment" than it is under the various approaches this Court now uses. The Framers understood an establishment "necessarily [to] involve actual legal coercion." "In other words, establishment at the founding involved, for example, mandatory observance or mandatory payment of taxes supporting ministers." And "government practices that have nothing to do with creating or maintaining . . . coercive state establishments" simply do not "implicate the possible liberty interest of being free from coercive state establishments."

There is no question that, based on the original meaning of the Establishment Clause, the Ten Commandments display at issue here is constitutional. In no sense does Texas compel petitioner Van Orden to do anything. The only injury to him is that he takes offense at seeing the monument as he passes it on his way to the Texas Supreme Court Library. He need not stop to read it or even to look at it, let alone to express support for it or adopt the Commandments as guides for his life. The mere presence of the monument along his path involves no coercion and thus does not violate the Establishment Clause.

Returning to the original meaning would do more than simplify our task. It also would avoid the pitfalls present in the Court's current approach to such challenges. This Court's precedent elevates the trivial to the proverbial "federal case," by making benign signs and postings subject to challenge. Even worse, the incoherence of the Court's decisions in this area renders the Establishment Clause impenetrable and incapable of consistent application. All told, this Court's jurisprudence leaves courts, governments, and believers and nonbelievers alike confused—an observation that is hardly new.

Finally, the very "flexibility" of this Court's Establishment Clause precedent leaves it incapable of consistent application. The inconsistency between the decisions the Court reaches today in this case and in McCreary County v. American Civil Liberties Union of Ky. (2005) only compounds the confusion.

Much, if not all, of this would be avoided if the Court would return to the views of the Framers and adopt coercion as the touchstone for our Establishment Clause inquiry. Every acknowledgment of religion would not give rise to an Establishment Clause claim. Courts would not act as theological commissions, judging the meaning of religious matters. Most important, our precedent would be capable of consistent and coherent application. While the Court correctly rejects the challenge to the Ten Commandments monument on the Texas Capitol grounds, a more fundamental rethinking of our Establishment Clause jurisprudence remains in order.

Justice BREYER, concurring in the judgment.

In School Dist. of Abington Township v. Schempp (1963), Justice Goldberg, joined by Justice Harlan, wrote, in respect to the First Amendment's Religion Clauses, that there is "no simple and clear measure which by precise application can readily and invariably demark the permissible from the impermissible."

One must refer instead to the basic purposes of those Clauses. They seek to "assure the fullest possible scope of religious liberty and tolerance for all." They seek to avoid that divisiveness based upon religion that promotes social conflict, sapping the strength of government and religion alike. They seek to maintain that "separation of church and state" that has long been critical to the "peaceful dominion that religion exercises in [this] country," where the "spirit of religion" and the "spirit of freedom" are productively "united," "reign[ing] together" but in separate spheres "on the same soil."

The Court has made clear, as Justices Goldberg and Harlan noted, that the realization of these goals means that government must "neither engage in nor compel religious practices," that it must "effect no favoritism among sects or between religion and nonreligion," and that it must "work deterrence of no religious belief." The government must avoid excessive interference with, or promotion of, religion. But the Establishment Clause does not compel the government to purge from the public sphere all that in any way partakes of the religious. Such absolutism is not only inconsistent with our national traditions, but would also tend to promote the kind of social conflict the Establishment Clause seeks to avoid.

Thus, as Justices Goldberg and Harlan pointed out, the Court has found no single mechanical formula that can accurately draw the constitutional line in every case. Where the Establishment Clause is at issue, tests designed to measure "neutrality" alone are insufficient, both because it is sometimes difficult to determine when a legal rule is "neutral," and because "untutored devotion to the concept of neutrality can lead to invocation or approval of results which partake not simply of that noninterference and noninvolvement with the religious which the Constitution commands, but of a brooding and pervasive devotion to the secular and a passive, or even active, hostility to the religious."

The case before us is a borderline case. It concerns a large granite monument bearing the text of the Ten Commandments located on the grounds of the Texas State Capitol. On the one hand, the Commandments' text undeniably has a religious message, invoking, indeed emphasizing, the Diety. On the other hand, focusing on the text of the Commandments alone cannot conclusively resolve this case. Rather, to determine the message that the text here conveys, we must examine how the text is used. And that inquiry requires us to consider the context of the display.

In certain contexts, a display of the tablets of the Ten Commandments can convey not simply a religious message but also a secular moral message (about proper standards of social conduct). And in certain contexts, a display of the tablets can also convey a historical message (about a historic relation between those standards and the law)—a fact that helps to explain the display of those tablets in dozens of courthouses throughout the Nation, including the Supreme Court of the United States.

Here the tablets have been used as part of a display that communicates not simply a religious message, but a secular message as well. The circumstances surrounding the display's placement on the capitol grounds and its physical setting suggest that the State itself intended the latter, nonreligious aspects of the tablets' message to predominate. And the monument's 40-year history on the Texas state grounds indicates that that has been its effect.

The group that donated the monument, the Fraternal Order of Eagles, a private civic (and primarily secular) organization, while interested in the religious aspect of the Ten Commandments, sought to highlight the Commandments' role in shaping civic morality as part of that organization's efforts to combat juvenile delinquency. The Eagles' consultation with a committee composed of members of several faiths in order to find a nonsectarian text underscores the group's ethics-based motives. The tablets, as displayed on the monument, prominently acknowledge that the Eagles donated the display, a factor which, though not sufficient, thereby further distances the State itself from the religious aspect of the Commandments' message.

The physical setting of the monument, moreover, suggests little or nothing of the sacred. The monument sits in a large park containing 17 monuments and 21 historical markers, all designed to illustrate the "ideals" of those who settled in Texas and of those who have lived there since that time. The setting does not readily lend itself to meditation or any other religious activity. But it does provide a context of history and moral ideals. It (together with the display's inscription about its origin) communicates to visitors that the State sought to reflect moral principles, illustrating a relation between ethics and law that the State's citizens, historically speaking, have endorsed.

If these factors provide a strong, but not conclusive, indication that the Commandments' text on this monument conveys a predominantly secular message, a further factor is determinative here. As far as I can tell, 40 years passed in which the presence of this monument, legally speaking, went unchallenged (until the single legal objection raised by petitioner). And I am not aware of any evidence suggesting that this was due to a climate of intimidation. Hence, those 40 years suggest more strongly than can any set of formulaic tests that few individuals, whatever their system of beliefs, are likely to have understood the monument as amounting, in any significantly detrimental way, to a government effort to favor a particular religious sect, primarily to promote religion over nonreligion, to "engage in" any "religious practic[e]," to "compel" any "religious practic[e]," or to "work deterrence" of any "religious belief." Those 40 years suggest that the public visiting the capitol grounds has considered the religious aspect of the tablets' message as part of what is a broader moral and historical message reflective of a cultural heritage.

This case, moreover, is distinguishable from instances where the Court has found Ten Commandments displays impermissible. The display is not on the grounds of a public school, where, given the impressionability of the young, government must exercise particular care in separating church and state. This case also differs from *McCreary County*, where the short (and stormy) history of the courthouse Commandments' displays demonstrates the substantially religious objectives of those who mounted them, and the effect of this readily apparent objective upon those who view them. That history there indicates a governmental effort substantially to promote religion, not simply an effort primarily to reflect, historically, the secular impact of a religiously inspired document. And, in today's world, in a Nation of so many different religious and comparable nonreligious fundamental beliefs, a more contemporary state effort to focus attention upon a religious text is certainly likely to prove divisive in a way that this longstanding, pre-existing monument has not.

For these reasons, I believe that the Texas display—serving a mixed but primarily nonreligious purpose, not primarily "advanc[ing]" or "inhibit[ing] religion," and not creating an "excessive government entanglement with religion"—might satisfy this Court's more formal Establishment Clause tests. But, as I have said, in reaching the conclusion that the Texas display falls on the permissible side of the constitutional line, I rely less upon a literal application of any particular test than upon consideration of the basic purposes of the First Amendment's Religion Clauses themselves. This display has stood apparently uncontested for nearly two generations. That experience helps us understand that as a practical matter of degree this display is unlikely to prove divisive. And this matter of degree is, I believe, critical in a borderline case such as this one.

At the same time, to reach a contrary conclusion here, based primarily upon on the religious nature of the tablets' text would, I fear, lead the law to exhibit a hostility toward religion that has no place in our Establishment Clause traditions. Such a holding might well encourage disputes concerning the removal of longstanding depictions of the Ten Commandments from public buildings across the Nation. And it could thereby create the very kind of religiously based divisiveness that the Establishment Clause seeks to avoid.

Justice STEVENS, with whom Justice GINSBURG joins, dissenting.

The sole function of the monument on the grounds of Texas' State Capitol is to display the full text of one version of the Ten Commandments. The monument is not a work of art and does not refer to any event in the history of the State. Viewed on its face, Texas' display has no purported connection to God's role in the formation of Texas or the founding of our Nation; nor does it provide the reasonable observer with any basis to guess that it was erected to honor any individual or organization. The message transmitted by Texas' chosen display is quite plain: This State endorses the divine code of the "Judeo-Christian" God.

For those of us who learned to recite the King James version of the text long before we understood the meaning of some of its words, God's Commandments may seem like wise counsel. The question before this Court, however, is whether it is counsel that the State of Texas may proclaim without violating the Establishment Clause of the Constitution. If any fragment of Jefferson's metaphorical "wall of separation between church and State" is to be preserved—if there remains any meaning to the "wholesome 'neutrality' of which this Court's [Establishment Clause] cases speak"—a negative answer to that question is mandatory.

I

In my judgment, at the very least, the Establishment Clause has created a strong presumption against the display of religious symbols on public property. The adornment of our public spaces with displays of religious symbols and messages undoubtedly provides comfort, even inspiration, to many individuals who subscribe to particular faiths. Unfortunately, the practice also runs the risk of "offend[ing] nonmembers of the faith being advertised as well as adherents who consider the particular advertisement disrespectful." Government's obligation to avoid divisiveness and exclusion in the religious sphere is compelled by the Establishment and Free Exercise Clauses, which together erect a wall of separation between church and state.

This metaphorical wall protects principles long recognized and often recited in this Court's cases. The first and most fundamental of these principles, one that a majority of this Court today affirms, is that the Establishment Clause demands religious neutrality—government may not exercise a preference for one religious faith over another. This essential command, however, is not merely a prohibition against the government's differentiation among religious sects. We have repeatedly reaffirmed that neither a State nor the Federal Government "can constitutionally pass laws or impose requirements which aid all religions as against non-believers, and neither can aid those religions based on a belief in the existence of God as against those religions founded on different beliefs." This principle is based on the straightforward notion that governmental promotion of orthodoxy is not saved by the aggregation of several orthodoxies under the State's banner.

Acknowledgments of this broad understanding of the neutrality principle are legion in our cases. In restating this principle, I do not discount the importance of avoiding an overly strict interpretation of the metaphor so often used to define the reach of the Establishment Clause. The plurality is correct to note that "religion and religious traditions" have played a "strong role . . . throughout our nation's history." Given this history, it is unsurprising that a religious symbol may at times become an important feature of a familiar landscape or a reminder of an important event in the history of a community. The wall that separates the church from the State does not prohibit the government from acknowledging the religious beliefs and practices of the American people, nor does it require governments to hide works of art or historic memorabilia from public view just because they also have religious significance.

This case, however, is not about historic preservation or the mere recognition of religion. The issue is obfuscated rather than clarified by simplistic commentary on the various ways in which religion has played a role in American life, and by the recitation of the many extant governmental "acknowledgments" of the role the Ten Commandments played in our Nation's heritage. Surely, the mere compilation of religious symbols, none of which includes the full text of the Commandments and all of which are exhibited in different settings, has only marginal relevance to the question presented in this case.

The monolith displayed on Texas Capitol grounds cannot be discounted as a passive acknowledgment of religion, nor can the State's refusal to remove it upon objection be explained as a simple desire to preserve a historic relic. This Nation's resolute commitment to neutrality with respect to religion is flatly inconsistent with the plurality's wholehearted validation of an official state endorsement of the message that there is one, and only one, God.

II

When the Ten Commandments monument was donated to the State of Texas in 1961, it was not for the purpose of commemorating a noteworthy event in Texas history, signifying the Commandments' influence on the development of secular law, or even denoting the religious beliefs of Texans at that time. To the contrary, the donation was only one of over a hundred largely identical monoliths, and of over a thousand paper replicas, distributed to state and local governments throughout the Nation over the course of several decades. This ambitious project was the work of the Fraternal Order of Eagles, a well-respected benevolent organization whose good works have earned the praise of several Presidents.

As the story goes, the program was initiated by the late Judge E. J. Ruegemer, a Minnesota juvenile court judge and then-Chairman of the Eagles National Commission on Youth Guidance. Inspired by a juvenile offender who had never heard of the Ten Commandments, the judge approached the Minnesota Eagles with the idea of distributing paper copies of the Commandments to be posted in courthouses nationwide. The State's Aerie undertook this project and its popularity spread. When Cecil B. DeMille, who at that time was filming the movie *The Ten Commandments,* heard of the judge's endeavor, he teamed up with the Eagles to produce the type of granite monolith now displayed in front of the Texas Capitol and at courthouse squares, city halls, and public parks throughout the Nation. Granite was reportedly chosen over DeMille's original suggestion of bronze plaques to better replicate the original Ten Commandments. The donors were motivated by a desire to "inspire the youth" and curb juvenile delinquency by providing children with a "code of conduct or standards by which to govern their actions."

It is the Eagles' belief that disseminating the message conveyed by the Ten Commandments will help to persuade young men and women to observe civilized standards of behavior, and will lead to more productive lives.

The desire to combat juvenile delinquency by providing guidance to youths is both admirable and unquestionably secular. But achieving that goal through biblical teachings injects a religious purpose into an otherwise secular endeavor. By spreading the word of God and converting heathens to Christianity, missionaries expect to enlighten their converts, enhance their satisfaction with life, and improve their behavior. Similarly, by disseminating the "law of God"—directing fidelity to God and proscribing murder, theft, and adultery—the Eagles hope that this divine guidance will help wayward youths conform their behavior and improve their lives. In my judgment, the significant secular by-products that are intended consequences of religious instruction—indeed, of the establishment of most religions—are not the type of "secular" purposes that justify government promulgation of sacred religious messages.

Though the State of Texas may genuinely wish to combat juvenile delinquency, and may rightly want to honor the Eagles for their efforts, it cannot effectuate these admirable purposes through an explicitly religious medium. The reason this message stands apart is that the Decalogue is a venerable religious text. As we held 25 years ago, it is beyond dispute that "[t]he Ten Commandments are undeniably a sacred text in the Jewish and Christian faiths." For many followers, the Commandments represent the literal word of God as spoken to Moses and repeated to his followers after descending from Mount Sinai. Attempts to secularize what is unquestionably a sacred text defy credibility and disserve people of faith.

The profoundly sacred message embodied by the text inscribed on the Texas monument is emphasized by the especially large letters that identify its author: "I AM the LORD thy God." It commands present worship of Him and no other deity. It directs us to be guided by His teaching in the current and future conduct of all of our affairs. It instructs us to follow a code of divine law, some of which has informed and been integrated into our secular legal code ("Thou shalt not kill"), but much of which has not ("Thou shalt not make to thyself any graven images. . . . Thou shalt not covet").

Moreover, despite the Eagles' best efforts to choose a benign nondenominational text, the Ten Commandments display projects not just a religious, but an inherently sectarian message. There are many distinctive versions of the Decalogue, ascribed to by different religions and even different denominations within a particular faith; to a pious and learned observer, these differences may be of enormous religious significance. In choosing to display this version of the Commandments, Texas tells the observer that the State supports this side of the doctrinal religious debate.

Even if, however, the message of the monument, despite the inscribed text, fairly could be said to represent the belief system of all Judeo-Christians, it would still run afoul of the Establishment Clause by prescribing a compelled code of conduct from one God, namely a Judeo-Christian God, that is rejected by prominent polytheistic sects, such as Hinduism, as well as nontheistic religions, such as Buddhism. And, at the very least, the text of the Ten Commandments impermissibly commands a preference for religion over irreligion. Any of those bases, in my judgment, would be sufficient to conclude that the message should not be proclaimed by the State of Texas on a permanent monument at the seat of its government.

III

The plurality relies heavily on the fact that our Republic was founded, and has been governed since its nascence, by leaders who spoke then (and speak still) in plainly religious rhetoric. The speeches and rhetoric characteristic of the founding era, however, do not answer the question before us. I have already explained why Texas' display of the full text of the Ten Commandments, given the content of the actual display and the context in which it is situated, sets this case apart from the countless examples of benign government recognitions of religion. But there is another crucial difference. Our leaders, when delivering public addresses, often express their blessings simultaneously in the service of God and their constituents. Thus, when public officials deliver public speeches, we recognize that their words are not exclusively a transmission from the government because those oratories have embedded within them the inherently personal views of the speaker as an individual member of the polity. The permanent placement of a textual religious display on state property is different in kind; it amalgamates otherwise discordant individual views into a collective statement of government approval. Moreover, the message never ceases to transmit itself to objecting viewers whose only choices are to accept the message or to ignore the offense by averting their gaze. In this sense, although Thanksgiving Day proclamations and inaugural speeches undoubtedly seem official, in most circumstances they will not constitute the sort of governmental endorsement of religion at which the separation of church and state is aimed.

The plurality's reliance on early religious statements and proclamations made by the Founders is also problematic because those views were not espoused at the Constitutional Convention in 1787 nor enshrined in the Constitution's text. Thus, the presentation of these religious statements as a unified historical narrative is bound to paint a misleading picture. Ardent separationists aside, there is another critical nuance lost in the plurality's portrayal of history. Simply put, many of the Founders who are often cited as authoritative expositors of the Constitution's original meaning understood the Establishment Clause to stand for a narrower proposition than the plurality, for whatever reason, is willing to accept. Namely, many of the Framers understood the word "religion" in the Establishment Clause to encompass only the various sects of Christianity.

The original understanding of the type of "religion" that qualified for constitutional protection under the Establishment Clause likely did not include those followers of Judaism and Islam who are among the preferred "monotheistic" religions Justice Scalia has embraced in his *McCreary County* opinion. Given the original understanding of the men who championed our "Christian nation"—men who had no cause to view anti-Semitism or contempt for atheists as problems worthy of civic concern—one must ask whether Justice Scalia "has not had the courage (or the foolhardiness) to apply [his originalism] principle consistently."

Indeed, to constrict narrowly the reach of the Establishment Clause to the views of the Founders would lead to more than this unpalatable result; it would also leave us with an unincorporated constitutional provision—in other words, one that limits only the federal establishment of "a national religion." Under this view, not only could a State constitutionally adorn all of its public spaces with crucifixes or passages from the New Testament, it would also have full authority to prescribe the teachings of Martin Luther or Joseph Smith as the official state religion. Only the Federal Government would be prohibited from taking sides (and only then as between Christian sects).

A reading of the First Amendment dependent on either of the purported original meanings expressed above would eviscerate the heart of the Establishment Clause. It would replace Jefferson's "wall of separation" with a perverse wall of exclusion—Christians inside, non-Christians out. It would permit States to construct walls of their own choosing—Baptists inside, Mormons out; Jewish Orthodox inside, Jewish Reform out. A Clause so understood might be faithful to the expectations of some of our Founders, but it is plainly not worthy of a society whose enviable hallmark over the course of two centuries has been the continuing expansion of religious pluralism and tolerance.

It is our duty, therefore, to interpret the First Amendment's command that "Congress shall make no law respecting an establishment of religion" not by merely asking what those words meant to observers at the time of the founding, but instead by deriving from the Clause's text and history the broad principles that remain valid today. The principle that guides my analysis is neutrality. The basis for that principle is firmly rooted in our Nation's history and our Constitution's text. I recognize that the requirement that government must remain neutral between religion and irreligion would have seemed foreign to some of the Framers; so too would a requirement of neutrality between Jews and Christians. The evil of discriminating today against atheists, "polytheists[,] and believers in unconcerned deities," is in my view a direct descendent of the evil of discriminating among Christian sects. The Establishment Clause thus forbids it and, in turn, forbids Texas from displaying the Ten Commandments monument the plurality so casually affirms.

IV

The Eagles may donate as many monuments as they choose to be displayed in front of Protestant churches, benevolent organizations' meeting places, or on the front lawns of private citizens. The expurgated text of the King James version of the Ten Commandments that they have crafted is unlikely to be accepted by Catholic parishes, Jewish synagogues, or even some Protestant denominations, but the message they seek to convey is surely more compatible with church property than with property that is located on the government side of the metaphorical wall.

The judgment of the Court in this case stands for the proposition that the Constitution permits governmental displays of sacred religious texts. This makes a mockery of the constitutional ideal that government must remain neutral between religion and irreligion. If a State may endorse a particular deity's command to "have no other gods before me," it is difficult to conceive of any textual display that would run afoul of the Establishment Clause.

The disconnect between this Court's approval of Texas's monument and the constitutional prohibition against preferring religion to irreligion cannot be reduced to the exercise of plotting two adjacent locations on a slippery slope. Rather, it is the difference between the shelter of a fortress and exposure to "the winds that would blow" if the wall were allowed to crumble.

Justice SOUTER, with whom Justice STEVENS and Justice GINSBURG join, dissenting.

Although the First Amendment's Religion Clauses have not been read to mandate absolute governmental neutrality toward religion, the Establishment Clause requires neutrality as a general rule, and thus expresses Madison's condemnation of "employ[ing] Religion as an engine of Civil policy." A governmental display of an obviously religious text cannot be squared with neutrality, except in a setting that plausibly indicates that the statement is not placed in view with a predominant purpose on the part of government either to adopt the religious message or to urge its acceptance by others.

Until today, only one of our cases addressed the constitutionality of posting the Ten Commandments, Stone v. Graham (1980). A Kentucky statute required posting the Commandments on the walls of public school classrooms. [The Court stated:]

> The pre-eminent purpose for posting the Ten Commandments on schoolroom walls is plainly religious in nature. The Ten Commandments are undeniably a sacred text in the Jewish and Christian faiths, and no legislative recitation of a supposed secular purpose can blind us to that fact. The Commandments do not confine themselves to arguably secular matters, such as honoring one's parents, killing or murder, adultery, stealing, false witness, and covetousness. Rather, the first part of the Commandments concerns the religious duties of believers: worshipping the Lord God alone, avoiding idolatry, not using the Lord's name in vain, and observing the Sabbath Day.

What these observations underscore are the simple realities that the Ten Commandments constitute a religious statement, that their message is inherently religious, and that the purpose of singling them out in a display is clearly the same.

In the present case, the religious purpose was evident on the part of the donating organization. When the Fraternal Order of Eagles, the group that gave the monument to the State of Texas, donated identical monuments to other jurisdictions, it was seeking to impart a religious message. Accordingly, it was not just the terms of the moral code, but the proclamation that the terms of the code were enjoined by God, that the Eagles put forward in the monuments they donated.

Thus, a pedestrian happening upon the monument at issue here needs no training in religious doctrine to realize that the statement of the Commandments, quoting God himself, proclaims that the will of the divine being is the source of obligation to obey the rules, including the facially secular ones. In this case, moreover, the text is presented to give particular prominence to the Commandments' first sectarian reference, "I am the Lord thy God." That proclamation is centered on the stone and written in slightly larger letters than the subsequent recitation. To ensure that the religious nature of the monument is clear to even the most casual passerby, the word "Lord" appears in all capital letters (as does the word "am"), so that the most eye-catching segment of the quotation is the declaration "I AM the LORD thy God." What follows, of course, are the rules against other gods, graven images, vain swearing, and Sabbath breaking. And the full text of the fifth Commandment puts forward filial respect as a condition of long life in the land "which the Lord they God giveth thee." These "[w]ords . . . make [the] . . . religious meaning unmistakably clear."

To drive the religious point home, and identify the message as religious to any viewer who failed to read the text, the engraved quotation is framed by religious symbols: two tablets with what appears to be ancient script on them, two Stars of David, and the superimposed Greek letters Chi and Rho as the familiar monogram of Christ. Nothing on the monument, in fact, detracts from its religious nature, and the plurality does not suggest otherwise. It would therefore be difficult to miss the point that the government of Texas is telling everyone who sees the monument to live up to a moral code because God requires it, with both code and conception of God being rightly understood as the inheritances specifically of Jews and Christians. And it is likewise unsurprising that the District Court expressly rejected Texas's argument that the State's purpose in placing the monument on the capitol grounds was related to the Commandments' role as "part of the foundation of modern secular law in Texas and elsewhere."

The monument's presentation of the Commandments with religious text emphasized and enhanced stands in contrast to any number of perfectly constitutional depictions of them, the frieze of our own Courtroom providing a good example, where the figure of Moses stands among history's great lawgivers. While Moses holds the tablets of the Commandments showing some Hebrew text, no one looking at the lines of figures in marble relief is likely to see a religious purpose behind the assemblage or take away a religious message from it. Only one other depiction represents a religious leader, and the historical personages are mixed with symbols of moral and intellectual abstractions like Equity and Authority. Since Moses enjoys no especial prominence on the frieze, viewers can readily take him to be there as a lawgiver in the company of other lawgivers; and the viewers may just as naturally see the tablets of the Commandments (showing the later ones, forbidding things like killing and theft, but without the divine preface) as background from which the concept of law emerged, ultimately having a secular influence in the history of the Nation. Government may, of course, constitutionally call attention to this influence, and may post displays or erect monuments recounting this aspect of our history no less than any other, so long as there is a context and that context is historical. Hence, a display of the Commandments accompanied by an exposition of how they have influenced modern law would most likely be constitutionally unobjectionable. And the Decalogue could, as *Stone* suggested, be integrated constitutionally into a course of study in public schools.

Texas seeks to take advantage of the recognition that visual symbol and written text can manifest a secular purpose in secular company, when it argues that its monument (like Moses in the frieze) is not alone and ought to be viewed as only 1 among 17 placed on the 22 acres surrounding the state capitol. Texas, indeed, says that the Capitol grounds are like a museum for a collection of exhibits, the kind of setting that several Members of the Court have said can render the exhibition of religious artifacts permissible, even though in other circumstances their display would be seen as meant to convey a religious message forbidden to the State.

But 17 monuments with no common appearance, history, or esthetic role scattered over 22 acres is not a museum, and anyone strolling around the lawn would surely take each memorial on its own terms without any dawning sense that some purpose held the miscellany together more coherently than fortuity and the edge of the grass. One monument expresses admiration for pioneer women. One pays respect to the fighters of World War II. And one quotes the God of Abraham whose command is the sanction for moral law. The themes are individual grit, patriotic courage, and God as the source of Jewish and Christian morality; there is no common denominator. In like circumstances, we rejected an argument similar to the State's, noting in *County of Allegheny* that "[t]he presence of Santas or other Christmas decorations elsewhere in the . . . [c]ourthouse, and of the nearby gallery forum, fail to negate the [crèche's] endorsement effect. . . . The record demonstrates . . . that the crèche, with its floral frame, was its own display distinct from any other decorations or exhibitions in the building."

Nor can the plurality deflect *Stone* by calling the Texas monument "a far more passive use of [the Decalogue] than was the case in *Stone*, where the text confronted elementary school students every day." Placing a monument on the ground is not more "passive" than hanging a sheet of paper on a wall when both contain the same text to be read by anyone who looks at it. The problem in *Stone* was simply that the State was putting the Commandments there to be seen, just as the monument's inscription is there for those who walk by it.

The monument in this case sits on the grounds of the Texas State Capitol. There is something significant in the common term "statehouse" to refer to a state capitol building: it is the civic home of every one of the State's citizens. If neutrality in religion means something, any citizen should be able to visit that civic home without having to confront religious expressions clearly meant to convey an official religious position that may be at odds with his own religion, or with rejection of religion.

Finally, though this too is a point on which judgment will vary, I do not see a persuasive argument for constitutionality in the plurality's observation that Van Orden's lawsuit comes "[f]orty years after the monument's erection . . . ." It is not that I think the passage of time is necessarily irrelevant in Establishment Clause analysis. Suing a State over religion puts nothing in a plaintiff's pocket and can take a great deal out, and even with volunteer litigators to supply time and energy, the risk of social ostracism can be powerfully deterrent. I doubt that a slow walk to the courthouse, even one that took 40 years, is much evidentiary help in applying the Establishment Clause.